Global Communication

Theories, Stakeholders, and Trends

SECOND EDITION

Thomas L. McPhail

Blackwell
Publishing

© 2006 by Thomas L. McPhail

BLACKWELL PUBLISHING
350 Main Street, Malden, MA 02148-5020, USA
9600 Garsington Road, Oxford OX4 2DQ, UK
550 Swanston Street, Carlton, Victoria 3053, Australia

First published 2002 by Allyn & Bacon
Second edition published 2006 by Blackwell Publishing Ltd

1   2006

Library of Congress Cataloging-in-Publication Data

McPhail, Thomas L.
  Global communication : theories, stakeholders, and trends / Thomas
L. McPhail.—2nd ed.
      p. cm.
  Includes bibliographical references and index.
  ISBN-13: 978–1–4051–3466–8 (hardcover : alk. paper)
  ISBN-10: 1–4051–3466–6 (hardcover : alk. paper)
  ISBN-13: 978–1–4051–3427–9 (pbk. : alk. paper)
  ISBN-10: 1–4051–3427–5 (pbk. : alk. paper)   1. Communication,
International.   2. Communication—International cooperation.   I. Title.
  P96.I5M37   2006
  302.2—dc22
                                                        2005016754

A catalogue record for this title is available from the British Library.

Set in 10/12.5pt Galliard
by Graphicraft Limited, Hong Kong
Printed and bound in the United Kingdom
by T J International Ltd, Padstow, Cornwall

The publisher's policy is to use permanent paper from mills that operate
a sustainable forestry policy, and which has been manufactured from
pulp processed using acid-free and elementary chlorine-free practices.
Furthermore, the publisher ensures that the text paper and cover board
used have met acceptable environmental accreditation standards.

For further information on
Blackwell Publishing, visit our website:
www.blackwellpublishing.com

Contents

Preface

After September 11, 2001, the peaceful satisfaction of many nations that began with the end of the Cold War and the demise of communism came to an early and abrupt end, foreshadowing the rise of a new enemy – global terrorism. Along with this new elusive enemy came new wars and a profound increase in global communication. From embedded journalists with videophones covering the wars, to new media outlets, such as al-Jazeera, al-Arabiyya, and al-Hurra, to photos being sent home and around the world on the internet, the role and scope of international media shifted dramatically. This second edition captures the major aspects of this new and in many cases disturbing era, updates the materials contained in the first edition, plus contains a totally new chapter on the volatile Arabic media scene (chapter 8).

This book portrays international communication from differing perspectives – it examines a number of major trends, stakeholders, and global activities, while promoting no particular philosophical or ideological school, whether of the Left or the Right. Rather, it seeks to provide information about major international trends of a theoretical, cultural, economic, public policy, or foreign relations nature. Moreover, in order to provide a framework for understanding the interconnection between the international communication environment and the global economy, *Global Communication* documents major historical events that connect the two. It also highlights communication-industry mergers and acquisitions that frequently transcend national boundaries.

Just as the printing press and the assembly-line were necessary events for the industrial revolution, so also the internet and modern communication technologies are essential for the international communication revolution. This book traces the influence and roles of major global communication technologies such as satellites, videophones, and personal computers. Collectively, these and other technologies have transformed the international communication environment, making possible the advent of global media systems such as CNN, MTV, the BBC, and the internet.

As part of the background needed to examine global media and related sectors, it is important to understand the history of the international communication debate, which developed initially within the halls of the United Nations Educational, Scientific, and Cultural Organization (UNESCO). This debate about the New World Information and Communication Order (NWICO) is important because it identified two significantly different philosophies, each supported by a different set of scholars and nations. Because the debate reflects much of the concern about the philosophical, cultural, and artistic threats that are of paramount concern to many nation-states, the phenomenon of "electronic colonialism" – the impact and influence of Hollywood feature films and television, plus other media from industrial nations – is also detailed. One large and vocal group supports a free-press perspective without regard to its economic and cultural consequences; the other group supports a more interventionist approach, calling on governments and other organizations to be concerned with essentially noncommercial dimensions of the international communication environment. Because of the roles each group played, the policy positions, agencies, and leaders on both sides of the debate are examined extensively. Several new major global stakeholders, including the significant role of the global advertising industry, are also detailed.

A second major theme of the book concerns the economic implications of international communication. Although the economies of the international communications industries cannot be separated from governmental and cultural policy debates, it is important to recognize that most communication organizations are independent, active, commercial, and aggressive players in the international communication arena. They have global influence and they affect the communication environment both at home and abroad. As such, attention is also given to communication enterprises such as the Hollywood feature film industry; media giants such as Time Warner, Disney, Viacom, Bertlesmann, Sony, and News Corporation; as well as the internet, international wire services, such as the Associated Press and Reuters, and several multinational advertising agencies. As will be demonstrated, some of these organizations appear to be oblivious to the global policy debate and are willing to let the marketplace alone determine the winners and losers, whereas others are very concerned about the non-economic aspects of "trade" emerging from international communication.

All major global multimedia conglomerates are based in the United States, Europe, and Japan. Most of the concern about cultural issues emanates from nations in Latin America, Africa, and Asia. Therefore, I outline a world-system theory perspective in chapter 1 to decipher some of the structural cleavages in the international communication field. Throughout this book, electronic colonialism and world-system theories are identified as a crucial part of the discussion and analysis concerning global stakeholders in the communication sector. These two theories help unify the various stakeholders as well as identify their collective impact on globalization.

Any book about international communication would be deficient if it examined only one of these two major themes. A review focused solely on the NWICO without mention of CNN or the BBC, for example, would ignore the contemporary reality and economic aspects of global communication. Similarly, a book that emphasized the internet and other new communication options and opportunities to the exclusion of the philosophical debate would fail to provide the necessary historical and cultural perspectives. To a surprising extent, the end of the cold war and the collapse of the Soviet Union have shifted the debate in favor of the trade-focused parties. Only by detailing major themes and examining their interrelationships can a student of international communication come to understand the complexities of the global communication scene and the implications of the rapid change in global communication landscape that continues on a daily basis worldwide.

We should not underestimate the nature and depth of the transformation taking place in global communication. The era of the Enlightenment (ca. 1600–1800) contributed to the intellectual transformation of Western societies, and so today we are going through a similarly profound alteration in our societies, fueled by the major structural changes in global communication. Just as the major contributors to the Enlightenment era were Francis Bacon, John Locke, Adam Smith, Jean-Jacques Rousseau, Sir Isaac Newton, Catherine the Great, and others, so also today we have a critical mass of change agents who are forming the intellectual nucleus to create a new type of society with their profound insights and innovations. People such as Marshall McLuhan, Bill Gates, Steve Jobs, Charles Saatchi, Tim Berners-Lee, Patricia Russo, Margaret Whitman, Larry Page and Sergey Brin of Google, and others, are collectively providing the intellectual architecture and means to transform and create a new information era. Hundreds more working in their homes, laboratories, or universities in various nations around the world have contributed to the ongoing revolution in international communication. Yet few of these individuals responsible for creating a new media framework or paradigm have truly understood the long-run ramifications of their contributions on the type of society we will have in 50 years' time. In all likelihood, our future society will be dramatically different from the industrial society of even a mere 60 years ago at the end of the Second World War.

It is important to keep in mind that this intellectual transformation is not limited to economics, politics, trade, or education; rather, it will affect all of these areas as well as transform our concept of self and of community. Yet one major problem with this transformation is appearing already: this new society changed by the media is located only in select parts of the globe; primarily in those core nations that have already benefited from the previous industrial era. This overall intellectual transformation is occurring at the same time a large number of poor nations are still attempting to come to grips with enormous social problems such as illiteracy, poverty, subjugation, famine, civil wars, and poor health, particularly HIV/AIDS. As we move forward into a new era transformed by global media, one might also consider dichotomies created by the reality of a relatively small cluster of nations with full access to the internet, digital television, and wireless telephony, and, at the other extreme, millions of people on the other side of the Digital Divide who have yet to make a phone call, or read a newspaper, or use a PC "mouse." One cannot be certain how parts of a world so intrinsically linked to media will interact with the vast numbers of individuals who so far have lived without it; we will be watching closely.

Acknowledgments

I would like to thank my students, who tested the materials in class and provided useful feedback. I also want to thank Brenda McPhail for her assistance, patience, and feedback. I want to thank Ralph Berenger of the American University in Cairo, (Egypt), a Middle East media expert, for chapter 8, titled "Media in the Middle East and North Africa (MENA)." I also want to thank my research assistant, James Lambert, for his excellent research and proofreading skills. Finally I want to thank Rebecca and R. T. McPhail for keeping me abreast of the significance of MTV, blogging, and the latest in technologies, like the iPod.

List of Abbreviations

AP	Associated Press
BBC	British Broadcasting Corporation
CNN	Cable News Network
ECT	electronic colonialism theory
EU	European Union
GNP	gross national product
ICANN	Internet Corporation for Assigning Names and Numbers
IMF	International Monetary Fund
INCD	International Network for Cultural Development
Intelsat	International Telecommunications Satellite Organization
IPDC	International Program for the Development of Communication
ITU	International Telecommunication Union
LDC	less-developed country
MENA	Middle East and North Africa
NGO	nongovernmental organization
NIEO	New International Economic Order
NWICO	New World Information and Communication Order
OPEC	Organization of Petroleum Exporting Countries
TQM	total quality management
TWE	Time Warner Entertainment
UNESCO	United Nations Educational, Scientific, and Cultural Organization
UPI	United Press International
USE	United States of Europe
WMD	weapon of mass destruction
WSIS	World Summit on the Information Society
WST	world-system theory
WTO	World Trade Organization

Chapter 1

Global Communication

Introduction

The world of international communication has changed rapidly in recent years. Following the Second World War, global communication was dominated by the tensions arising from the Cold War. Much of the rhetoric, news space, and concern dealt with some aspect of government control of mass communication and the impact of governments and other entities on free speech, or the free flow of information or data across international borders. Likewise, much of international coverage had an East–West tone, reflecting a communism-versus-democracy wedge. In the 1990s, with the demise of the former Soviet Union and communism as a major global force, the factors underpinning international communication shifted dramatically. No longer did crises in Cuba, China, Japan, or Germany create major confrontations between the two superpowers. What's more, the end of communism spelled the demise of the Soviet enemy of the free press and of the free flow of information. In many editors' and producers' opinions, it also spelled the end, or at least a downgrading, of the importance of foreign news coverage. Yet clearly much of that changed on 9/11.

Today, the United States stands alone as the world's only superpower. While other economic entities such as the European Union and parts of Asia compete daily with the United States in the global marketplace, there is no large-scale foreign military threat to the United States. But today there are new enemies out there. The Taliban, al-Qaeda, Osama bin Laden, the Islamic Jihad, suicide bombers, and a vast array of terrorist cells around the world have taken up new weapons to confront the US and other nations. This has ironically once again seen an editorial shift to greater coverage of international affairs. The Good Guys versus Bad Guys mentality has returned. Terrorists of many stripes are replacing communism as the evil force. In the 1990s, even *Time* magazine and the *New York Times* had been replacing their foreign bureaus and coverage with a domestic agenda and concerns. Now Afghanistan and Iraq are front-page news on an almost daily basis. Until 9/11, evening television newscasts by the major US networks had been carrying less foreign news than in previous decades. But the war on terrorism and its successors have put international news back in primetime. In addition to the various government investigations into issues like weapons of mass destruction, the 9/11 Commission, the Abu Ghraib and Guantanamo Bay prisoner scandals, and public safety, the global agenda and media interest have returned to Cold War-era coverage levels.

International communication refers to the cultural, economic, political, social, and technical analysis of communication patterns and effects across and between nation-states. International communication focuses more on global aspects of media and communication systems and technologies and, as a result, less on local or even national aspects or issues. Since the 1990s, this global focus or prism through which interactions are viewed or analyzed has been altered substantially by two related events. The first is the end of the Cold War and the sweeping changes this has brought; the second is increasing global interdependence, which is a fixture of the expanding global economy. But this interdependence has more than an economic orientation; it also has a cultural dimension. This cultural dimension, in turn, has two important traits: (1) how much foreign content is contained, absorbed, or assimilated within the cultural domain, and (2) how this foreign content is being transmitted (e.g., by books, movies, music, DVDs, television, commercials, or the internet).

These aspects, issues, and questions are what this book is about. *Global Communication* highlights an international or global approach to the broad range of components that collectively make up the discipline of international communication. Because "[w]e live in an era of new cultural conditions that are characterized by faster adoption and assimilation of foreign cultural products than ever before,"[1] this book investigates in some detail who and where these cultural products are coming from and why, and addresses issues and concerns about their impact in foreign lands.

Historically, the United States government has orchestrated international communication policy and the many activities relating to transborder communication activities. During the 1950s and 1960s, the US State Department, the Central Intelligence Agency (CIA), the National Security Council, and the Pentagon played central roles within international organizations to suit Cold War objectives. This behavior was evident at a number of international conferences, but it was particularly clear in the US position regarding the

New World Information and Communication Order (NWICO). Ultimately, the hostile rhetoric became so intense that the United States under President Reagan withdrew from the United Nations Educational, Scientific, and Cultural Organization (UNESCO) in the 1980s. The United States remained outside UNESCO until 2004.

When the Soviet Union disintegrated in the early 1990s, the counterpoint to much US rhetoric and foreign policy, whether overt or covert, disappeared. The old rationales – Cold War rhetoric, concern about communism, fear of nuclear destruction, and national security objectives – became less prominent in the new environment of openness and cooperation. Foreign trade replaced concern about foreign media initiatives. Hardline Soviet-style journalists were either forced into retirement, or they quickly claimed adherence to free press traditions and practices. By 2004 several former Soviet-dominated nations had become members of the European Union. This included a move to market economies and a system supporting a free press.

The current international communication landscape is in a state of flux. The vacuum created by the demise of the Soviet Union had been filled by an atmosphere of economic determinism influenced by the reality of the increasing global economy. Economic determinism, including global mergers and the pursuit of foreign markets, had moved the focus of power and discussion from Washington to Wall Street, and to what affects the stock markets. For example, US companies now make more than $200 billion in annual income from abroad. More and more American firms, from Hollywood films, to music, to Microsoft, now earn more than 50 percent of their profits from abroad; 80 percent of MTV's total audience is non-US. And this percentage will only continue to expand as the global economy continues to grow in size and importance. Yet now this economic-based media orientation has to be shared with terrorism topics and the heavy costs associated with covering foreign wars, widely scattered terrorist bombings, and global disasters like the Asian tsunami.

Following are three examples of different global communication issues, one concerning terrorism, one from Latin America, and the other from China. These vignettes reflect the breadth and diversity of global communication issues.

Global War on Terrorism and 9/11

Not only did the world change as result of the attacks on the World Trade Center and the Pentagon; the global media changed as well. In New York City alone, the estimated costs of the terrorist attack exceeded $17 billion, over 100,000 jobs, and nearly 3,000 lives. All major US news outlets, print and electronic, created special programming or special editions to cover not only the attack itself, but its aftermath. In particular, CNN and the *New York Times* devoted significant coverage, news space, and attention to the global war on terrorism. Major television network shows, such as the Emmys, were rescheduled, and Hollywood producers assisted federal government officials in designing propaganda to counter global terrorism. Many overseas tours of leading orchestras, actors, and actresses were curtailed because of post-9/11 fears concerning the safety of world travel.

Related events also kept the 9/11 and War on Terrorism themes alive. Events such as Al Jazeera's showing of various Osama bin Laden and other Al-Qaeda videotapes became an issue within the Pentagon, as well as major US television outlets. The January 2002 kidnapping and murder of *Wall Street Journal* reporter Daniel Pearl also became part of the terrorism coverage. The wars in Afghanistan and Iraq, the train bombing in Spain, terrorist actions in the Philippines, and the school massacre in Belsen, Russia, gave global media outlets a plethora of new material and evidence of an altered and more dangerous world.

The National Commission of Terrorist Attacks upon the United States (9/11 Commission) held numerous open hearings, and its widely read final report in July 2004 gave further life to the post-9/11 media frenzy. In particular, former US National Security Adviser Condoleezza Rice's initial refusal to appear and her eventual testimony, along with terrorism expert Richard Clarke's strong statements against the Republican administration, also kept the commission and terrorism on the front pages and provided a daily windfall for the all-news networks.

The global media coverage also shifted, putting on the radar renewed emphasis on the Arab–Israeli conflict, Muslim culture and communities, and the divisive debate leading to the buildup to the second Iraq war. The United Nations, the weapons inspection, as well as the international media, exhibited considerable interest in the buildup to the war. It was frequently dominated by the considerable cleavage in the reporting as well as the ultimate accuracy of various claims concerning weapons of mass destruction (WMDs). The war itself began in March 2003, and President Bush announced the end of combat in May 2003. Yet well over 1,700 US soldiers were killed in Iraq, the majority of those casualties occurring after the declaration of the end of combat phase. The mass media also began running pieces about the disastrous Vietnam War, making quagmire analogies with the Iraq War, to the disappointment of the White House and the Pentagon.

The BBC also got caught up in the war coverage issue. The BBC presented a piece about the contentious WMD rationale and interviewed a British expert, David Kelly. He claimed that the evidence was "sexed up" to support the WMD claim. Shortly thereafter he committed suicide as a direct result of the stress caused by the media frenzy surrounding his testimony. Following that, the BBC management began a formal investigation, known as the Hutton Report, and several lapses in journalistic integrity by the BBC were noted. Senior BBC officials resigned as a result of the report as well.

In terms of the mass media itself, prior to 9/11 much of the literature on network television news focused on the preponderance of bad news. Phrases like "if it bleeds it leads" were common in terms of framing and understanding what was going to dominate the nightly newscasts, both locally and nationally. Post September 11, this news mantra became the global mantra, and other world broadcasters became either enthralled or captivated with the horrors of war and scattered terrorist acts, beginning with Afghanistan and the raids on Taliban resistance fighters. Iraq and the gruesome beheadings of kidnap victims became common fare on the BBC World Television Service and CNN, as did the horrific pictures and tales of abuse and torture by US military coming out of the Abu Ghraib prison scandal. In fact, the internet was central to exposing the prison scandal. In Iraq US soldiers were sending pictures and emails back home to their family and friends. This is how the circulation of pictures moved from the internet to mainstream mass media, such as CBS's *60 Minutes*. The US military also tried to adapt and come up with a reasonable policy, which appeared elusive, concerning soldiers that were blogging their daily activities in Iraq on the internet, much to the chagrin of not only their field commanders, but also the Pentagon in Washington. The Iraq war became known as the first internet war.

In 2005 British soldiers were prosecuted for Abu Ghraib-type torture in a jail near Basra. The European media were outraged at the abuse photographs. Some media began referring to the US and British military in Iraq as a coalition of the shameful.

Finally, the post-9/11 media environment, which was dominated by a great deal of sympathy for the position and activities of the Bush administration, has come under some criticism. Fox networks and Sinclair Broadcasting were labeled as public relations extensions of the White House and Pentagon. There was also the failure by the mainstream media in examining critically the Patriot Act, ghost detainees, or military oversight at the Guantanamo Bay holding jail, and basically no tough questioning of former Attorney General Ashcroft or the FBI and CIA for their anti-civil liberties stances. CBS news anchor Dan Rather openly accused his fellow journalists of laying down and fearing White House or FBI subpoenas, or other retribution, if they pursued high-profile stories or questioned the War on Terrorism.[2] A notable exception was *The New Yorker*'s Seymour Hersh. He withstood the orchestrated criticism of his magazine pieces and his book, *Chain of Command: The Road from 9/11 to Abu Ghraib*. In the book, he details how the torture and acts of humiliation by the US military in Iraq were an outcome or fallout of the US disregarding the Geneva Convention and proceeding without the United Nations' full support. Speaking at Columbia University's Graduate School of Journalism in the Fall of 2004, Richard Sambrook, Director of the BBC's World Service and Global News Division, made critical comments about the US media being less than objective in their post-9/11 coverage, particularly of the war in Iraq (Sambrook, 2004).

Latin American Media

Latin American media markets are significantly different from those in North America. Several countries in Latin America, such as Argentina, Brazil, Chile, and Colombia, have experienced political and social turmoil since the end of the Second World War. Some other nations continue to be controlled by dictators with military backing. Given this environment, the radio and television industries in these nations tend to be either government owned and controlled or heavily regulated. In other Latin American nations, the independent print press frequently is allied with the political and religious elites, plus there is little investigative journalism. Although Latin American markets are substantial in terms of population and consumer base, they still are relatively underdeveloped compared to their North American counterparts. But that is changing.

In the 1990s, the Latin American environment changed substantially in terms of governments and mass communication. Many governments moved to a more open and democratic way of attempting to improve overall social and economic conditions for the populace. In telecommunications and mass-media systems, there was a noticeable liberalization, deregulation, and privatization as reform legislation was passed in almost all Latin American nations. These countries clearly are at a crossroad; they must decide whether they will follow this new path or revert to the historical tendency of military coups, government control, and heavy censorship.

Despite the uneasy balance between old and new, the Latin American market is characterized by two significant phenomena. First, by virtue of the domination of the Spanish language (with the exception of Brazil, which speaks Portuguese), Latin America has not been as readily inundated with US television shows, which carry English-language soundtracks. In contrast, English-speaking nations such as Canada, Australia, and Great Britain were easy international markets for, first, Hollywood feature films, and then US television programs, followed by music. This language difference led to a second important Latin American media phenomenon. Because these countries were forced to create their own programming, they created an interesting and successful genre known as telenovelas. They are Spanish soap operas that are extremely popular from Mexico to the tip of South America. They have been successful enough to be exported to Spain, Russia, Cuba, Puerto Rico, and other non-English-speaking European countries, as well as Florida and California. Many of the leading actors and actresses are national celebrities, like soccer stars, in the various regions of Latin America. The export market is expanding rapidly for telenovelas because they cost much less to produce than their Hollywood and New York counterparts. On the feature film front the scene is not as encouraging. Over 60 percent of the theater screens across Latin America regularly show Hollywood films. In Latin America there are few film houses that can mount and finance blockbuster films to rival Hollywood.

Another difference between North America and Latin America is the role and success of newspapers. In North America, many newspapers have folded over the last decade, and single-newspaper cities are the norm rather than the exception. By contrast, Latin American newspapers are still a substantially growing market, with over a thousand newspapers in circulation and a readership, on a daily basis, in excess of 100 million people. Because of the high circulation figures, newspaper advertising is competitive with radio and television, making it a challenge for start-up private stations to succeed. Finally, because newspapers are privately owned, the owners and publishers generally support the movement toward greater democratization as well as government reforms to privatize the communication sector.

The left-wing connection: Latin America

In the postwar era, Latin America displayed a unique joint interest between labor unions and academics, which were frequently of like mind as they sought Marxist or left-wing solutions to corrupt regimes, many of which had military connections. Ideological fervor and rhetoric spread across Latin America as unions and academics sought to use the discontent of the peasants to mobilize support for Marxist economic and political solutions. For the most part, these failed, one of the prime exceptions being Cuba. There were occasional major confrontations, such as the uprising in Chiapas, Mexico. In this revolt, the rebels went so far as to exclude the major Mexican broadcaster, Televisia, from their various press conferences. Latin American academics were particularly critical of North American models, such as open markets, private ownership, and advertising-supported media, and they frequently attacked the violence of Hollywood feature films or the wasteland of television shows ranging from *The Simpsons*, to *Baywatch*, to reality shows, to MTV videos. They saw American junk culture with the same prism through which they saw American junk food.

With the demise of Marxism and the end of the Cold War, these same Latin American groups have lost steam and credibility. Labor unions are becoming isolated as democratization begins to take hold in several nations, along with greater economic prosperity. Leftist academics are finding fewer opportunities to promote anti-US media criticism as liberalization, privatization, and de-regulation sweep across the communication sectors. Latin American academics tend to write flourishing and lengthy essays critical of American culture with little, if any, empirical data to support their assertions. Today, change is bringing greater media choice, more advertising, less government owner-ship, and reduced regulatory control of electronic media across Latin America.

The role of media and culture, plus their impact on economic growth in Latin America, has been demonstrated in the literature. Cultural change and economic change are linked, but as David Hojman points out, "[T]he 'McDonaldisation' of all societies is possibly inevitable, but it is possible to eat McDonald burgers, and to wear jeans, without losing any of the most cherished aspects of the national culture."[3] Yet historically Latin American communication scholars have been among the most critical, and particularly anti-United States, in their writings. The vast majority work from a Marxist platform, which is now stale and suspect with the end of the Cold War. Yet some continue their diatribes, not appreciating how substantially the global communication scene has changed.

What follows is a dramatic example of how the Cold War atmosphere invaded media activities involving Washington and a Latin American nation, in this case Chile.

Chile: US government media interaction

The 1973 military coup in Chile during the Cold War provides an example of the US government's concern, influence, and backstage role in the US media when dealing with foreign events. In this case, as in others, it is im-portant to realize that frequently the US press corps has little background knowledge, local information or sources, cultural awareness, or even native language skills as preparation for breaking foreign stories. In the past, this weakness frequently was addressed by willing and well-trained US embassy staffers who provided background briefings to visiting US journalists in order to furnish them with "off the record" information and help them establish meetings and interviews. The information generally was selected to support and promote US positions and foreign policy objectives abroad. Although there is nothing intrinsically wrong with this practice, problems develop when journalists write their stories or file their videoclips without acknowledging the substantial influence or assistance of US embassy personnel.

From 1970 to 1973, the United States government sought to assist in the overthrow of Chile's leftist government. The US was hostile to Chilean president Salvadore Allende, whom US President Richard Nixon had labeled a communist threat. According to the US State Department, Allende had to be removed, or communism could spread across South America. When the Chilean military seized power in September 1973, the US government supported General Augusto Pinochet, despite the fact that he had been associated with many nefarious crimes, including supporting Chilean death squads. Pinochet subsequently ruled Chile for 17 years.

Without detailing the specific role of the Central Intelligence Agency (CIA), it is instructive to examine its relationship with the US media in Chile. Prior to and during the revolution, the CIA directed its Chilean station chief to engage in propaganda. He was to spread misinformation when it suited US objectives. According to the *New York Times*:

> The CIA's propaganda efforts included special intelligence and "inside" briefings given to the U.S. journalist. . . . Particularly noteworthy in this connection is the *Time* cover story which owed a great deal to written materials provided by the CIA. [Moreover,] CIA briefings in Washington changed the basic thrust of the story in the final stages, according to another *Time* correspondent.[4]

The result of this cozy relationship between US foreign affairs officials and foreign correspondents was a *Time* magazine cover story openly calling for an invasion of Chile to thwart the Marxist president and to stop the spread of communism throughout South America.

The point of this example is not to debate the role of the CIA in ultimately assisting in the overthrow of a democratically elected leader, but rather to focus on the role of foreign correspondents during the height of the Cold War. The US State Department, Department of Defense, and CIA all actively courted US foreign correspondents. The foreign correspondents in turn were to varying degrees willing to accept advice, leads, and in some cases copy from US embassies around the world. This situation was particularly true in countries where English-speaking US journalists did not speak the native language. In these cases, embassy staff and CIA operatives had enormous clout and access. They knew which locals spoke English and were sympathetic to the US position. American embassies set up media interviews and assisted journalists with logistics and acquisition of compatible equipment and other necessities for gathering pro-US news in foreign venues.

For over a decade, without the *raison d'être* of the Cold War and the anticommunist fervor that once dominated the agenda and mindset at the

US State Department and its network of foreign embassies, CIA operatives have been marginalized and replaced by trade representatives. US ambassadors and their staffs courted economists, investors, and the business community. Journalists no longer received priority access or assistance. Indeed, unless journalists are reporting on successful business ventures by US investors or corporations, they have difficulty getting their phone calls returned.

In the post-Cold War era, US embassies focused on trade and the provision of the organizational and logistical work necessary for US corporations to expand exports in these countries or regions. Senior embassy personnel spent the majority of their time seeking out investment opportunities, organizing trade fairs, or identifying new export markets while nurturing existing ones. Within the new reality of US embassy culture and foreign policy there is now a shared emphasis. The business press now shares media attention with security, terror, or war issues. Some US journalists abroad deal with foreign policy and the global war on terrorism while others still look at foreign profits, mergers, and acquisitions in the post-Cold War environment.

China: The Growing Impact of the Media

China presents another example of the changing role of the media. During his 1998 trip to China, noted media critic Max Frankel discovered that "a thousand television stations convey American style talk shows and western soaps to poor slums."[5] In response he wondered, "Can the internet scale the Great Wall? Can the global flow of information and images penetrate the defenses of a rigid old oligarchy? Can China run a free market economy without a free market in ideas?"[6] If China, with its bureaucratic government representing one of the last bastions of communism, is being influenced by the internet, fax machines, and satellite dishes, then how much more is the rest of the world being affected by these technological advances?

In China, journalists from CNN, the BBC, and other foreign networks once were limited to exclusive hotels frequented solely by foreigners. Today Chinese society and foreign media representatives are finding ways to obtain permission for more and more ventures. Although widespread access to foreign information and news is restricted in China, it is not as limited as many Westerners think. Even the government itself is party to the inexorable lure of Western media. Witness its agreement with Rupert Murdoch to broadcast Star TV, and in 2004 deals were announced to allow the National Geographic channel and HBO Asia to be available on Chinese cable television. As Frankel concludes, "Whether government in China evolves, dissolves or convulses, the chances are that it can never again seal its borders against the global Babel of voices, including the voices of freedom."[7] Yet beginning in March 2001, Chinese authorities banned *Time* magazine for several months for carrying a favorable story on the Falun Gong movement. Cybercafes are closed frequently. In 2004 Chinese authorities arrested a *New York Times* researcher for doing political research involving criticism of China's human rights record.

But on the positive side, China has joined the World Trade Organization, the newest Disney theme park is in China, and the 2008 Summer Olympic Games will be held in Beijing, with NBC holding the US broadcasting rights. Finally, in 2004 China International TV Corp. introduced "Great Wall TV Package" in the US and is carried by DISH network. The package consists of 17 television channels from mainland China and Hong Kong. The channels are in English, Mandarin, Cantonese, and the Min Dialect. In 2005 this service was extended to all of East Asia. In the future the Great Wall satellite package will be made available across Europe and Africa.

The terrorist piece, Chilean, and Chinese examples reflect the dramatically changing landscape confronting international communication. This book looks at global media, global communication technologies such as the internet, global advertising, multimedia organizations, Middle East broadcasting, and global events from post-Cold War and 9/11 vantage points. But some historical themes of concern continue to shape the scope and impact of global communication. These themes are best understood by examining where, why, and in what context NWICO emerged. But before discussing NWICO, I wish to look at how, from an historical perspective, the role or invention of the telegraph in the mid-nineteenth century had profound consequences for international communication. This new technology resulted in a paradigm shift from national to international communication (Hills, 2002).[8] It resulted in information becoming a commodity, particularly for the expanding print press. Finally, it also fostered a new breed of journalists – the war correspondent.

History of the war correspondent

Prior to the Crimean War (1853–6) there had been many wars. What would separate the Crimean War was the impressive fact that this war was the first to be covered by a foreign correspondent. For example, the earlier War of 1812, between Canada and Great Britain against the US, ended in 1815. Canada and Great Britain won the war, and the Treaty of Ghent, ending the war, was signed in Europe in December 1814. But this agreement did not reach North America until February 1815. With the newly invented telegraph, however, it was possible during the Crimean War for reporters to send daily dispatches. The necessary technology was patented in Europe by Charles Wheatstone in 1838.

The background to the war was a dispute between Russia and France, under Napoleon, over the Middle East. The British also had a vested interest in the conflict since they controlled the seas and trade routes, and aspired to continue their colonial expansion in the Middle East region. The Russians lost the Crimean War under the Treaty of Paris. Following this loss the Russians pulled back from expansionist goals. They soon sold Alaska in 1867 to the US for $7.2 million.

William Harold Russell was the first foreign war correspondent for the London-based *Times*, which was founded in 1785 and now is controlled by the conservative News Corp. Three interesting factors emerged from this coverage. First, Florence Nightingale, the legionary nursing pioneer, complained to the British press about how poorly the British war casualties were treated, and the horrific battlefield conditions compared to the excellent French facilities. The coverage in the *Times* eventually led to the dismissal of the Cabinet Minister responsible for the conduct of the war. Second, Queen Victoria of Britain called for a Royal Commission on Health and War (1856–7), but Nightingale was not appointed to the Commission because only males were eligible. Third, the impact of the *Times* coverage was so important and explosive that the number of journalists assigned to cover the US Civil War (1861–5) skyrocketed. The London *Times* circulation nearly doubled. In the US, with over half a million deaths, the pictures and accounts were major copy for the infant print press across the north and south. Several foreign correspondents from Europe covered the Civil War as well. For example, the UK reporters supported the slavery-afflicted South to protect the cheap source of cotton for British factories. The UK press for centuries has been blindly supportive of the national government's policies, right or wrong. Without going into details here, the trend continues today concerning the UK supplying troops to the Iraq war despite a substantial opposition among the majority of British people.

The New World Information and Communication Order (NWICO)

The foregoing examples are indicative of the major issues in international communication. In the past, much of this debate focused on the New World Information and Communication Order, which represents (1) an evolutionary process seeking a more just and equitable balance in the flow and content of information, (2) a right to national self-determination of domestic communication policies, and (3), at the international level, a two-way information flow reflecting more accurately the aspirations and activities of less-developed countries (LDCs).[9] Despite the fact that some proponents still champion this vision, many believe that NWICO is no longer a serious international issue. Even UNESCO has abandoned it. However, an appreciation of its basic premises and of the issues that divided nations remains an important and relevant element in a complete understanding of international communication.

NWICO's ultimate goal is a restructured system of media and telecommunication priorities in order for LDCs to obtain greater influence over their media, information, economic, cultural, and political systems. For LDCs or peripheral nations, the current world communication system is an outgrowth of prior colonial patterns reflecting commercial and market imperatives. NWICO provides a way to remove this vestige of colonial control. However, Western governments and news organizations vigorously oppose any such plan, fearing it will bring increased interference with the press, thus ultimately reducing market share and profitability.

In seeking to gain a more balanced flow of information, LDCs postulate potential mechanisms that clash with strongly held journalistic traditions and practices in the West. LDCs call for government control of the media, limited reporter access to events, journalistic codes, licensing of reporters, and taxation of the broadcast spectrum – all ideas that Western journalists, media owners, and policy-makers abhor. Even the call for a "balanced flow" of information, which was approved by UNESCO in the 1970s, is criticized as interference with free flow and free market mechanisms. Only an open and free flow of information is consistent with the goals of a truly free press.

The concerns of the Western press about NWICO are not merely theoretical. Because it legitimates a governmental role in the dissemination of information, several nation-states continue to support and implement policies based on NWICO. In Africa, for example, the government of Liberia, through its Ministry of Information, released an edict restricting press access to the internet. Journalists need a government permit, which limits the information they can cover. Because no permit or license has ever been issued for use of the internet, this activity basically is prohibited. As explained by the Honorable Joe W. Mulbah, Minister of Information for the government of Liberia:

> In sharp contrast to broadcast and journalism ethics requiring the truthfulness of information so disseminated, some radio stations and newspapers have begun running unauthenticated newspaper articles and gossip columns from Liberia on the Internet. Additionally, contrary to stipulations contained in the guidelines requiring the submission of broadcast program logs quarterly, radio and television stations have neglected their compliance in this respect thereby

making it impossible for the government to undertake the requisite monitoring of such program logs.[10]

The nations of Africa are not alone in their attempts to intervene and establish restrictive regulations concerning international websites. For example, in the Middle East, Islamic opposition to media, including the internet, is widespread:

> First satellite television, now the Internet. Computer-literate Saudi citizens, already spoilt for satellite choice, are about to be swamped by a wave of imported material on the Internet. After considerable delay, the government is expected to announce on October 19th [1998] which local companies have been chosen to deliver this Trojan horse of miscellaneous information into Saudi Arabia's pristine households. The Saudi government long ago decided that unfettered access to foreign websites would introduce a torrent of political and religious debate, not all of which would be welcomed by the regime.[11]

Many LDC critics attack the Western press as if it were a monolithic, rational system. They fail to realize that what eventually winds up in Western newspapers, on radio, or on television is determined by a complex, and not entirely consistent, process of decision-making. As Mort Rosenblum explains:

> Correspondents play an important part in selection by determining what to cover in the first place. But most of the process is in the hands of editors at different stages. These are the gatekeepers. Each medium and each type of correspondent operates in a different fashion, but the principle is the same. A correspondent's dispatch first goes to one gatekeeper and then what emerges – if anything – goes on to others. All along the way; the original dispatch may be shortened, lengthened, rewritten, or thrown away entirely. This series of editors determines what is to be eventually shared with the public; and they decide what the American people may never know.[12]

This is an important point. What people in Western or core societies learn about peripheral regions is meager and the result of several gatekeepers. What makes this successive diminution of information about poor nations so paradoxical is that both technically and theoretically there is more international information available today than ever before. The internet, satellites, fax machines, videodiscs, portable computers, radio, and direct long-distance dialing have collectively replaced the slow and cumbersome dispatches of the past.

But practically, the story is quite different. There are several contributing factors. The major one is simply the high cost of international reporting. The estimated cost to place and equip a single foreign correspondent abroad for one year is $300,000. This has led to a net reduction in the number of reporters that wire services, networks, or individual papers are willing to post abroad. Second, restrictions ranging from censorship and outright bans to withholding critical interviews past filing time, threats of physical abuse unless proper slants are evident, jailing, or even death all serve to reduce or limit the amount of available copy. Third, the high turnover of foreign correspondents and the pack journalism phenomenon make editors and publishers reluctant to expend time and money to significantly increase foreign coverage. Fourth, the trend toward "parachute journalism," in which large numbers of foreign correspondents, assorted paparazzi, and belligerent camera crews descend by the planeload on international scenes of conflict, tends to trivialize or sensationalize events that are far more complex than a 30-second clip can capture. Finally, the lack of public concern, as reflected in the trend toward light, fluffy, gossipy, and trendy journalism, reduces the incentive for editors to provide in-depth and continuous coverage of a broad range of foreign issues and conflicts. On the print side *The New Yorker* magazine, the *New York Times*, and the *Washington Post* are clear exceptions.

The reason for this shift in newspapers has been a mix of accounting and fiscal concerns related directly to declining circulation numbers and a movement toward local community journalism. The policies of the media are increasingly governed by marketing experts, who make news decisions to reflect focus-group results, rather than by editors. Without the Cold War, there was no strong focus for international news. With no counterpoint or dramatic confrontations between East and West, there were no engaging images to attract the public's attention to international coverage. The terrorist attacks of 9/11 and the aftermath have changed all that.

Clearly, the exceptional and unusual still dominate what is reported. In-depth front-page pieces on population, education, healthcare, environment, and other development successes are still rare. Rosenblum, in talking about "the System," makes this point:

> Foreign correspondents do often seem to be mad as loons, waiting on some source for hours in the rain so they can write a dispatch which might well end up blotting spilled coffee on an editorial desk back home. Editors seem madder still, suffering hypertension over whether their own man reached some obscure capital in time to duplicate stories available to them by other means. And their combined effort, when it reaches breakfast tables and living rooms across the United States, often appears to be supercilious and sloppy.
>
> This system is geared as much to amuse and divert as it is to inform, and it responds inadequately when suddenly called upon to explain something so complex and menacing as a dollar collapse or a war in Asia. Yet it is the American citizen's only alternative to ignorance about the world.
>
> Because of the system – and in spite of it – most Americans are out of touch with events that directly affect their lives. When crisis impends, they are not warned. When it strikes, they are not prepared. They know little about decisions

taken on their behalf which lessen their earnings, restrict their freedoms and threaten their security.[13]

Why is this the case? What are the implications? In an era of so much information, why is there so little useful information? The Western press warns that this situation would worsen under NWICO. The idea of licensing foreign correspondents is seen as the first of many steps that collectively will result in fewer reporters being acceptable to authoritarian nations and only favorable, pro-government news stories being permitted out of many of them. As this book describes in detail, international news coverage is going to change. The question is whether it is going to improve in accuracy, quantity, and quality, or whether gatekeepers will ignore it, and it will be restricted, biased, or heavily censored. That is why awareness of global media issues and positions is central to understanding international communication.

Two major theoretical outlooks will assist in organizing and understanding the events, trends, and major stakeholders in the rapidly changing field of international communication: electronic colonialism and world-system theories. Both are described in the following section, and then their interrelationships are outlined. In addition, throughout *Global Communication* certain examples of the media scene or global operations as they reflect and apply to these underlying two theories are commented on.

Electronic Colonialism Theory (ECT)

Traditionally, mass-media research looks either at select micro issues, such as agenda-setting, ownership, or violence, or at a specific medium, such as print or television. Only occasionally do scholars examine the macro aspects of the overall mass communication system. Harold Innis, Marshall McLuhan, Armand Mattelart, Jacques Ellul, Ben Bagdikian, and George Barnett are representative of the macro research school. The concept of NWICO offers another macro approach. The theory of electronic colonialism reflects much of the current concern and is a good theoretical concept with which to begin.

Four epochs of global colonization

Over the course of history, there have been only a few major successful trends in empire building. The first era was characterized by military conquests. These occurred during the Greco-Roman period and witnessed the expansion of the Roman Empire throughout most of what is modern Europe, including North Africa. This early era is labeled military colonialism.

The militant Christianity of the Crusades represented the second era during the Middle Ages. The Crusades, with the Catholic Pope as patron, sought to control territory from Europe, across Northern Africa, to the Middle East. Beginning around 1095, a series of crusades over 200 years resulted in eastern expansion and the establishment of new European colonies promoting Christianity in the Middle East. The territories were seized from Muslims, as Western civilization became the dominant international force or hegemony. Relics and treasures from the Greek Orthodox Church were plundered and returned to the Vatican as gifts. For example, in 1204 the Crusaders sacked and desecrated Constantinople's holiest cathedrals and shrines. To this day much of the history and treasures of the eastern Greek Orthodox Church are locked in the Vatican's basement. In 2004 Pope John Paul II returned the bones of two early Greek theologians but many Greeks are still waiting for the plundered gold, silver, and art works from this era. This era is labeled Christian colonialism.

Beginning with the invention of significant mechanical advances in the seventeenth century, the third era – mercantile colonialism – continued untamed until the mid-twentieth century. Spawned by a desire for cheap importation of raw materials, along with ready export markets for finished products, the industrial revolution created mercantile colonialism. Asia, Africa, the Caribbean, and the Americas became objects of conquest by European powers. France, Great Britain, Spain, Portugal, the Netherlands, Belgium, Italy, and the Nordic nations systematically set about extending their commercial and political influence. These expanding empires of Europe sought markets, raw materials, and other goods unavailable at home. In return, they sent colonial administrators, immigrants, a language, educational system, religion, philosophy, high culture, laws, and a lifestyle that frequently were inappropriate for the invaded country. None of this concerned the conquerors, such as the vast British empire, which thought it was doing the conquered a favor. International status was a function of the number and location of one's foreign colonies.

During the latter part of this era, industrialized nations sought to extend their influence through transnational corporations that supplemented and extended more traditional means of control. But the common denominator remained a desire for economic advantage – plentiful raw materials, cheap labor, and expanding markets. Mercantile colonialism also included other commercial imperatives such as advertising, government regulation, and laws, including contract and property rights, that better suited the larger and more powerful industrialized nations than their weaker foreign colonies.

A key element in the success of mercantile colonialism was the invention of the printing press by Johannes Gutenberg. In the early 1450s, he produced 200 copies of the Bible. Despite their high cost, the bibles completely sold out, ushering in a new era of communication. Although Gutenberg was forced into bankruptcy and eventually died a poor man, his invention provided the means for others to amass incredible wealth and power. Initially, the presses were used to mass-produce religious materials in the vernacular, and soon "penny press" newspapers appeared. Over time the printing press undermined the absolute authority and control of the Roman Catholic Church and monarchies alike. Also, the demand grew for a literate workforce capable of operating the increasingly sophisticated technology of factory production. Mass societies were created with greater literacy and some disposable factory income that permitted the purchase of newspapers, movie tickets, telegrams, books, and radios.

The First and Second World Wars brought an end to major military expansion and positioned the industrialized nations of the West in command of international organizations, vital trade routes, and global commercial practices. During the 1950s, the business and economic climate encouraged transnational corporations to increase and solidify domestic and foreign markets based on the production of mass-produced goods, from breakfast cereals to cars. As the industrial revolution ran its course, two major changes occurred during the late 1950s and early 1960s that set the stage for the fourth and current era of empire expansion.

These two changes were the rise of nationalism, centered mainly in developing nations, and the shift to a service-based, information economy in the West. The service economy relies substantially on telecommunications and computer technology to transfer and communicate information. It renders obsolete traditional national borders and technological barriers to communication. This fact has significant implications for industrial and non-industrial nations alike as the military, religious, and mercantile colonialism of the past is replaced by the "electronic colonialism" of today and tomorrow. (See figure 1.1.)

Eras	Dates
Military colonialism	BC–1000 AD
Christian colonialism	1000–1600
Mercantile colonialism	1600–1950
Electronic colonialism	1950–Present

Figure 1.1   Electronic colonialism theory

Electronic colonialism represents the dependent relationship of poorer regions on the postindustrial nations established by the importation of communication hardware and foreign-produced software, along with engineers, technicians, and related information protocols, that establish a set of foreign norms, values, and expectations that, to varying degrees, alter domestic cultures, habits, values, and the socialization process itself. From comic books to satellites, computers to fax machines, CDs and DVDs, to the internet, a wide range of information technologies makes it easy to send and thus receive information.

The issue of how much imported material the receiver retains is critical. The concern is that this new foreign information will cause the displacement, rejection, alteration, or forgetting of native or indigenous customs, domestic messages, and cultural history. Now poorer regions fear electronic colonialism as much as, and perhaps even more, than they feared the mercantile colonialism of the eighteenth and nineteenth centuries. Whereas mercantile colonialism sought to control cheap labor, electronic colonialism seeks to influence and control the mind. It is aimed at influencing attitudes, desires, beliefs, lifestyles, and consumer behavior. As the citizens of peripheral nations are increasingly viewed through the prism of consumerism, influencing and controlling their values and purchasing patterns becomes increasingly important to multinational firms.[14]

When viewers watch the television show *Baywatch*, they vicariously learn about Western society and mores. *Baywatch*, which began in 1989, hit a peak in the mid-1990s when more than a billion people a week in nearly 150 countries viewed it. With shows like this, along with *Dallas*, *Knots Landing*, *All in the Family*, *Maude*, or *Fresh Prince of Bel-Air*, foreign viewers began to develop a different mental set and impression of the United States. Another example is *The Simpsons*, the longest-running primetime animated cartoon ever developed. The show has now surpassed 300 episodes and is widely distributed around the globe. It has a leading cartoon character, Homer Simpson, who thrives on being a moron and placing his family and friends in bizarre situations. The show and characters thrive on portraying the distasteful aspects of US life, culture, education, and community. Yet the program has been so successful that not only does it continue, but it has also spawned other weekly animation shows such as *South Park*. Likewise, movies such as *Basic Instinct* or *Rambo* deliver the trappings of an alternative lifestyle, culture, language, economy, or political system that go far beyond the momentary images flickering on the screen. Electronic colonialism theory details the possible long-term consequences of exposure to these media images and messages to extend the powerful multinational media empires' markets, power, and influence.

Not surprisingly, the recent rise of nationalism in many areas of the world seeks to counter these colonialist effects. Many of these newer nations are former colonies of European powers. Their goal is to maintain political, economic, and cultural control of their own history, images, and national destiny. It is within these cultural issues that students of journalism, cultural studies, communication, and telecommunications find theoretical, policy, and research interest. For example, issues that concern both developing nations and the industrial ones, and frequently find them on opposing sides, are the performance and role of international wire services, global television networks, advertising agencies, and the internet.[15]

History of electronic colonialism theory

Prior to the First World War, when international communication consisted primarily of mail, some newspapers crossed national borders, along with limited electronic communication, which was a mixture of wireless and telegraph systems using Morse code, also crossing international boundaries. There was no international communication theory.[16] Also, the feature film industry was in its infancy, but there were examples of movies created in one nation being shown in another nation. For example, Hollywood exported to both Canada and Mexico some of its major films, even at this early stage.

This early era was dominated by the systematic exploitation by powerful European nations of foreign colonies that were to be a source of cheap labor and raw materials. In turn, these resources were manufactured into finished goods and sent back to the various colonies. Many of the on-site colonial leaders were either government officials or wealthy European families who displaced many locals to rural or remote areas. Examples of this phenomenon are the Maori tribes in Australia and New Zealand, Native Americans across North America, Zapatistas in Mexico, French Canadians in Québec, and many tribes across Africa. Given the pervasiveness of Great Britain's colonial empire, the noncommercial British Broadcasting Corporation (BBC), which was founded in 1922, was also exported as the operating model for many new radio systems that were being started across the globe.

During the late 1920s and the 1930s, there did emerge an alternative workers' culture which promoted a grassroots orientation to art, culture, and some local media. Labor organizations sought to promote folk art, decentralize the bourgeoisie orientation of the elite cultural industries, and promote local media with a noncommercial orientation. During this phase there emerged a European group of critical scholars, now referred to in the literature as the Frankfurt School. A group of philosophers which included Herbert Marcuse, Jürgen Habermas, Max Horkheimer, and Theodor Adorno developed a body of theory critical of power elites. To some extent they planted the seeds of electronic colonialism theory by focusing academic attention on ownership and power issues.

Many of these labor-based and critical initiatives became mute for two major structural reasons: the Great Depression and the Second World War. It was only after the end of the war in 1945 that there was substantial international expansion of the mass media and transborder activities involving communication as well as cultural products. In addition, many of the academics associated with the Frankfurt School relocated to North American universities.

After the Second World War, the United Nations, on December 10, 1948, recognized the growing importance of the interaction of culture and the arts within the Universal Declaration of Human Rights. Article 27 of the 30-article proclamation states "(1) Everyone has the right freely to participate in the cultural life of the community, to enjoy the arts and to share in scientific advancement and its benefits. (2) Everyone has the right to the protection of the moral and material interests resulting from any scientific, literary or artistic production of which he is author."[17]

National government media services, such as the BBC, the US's Voice of America, or Canada's Radio Canada International, along with many others, began to expand their activities into multiple languages with a strong desire to promote fundamental concepts of free speech, free press, and democracy, particularly in light of a campaign to thwart, counter, or indeed stop the growing threat and rise of communism. Most shortwave, government-backed radio services pushed a Cold War agenda in their broadcasts.

In the late 1960s and throughout the 1970s, the debate about international communication moved to the halls of United Nations Educational, Scientific, and Cultural Organization (UNESCO) in Paris, France. Certain constituencies, such as the old Soviet Union countries, academics in Nordic and Latin America countries, and some social-democratic party forces across Europe, began to express early concern about the impact of Western culture and the global economy. Although there was significant support for non-commercial media systems, there was also concern expressed about global syndication of Hollywood films and television shows, along with the impact of music, particularly that emanating from the United Kingdom and the United States under the banner of rock-and-roll. This debate about the importation of junk culture, much like junk food, hit a responsive chord at UNESCO. A major UNESCO-sponsored research report, which confirmed the imbalances in global media flows, is known as the MacBride Report (1980). The Report added momentum to the anti-one-way-flow debate. Eventually the debate about NWICO and its various elements by 1985 led the United States and Great Britain to withdraw from UNESCO in protest.

During the 1980s, under the philosophical mantra of US President Ronald Reagan, a new era of privatization, liberalization, and deregulation not only took hold in North America, but also across Europe, strongly promoted by Prime Minister Margaret Thatcher in the United Kingdom. There was a significant emphasis on market forces, free enterprise, and entrepreneurship, and a strong reversal of any type of sympathy or support for noncommercial media or telecommunication undertakings. Market forces also led to a flurry of mergers and acquisitions across the communication sector. Consolidation created global giants and this trend continues. In 2004 WPP, a British-based advertising firm, purchased the US-based Grey Global, and SONY of Japan bought MGM. One new global player deserves to be singled out: namely the creation of a satellite-delivered all news network, Cable News Network (CNN), by Ted Turner in 1980, which would come to significantly alter the global news as well as other broadcasting practices.

Finally, during this period, there were three seminal documents that formed the basis for a school of cultural imperialism. To some extent these were forerunners to eventual development of the electronic colonialism theory. In particular, Herbert Schiller's 1969 work entitled *Mass Communication and American Empire*, Tapio Varis's work for UNESCO and his 1974 article entitled "Global Traffic in Television," and Jeremy Tunstall's 1977 book *The Media are American*, served as a new catalyst and basis for promoting critical research in terms of analyzing international communication flows, impact, and imbalances. Critical scholars such as Dan Schiller and Bob McChesney along with others are still conducting research with a liberal perspective. Yet it would not be until the 1990s that a major new group finally emerged as a global nongovernmental organization (NGO).

The International Network for Cultural Development (INCD) was established in 1998 to defend cultural expression, cultural diversity, and promote national and multilingual cultural expression. It sought to promote genuine authentic media, rather than or indeed to counter the impact of the dominance of English-language mass media which controlled the flow of cultural products across national boundaries. The INCD took up the debate on international communication with new vigor and sought out new global participants, including senior government officials. They were opposed to multinational communication corporations promoting a homogenized global culture. INCD, along with UNESCO and several academics, sought to align themselves with government officials to promote an alternative to the market-based, free enterprise capitalist system, which was clearly dominating global communication. A major goal of INCD is to promote through the auspices of UNESCO an international convention that will define and protect cultural and linguistic diversity along with support for open artistic expression.

Much of the dominance that occurred since the middle of the twentieth century has been documented in a 1981 work entitled *Electronic Colonialism: The Future of International Broadcasting and Communication*, which was revised and updated in 1986. These early works along with the first edition of *Global Communication* both documented and expanded the literature and debates, which laid the groundwork and further amplified the theory of electronic colonialism. It is this theory to which we now turn.

What is Electronic Colonialism Theory (ECT)?

Just as Mercantile Colonialism focused on empires seeking the toil and soil of others, frequently as colonies, so now ECT looks at how to capture the minds and to some extent the consumer habits of others. ECT focuses on the global media influence on how people think and act. The aim of ECT is to account for how the mass media influence the mind. Just as the era of the Industrial Revolution focused on manual labor, raw materials and finished products, so also the Information Revolution now seeks to focus on the role and consequences concerning the mind and global consumer behavior.

Consider how culture is conveyed in a multimedia world. Historically grandparents and tribal elders played a central role in recreating, transmitting, and transferring culture. They relied on oral communication along with family, community, or tribal connections. Culture is basically an attitude. It is also learned. It is the learning of shared language and perceptions, which are incorporated in the mind through education, repetition, ritual, history, media, or mimicking. In terms of the media's expanding role, it becomes a shared media culture including influencing perceptions and values. Examples of media systems that attract heavy users are MTV, ESPN, soap operas, CNN, the internet, or video games. These systems tend to be the output of global communication giants, such as Time Warner, Disney, Viacom, SONY, and News Corp. Collectively they have the real potential to displace or alter previous cultural values, habits, activities, or family rituals. This is particularly true for heavy users of one or two external media. Over time, ECT states that these changes can and usually do impact friends, family, and community ties. A virtual community or new friends who share two things replace the latter. First, a preoccupation with identical media, such as MTV, talk radio, or Al Jazeera, and second, the embedded media culture that involves new or different messages, perception, learning, and habits. An example of this is the new subculture of black slang. It is at the core of the new media-induced culture for this group. Rap music, movies, concerts, dress, and playgrounds repeat and reinforce this linguistic trend.

A way to look at ECT is to think that we go through life wearing various masks or face paintings. We come to play out the appropriate roles, such as child, parent, student, immigrant, minority, athlete, or boss.[18] But with ECT the masks become largely invisible yet we feel different, as we become what we watch, do, or listen to. They become a veil of collective media images, which we absorb into our minds and eventually, even if subtly, begin to act out or speak differently as we consume input from the mass media rather than from family or former friends. The socialization process is hijacked by the media empires rather than colonial empires of days gone by. It is as if we have moved with modernization from a tribal state where culture was located in a fixed territory, region, or nation to a mediated state of mind where we might have more in common with someone or some group halfway around the world rather than in our own house, school, or neighborhood. What we are in is the early stages of a new "Empire of the Mind." Not an empire based on land or territory, but an empire based on taking over the minds of global listeners, viewers, readers, or users. This new empire is the long-run logical outcome or consequence of the validity of electronic colonialism theory.

Now with ECT a new culture has emerged that is a global phenomenon driven primarily by large multimedia conglomerates. They control, reproduce, and spread the global flow of images and sounds. They seek to impact the audiences' minds without regard to geography.[19] Their audiovisual products become sold and standardized without regard to time or space. They are marketed to international consumers who come to view their world outlook and buying habits as the logical outcome of a new media culture, as outlined and identified by ECT. For example, many Hollywood films and DVD sales now make more revenue outside the United States than at home; or MTV and Blockbuster have more aggressive expansion plans outside the US than inside. For many media products the US domestic market is saturated, and thus off-shore sales, audiences, consumers, or expansion is a logical trend that is enabled and explained by the phenomenon of ECT. The leading American communication giants describe themselves as global companies and not US companies. Their corporate strategic plans all focus on expanding global markets and developing products and services for international consumption. They position themselves as stakeholders, beneficiaries, and advocates of the global economy.

World-System Theory (WST)

World-system theory provides the concepts, ideas, and language for structuring international communication. World-system theory was proposed and developed by Immanuel Wallerstein.[20] The theory has also been linked to dependency theory[21] in that some of the criticisms are similar to the rhetoric and writings of the critical school of media scholars. Others have applied world-system theory to specific sectors, as Thomas Clayton did to comparative education, or George Barnett did to telecommunications.[22] This chapter develops world-system theory as it applies to international communication. The previously developed theory of electronic colonialism applies directly to the actions and reactions in the "semiperiphery" and "periphery" zones, as developed by Wallerstein and others.

World-system theory states that global economic expansion takes place from a relatively small group of core-zone nation-states out to two other zones of nation-states, these being in the semiperipheral and peripheral zones. These three groupings or sectors of nation-states have varying degrees of interaction on economic, political, cultural, media, technical, labor, capital, and social levels. The contemporary world structure follows the logic of economic determinism in which market forces rule in order to place as well as determine the winners and losers whether they are individuals, corporations, or nation-states.[23] It is assumed that the zones exhibit unequal and uneven economic relations, with the core nation being the dominant and controlling economic entity. The core nations are essentially the major Western industrialized nations. The semiperiphery and periphery nations are in a subordinate position when interacting with core nations. Core nations exert control and define the nature and extent of interactions with the other two zones. Core nations define the relations between the core and the semiperiphery as well as the core and the periphery. The core provides technology, software, capital, knowledge, finished goods, and services to the other zones, which function as consumers and markets. The semiperiphery and periphery zones engage in the relationship with core nations primarily through providing low-cost labor, raw materials, mass markets, or low-cost venues for feature films. Mass-media technology (hardware) or products (software) represent finished goods or services that reinforce and frequently dominate relations between the three sectors. World-system theory is useful in examining cultural industries, mass-media systems, audiovisual industries, technology transfer, knowledge, and activities of the biggest global stakeholders, which pursue interrelated strategies to maximize corporate growth, market share, revenues, and profits.

Thomas Shannon describes the economic, labor, technology, and other processes among the three zones, as shown in figure 1.2. Central to these relationships is the learning of appropriate economic values that facilitate modernization. Some of these values are conveyed through advertising as well as in the content of Western, core-produced mass-media exports. Also central to the relationships among the sectors is a mass communication

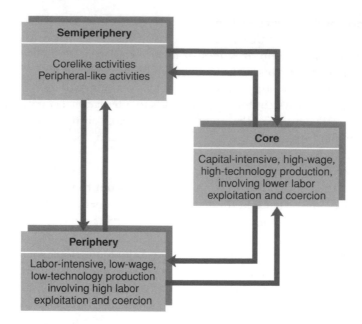

Figure 1.2 Relationships in the capitalist world economy
Source: Thomas Shannon, *An Introduction to the World-System Perspective* (Boulder, CO: Westview Press, 1989), p. 29. © 1989, 1996 by Westview Press. Reprinted by permission of Westview Press, a member of Perseus Books, LLC.

system that allows the transfer of media materials to create either a broadly based popular culture for a mass market or audience, or alternative cultures for a niche market large enough to encourage imports of select media products or services. The essential point is that despite criticisms of modernization theory and goals, there are nevertheless clear stages and goals that periphery nations need to learn, pass through, adopt, or clear as a precondition for advancing to the next zone, the semiperiphery. The nations in the semiperiphery engage in both core-like and periphery-like economic and media behavior. They strive to emulate core values over periphery values in order to become a core nation over time.

The core nations are generally considered to be the US, the European Union (EU) (without the most recent 10 entrants, which are considered to still be semiperipheral nations), Canada, Japan, Norway, Israel, Australia, New Zealand, South Korea, Switzerland, and South Africa.

The semiperipheral nations are China, Brazil, India, Chile, Turkey, Mexico, Venezuela, Argentina, Russia, Saudi Arabia, Egypt, Oman, Pakistan, Croatia,

Iceland, Philippines, and the 10 new members of the EU. They are Cyprus, the Czech Republic, Estonia, Hungary, Latvia, Lithuania, Malta, Poland, the Slovak Republic, and Slovenia. This latter group is now on the fast track to become core nations since the EU provides the necessary leadership and access to capital and consumer markets to rapidly improve their economies as compared to their former status of being small and marginal nations on the world's stage. Over the next few decades China, Brazil, and India are also likely to become core nations and rival both the United States and the EU as world powers.

The peripheral nations are the least-developed nations, frequently referred to as the Third World or developing countries. Most of Africa, Latin America, large parts of Asia, and the least-developed member states of the former Soviet Union are in this third zone. This zone has the least trade, weakest economies, and fewest news stories written or broadcast about it, plus the worst internet connectivity on the planet. The news stories that do appear about these countries are frequently negative, focusing on coups or natural disasters. Industrialization, which is central to the rise of capitalism and capitalists, has yet to reach this peripheral zone. Literacy – the ability to read newspapers, books, or magazines – is also lacking in this last zone. A defining characteristic of the peripheral zone is the agrarian nature of their economies. They lack influence or power in defining their relations with the core, with the major exception of being able to ban all foreign media imports, as Iran and other authoritarian regimes have done. (See figure 1.3.)

World-system theory explains well the expansion being played out in international communication. Mass media, including television and feature

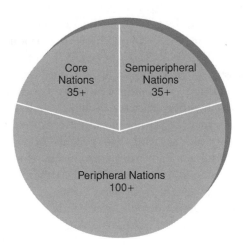

Figure 1.3 Breakdown of nations in the three world-system zones

films, are major vehicles (sound, print, video, and data) for conveying and indoctrinating the two subordinate zones. The dominant capitalist ideology is embedded within the transactional structure, marketing, and strategic plans of the major core cultural industries. The major multinational media conglomerates come from core nations, particularly the United States and the European Union. They seek to influence, expand, and promote their range of cultural products, including books, magazines, movies, music, and so forth, in the two subordinate zones for profit. The software and hardware of international communication are constructed and marketed by core industries and enterprises. They are then sold directly or indirectly (co-productions, minority ownership, licensing agreements, etc.) to semiperipheral and peripheral nations as quickly as markets can absorb and pay for them. Just as general world-system theory explains that capitalist ideologies are necessary for the working and expansion of the global economy, so also the major multimedia conglomerates have a parallel goal of directly enhancing their performance, both at home and abroad, by promoting and endorsing core capitalist mechanisms and values within the two subordinate zones. Jim Collins, for example, describes Walt Disney as a visionary who used his company's products "to shape society and its values." Collins continues: "From Israel to Brazil, Sweden to Australia, children grow up with the guiding hand of Walt Disney partly shaping their imaginations and world outlook."[24] This is a classic example of what electronic colonialism is all about. The business leaders of core multinational media firms seek to convert and capture the attitudes, minds, and purchasing behavior of global customers in such a fashion that their products are purchased first and frequently.

If the economic, social, and cultural values of core nations are not accepted and internalized by the subordinate zones, then the necessary attitudes and required behavior to purchase core-produced CDs, movies, videos, cassettes, DVDs, iPods, and books will not develop. Consumer spending is ultimately required in all zones. Core-based cultural industries and ideologies require the successful sale of core goods and services across the other two zones in order to increase market share as well as join with other core industries such as automobiles, fast food, equipment, airplanes, computers, and so on in enjoying the benefits of an expanding global economy. The utilization of advertising campaigns for cultural products, which are in many instances customized for the other zones, is also part of the overall capitalist movement.

Advertising itself represents a mini "case study" of world-system theory and is covered in a later chapter. Without going into excessive detail here, it is worth noting that almost all new media outlets worldwide are commercial stations, or networks, which rely solely on advertising revenue for their income and profits. This gives advertising enormous influence and a central role in the ultimate success of new ventures. Further compounding this dependency is the fact that all of the advertising agencies are multinational corporations from core nations. These core headquartered agencies bring with them everything from accounting practices, research, graphics, and artwork, along with placement strategies that are imposed on media customers in the subordinate zones, as part of their comprehensive full-service contracts. Whether the enterprises are in print, radio, television, outdoor billboards, or the internet, multinational advertising agencies frequently rule in the crucial component of the communication enterprise.

World-system theory carries an implied belief that prosperity will accrue to the two subordinate zones as they become more pro-capitalist and expand their markets to include the core nations. But a major part of the prosperity problem is that as core nations expand their cultural artifacts and products to the other zones, these economic transactions often do two things. First, they require foreign customers to purchase core products, with the eventual profits returning to the multimedia conglomerates, most of which are based in Europe or the United States. Second, core communication products usually displace or replace indigenous cultural products with foreign altern-atives and values. Local films, music, books, and so forth in the two subordinate zones must compete with major advertising and promotion campaigns affiliated with the core products; this local firms simply are not able to afford. So when discussing prosperity, one needs to ask, prosperity for whom? Who is being rewarded? A local person or a foreign firm? As core enterprises expand into the subordinate zones, it is the multimedia firms that reap the prosperity in a measure not commensurate with their impact on or assistance in the subordinate zones.

One argument in favor of this imbalance of influence makes the case that labor, central to world-system research, does benefit in the two subordinate zones. For example, when movies or television series are produced in the sub-ordinate zones, extras, drivers, local restaurants, and merchants of all trades are involved; or when newspapers, magazines, or records are sold, a com-mission is paid to the local shopkeeper. Many other examples also illustrate that the subordinate zones do profit by being part of core-nation transactions. In fact, core nations actively court other core nations' media firms to under-take business in their countries. Consider the following, which deals with the film industry and Canada–US relations, both of which are core nations.

Many Canadian nationalists lament endlessly US media and cultural influ-ences. Since the early introduction of radio in Canada, there has been a con-stant concern about the US media spillover into Canadian homes and theaters. Yet as media giants become more concerned about and focused on global markets and profitability, Canada has increasingly welcomed film-making by

Hollywood movie studios and US television networks. Montreal, Toronto, and Vancouver are prime locations for US companies producing movies and television series. These productions create thousands of jobs annually and contribute millions to the Canadian economy. Canada, as the core nation physically closest to the leading core nation, the United States, has to accept the growing role that US, particularly Hollywood, studios play in its economy, employment, and culture. As media costs escalate, particularly for leading stars, Canada begins to look like Hollywood North. A *Maclean's* (Canada's weekly newsmagazine) Special Report entitled "Northern Exposure" sums up the situation like this: "Stars want good roles, studios want to save money and create good entertainment. By filming in the Great White North, they can have it all."[25]

Finally, although there is not much specific empirical media research[26] with a world-system theory focus, one notable exception is a study by Kyungmo Kim and George Barnett. Their article, "The Determinants of International News Flow: A Network Analysis,"[27] is a good example of the utility of world-system theory. They apply both world-system and dependency theories. Following a detailed examination of international news flow across 132 nations, they conclude, "[T]he findings of this research reveal the inequality in international news flow between the core and periphery. The Western industrialized countries are at the center, dominating international news flow. Most African, Asian, Latin American, and Oceania countries are at the periphery."[28] Based on a regression analysis of their data, they further conclude:

> This center–periphery structure of the international news flow network has two implications for communication dependency. First, Western industrialized countries are at the position in which they produce and sell international news. In contrast, the peripheral countries consume and depend on their information from the core countries. One way this happens is through the maintenance of historical colonial relationships.[29]

The authors point out that not much truly global research on international news flow has been undertaken for a variety of structural reasons; their study is a major exception.

The Connection: Electronic Colonialism and World-System Theories

There is a substantial and important link between the electronic colonialism theory (ECT) and world-system theory (WST). ECT posits that when exported the mass media carry with them a broad range of values. These values are economic, social, cultural, and sometimes political or religious in nature. WST theory elaborates and extends ECT by dividing the nations of the globe into three categories; it then expands on how the core category works to influence the two subordinate categories. Some core nations are concerned about the impact and penetration of ECT as well. Canada, France, the UK, Israel, and Australia are prime core nations that continually worry about the Americanization of their domestic cultural industries and consumer behavior. Nations in the subordinate categories, mainly the semiperiphery and periphery, have a multitude of reasons, whether they be economic, social, cultural, or moral, to be concerned about the implications of ECT. Dependency theory, when referring to attitudinal shifts brought about by repetitive interactions with core businesses, is an example of ECT. For example, since the 1980s there has been a steady stream of research from Latin America on the structural impact, mostly negative, of relations with core nations, particularly the United States, but also with former colonial powers in Europe, particularly Spain. Although much of this research failed to utilize or identify either EC or WS theories as being relevant, in retrospect both theoretical constructs have much to offer in terms of organizing and explaining the phenomena under consideration.

Just as WST applies to all three zones, so also ECT has different applications in each zone. Basically, WST looks at the world through an economic lens and ECT looks at the same world through a cultural lens. Utilizing appropriate aspects of both theories will significantly enhance future research in international communication. EC and WS theories are well suited for examining the global activities of multinational cultural industries.

Communication Forces Among Nations

International communication as a commercial sector acts as an ideal case study of the application of world-system theory. Multinational communication conglomerates as well as major advertising agencies are all based in the core zone. When operating in other core nations or in semiperipheral and peripheral nations, they do so with a well-refined and strategically set agenda drawn from the capitalist economic system. The semiperipheral and peripheral zones are viewed as prime potential markets for core-based multimedia corporations, which define the relations among the semiperiphery and periphery nations. Part of the corporate goal is to influence the attitudes and values of potential customers as explained by the theory of electronic colonialism. There is no threat of force, such as military conquest, yet marketing strategies, research, advertising, and economic savvy permit core-zone businesses to influence consumer behavior by creating appropriate global mindsets toward their cultural products and services. Core nations thrive on market-based activities since they make the rules.

To understand the post-Cold War global communication environment, it is necessary to understand the evolution of the two quite different views of the core industrialized nations, and why the peripheral regions are, after decades of modernization efforts, still locked into the peripheral zone. Indeed, some peripheral nations are now worse off than they were when they had European colonial masters. Their situation – in terms of economy, health, education, indigenous media, and technology – has only deteriorated over time. In order to understand this lag and fundamental dichotomy, it is necessary to review the role UNESCO played as the major global forum for many of the stakeholders to set out their views, take sides, and establish how deep-seated and structurally different their views and concerns are about international communication.

Also, during the 1990s the movements toward liberalization and privatization witnessed many nations' state-controlled and -owned media monopolies under siege. The siege was not from an armed military intruder; rather, it was a mix of two new strong, hegemonic communication forces. These forces were (1) cable and satellite broadcasting systems and (2) an avalanche of Western, primarily American, television programming. The two forces, hardware and software, radically altered the media environment and balance in a vast number of core and semiperipheral nations between 1980 and today. Whereas only one or two public television channels were the norm for years, suddenly dozens of new channels and choices appeared on television sets as cable or satellite services became available around the globe. The impact was to create electronic colonies, built mostly around US shows, out of a new generation of viewers around the world.

For years, public broadcasting systems, particularly in Europe, had attempted to enlighten and inform their audiences. But with new channels came new opportunities to promote entertainment, advertising, and market forces. Commercial channels sought out popular programming ranging from *Big Brother*, *Millionaire*, *Weakest Link*, *Survivor*, *The Simpsons*, to soap operas and reality shows, to *Baywatch*. In their wake, they left smaller audiences for the public broadcasters, which in turn were coming under increasing pressure from politicians and regulatory authorities to do something about their shrinking audiences. At the same rime, many commercial broadcasters were seeking increased revenues from public sources. Every new commercial channel that is introduced steals away a portion of the audience from the public channels, which are being challenged seriously by three forces: financial, technological, and regulatory. The new forces all emanate from core nations to the semiperipheral and peripheral zones. In these nations, the consumption of media from local, sometimes bland, monopolies is frequently being replaced with Western media and foreign values that have had considerable cultural, economic, regulatory, and political repercussions.

Breadth of the problem

The range of global communication activities is extensive indeed. At one end of the spectrum is the large group of developing, or peripheral, nations concerned about basic communication infrastructures such as the introduction of radio or telephone services. At the other end are core nations, some of which have been industrialized for over a century, that have concerns about their own survival in the information age. They do not want to become information colonies of other nations. Communication issues related to mergers, transnational data flows, computers, censorship, privacy, and employment in cultural industries are central policy concerns of several industrialized nations. This is highlighted by the fact that today more than 50 percent of the US gross national product (GNP) depends on information-based services. This means that employment is directly related to the ability to supply all aspects of the information process – both hardware and software – necessary to participate in the information age.

Clearly, for Western core nations, such as Canada, France, Switzerland, and Australia, the notion that some of them may become electronic colonies of the US represents a serious threat and is forcing a rethinking of their own media philosophies. Issues related to national sovereignty, culture, language, and electronic colonialism are once again raising questions about the appropriate role of government intervention, fiscal assistance to cultural industries, and media ownership regulations. The emergence of the electronic newspaper, interactive cable, the internet, and direct satellite broadcasting is raising questions about the role of regulation and the concept of national borders or boundaries. Although the specific questions may differ, the basic issues are not far removed from the scope of concerns that peripheral nations experience about their communication disparities and problems.

Another issue for industrialized countries relates to the growing conflict between economic and national-security imperatives. From the beginning, competitive and commercial pressures have affected information flows as media outlets tried to silence the voices of their competitors. Today, the major supporters of the free-flow philosophy are governments responding to pressures from multinational corporate interests, ranging from American Express to Microsoft, IBM, and Time Warner, that are seeking to protect or extend their corporate and not necessarily US national interests. What is good for IBM in selling computer systems to Iran, China, or Russia, for example, may not necessarily be good for the national, or indeed international, interests of the United States. Yet these corporations and their advertising agencies rely on open borders and open markets, backed by the World Trade Organization, in order to compete effectively in the global economy.

Finally, it should be recognized that much of the pressure and support for the free-flow philosophy is coming from print media, both daily newspapers and major weekly magazines. Their concern is intense and historically genuine. But technology is quickly moving them toward government involvement in the dissemination of their messages. Although print and electronic media are still running on separate legal and regulatory tracks, their paths are expected to converge as print media increasingly rely on electronic information systems such as the internet to take their messages to consumers. Although always regulated to some degree,[30] the print media will find themselves increasingly restrained by legislative, regulatory, or court actions that are clearly inconsistent with the spirit of the United States' First Amendment rights.

What is significant, then, is that international communication is no longer solely focused on the role of the print press and the newsgathering habits of the international news agencies. It is growing to encompass a broad range of issues that arise from the emergence of global broadcasting, global advertising, and the global economy. The further economic deterioration of LDCs, the pervasiveness of satellite-delivered television programming, and the ability of the internet to defy traditional means of control are all reigniting the debate about the appropriate environment for international communication and the role of government in global communication policy. This role is no longer limited to national governments but has clearly moved into international forums, particularly the specialized agencies of the United Nations.[31]

Format for the Balance of the Book

The foregoing highlights the themes of this book, which examines broadcasting and news services ranging from MSNBC, MTV, and CNN to television sitcom and Hollywood export markets. It investigates the roles of the major players, whether they are Rupert Murdoch, Disney, Bertelsmann, Viacom, or Time Warner. It probes the role of advertising and the influences as well as future of the internet and their ability to transcend boundaries and beliefs. The growing importance of the Middle East media, particularly Al Jazeera, is detailed in chapter 8.

Global communication of all types is undergoing major reexamination. In order to be knowledgeable and understand the various factors influencing the processes of international communication, we need to know who the major stakeholders are and how certain economic and technical forces are changing the global media landscape. This book details the changes in the nature, flow, and control of all types of international communication, including news, in the future.

In order to accomplish this, the remainder of *Global Communication* outlines the major institutions, individuals, corporations, technologies, and issues that are altering the international information, telecommunication, and broadcasting order. This includes all types of media activities – wire services, internet, fax machines, electronic data, satellites, journalists, film, radio, television, and advertising. Traditional assumptions about media flows and priorities are being challenged and altered daily. What follows is a descriptive and analytical portrayal of how certain events, some very recent, are affecting the domestic and foreign information environments of today and tomorrow. Central to the discussion is the collapse of communism and the removal of the Soviet Union as a major global player in global communication policy, the importance of global media organizations, the global war on terror, the influence of global advertisers, and, finally, the substantial and somewhat unanticipated impact of personal computers and the internet.

These issues are explained and interpreted through three major theories or movements: NWICO, electronic colonialism, and world-system theories. Collectively, they help organize the trends, economics, technologies, and stakeholders involved in the dynamic, globally significant, and expanding role of international communication. Part of the dynamic is the pace of mergers and acquisitions affecting several of the global communication stakeholders. As the global economy evolves and increases in influence, international communication moves in unison with it. International communication will have a greater impact on the future of the planet than exploration and transportation combined.

Notes

1   Hong-Won Park, "A Gramacian Approach to Interpreting International Communication," *Journal of Communication* 48(4) (1998), p. 79.
2   *USA Today*, Sept. 16, 2004, p. 7A.
3   David Holman, "Economic Policy and Latin America Culture: Is a Virtuous Circle Possible?" *Journal of Latin American Studies* 31 (Feb. 1999), p. 176.
4   *New York Times*, Sept. 13, 1998, sec. WK, p. 7.
5   *New York Times*, Oct. 25, 1998, sec. 6, p. 36.
6   *New York Times*, Oct. 25, 1998, sec. 6, p. 38.
7   *New York Times*, Oct. 25, 1998, sec. 6, p 38.

8   Jill Hills, *The Struggle for Control of Global Communication: The Formative Century* (Urbana, IL: University of Illinois Press, 2002).

9   There are several ways of defining and categorizing the nations of the world. Frequent dichotomies include north–south, east–west, developed–underdeveloped, socialist–capitalist, industrialized–Third World. Another system categorizes according to core, semiperipheral, and peripheral. Although the system is far from perfect, this book will use the following: Western nations include the industrialized nations, which according to the World Bank are Australia, the UK, Canada, Finland, France, Italy, Japan, Netherlands, Sweden, Switzerland, United States, and Germany. Most of these are situated in the North and are core nations. The peripheral nations are located mainly in Asia, Africa, and Latin America – generally to the South.

It also should be noted that nations are continually obtaining independence or moving back and forth on both the political and economic continua. Examples include Russia, Indonesia, Iran, Iraq, Mexico, Brazil, Yugoslavia, Venezuela, and Poland. No definition will fit accurately over time. Therefore, the terms are used for the sake of convenience because they reflect the major global parties involved in the NWICO debate. These categories also apply to the theories of electronic colonialism and world system that will be detailed later.

10 Committee to Protect Journalists (CPJ), New York, Oct. 28, 1998: wwwcpj.org/ pg. 1.

11 *The Economist*, Oct. 17, 1998, p. 50.

12 Morton Rosenblum, *Coups and Earthquakes* (New York: Harper & Row, 1979), pp. 1–2.

13 Ibid., pp. 1–2.

14 Cultural reproduction theorists view international media initiatives as a means of reproducing and socializing students in peripheral nations into knowledge systems that make them more compatible with Western ideals and, equally important, Western consumer values. Cultural reproduction theorists see foreign mass media as reproducing and socializing the populace of other nations into a knowledge system or frame of mind that will make them more compatible with or sympathetic to foreign ideas and consumer values. See Alan Hedley, "Technological Diffusion or Cultural Imperialism? Measuring the Information Revolution," *International Journal of Comparative Sociology* 39(2) (June 1998), pp. 198–213. Hedley states, "Also flowing from this analysis is the potential for cultural dominance that the information revolution may foster. However, unlike previous technological revolutions, what are at stake are the very minds and thought processes of those dominated. Only powerful nations currently have the ability to choose the type of information society most compatible with their cultural institutions" (p. 210). Edward Goldsmith, "Development as Colonialism," *The Ecologist* 27(2) (March–April 1997), pp. 69–78, focuses on the role of transnational corporations and their expanding development of the global economy. He concludes, "The new corporate colonialism is thus likely to be far more cynical and more ruthless than anything we have seen so far. It is likely to dispossess, impoverish and marginalize more people, destroy more cultures and

cause more environmental devastation than either the colonialism of old or the development of the last fifty years. The only question is. How long can it last?" (p. 76).

15 The major global stakeholders for all these sectors are detailed in later chapters. Some readers may want to refer to these chapters now.

16 Jill Hills, *The Struggle for Control of Global Communication* (Chicago: University of Illinois Press, 2002).

17 United Nations, *Universal Declaration of Human Rights*, 1948.

18 David Napier, *Righting the Passage: Perceptions of Change after Modernity* (Philadelphia: University of Pennsylvania Press, 2004).

19 Al Reis and Jack Trout, *Positioning: The Battle for your Mind* (New York: McGraw Hill, 2001).

20 Immanuel Wallerstein, *The Modern World System* (New York: Academic Press, 1974), *The Modern World System III* (San Diego: Academic Press, 1989), and "National Development and the World System at the End of the Cold War," in *Comparing Nations and Cultures: Readings in a Cross-disciplinary Perspective*, eds. A. Inkeles and M. Sasaki (Englewood Cliffs, NJ: Prentice-Hall, 1996), pp. 484–97. A definition of world-system theory, along with a fine review of research trends, is contained in Thomas Hall's "The World System Perspective: A Small Sample from a Large Universe," *Sociological Inquiry* 66(4) (Nov. 1996), pp. 440–54.

21 Andre Frank, *Capitalism and Underdevelopment in Latin America* (New York: Monthly Review Press, 1969); Barnett Singer and John Langdon, "France's Imperial Legacy," *Contemporary Review* 272 (May 1998), pp. 231–8; Alvin So, *Social Change and Development: Modernization, Dependency, and World System Theory* (Newbury Park, CA: Sage, 1990).

22 Thomas Clayton, "Beyond Mystification: Reconnecting World System Theory for Comparative Education," *Comparative Education Review* 42 (Nov. 1998), pp. 479–94; George Barnett and Young Choi, "Physical Distance and Language as Determinants of the International Telecommunications Network," *International Political Science Review* 16(3) (1995), pp. 249–65.

23 Or groups of nation-states such as those in NAFTA, the European Union, ASEAN, or MERCOSUR.

24 Jim Collins, "Shaping Society," *USA Today*, Sept. 23, 1999, p. 19A.

25 "Northern Exposure," *Maclean's*, Oct. 11, 1999, p. 71.

26 John Comer, Philip Schlesinger, and Roger Silverstone, eds., *International Media Research: A Critical Survey* (London: Routledge, 1997).

27 Kyungmo Kim and George Barnett, "The Determinants of International News Flow: A Network Analysis," *Communication Research* 23 (June 1996), pp. 323–52; G. Barnett, T. Jacobson, and S. Sun-Millar, "An Examination of the International Communication Network," *The Journal of International Communication* 3 (1996), pp. 19–43; G. Barnett, "A Longitudinal Analysis of the International Telecommunications Network: 1978–1996," *American Behavioral Scientist* 44(10) (June 2001), pp. 1638–55; G. Barnett, B. S. Chon, and D. Rosen, "The Structure of International Internet Flows in Cyberspace,"

NETCOM (Network and Communication Studies) 15(1–2) (Sept. 2001), pp. 61–80.

28 Kim and Barnett, p. 344.

29 Kim and Barnett, p. 346.

30 This refers to journalistic limitations. Most agree that there should be no limitations on the political, economic, or social consequences of investigative journalism, but clearly there are legal limitations. These include the laws related to libel, slander, defamation, obscenity, and so forth that do constrain what is printed or aired. For example, in 2004, US Federal officials in order to charge journalists from major media outlets with illegal activities used the Intelligence Identities Protection Act of 1982.

31 Another forum is the 46-nation International Network for Cultural Diversity (INCD), which began with a meeting in Canada in 1998, followed by meetings in Mexico, Greece, Switzerland, South Africa, and Croatia, plus a growing number of regional meetings. These meetings focus on cultural identity, cultural policy, and the impact of cultural globalization. A growing concern of the member nations is the treatment of cultural industries, particularly television, film, and magazines by the World Trade Organization (WTO). The INCD group, which does not include the United States, view the WTO's policies as favoring the one-way flow of American products around the globe to the detriment of local cultures. One policy option being floated at INCD meetings is to remove cultural goods and services from WTO agreements. This initiative has major implications concerning global trade for the major stakeholders, detailed in future chapters.

Finally, Canada is providing leadership for the INCD group for the obvious reason that it is, to a large extent, on the leading edge of becoming an electronic colony of the US. They have become a branch plant of US media empires. The foreign content of Canada's mass media is staggering. Consider the following: 98% of theater revenues are for foreign, mainly Hollywood, films; 83% of magazines, such as *Time*, *Newsweek*, and *Sports Illustrated*, sold are foreign; 80% of music sales in all formats are foreign; and more than 60% of television programming on the three national networks comes from other nations, despite decades of electronic media content regulations, along with handsome financial subsidies, from the Canadian federal government.

Chapter 2

Development Research Traditions and Global Communication

Introduction

During the 1980s, several apparently unrelated factors came together to further the movement questioning Western aid, values, and media. Among these factors was the failure and subsequent rejection of the theory of modernization promulgated by major industrialized core nations and aid agencies since the close of the Second World War. Implementation of that model had failed to produce positive results in the eyes of peripheral nations. In reality, after decades of core-based modernization attempts, some peripheral nations were worse off and others had made little progress. Within the overall theoretical framework, the mass communication system was a substantial component among the mix of factors that cumulatively should have moved peripheral nations to at least semiperipheral status and then to industrialization and modernization. Herein lies the connection between modernization theory and development communication. In theory, development communication should work in concert with other growth factors to lead poorer nations to modernization or, at least, to move them from the peripheral zone to the semiperipheral zone. In practice, those peripheral nations that did invest in media infrastructures realized too late that these systems were bringing in more foreign, not local, content. For example, where cable or satellite media were introduced, affluent locals watched CNN or MTV rather than domestic broadcasters.[1]

In retrospect, just as educational television in the West failed to bring about the projected revolution in the classroom, the prediction that broadcasting was the means by which poor nations could rapidly transform into industrialized nations was similarly off course. Indeed, during the last decade, some peripheral nations moved in the opposite direction with regard to their environment, currency, literacy, and healthcare, particularly with respect to AIDS.

Some poor nations, for example, assume that the introduction of color television is the appropriate medium to foster economic and cultural development. But color television is expensive and has limited applications. In peripheral nations where color television broadcasting is available, few households even have access to black-and-white television sets. Digital television, which is making its entry in core nations, is raising a new issue and barrier. This new technology will render existing analog broadcasting systems and their receivers obsolete. Because of its cost, it is likely to take decades for the diffusion of digital television to be complete – even in industrialized nations. In their eagerness to "measure up," many peripheral nations are likely to desire the digital format and related new technology, but its costly introduction is likely to set back, rather than promote, development.

The balance of this chapter traces the various streams of the major theories of communication, both American and European, as well as major research trends that underpin the knowledge base for students of international communication. Beginning with development theory, the review highlights major contributions to the theoretical and applied international media research literature. The chapter concludes with a discussion of the application of the theories of electronic colonialism and world-system theory.

Development Journalism/Communication

Development journalism and communication are attempts to counterbalance the thrust toward electronic colonialism. They acknowledge that the demands of an infant press differ from those of a mature press. To impose the legal, economic, or regulatory models of one onto the other results in a failure to appreciate the underlying differences that are a result of a combination of historical and cultural factors. Development journalism is the concept that attempts to deal with the needs, strengths, and aspirations of journalistic endeavors in the emerging developing nation-states.[2] It is a media theory that encourages an engineered press – a press committed to government-set priorities and objectives. It assumes that all efforts, including local media, need to work in unison to support national goals. Totalitarian regimes in a substantial number of peripheral nations follow and enforce this media theory and approach.

Consequently, development journalism essentially serves to promote the needs of developing countries. It encourages indigenous media and discourages reproduction of Western media models, which debase or marginalize local and traditional cultures. Most peripheral media systems are underdeveloped, with few newspapers, some radio outlets, and usually one television system, at most. Under these conditions, administrators, editors, and reporters in peripheral regions find little relevance in Western media values and systems, which do not serve the needs of peripheral nations or highlight their interests or concerns. Except for the occasional political coup or natural disaster, few of their stories are told in the mainstream media and even less is revealed from the peripheral nations' own perspective. In fact, research indicates that the vast majority of international media offerings emanate from a few core nations as sources. Consider the following:

1   Major Western news agencies such as the Associated Press (New York), Reuters (London), and Agence France Presse (Paris) provide about 90 percent of all the world's wire-service information. They are all based in core nations.
2   Major Western newspapers, magazines, and journals are virtually all published in the US or Europe. In Europe, most of these media come from foreign colonial powers and still enjoy significant sales in current or former colonies.
3   International radio programming such as Voice of America (US), the BBC (United Kingdom), Deutsche Welle (Germany), and other Western shortwave services transmit programming specifically designed for international audiences. The perspective is invariably that of the Western, core industrial nations, but the majority of the global audience is in noncore nations.
4   Global television news and newsreels such as CNN, BBC, AP, and Reuters have established worldwide markets for their products using video material produced or designed for initial use in the US, Great Britain, or other Western media systems.
5   Television programming and feature films are almost exclusively the province of Western nations. Over two-thirds of available global video programming comes from the US alone.
6   All major global advertising agencies are based in the US, Europe, or Japan. If there is any physical presence at all in semiperipheral or peripheral nations, it is only in the form of small branch offices.

Although the seeds of a theory of development journalism were sown in the 1950s, it was decades before the debate about the role of the mass media reached the West. Originally, the dominant paradigm for development communication reflected a mainstream consensus of opinion that encouraged industrial growth. It was assumed that as the gross domestic product (GDP) increased, so too would communication activities of all types, including the development of telecommunication as well as mass-media systems. This "growth is good" model ignored the fact that enormous capital investment was required to finance communication development. Without adequate domestic professional and fiscal resources, peripheral nations found themselves even more dependent on external foreign aid, which invariably had strings attached.

Over time, piecemeal programs evolved to encourage development. However, it soon became clear that foreign aid turned out to be little more than a weapon on the Cold War battlefield. The Soviet Union supported communist-oriented nations and regions, and the US assisted fledgling democracies ostensibly committed to a free-enterprise model. Moreover, uncounted sums of this aid were skimmed off by corrupt regimes or wasted by inept, untrained bureaucrats with good intentions but little experience with large-scale development projects. This blatant failure to improve the conditions in developing countries led to a rethinking of development communication.

> The immediate result of such rethinking was manifest in sensitivity to the structural and cultural constraints on the impact of communication, in addition to conscious awareness that the mass media were just a part of the total communication infrastructure. It became evident that successful and effective use of communication in any community requires adequate knowledge of the availability, accessibility, relationships, and utilization of communication infrastructure and software in that community.[3]

The problems were not limited to the lack of communication progress in developing nations; some critics found fault with Western researchers who ignored indigenous media and failed to stress the importance of sustaining local cultures. African scholar Kwasi Ansu-Kyeremeh states, "[T]he paltry literature regarding various interpretations of indigenous communication systems elsewhere and in Africa"[4] is a problem in itself. And this lack of relevant models is only part of the problem in peripheral nations. Ank Linden points out, "Governmental authorities in Third World countries often seem to be more interested in maintaining the status quo than in strengthening the communication capacity of the people."[5]

Concern about the sociology and culture of communication, whether in the form of folklore transmitted orally or as color television transmitted live via satellite, heightened the need for a revised vision of cultural development and the role of communication in it. Whereas the Western media valued freedom of the press, free speech, and the free flow of information, most peripheral nations began to reject these and related values as luxuries they could not afford. They had no multitude of competing views and media systems. Most of these countries were fortunate to have a single electronic medium, usually radio. What is more, as illiteracy on a world scale continues to increase, a widely accessible printed press remains a distant dream, if not an illusion, for many emerging nation-states. Finally, of course, virtually all peripheral regions lack the necessary telecommunications infrastructure required for modem media systems, including cellular phones and access to the internet.

Moreover, the position of peripheral nations on the role of government control conflicted with that of the core and democratic nations. In some cases, the development media sought the support of government, and in others the government imposed control. In both, the media had little choice but to accept and repeat the messages those in control wished to disseminate. The result was two diametrically opposed journalism philosophies about the relationship between the media and government. The Western journalists favored a free press, and less-developed country (LDC) journalists followed a development journalism approach.

Development journalism/communication is a pivotal concept in this new environment. Its proponents are newly emerging nations, all in the periphery, primarily in Africa, Latin America, and Asia, with low income, high illiteracy rates, and virtually no modern media systems. The infrastructure to support an advanced telecommunications system simply does not exist. As the poor countries see it, in order to rapidly improve the economic and social position of peripheral nations, a concerted effort by both government and media is required. The "luxury" of competing and critical views on government policies and programs within the national media is viewed as detrimental to the colossal task of "catching up."

In order to correct the imbalances and mistaken impressions created by the Western press, peripheral nations continue to promote their media theory of development journalism. At a practical level, they reject neutrality and objectivity in favor of active roles as promoters of government objectives. They engage in advocacy journalism. Their reporting reflects the stated objectives of their governments, and they see no conflict with this. In some instances, they go so far as to avoid any positive reporting of Western activities. Only negative stories are disseminated in order to reinforce the view of the West as the "Great Satan." Unfortunately, in doing so, the development press commits the same grievous crime it so readily attributes to the Western press.

Finally, many media corporations based in Europe and North America have reduced their number of reporters in Africa, Asia, and Latin America in particular for three significant reasons (see figure 2.1). First, the cost of stationing full-time reporters in foreign bureaus has increased dramatically.

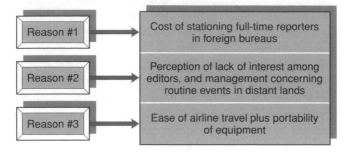

Figure 2.1   Declining foreign bureaus

These media corporations are profit driven and they seek ways to reduce costs, so they close foreign bureaus. Second, with the lack of Cold War tension, there is at least a perception of a lack of interest on the part of editors and management about events in distant lands. Less space and time is allotted to foreign news. Many media corporations based in Europe and North America have reduced the numbers of reporters in Africa, Asia, and Latin America across all media. Third, core-based editors realize that when a mostly negative major news story breaks somewhere in a peripheral nation, they can dispatch a crew and reporters in a relatively short period of time due to the ease of airline travel and the portability of equipment. This phenomenon further exacerbates the criticism and antagonizes the critics of Western media because it contributes to the largely negative media coverage of peripheral nations and regions. Ultimately, the notion of development is entwined with economic issues that lead to a consideration of economic models of growth and modernization.

The Economic Growth Model

Perhaps the best-known categorization of stages of development is the one advanced by US economist Walter Rostow in *The Stages of Economic Growth*. Rostow asserts that the development process can be divided into five stages: traditional society, establishment of preconditions to takeoff, takeoff into sustained growth, the drive to maturity, and the age of high mass consumption (see figure 2.2).[6] In most versions of this scheme, traditional and modern societies are placed at opposite ends of an evolutionary scale. Development is viewed as evolution beyond traditional structures that supposedly cannot accommodate rapid social change or produce sufficient economic growth.

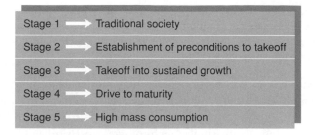

Stage 1 ⟶ Traditional society

Stage 2 ⟶ Establishment of preconditions to takeoff

Stage 3 ⟶ Takeoff into sustained growth

Stage 4 ⟶ Drive to maturity

Stage 5 ⟶ High mass consumption

Figure 2.2 Walter Rostow's stages of economic growth

The new attitudes, values, and social relationships that support social change are frequently conveyed through mass media as well as educational systems.

The economic growth model assumes development to be irreversible, like biological evolution. Modernization occurred when the necessary conditions for change were established, and the process continued inexorably. Societies absorbed the stress and adapted themselves and their institutions to the change in order to prosper. In reality, however, this dominant paradigm of development did not produce the success stories that governments and aid agencies had promised. The complex processes and depth of traditional behaviors rendered most development efforts futile. Criticism of the model mounted and continues today.

To understand the role that mass media was thought to play in development under the dominant paradigm, it is important to note that one of the most prominent features of the paradigm was the assumption that development could be equated with economic growth, the type of rapid growth that core nations experienced through capital-intensive, technology-driven industrialization. As Everett Rogers points out, "economists were firmly in the driver's seat of development programs. They defined the problem of underdevelopment largely in economic terms, and in turn this perception of the problem as predominantly economic in nature helped to put and to keep economists in charge."[7] Despite criticisms, theorists and aid practitioners continued to be preoccupied with the economic determinism of Western models of modernization, in large part because they produced measurable phenomena.

Yet, as nations struggled to move from the peripheral to the semi-peripheral zone and finally to elite core status, the nations and their citizens needed to adopt the trappings and values of a modernized state. Embedded in the modernization process is the ever-pervasive and influential role of mass-media and communication technologies. Anthony Giddens states,

The media, printed and electronic, obviously play a central role in this respect. Mediated experience, since the first experience of writing, has long influenced both self-identity and the basic organization of social relations. With the development of mass communication, particularly electronic communication, the interpenetration of self-development and social systems up to and including global systems becomes even more pronounced.[8]

To some extent, Giddens is speculating that modernization will ultimately lead to Marshall McLuhan's "global village," where communication systems are capable of importing images, data, and sounds from around the corner or around the globe, with similar technologies and similar effects. One of the most profound effects will be that the language of the "global village" will be English.[9]

In summary, development has been viewed as "a type of social change in which new ideas are introduced into a social system in order to produce higher per capita incomes and levels of living through modem product methods and improved social organization."[10] But after decades, a growing chorus of critics began to make themselves heard.

The inadequacy of the economic growth model

For the most part, attempts at direct social and economic change in peripheral regions never materialized, and the effort of core nations to engineer change in peripheral nations has been largely unsuccessful. In fact, a recent World Bank *World Development Report*[11] points out that developing countries are still relatively worse off, *vis-à-vis* the core nations, in terms of growth. One only has to look at the relative penetration of information technologies per capita to glean how far behind peripheral nations are in participating in the information revolution and global economy. Some critics, such as Kevin Danaher, go so far as to claim that the World Bank and the International Monetary Fund (IMF) have been counterproductive in terms of global development. Moreover, critics, such as those opposing trade agreements, point out that economic life simply has not improved through World Bank intervention and that local private enterprises in peripheral nations are frequently squeezed out by large IMF projects or multinationals entering peripheral regions in cooperation with the IMF or other aid agencies.[12]

Another major problem is illiteracy. Along with economic stagnation, many peripheral nations have increasing illiteracy rates. Peripheral regions are defined in part by their high illiteracy rates. Illiteracy makes access to consumption of certain mass media such as newspapers, magazines, and books irrelevant to a large proportion of the population in peripheral areas, particularly the younger generation.

Many peripheral-based critics began questioning the entire functional school of media theory. In general, the functional theorists uncritically accepted the position of media elites and the reinforcement of the status quo as legitimate and rational behavior for the media systems. But today, the relevant question about placing communication systems in peripheral nations is, "Functional for whom?"

Imported economic practices, technologies, and media often created confusion because traditional systems were unable to support the required change. In turn, some analysts shifted to non-economic explanations of development, identifying variables such as mass-media exposure, telecommunications, political and social structural changes, social mobility, and individual psychology as preconditions for development and eventual modernization.

The development of mass communication was portrayed under the dominant paradigm as part of a universal, inevitable sequence of changes that traditional societies undergo in the transition to modernity. Mass communication was thought to function best in the service of centralized government development agencies when geared toward raising the public's aspirations and facilitating the acceptance of new ideas, values, and inventions for the purposes of overall economic growth and higher gross national product (GNP). Critical questions about the violence, tastes, values, language, history, role models, or cultures inherent in foreign mass media were simply not addressed.

The Research Traditions

When communication researchers turned their attention to development and modernity, they had a dual heritage. First, they were influenced strongly by the body of theory on the development process that had been built up in other fields, namely economics, political science, and sociology. But equally strong influences on development communication research were the well-established traditions and orientation of social-science research in the communication field. The following sections briefly review the major research traditions in the discipline of communication – functionalism, structuralism, and professionalism. Almost the entire body of literature dealing with international communication since the post-Second World War era was guided and influenced by these schools of thought.

Functionalism

The traditions of functionalism began to take shape with the commercially oriented early mass communication research of the 1930s and 1940s in the US. Functionalism reflected the marketing concerns of a consumer society.

Lazarsfeld, one of the pioneers of mass communication research, described this type of work as "administrative research."[13]

Historically, US mass communication research isolated specific media purposes, messages, or effects from the overall social process. It did not attempt to relate communication to the social, ideological, political, cultural, and economic systems in which it operated. Explanations about the specific communication data were seldom discussed in terms of the larger communication system, or from a macrotheoretical perspective. A linear, one-time analysis was typical of the early stages of research and still afflicts the discipline today.

US mass communication researchers concentrated on collecting and classifying data in order to illuminate new forms of social control, persuasion, or attitude change. They did not see it as their function to interpret these facts or build grand theories about structural and systemic determinants of the communication process. This early trend continues, with a focus on quantitative, empirical, behavioral-science methods as opposed to highly conceptual, speculative, theoretical, or philosophically discursive approaches to mass communication research. There are a few noticeable exceptions.[14]

This emphasis on quantitative, empirical methodology at the micro level is not surprising, considering that most early mass communication research studies were commissioned by broadcast, political, or advertising organizations. They were to deal with specifically defined concerns about message effectiveness. These sponsors wanted to know what kind of political propaganda or persuasion technique would produce the desired effect. They were interested in the influence of such things as votes, purchases, and conformity on the behavior of individuals. They wanted hard data about particular messages. They had no interest in how these findings fit into a greater social, ideological, or cultural scheme. Melvin Defleur and Sandra Ball-Rokeach note that as a result, the study of audiences to discover effects almost monopolized mass communication research.[15] Following the functionalism approach, US researchers have tended to accept the system as a given and implicitly endorse it by failing to examine how their understanding of communication could be enriched by questioning other basic characteristics of the system such as ownership and power.

Structuralism

Some critics, such as Herbert and Dan Schiller, Dallas Smythe, Bob McChesney, and Howard Frederick, probed more deeply into the question of who communicates and for what purposes. They found that the real shaper of peripheral nations' communication systems and the messages they produce is media from core nations. Most peripheral regimes do not have the expertise or resources to establish domestic communication systems that genuinely reflect their history, needs, concerns, values, and culture. Consequently, they rely on the transfer (usually through foreign-aid programs) of core-nation communication technology and software. Imported TV series and sitcoms, feature films, and wire-service copy are far cheaper to acquire than the equivalent domestically produced media fare.

In addition, it is important to note that most of the international communication industry is owned and controlled by giant core nations, mainly in the form of European, US, or Japanese transnational communication conglomerates. Good examples are Time Warner, Disney, Viacom, General Electric (NBC), the News Corporation (FOX), Sony, and Bertelsmann. These corporations are tied closely into a subtle and invisible network of core-based political, ideological, and economic elites, and they use the communication industry to perpetuate certain "needs," tastes, values, and attitudes so as to increase profits. When a peripheral nation imports, either through purchase, loan, or donation, telecommunication technologies (from simple shortwave radio equipment, to printing presses, to ground stations for color television by means of satellite or the internet), plus software, it imports an alternative way of life. Schiller describes this as cultural imperialism and claims that it is becoming steadily more important in the exercise of global economic power:

> The marketing system developed to sell industry's outpouring of (largely inauthentic) consumer goods is now applied as well to globally selling ideas, tastes, preferences, and beliefs. In fact, in advanced capitalism's present stage, the production and dissemination of what it likes to term "information" become major and indispensable activities, by any measure, in the overall system. Made-in-America messages, imagery, lifestyles, and information techniques are being internationally circulated and, equally important, globally imitated. Multinational media corporations are major players in the world economy. Information and communications are vital components in the system of administration and control. Communication, it needs to be said, includes much more than messages and the recognizable circuits through which the messages flow. It defines social reality and thus influences the organization of work, the character of technology, the curriculum of the educational system, formal and informal, and the use of "free" time – actually, the basic social arrangements of living.[16]

A substantial body of literature deals with the central concept of cultural imperialism,[17] which usually applies either to specific peripheral nations or to specific communication industries such as feature films, advertising, television sitcoms, or mass circulation magazines. The central finding of the research is that exporting corporations establish ground rules in such a way that the peripheral nations are at a structural disadvantage from the start. Yet this is considered a crucial process in world-system theory. Somehow, this imbalance is supposed to exist in order for core nations to grow and succeed even more. A good example of this process is the global leader in video rentals, the US retailer Blockbuster. In addition to its US stores, Blockbuster has more than 2,600 stores in 28 foreign nations. Many of these stores are in semiperipheral and peripheral nations. One can easily imagine what happens to a small, local, family-owned and -operated video store in peripheral nations such as Thailand, Argentina, Brazil, Mexico, or Chile when a Blockbuster store opens in the same community. Finally, as it seeks to become the leading global provider of home video rentals, Block-buster also brings with it a vast library of Hollywood feature films and US marketing and advertising expertise, with little room or interest for low-volume video rentals of indigenous productions.

Professionalism

An integral but seldom discussed instrument of cultural imperialism is the technocratic baggage, including technicians, engineers, producers, directors, behind-the-scenes personnel, and writers, that are required for the technical maintenance and operation of an imported communication infrastructure. These technocrats usually are on loan from the industrialized nations or are trained and educated in core nations. They bring to peripheral countries value systems and attitudes associated with Western professionalism about how communication systems should be properly run. This socialization frequently adds another layer to the software that portrays a foreign culture. Moreover, technological personnel are frequently in the employ of various core-nation aid agencies – governmental, educational, or religious organizations – that also are heavily value-laden enterprises with a proselytizing agenda.

These realities may help to explain why the introduction of mass media in many peripheral nations failed to produce substantial results. Although there was some effort to promote cultural sovereignty and indigenous productions, in the final analysis these efforts produced little of substance on a national level. A noted authority in the field, Robert Stevenson, states:

> Development journalism – very much a part of the New World Information Order debate at the United Nations Educational, Scientific and Cultural Organization (UNESCO) in the 1970s – now has a record, and it is not impressive.[18]

Given its preoccupation with audience research, US communication studies have not investigated the ties that bind media institutions to other sources and structures of power, whether domestic or international. In essence, communication experts have taken for granted that more modern technology, including communication hardware and software, will be beneficial and will promote more economic growth. In fact, the policies they support do not advance development or improve their quality of life, but tend to foster a neocolonial-like dependence on the core nations. Increasing amounts of media and information technologies often contribute to the already unbalanced distribution of benefits by concentrating additional communication power in the hands of ruling elites. These elites may be political, religious, or military in nature. This further creates tension and frustration in peripheral regions by promoting inappropriate and inaccessible consumer products and values, further expanding the economic gap between core and peripheral nations.

Professionalism, as a body of research, did not have a parallel counterpart in European communication studies. The European tradition differs in two dramatic ways. First, many of the studies undertaken by European communication scholars deal with either critical theory emerging from the Frankfurt School of the 1930s, or with cultural studies that examine issues from a far different perspective than the North American traditions. Furthermore, practicing media professionals in Europe have distinctly different training than their US counterparts. Whereas most US professionals are required to have a university degree, preferably from one of the leading schools of journalism, European media outlets prefer to train their personnel through apprenticeships at regional media outlets, such as provincial newspapers. Thus, European media professionals learn their craft by doing rather than by studying.

Despite the substantial difference between European and US socialization of media professionals and technicians, it is important to note that the critical school frequently examines ownership by media elites or economic aspects of the industry. These European researchers often reach conclusions similar to those of US scholars. Basically they have found dysfunctional elements in the exportation of considerable amounts of communication hardware, software, and related cultural products.

Western Research Failings

More exhaustive approaches focusing on structural, contextual, and procedural determinants of communication have been low-priority research concerns in the US. US students of communication have never sought a conceptual inventory that would provide a complete basis for explaining communication in the context of an overall social system. This failure to recognize communication as inextricably tied to social structure and power has hampered the field. Even the diffusion-of-innovation research tradition has flawed assumptions. Luis Beltran writes,

> One basic assumption of the diffusion approach is that communication by itself can generate development, regardless of socioeconomic and political conditions. Another assumption is that increased production and consumption of goods and services constitute the essence of development, and that a fair distribution of income and opportunities will necessarily derive in due time. A third assumption is that the key to increased productivity is technological innovation, regardless of whom it may benefit and whom it may harm.[19]

The dominant research tools of diffusion studies – interview, sample survey, and content analysis – are another obstacle to the exploration of social structure as a key factor in the communication process. A preoccupation with methodological precision and small samples has taken precedence over macrotheoretical formulations.

This brings us to another feature of communication research that militates against the adoption of a macrosocial approach that encompasses the roles of structural and organizational variables. Most theoretical models of development tend to locate internal sources of problems in developing countries and seldom look at external agencies or practices, such as the World Bank or World Trade Organization, or at foreign ownership of media, ad agencies, and telecommunication systems. Many of the peripheral nations have simply been glad to be the recipients of foreign aid or to have a global corporation build a plant or office in their country and create new employment opportunities.

It was suggested earlier that the lack of an adequate focus on structure in development communication research in particular, and US communication studies in general, is related to researchers' acceptance of the premise that the system is in synch. Basically, researchers did not question the system since they viewed it as working for everyone's benefit. This acceptance makes it difficult for researchers to question the structure and organization of that system, instead encouraging them to concentrate their attention on how mass communication could act on audiences in a way that promotes conformity, purchases, and adjustment to a larger consumption-driven social order.

One could argue that the lack of a structural focus stems also from the empirical, quantitative slant of US communication research and a corresponding reluctance to theorize at the macro level, as Marshall McLuhan did. The influences of communication on ideological and value systems, patterns of social organization, or subtle, difficult-to-measure matrices of power and social interaction are much harder to handle with empirical precision. These variables are less subject to rigorous measurements than the effects of specific messages on specific audiences. Study of those influences necessarily involves some theorizing, hypothesizing, and a speculative thinking not always firmly rooted in hard data. But such modes of understanding run against the grain of the exactness of the behavioral-science tradition of US communication research as promoted and reinforced at universities.

Recently, the claim of scientific neutrality and objectivity is being challenged by a growing number of critics in the communication and journalism fields. Some comparative research is also appearing. In the foreword to *Images of the U.S. Around the World: A Multicultural Perspective*, Majid Tehranian makes the following point concerning the image of the US in a global context:

> The image of the United States thus gradually deteriorated from a friend to a foe. In the meantime, however, the flow of American soft power in the spread of its cultural influence around the world through its cultural exports (English language, books, films, music, radio and TV programs, blue jeans, Coca-Cola, Madonna, and Michael Jackson) has seduced the younger generation nearly everywhere into emulating the American ways. The repugnance against Americanization has led some critics of US cultural influences to call it westoxification. Just like intoxication, the afflicted not only fall victim to its influence but revel in it.[20]

New Departures

Current students of the discipline have found development communication theory and research methodology wanting in several respects, and they are undergoing a reexamination. To overcome these limitations, efforts are underway to find more sophisticated tools for measuring the influence of social structure; for example, the non-economic variables of social life and culture, at both macro and micro levels.

In addition, Marxist theories of communication and development gained attention during the 1960s and 1970s. In these models, the causes of underdevelopment are traced back to international imbalances caused by the dominance of capitalist systems and the imperialist control they exercise over peripheral regions. There is a growing consciousness of the role that multinationals play in perpetuating colonial dependence both culturally and ideologically through their economic and political control of the international communication industry. This understanding is reflected in many new models that consider the influence of global political and economic power structures on development in their attempts to describe the causes of and solutions to underdevelopment. But in the early 1990s, with the failure of communism and its champion, the Soviet Union, much of the interest in and research with a Marxist underpinning quickly lost advocates and viability. The Marxist body of communication literature became stale. Still, the predominately European-based critical school of cultural studies is gaining broader attention. Although it offers a significant alternative, the problems of operationalizing its premises make large-scale research projects difficult and very costly.

For decades, communication scholars such as Schiller and Rogers pointed out the centrality of communication in the development process, but their research and scholarship had little impact outside the discipline of communication. Most of the aid agencies and government organizations responsible for implementing development policies are controlled and dominated by economists or political scientists, and these academics failed to understand the crucial role of communication in the development cycle. If they had, they might have been more successful, and the voices of criticism might have been fewer and less vociferous.

The good news is that there is evidence of a growing movement toward change. The World Bank provides a good example. Long focused on the more easily measured economic indices of development such as miles of asphalt or tons of concrete, the World Bank is reconsidering its focus. It has discovered the centrality of communication within the overall development process. Each year the World Bank publishes its *World Development Report*, which identifies factors that promote sustainable development. It also reflects the thinking of the bank's senior staff. Historically, the reports have focused on large-scale projects, some of which relate to transportation and agrarian infrastructures. However, the 1998 report marks a dramatic shift by including communication as central to future development:

> The Report suggests three lessons that are particularly important to the welfare of the billions of people in developing countries.
>
> 1. First, developing countries must institute policies that enable them to narrow the knowledge gaps separating poor countries from rich.
>
> 2. Second, developing country governments, multilateral institutions, nongovernmental organizations, and the private sector must work together to strengthen the institutions needed to address the information problems that cause markets and governments to fail.

3. Third, no matter how effective these endeavors are, problems with knowledge will persist. But recognizing that knowledge is at the core of all our development effort will allow us to discover unexpected solutions to seemingly intractable problems.[21]

In the face of its critics, the World Bank is attempting to reposition itself as an institution that understands and fosters the central role of information, knowledge, and communication in its expanding global mandate.

Finally, a new movement under the umbrella of participatory communication has emerged. It seeks to use communication as a tool at the grassroots level. A goal is to bring about social change by using nonformal education methods. Nongovernmental organizations (NGOs), in particular, attempt to work with local people in peripheral regions to share efforts and goals. This approach seeks to promote ownership at the community level. Participatory communication is not top-down but aims at being sensitive to local traditions, culture, and language by engaging locals at every stage of both planning and implementation.[22] The regions of Africa, Latin America, and Asia have attempted with varying degrees of success to implement social change along the lines of participatory communication strategies.

Postscript

As noted earlier, the criticisms identified here created widespread cause for concern among academics, professionals, and policy-makers. Some are calling for a new definition of development journalism/communication in light of the failure of dominant models.[23] The many nations in the peripheral zone are still stuck in that most marginal, least desirable zone, with little if any power. In a later chapter, we will examine the role of UNESCO in bringing communication concerns to the forefront of the international arena. Although NWICO is not a research methodology, it does represent some theoretical alternatives for media flows, indigenous practices, and cultural sovereignty. These issues deserve the attention of students of development and the media, as well as professionals actively involved in the collection, observation, and reporting of foreign news, cultures, and viewpoints.

In its infancy, discussions about NWICO were marginal, manifesting themselves in a few academic departments and marginal textbooks. But when UNESCO championed the cause for a reexamination of international communication flows, the debates surrounding NWICO took on a life of their own. By introducing communication issues into global political discourse, UNESCO simultaneously found both supporters and detractors.

Whereas some nations recognized the validity of the arguments and concerns, others interpreted them in terms of Cold War rhetoric and divisions. In fact, the latter position ultimately led to the withdrawal from UNESCO of the UK, under Prime Minister Margaret Thatcher, and the US, under President Ronald Reagan. Both countries have now returned to UNESCO. The main point is that communication research with an international focus is changing, complex, and in some cases controversial. Previous theories and approaches appear limited, which is why the application of world-system theory, as well as the theory of electronic colonialism, to global communication trends is a welcome addition to the discipline. Electronic colonialism theory examines the cultural forces influencing individual's attitudes and behaviors in foreign countries, whereas world-system theory attempts to explain and separate the different nations or regions of the world into a three-stage or platform construct.

We now turn to major global stakeholders, including US and foreign multimedia conglomerates. An important point to keep in mind is that new digital technologies are blurring the old boundaries between software and hardware, between broadcasting and telecommunication. Old divisions and distinctions are becoming meaningless as giant communication firms morph into digital providers of a broad array of products and services to end users – customers – around the globe without concern for national boundaries. The convergence of delivery systems in a broadband environment will force regulators and multimedia firms to rethink their global strategies in the near future.

Notes

1 Normandy Madden, "Cable, Satellite Media Lure Influential Viewers," *Advertising Age International* (Oct. 1999), p. 36.
2 The history of development journalism may be traced to the Department of Development Communication in the College of Agriculture at the University of the Philippines. It was established in 1973 for the purpose of training students to assist in the communication process of transmitting, by way of the media, the government's policies on agricultural development projects.
3 Andrew Moemeka, "Development Communication: A Historical and Conceptual Overview," in *Communication for Development*, ed. Andrew Moemeka (Albany: State University of New York Press, 1994), p. 7.
4 Kwasi Ansu-Kyeremeh, "Indigenous Communication in Africa: A Conceptual Framework," in *Perspective on Indigenous Communication in Africa*, ed. Kwasi Ansu-Kyeremeh (Legon, Ghana: School of Communication Studies Printing Press, 1998), p. 1.
5 Ank Linden, "Overt Intentions and Covert Agendas," *Gazette* 61(2) (1999), p. 153.

6   Walter Rostow, *The Stages of Economic Growth* (New York: Cambridge University Press, 1960).

7   Everett Rogers, "Communication and Development: The Passing of the Dominant Paradigm," *Communication Research* 3 (1976), p. 215. Rogers wrote the "Introduction" to the first edition of *Electronic Colonialism*. He died in 2004.

8   Anthony Giddens, *Modernity and Self-Identity* (Stanford: Stanford University Press, 1991), p. 4.

9   David Crystal, *English as a Global Language* (Cambridge: Cambridge University Press, 1997).

10 Everett Rogers, *Modernization Among Peasants: The Impact of Communication* (New York: Holt, Rinehart, and Winston, 1969), pp. 8–9.

11 *World Development Report 1998/99: Knowledge for Development* (New York: Oxford University Press, 1998).

12 See, for example, the following collection of essays, which dissect the role of the World Bank and the International Monetary Fund in promoting the politicization of economic life, inhibiting private enterprise, and delaying the emergence from poverty. The contributions argue that because of the nature of their structure, the World Bank and the IMF cannot change pro-market policies. Doug Bandow and Ian Vasques, *Perpetuating Poverty: The World Bank, the IMF, and the Developing World* (Washington, DC: Cato Institute, 1994), p. 362. Also Kevin Danaher, *10 Reasons to Abolish the IMF and World Bank* (New York: Seven Stories Press, 2001).

13 Paul Lazarsfeld, "Remarks on Administrative and Critical Communication Research," *Studies in Philosophy and Social Science* 9 (1941), pp. 2–16.

14 Two of the most notable exceptions are Kyumyruo Kim and George Barnett, "The Determinants of International News Flows: A Network Analysis," *Communication Research* 23(3) (1996), pp. 323–52, and Jianguo Zhu, "Comparing the Effects of Mass Media and Telecommunications on Economic Development: A Pooling Time Series Analysis," *Gazette* 57 (1996), pp. 17–28.

15 Melvin Defleur and Sandra Ball-Rokeach, *Theories of Mass Communication* (New York: Longman, 1975).

16 Herbert Schiller, *Communication and Cultural Domination* (White Plains, NY: International Arts and Sciences Press, 1976), p. 3.

17 Some scholars see this substantial body of literature as being overly representative of the body of knowledge in international communication. One critic refers to this aspect in the following way: "The root of the problem is that the research paradigm of the field of international communication is dominantly critical" (p. 382). After applying a meta-analysis, the author claimed that the majority of writers used polemics rather than empirical evidence to support their conclusions. In the same piece, the author also called for the utilization of more meta-analysis in order to move the field of international communication to a higher plateau. Michael G. Elasmar, "Opportunities and Challenges of Meta-Analysis in the Field of International Communication," *Critical Studies in Mass Communication* 16(3) (Sept. 1999), pp. 379–84.

18 Robert Stevenson, *Global Communication in the Twenty-First Century* (New York: Longman Publishing Group, 1994), p. 13.

19 Luis Beltran, "Allen Premises, Objects and Methods in Latin American Communication Research," *Communication Research* 3 (1976), pp. 107–34.
20 Majid Tehranian, "Foreword," in *Images of the U.S. Around the World: A Multicultural Perspective*, ed. Y. Kamalipour (Albany: State University of New York Press, 1999), pp. xvi–xvii.
21 World Bank, *World Development Report 1998/99*, p. 1.
22 For further details see: J. Servaes, T. Jacobson, and S. White, eds., *Participatory Communication for Social Change* (London: Sage Publications, 1996), and T. Jacobson and J. Servaes, eds., *Theoretical Approaches to Participatory Communication* (Cresskill, NJ: Hampton Press, 1999).
23 Hermant Shah, "Modernization, Marginalization, and Emancipation: Toward a Normative Model of Journalism and National Development," *Communication Theory* 6(2) (May 1998), pp. 143–67.

Chapter 3

American Multimedia Giants

Introduction

Not long ago, US productions, particularly feature films and television shows, dominated theater screens and television sets around the globe.[1] Foreign productions provided relatively little competition. Today, other major global firms either own US production houses, or they produce elsewhere world-class competitive products for a global media market. Sony of Japan and Bertelsmann of Germany are good examples of foreign multimedia firms which compete daily with US media companies. Yet US firms still control a majority of foreign sales in the global communication market. They are also expanding through regional partnerships, international joint ventures, or outright takeovers. Time Warner, Disney, Viacom, News Corporation, and General Electric represent the major US media owners that dominate many global media and global media-related markets. (See figure 3.1.)

Time Warner controls CNN, HBO, Warner Brothers Records, AOL, and several other media properties. Disney controls ABC; Viacom owns MTV, CBS, BET, and Blockbuster. News Corp. owns the Fox properties, and General Electric owns NBC Universal. All are headquartered in the United States, the dominant core nation, with extensive semiperipheral and some peripheral market activities. This chapter details origins, assets, and global interests of major US multimedia firms.

It is important to note the profiles of such multimedia firms. First, in terms of revenue, the three largest global media empires are all American. Time Warner, which owns several major properties, is by far the largest, but it does not own a general-interest national television network such as ABC, CBS, FOX, or NBC. Disney is second and owns ABC radio and television,

1. Time Warner (US)

2. Disney (US)

3. Viacom (US)

4. Bertelsmann (Germany)

5. News Corporation (US)

6. Sony (Japan)

7. General Electric–NBC Universal (US)

8. VNU (Netherlands)

9. Dow Jones (US)

10. Vivendi (France)

Figure 3.1   Global media leaders

as well as ESPN. Viacom is third and owns CBS radio and television, along with MTV and BET. The fourth largest global media empire is the News Corporation, which domestically controls the FOX television network, 20th Century Fox, and has many other global properties. NBC network is owned by General Electric and is detailed in this chapter. NBC also has global activities such as CNBC, MSNBC, which is a partnership with Microsoft, and cable TV channels in Europe and Asia.

Second, in terms of electronic colonialism theory, all of the US multimedia empires, along with their extensive advertising networks, project and encourage US tastes, values, mores, history, culture, and language around the world. To a considerable extent, it is this influence that concerns other core,[2] semiperipheral, and peripheral countries because of the impact of US multimedia fare on those countries' domestic media. Their concern covers a vast range of cultural products such as music, movies, television series, magazines, books, and now the internet. In terms of world-system theory, the United States' activities in semiperipheral nations, which have large, accessible markets with growing disposable incomes, as well its activities in some peripheral nations, illustrate well the model explaining the broad range of offshore economic activities undertaken by major US communication corporations. Major US global multimedia empires define relations with other nations along several product lines, as well as advertising, on an expanding number of foreign commercial television, radio networks, and print publications.

Hollywood- and New York-based communication corporations do well on a global scale because they have four substantial advantages. First, they operate in English, the language of the largest global segment of media outlets with purchasing power. Second, they have access to substantial fiscal resources and capital markets, allowing them to finance multimillion-dollar productions. A single Hollywood feature film costs more than most other nations spend annually on all their feature films. Third, US television networks overwhelmingly prefer US made primetime shows. ABC, CBS, FOX, and NBC seldom purchase foreign-made programs. Fourth, Hollywood and New York have access to the broadest range of acting talent, producers, writers, and directors. Some of the talent is from other core nations such as Australia, Canada, Britain, France, or Japan. The best global actors and actresses work primarily or exclusively on US productions. The critics of US cultural imperialism are at a virtual loss about what to do. Some call for media protectionist policies, which emerge from time to time around the globe. Quotas limiting US media imports are a good example. Others simply lament the fact that the business is all about economics and job opportunities and that there are scant opportunities for actors, writers, or producers from semiperiphal and peripheral nations to obtain employment and needed exposure in core nations. Most foreign commercial markets buy US television and movies for their television and theater outlets. For example, across Europe, 60 to 80 percent of their purchases of foreign television programming are native to the US. At least 50 percent of the movie screens in Europe show Hollywood productions as well. Across Latin America 60 percent of the movie screens show Hollywood productions. In the future, as the number of channels increases in other core and semiperipheral nations thanks to cable, satellite, and digital technologies, the need for content will only increase the demand for American productions of all genres.

The three largest media conglomerates in the world are all US owned. They are Time Warner, Disney, and Viacom. They and other significant US multimedia enterprises are detailed as follows.

Time Warner

The merger of American Online and Time Warner created the largest communication organization in the world. It was a US$350 billion deal completed in 2000. The merger and anticipated synergies have not gone nearly as well as expected. Initially, the merger faced serious regulatory hurdles in both Europe and the United States, but for different reasons. In Europe the European Commission's antitrust enforcers focused primarily on Time Warner's music holdings in considering whether to approve the deal. For them it was a culturally charged issue. Eventually Time Warner agreed not to pursue the purchase of the major British music empire EMI, and made other concessions, in order to obtain European approval. On the other hand, in the United States the merger had to survive two separate reviews, one by the Federal Trade Commission (FTC) and the other by the Federal Communications Commission (FCC). Their concerns focused primarily on the issue of access, which was a concern on two fronts: (1) access to the vast Time Warner cable systems across the United States, and (2) access to America Online properties, particularly their email and other e-properties contained in AOL.

Essentially, US regulators were concerned about providing a level playing field for competitors who had to deal with the giant merged companies of AOL and Time Warner. Washington powerbrokers remembered that Time Warner cable division had pulled the cable plug affecting Disney's ABC TV network. This involved millions of subscribers in 1999. The lengthy review process was dominated by negotiations to protect competitors from either of two possible scenarios. First, AOL providing monopolistic preference for Time Warner's vast product lines, and second, Time Warner's cable systems providing clear preference for AOL's internet activities. Even so, after the approval, AOL, formerly headed by Steve Case, owns 55 percent of the newly merged firm, and Time Warner owns the balance, 45 percent. In January 2003, Case was removed as Chairman in a major executive shake-up. AOL still has about 80,000 employees around the globe.

This concern about Time Warner being unfair to a competitor such as Disney's ABC was a defining moment for all other nations. If AOL and Time Warner were willing to obstruct a major stakeholder such as Disney, then what chance did the distinctly smaller stakeholders in other core, semipe-ripheral, and peripheral nations have to withstand the enlarged Time Warner juggernaut? They perceived the merger as exemplifying the way in which electronic colonialism was reaching not just a new, broader, and more sophisticated level, but moving into a more pervasive phase of global commu-nication, through the internet, which AOL personifies. Time Warner man-agement and shareholders applauded the marriage, while end users outside the US hardly realized that their domestic or indigenous productions and networks would be fighting for their very survival. The merger also turned out to be a fiscal mess since the synergies failed to appear and the stock took a big dive. In fact, senior management took the "AOL" part of their corpo-rate name off the masthead to improve the image of their core assets. So today the combined company is known simply as Time Warner. Ted Turner of CNN fame, a major shareholder, quit their board of directors in disgust. Generally, the analysis of world-system theory pits the core nations against the values and interests of the semiperipheral and peripheral nations. But the high-profile merger of AOL and Time Warner clearly presented a

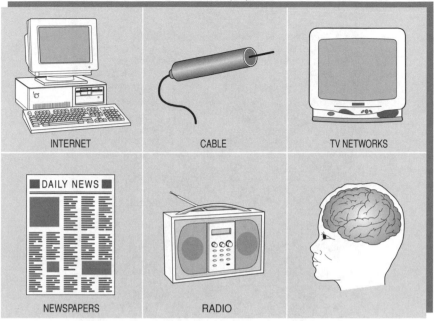

Figure 3.2a   Time Warner and AOL's strategic goals
Source: St. Louis Post-Dispatch editorial cartoon, Feb. 26, 2002. Reproduced by kind permission.

situation in which a single core nation – the US – is influencing all other core nations, including Canada, Australia, Japan, the European Union, Latin America, and eventually every other nation on the planet. (See figure 3.2a.)

Before describing the various media assets of Time Warner, it is important to note that the merger is part of the internet revolution. AOL brings the technological advances necessary to push Time Warner to a more sophisticated level of promoting on a global scale its substantial portfolio of communication holdings. AOL had previously merged with other internet companies such as Netscape and CompuServe. The combined company is seeking to take advantage of the global growth of advertising that utilizes e-commerce as a major revenue stream. Finally, an interesting byproduct of the merger is that this marriage of old media (Time Warner) and new media (AOL) is putting all other companies under a microscope, as customers and shareholders alike begin to expect that other old media stakeholders will join with relatively new media enterprise to become more internet savvy. Time Warner brings to the AOL merger a vast array of media and subsidiaries. (See figure 3.2b.)

AOL	Warner Books
AOL Europe	Turner Entertainment
AOL Latin America	Turner Classic Movies
Compuserve	TBS
CNN	TNT
HBO	New Line Cinema
Cinemax	Little, Brown & Company
Time Inc.	Fine Line Features
Time4 Media	Cartoon Network
Time Warner Books UK	Atlantic Recording Corp.
Time Warner Cable	Elektra Entertainment Group
Warner Music Group	IPC Group Limited (Europe)
Warner Bros. Pictures	Comedy Central (50%)
WB Network	Court TV (50%)

Figure 3.2b   Major Time Warner properties

Its major properties include CNN, Warner Bros., HBO, Cinemax, Time Warner Cable, Time Warner Books, Warner Music Group, Time Inc., its publishing arm, and TBS. Time Warner's 2003 global revenues were close to $40 billion. Time Inc. accounts for 15 percent of Time Warner's sales. Warner Bros.' movies and WB television network generate almost 50 percent of Time Warner's sales. They also publish over 30 feature magazines such as *Time, People*, and *Sports Illustrated*. The Time Warner video group controls close to 6,000 feature films, including *Austin Powers: International Man of Mystery* and *Pokemon*; 32,000 television shows, and 14,000 animated titles. During the 1990s, Time Warner launched 9 new magazine titles; it sees a strong future for print media. It operates major book clubs and book publishing through Warner Books and Little, Brown, and promotes print and videos through the Time Life series. Finally, Time Warner controls 50 percent of both Comedy Central and Court TV.

A major Time Warner acquisition was the 1996 takeover of Ted Turner's Turner Broadcasting System (TBS) for $8 billion, which brought all of Turner's properties, including the prestigious global broadcasting news network CNN, as well as TNT, TBS, and Atlanta's three professional sports teams, into the Time Warner family.

Time Warner Entertainment history

In 1922, 24-year-old Henry Robinson Luce founded Time Inc.[3] Beginning with *Time* magazine and later *Life*, *Fortune*, and *Sports Illustrated*, Luce became the leading global magazine publisher. Time Inc. lost its print persona almost overnight when in 1989 it merged with Warner Communications. Warner brought a major video culture to the print culture of Time. The new, combined entity, Time Warner Entertainment (TWE), experienced some merger woes. The two different corporate cultures took time to blend, and senior management experienced turmoil, but eventually Gerald Levin of Time Inc. became chairman and CEO of Time Warner in 1992.

The new focus for TWE was expanded further with the addition of Ted Turner's empire in 1996. Today, journalism and entertainment history co-exist at TWE. Gerald Levin recalls Luce's legacy at TWE:

> Luce was adamant that economic progress was inextricably linked to political systems that actively encouraged individual initiative and free enterprise. For me, the advent of a digitally based economy gives Luce's view fresh urgency.
>
> Luce also insisted it wasn't enough for business leaders to pursue efficiency and productivity. Those who entered the executive suites of American business had to have a heightened sense of their responsibility to the common good.
>
> I share this conviction.[4]

Levin also comments on his grasp on the new role for video and cable at Time: "At the heart of what I envisioned was a world-class news operation in print and electronic media, with the size and resources to immunize it from those who had no regard for its heritage."[5]

> I believe that if Luce had entered the media business when Ted Turner did, his instincts as an entrepreneur and journalist would have led him to grasp cable's potential for creating a new kind of global journalism. In the same way I believe that the 24-year-old Luce who conceived Time or the media revolutionary who proclaimed that Life was more than a news magazine – that it was a new way of seeing – would have jumped on the Internet and been a formative influence on its evolution as a news medium.[6]

Luce was a print man, whereas Levin brought expertise in video, and through the merger with AOL, he also brought internet expertise. Levin was sacked in 2002 and AOL's Steve Case a short time later.[7] Also, Time Warner's major competitors – Disney, Viacom, News Corporation, Sony, Bertelsmann, NBC Universal, and others – compete in the same global communication market with many competing brands.

CNN connection

Although CNN, a Time Warner enterprise, is discussed more thoroughly in chapter 6, an important issue involving CNN is relevant here. Ted Turner's video empire competed with Time's print focus and culture. Turner's various media properties greatly supplemented Time Warner's strategic moves in the video business. Turner brought with him not only a 24-hour cable news network and other media properties, but also the Goodwill Games, which Turner himself established in 1986 to provide an international platform for amateur athletes while at the same time ignoring Cold War rhetoric and sanctions. Turner had a global model in mind for both his media properties and his amateur athletics endeavors. He sought to use the games as a way to enrich all humanity, regardless of politics, national boundaries, and historical feuds. Turner thought globally and had a vision of world peace. He was a strong supporter of the United Nations as well.

The Goodwill Games have been held in the following cities: 1986, Moscow, Soviet Union; 1990, Seattle, United States; 1994, St. Petersburg, Russia; 1998, New York, United States; 2000, Lake Placid, United States; 2001, Brisbane, Australia. The TNT network provided extensive coverage of the events in over 100 countries. Time Warner finally closed the Goodwill Games in 2002, after holding them in Brisbane.

Turner's global perspective is manifest in several philanthropic undertakings. In 1990 Turner established the Turner Foundation with a $150 million endowment; it focuses on environmental and global population issues. In 1997 Turner also gave the United Nations Foundation $1 billion to encourage greater global cooperation. He resigned from Time Warner in 2003. Since that time Turner has been giving speeches and media interviews which are critical of Time Warner's strategic planning as well as the excessive power of media conglomerates. [8]

America Online (AOL)

The AOL side of the merger brings global leadership covering web brands, interactive services, internet connectivity, branded portals, and an expanding range of e-commerce services. The AOL network's handling of over two billion instant messages per day indicates an example of their size. AOL was founded in 1985 and has four major product lines:

1 Interactive Services Group includes AOL's major internet provider activities including CompuServe and Netscape, which are internet portals. This business group also contains AOL Wireless Services, which is designed to deliver AOL properties to an expanding global group of

wireless customers. Whereas most AOL customers today hook up to the internet through a PC, in the future, particularly in Europe and Asia, more and more clients will opt for wireless internet connectivity.

2   Interactive Properties Group contains branded properties such as Digital City; ICQ, a portal; AOL Instant Messenger, which is a popular electronic text message service; as well as Moviefone, Inc., and MapQuest.

3   AOL International Group is responsible for all AOL, CompuServe, and Netscape operations outside the United States. This is a rapidly expanding segment of AOL's overall business. AOL outside the US has more than 9 million subscribers. In many nations, AOL properties are the second leading internet provider. In foreign countries, the main internet provider is generally the domestic telecommunications company, such as France Telecom or Bell Canada. AOL Worldwide has the following divisions: UK, Canada, France, Brazil, Latino, Japan, Germany, Puerto Rico, and Argentina.

4   Netscape Enterprise Group includes software products, technical support, and consulting and training services.

The number of AOL subscribers around the world is close to 30 million, approximately 24 million of whom are in the United States. AOL is growing by approximately 5 million new subscribers a year, and it is engaging in more extensive joint ventures overseas. This is particularly true for wireless devices being developed in Europe and Asia.

AOL competes directly for internet subscription revenues with Microsoft, AT&T, Prodigy, and others. Their web-based search services and portals also face considerable competition from Google, Yahoo!, Lycos, Disney's portal, and Excite At Home. Even though it functions in a highly competitive environment, AOL has structurally maintained a distinct global lead as the major internet provider. By merging with Time Warner, AOL had hoped to move to a new level in its ability not only to provide connectivity and e-commerce services, but also to deliver around the globe a vast array of content through a mix of free and subscriber services. This major corporate merger is not being universally applauded. A number of key executives have been replaced. The firm still does not have a national television network among its properties. Some major competitors have expressed concern about being excluded or treated as second-class corporate citizens within the vast array of AOL services.

Synopsis

Time Warner became the world's largest media company through a long-term strategic plan involving major mergers. In 1989 it merged with Warner

Communications; in 1996, it merged with Turner Broadcasting; and in 2000 it merged with America Online. Time Warner now operates in six major communication sectors: cable, publishing, films, music, broadcasting, and the internet. Its cable systems provide some of the most technologically sophisticated digital fiberoptic systems available anywhere. The company has also focused on global markets. This is especially true of its broadcasting undertaking, particularly CNN International, which produces exclusive programming designed for Asia and Europe and reaches over 150 million TV-viewing households in over 212 countries and territories. A major part of AOL Time Warner's current strategic plan is aimed at expanding markets in other core nations, particularly European countries, as well as in semiperipheral nations, primarily in Asia. It is undertaking this without the advantage of a national television network based in the United States such as ABC, CBS, FOX, or NBC.

Disney

Disney is the world's second largest communication empire, after Time Warner, with annual revenues of $27 billion, just slightly more than third-place Viacom's $26.6 billion. Disney started early last century under the leadership of Walter Disney, who had a professional vision of using animated cartoons and feature films as major commercial ventures.[9] His brother, Roy Disney, provided the financial acumen to help build a media giant.[10] The venture produced global icons including widely recognized characters such as Mickey Mouse and Donald Duck. During the 1950s, the major film subsidiary Buena Vista was established, and a number of Disney shows were made for television. Disneyland opened in 1955 in California. In the 1960s, Disney had several successful feature films including *101 Dalmatians*, *Mary Poppins*, *The Jungle Book*, and *The Love Bug*. In the 1970s, further theatrical successes included *The Aristocats*, *Robin Hood*, and *The Rescuers*. Walt Disney World, another major theme park, opened in Orlando, Florida, in 1971. In 1983 Tokyo Disneyland opened, and that same year the Disney Channel began as a cable TV service. In the early 1990s, Disneyland Paris opened and quickly became controversial because of its US cultural orientation. Also, the Disney corporation purchased Capital Cities/ABC in 1995 and became a major television broadcasting network owner (see figure 3.3). In the late 1990s, several Disney subsidiaries started websites that include the ability to purchase products directly from Disney anywhere in the world. Disney currently operates as a global entertainment company with four major business divisions: Media Networks, Parks and Resorts, Studio Entertainment, and Consumer Products.

ABC Television Network	Walt Disney Internet Group
ABC Radio Network	Toon Channel
ESPN (80%)	Hollywood Pictures
Biography Channel	Touchstone
E! Entertainment	Miramax
Disney Publishing Worldwide	Buena Vista International
Euro Disney (39%)	Citadel Broadcasting
A&E Television Networks (38%)	Disney Stores Worldwide
Walt Disney Studios	Walt Disney Parks and Resorts
Walt Disney Television International	

Figure 3.3 Major Disney properties

A major global asset is Walt Disney Television International (WDTV-I). Now WDTV-I is available in 68 countries with over 600 million viewers worldwide per week. Part of the media fare is a cartoon channel for children, named Toon Disney. It carries Disney animation shows, movies, and cartoons. Internationally it is offered as part of cable or satellite packages aimed at children's audiences. Given Disney's vast library of video productions, much of it decades old, non-American networks have considerable difficulty competing with WDTV-I and the Toon Channel appeal.

The Walt Disney Internet Group has two main interests: entertainment websites and news websites. Combined, the sites attract close to 25 million viewers a month; sites include Disney Online, ESPN.com, ABC.com, and ABC news.com. The Internet Group also offers searches, chatrooms, message boards, and email. As a full-service internet provider, it competes directly with other major portals such as AOL, Microsoft, and Yahoo! Today Disney is a highly diversified communication conglomerate, ranging from broadcasting, to feature films, to the internet, to theme parks and resorts, to Disney stores, which operate in hundreds of locations worldwide.

History

The roots of Disney date back to December 30, 1890, when Walter Disney was born in Chicago, Illinois. Through his early years, Disney held several jobs including volunteering for the American Ambulance Corps, sorting and delivering Christmas mail for the Kansas City Post Office, and eventually forming a company with Ubbe Iwerks called Iwerks-Disney Commercial Artists. By 1920, Disney and Iwerks joined the Kansas City Slide Company, which was renamed the Kansas City Film Ad Service. That same year, Disney produced what he called "Laugh-O-Grams." Essentially, the production of Laugh-O-Grams was Disney's introduction to the world of animated film and the beginning of the Disney Empire. In 1937, *Snow White and the Seven Dwarfs* arrived in cinemas. It represented a new breed of film because it was full-length animation. After *Snow White*, Disney went on to produce 35 animated feature films. Some of Disney's most famous works include *Cinderella, Sleeping Beauty, Pinocchio, Dumbo, Peter Pan, Mary Poppins, The Jungle Book, The Little Mermaid, Beauty and the Beast, Aladdin, The Lion King, Toy Story,* and *Hercules.*

To increase exposure and sales, Disney opened several theme parks, which today are the most attended theme parks in the world. The theme parks are Magic Kingdom, Disney-MGM Studios, Epcot, Disneyland, Disney's Animal Kingdom, Tokyo Disneyland, and EuroDisney. In 2001 Disney opened California Adventure and Tokyo's Disney Sea, and has a theme park in Hong Kong. Disney has 11 theme parks worldwide.

When the Walt Disney Company bought Capital Cities/ABC for $19 billion in the mid-1990s, it entered network broadcasting in a big way. Disney bought Capital Cities/ABC because the Disney Company was having problems getting its programs on television at desirable times. The purchase of Capital Cities/ABC allowed Disney to reach larger primetime audiences. After all, ABC was the network credited with the highly rated primetime shows – and audience favorites – *Home Improvement, The Drew Carey Show,* and *Monday Night Football.* ABC's Wednesday-night lineup was just as popular with one of the network's newest and most watched programs, *Dharma & Greg.* ABC was also popular with Sunday-night primetime audiences, who enjoyed the return of *The Wonderful World of Disney.* Finally, the network picked a winner in *Who Wants to Be a Millionaire.*

News is another important element of ABC Broadcasting. ABC News continues to attract large audiences with *World News Tonight.* The news division was enhanced with a second launch of *20/20,* Ted Koppel's successful late-evening show *Nightline,* and *PrimeTime Live,* which is on Thursday evenings. *ABC World News* has always been the leader in foreign news coverage.

In 2002, senior Disney and ABC executives tried to cancel the award-winning *Nightline.* The newsmagazine, which began in the 1980s with coverage of the Iran hostage crisis, has a loyal following and is a credit to moderator Koppel and ABC's News Division. But the senior staffs of

Disney and ABC attempted to hire NBC late show star Jay Leno without informing Koppel or his producer. The industry and viewers alike were upset with the crass, secretive move. ABC was perceived to be abandoning its public-service mandate in pursuit of a few more dollars. Leno quickly declined the offer, sensing that being part of a plot to end a high-quality news show in a post-9/11 environment would be a career mistake. But in the end, the "bean counters" at Disney are likely to prevail and quality broadcasting will take a hit in the name of profits.

ABC Broadcasting also has a vested interest in the following cable networks: A&E (37.5 percent), the History Channel (37.5 percent), Lifetime (50 percent), E! Entertainment (34.4 percent), and Walt Disney International. A&E has been the winner of 20 Emmy Awards, and the network has reached more than 70 million subscribers in North America. The History Channel serves more than 42 million subscribers and the History Channel International was launched in 1998 and is available in 50 countries. E! Entertainment has become a leading worldwide provider of entertainment and news information on both television and the internet. In fact, E! Online Entertainment is one of the leaders of the World Wide Web and has a large teenage audience.

ESPN Inc.

Disney-controlled ESPN is the worldwide leader in sports, reaching 77 million homes. All ESPN networks and services are 80 percent owned by ABC. It was founded in 1979. Its main telecast is *SportsCenter* and in 1987 it negotiated with the National Football League to broadcast Sunday night NFL football. ESPN's audience jumped dramatically and now they are a fixture in the global sports culture. ESPN2 was launched in 1992 and has 65 million subscribers and is one of the fastest growing cable networks in the United States. ESPN also reaches households internationally. This 20-year-old network now reaches 150 million households in more than 150 countries and territories and in 20 languages. In 2004 it launched a Spanish network, ESPNU. ESPN.com is one of the most visited websites in the world. In 2003 the US Office of Foreign Assets Control, as part of their anti-Castro preoccupation, fined ESPN for broadcasting sports in Cuba. Finally, Sega is licensing ESPN shows for its video games worldwide. ESPN is a 24-hour sports cable franchise that is a media wonder, much like CNN or HBO.

Disney's Buena Vista International (BVI) distributes globally ABC's original shows, as well as other programming initiatives. For the last five years, BVI has taken in over $1 billion in foreign box-office revenue. This makes BVI one of the premier international movie distribution companies. BVI represents the ideal model of a US network successfully going global. BVI markets shows in other core nations and all semiperipheral regions. Also, Disney offers content for both cable and theaters around the world. For example in the United Kingdom, in direct competition with the BBC, Disney offers Toon Disney, Playhouse Disney, the Disney Channel, all Disney feature films, and relevant Disney websites.

Theme parks: marketing media heroes

To further reach audiences internationally through television, radio, cable, and the internet, Disney is expanding its theme park business in Europe and Asia. Based on the success of Tokyo Disneyland, which opened in 1983, Disney opened Disneyland Paris in 1992 to further expand international markets. It currently owns 40 percent of the French-based theme park and resort, which has been renamed EuroDisney. EuroDisney operates two parks outside of Paris. They are Disneyland Paris and Walt Disney Studios. The Studios were constructed in 2002 at a cost of over $500 million. With close to 13 million annual visitors, the two parks are the largest vacation destinations and theme parks in Europe. Since inception they have welcomed over 100 million visitors. EuroDisney is now Europe's top tourist attraction, yet it is still losing money. Saudi Arabian Prince Alwaleed is the largest personal shareholder with 16 percent. EuroDisney also contains a McDonald's restaurant. Disneyland theme parks have been successful and profitable in the United States and in Tokyo because the "American" style of doing business worked; however, this was not the case during the early years in Europe. Europeans did not accept or understand the American way of doing business, nor did they like it. Cultural differences created some hostility in France, and the Walt Disney Company did not experience magical success in Europe. Disney executives also failed to do preliminary research, approaching France as though it were a foreign market similar to Japan.

Knowing a country's unique culture is vital to the success of a US company. The Disney training manual is a good example of the problems Disney encountered in France. Before Disneyland Paris opened, the Walt Disney Company built offices and a training center in order to recruit the park's cast members. After passing Disney's pre-hiring procedures, the candidates were then trained. Every employee hired needed to meet and pass Disney's strict personality requirements. Recruits practiced the "Disney smile" and saying "Have a nice day." They also had to follow the 13-page manual outlining Disney's dress code, otherwise known as the "Disney Look." The manual outlines the idealized American appearance: a well scrubbed, happy, all-American look. The manual spells out everything from the appropriate size of earrings, to the appropriate length of fingernail, to the no-tolerance rule on facial hair and dyed hair. The young European employees did not understand or appreciate the "Disney Look." It was difficult for them to adhere to an American look since they were not Americans. They also believed this requirement stripped them of their individuality. As a result of this major culture clash, the French, who contested the strict dress policy, took Disney to court. Ultimately, the Walt Disney Company modified and instituted a new, more relaxed European dress policy.

The Walt Disney Company also failed to research the pros and cons of selling alcohol at Disneyland Paris. Alcoholic beverages are not served in the California, Florida, and Tokyo theme parks, and Disney instituted the same no-alcohol policy at Disneyland Paris, failing to respect the European custom of drinking wine with lunch. Needless to say, the Europeans rebelled against the no-alcohol policy and stayed away in droves. As a result, in 1993 the Walt Disney Company changed its policy to allow the sale of wine and beer at Disneyland Paris. Despite several other examples of Disney's failure to understand local tastes and traditions, it has adjusted to make Disneyland Paris more of a success by adopting other European practices. It also recently expanded its hotel offerings, and the parks now feature 7 hotels, with a total of 8,000 rooms, plus two major convention centers.

Disney has embarked on another international theme park: Hong Kong Disneyland, which opened in 2005. This former British colony has experienced major tourism setbacks since 1997, when it once again became a part of China after a century of British rule. Chinese senior administration officials in Beijing approved the park and are aggressively courting Disney with a $3.6 billion investment. The Hong Kong authorities own 57 percent of the venture while Disney owns the minority stake. The new Disneyland will resemble Disney's Magic Kingdom and will include traditional Disney characters, along with a broad range of shops, restaurants, hotels, and theaters. Disney's expansion into Asia represents a straightforward example of a core-based multinational organization entering a semiperipheral area, in this case China, which has an enormous population of 1.2 billion; thus, China has the potential to become part of Disney's major global network in the twenty-first century. The Hong Kong investment is likely the tip of the iceberg in terms of Disney's future expansion plans across China – and all with the initial blessing of the communist Chinese government.[11]

Finally, Disney has reappeared in the animation scene with major successes such as *Toy Story*, *A Bug's Life*, *Monsters Inc.*, and *Finding Nemo*, the largest-grossing animated film ever. Disney made these films in collaboration with Pixar Studios, but Disney management failed to renew their contract with Pixar in 2004.

Synopsis

The Walt Disney Company began as a small, creative firm established by two brothers: Walter Disney, who was responsible for the animation activities, and his brother Roy Disney, who handled the company's finances and strategic planning. The initial years of the company were extremely successful with the creation of several popular culture icons such as Mickey Mouse and Donald Duck. After the Second World War, the company began to add theme parks, one in California and later one in Florida. They then expanded internationally with Disneylands in Japan and France. During the 1980s, the company expanded through Disney stores and greater diversification into related fields. Several highly successful children's and family films were produced during this period, and they ventured into new territory such as the NHL hockey team the Mighty Ducks, the addition of Disney cable channels, and the addition of Disney Music. In the 1990s, the takeover of the national television network ABC was a major move for the corporation. Currently, Disney's largest unit is its film labels, which include Disney, Touchstone, Buena Vista, Dimension Films, Hollywood Pictures, and Miramax Films. These units produce films for the global market, and they market select ABC shows. Finally, the move into Asia with a second theme park in Hong Kong represents a major global move for the Disney Company. Asia represents a vast new market, and Disney appears to be ahead of Viacom and Time Warner in strategically identifying new opportunities in Asia. But not all is well at the Magic Kingdom. In 2004 major shareholders, including Roy Disney, Walt Disney's nephew, were calling for the resignation of the CEO, Michael Eisner.[12] He resigned, and in 2005 Robert Iger, a former ABC executive, became chief executive of Disney.

Finally, in the context of ECT, Disney is a classic example. It operates on a global scale with cultural products across a broad range of media. It utilizes the latest marketing information to increase market share annually, whether through movies or theme parks. More children around the world know Mickey Mouse than any other cultural icon. For other non-American cultures, Mickey and Minnie represent a distinct challenge to indigenous practices and to sales of indigenous goods. For example, in Mexico, children's parties have traditionally featured a piñata, a papier-maché donkey, filled with candy. Now, most piñatas are made in the likeness of either Mickey Mouse or SpongeBob.

Viacom

History

In May 2000, the Federal Communications Commission (FCC) approved the merger of Viacom with CBS. Viacom, as part of the consolidation in the broadcasting industry, was able to purchase CBS Corp. for $30 billion. This immediately gave Viacom control of more than 35 percent of the US broadcasting market. The deal covered all CBS properties, which include 38 television stations, 163 radio stations, and interests in 13 internet companies. Now Viacom is the third largest (after Time Warner and Disney) communication giant in the world. The purchase constitutes an interesting role reversal. Originally CBS, like other networks, produced a great deal of in-house programming.[13] But in 1971, the FCC forced CBS to sell all internal production and cable programming units, which it did by creating Viacom.[14] Now 27 years later, Viacom has been so successful that it is in a position to buy its parent, CBS. The FCC dropped the prohibition against networks owning production houses in 1995. As a result, major television networks are now producing more in-house shows in order to contain costs, control the process, and reap the syndication income from successful dramatic series or sitcoms. Viacom is a massive video syndication company with a global reach, which includes properties such as MTV, Paramount Pictures, King World International (*Jeopardy* and *Wheel of Fortune*), United Paramount, Infinity Broadcasting, Simon & Schuster publishing, Blockbuster (80 percent), and hundreds of movie theaters in Canada, Europe, and South America. (See figure 3.4.)

Federal regulators' decision to allow the merger reflects a current policy of permitting competition among corporate giants in order to facilitate the efficient and effective use of the market, rather than letting federal regulators rule with a heavy hand. Now several Viacom brands will have to fight it out with the brands of other major conglomerates such as Disney, which owns ABC, News Corporation, which owns FOX, General Electric, which owns NBC, and the even larger giant Time Warner. All of these corporations have major international holdings. They are able to use their North American studio base to produce videos and movies for domestic and foreign television and theaters, as well as software for their internet sites. Their internet activities are expanding globally as these firms put greater resources and strategic emphasis on internet initiatives, many of which are joint ventures. These North American communication conglomerates almost always cover the costs of production through US revenues, and thus foreign markets, through syndication, represent substantial profits based on two large income streams – the US and global markets.

CBS Television Network	Showtime
CBS Enterprises	Infinity Radio Broadcasting
Paramount Pictures	Simon & Schuster Publishers
Paramount Television	King World Productions
United Paramount Network (UPN)	Famous Players theaters
MTV	Blockbuster (80%)
mtvU	Movielink
VHl	United International Pictures
Nickelodeon	Viacom Internet Group
BET	Viacom Outdoor, INC

Figure 3.4 Major Viacom properties

Viacom is an international stakeholder in major media markets ranging from motion pictures, to television, to publishing, to recreation, to video distribution through Blockbuster. Viacom owns Paramount Pictures, which began producing feature films in 1912. Viacom controls Paramount's 2,500- and-growing title library, which contains a number of classic feature films, along with the *Star Trek* and *Indiana Jones* movies, *Braveheart*, and *South Park*. Viacom holds 33 percent of United International Pictures, which manages foreign distribution of Paramount's vast feature film libraries to over 60 countries around the world.

In terms of television, the major products are produced through Paramount Television as well as CBS, MTV, Nickelodeon, VHl, Nick at Nite, BET, and Showtime. Through its holdings, Viacom controls the libraries of major series such as *I Love Lucy, The Honeymooners, Star Trek, Beverly Hills 90210*, and *Cheers*. It also controls Spelling Entertainment, which in turn controls the syndication rights of 16,000 television episodes, including international markets.

Viacom also offers the Paramount channel in Europe, distributed as part of a multichannel package on Rupert Murdoch's satellite system BSkyB. In television broadcasting, Viacom owns 19 TV stations in the United States through its subsidiary Paramount Stations Group. These stations are located primarily in major cities and reach 25 percent of US TV-viewing households.

Simon & Schuster, a major publisher, is also a Viacom property, publishing more than 2,400 titles a year. Simon & Schuster is one of the most influential publishing houses for the mass market in the world. It publishes major bestsellers, including books by Stephen King and Frank McCord, and has a strong presence in the children's book market.

In 1993 Viacom and Paramount announced their merger, and Blockbuster Entertainment Corporation announced it would start to invest millions in Viacom. In January 1994, Viacom and Blockbuster announced an $8.4 billion merger. In 2004 Blockbuster was spun off as a separate company. Blockbuster has more than 6,000 video and music stores in 26 foreign nations. Viacom took a majority control of Paramount in 1994, and soon thereafter began assembling the management team for the combined company. At the same time, Viacom announced the formation of the Viacom Entertainment Group, comprising the Paramount Motion Picture Group, Paramount Television, and the Paramount Stations Group.

In Latin America, Paramount, MCA, MGM, and FOX have a joint interest in Cinecanal for Spanish-speaking Latin America and in Telecine for Brazil. Combined, these two networks reach approximately 1.7 million subscribers.

Viacom is a diversified entertainment and publishing company with operations in four areas: networks and broadcasting, entertainment, video and music/theme parks, and publishing. Through the networks and broadcasting segment, Viacom operates MTV, Showtime, Nickelodeon, Nick at Nite, VH-1, and 111 broadcast television stations. Generally Viacom's networks are offered to customers of cable and direct home-satellite services.

Finally, Viacom controls Paramount Parks, which consists of five North American theme parks. One of the parks is based in Toronto, Canada, where Viacom also controls the largest theatrical exhibitor in Canada, Famous Players, which has in excess of 700 screens in over 100 locations.

Viacom's future plans are clear. The major changes will be dealing with the growth and expansion of Blockbuster, MTV, Nickelodeon, BET, and CBS. Nickelodeon and the Media Group have introduced plans to launch Nickelodeon in Turkey as well as other foreign countries. Viacom hopes to have Blockbuster and Nickelodeon spread worldwide so that it can meet the demand for expanding markets with network shows that have proved successful in the United States.

Synopsis

Viacom has major global interests ranging from Paramount Pictures and MTV, which are particularly attractive to advertisers because of its global niche market; strong publishing interests with Simon & Schuster; as well as packaged television programming on various global satellite systems. Viacom has been active in promoting regional global markets, including Australia, Latin America, and particularly Asia. It is also a major player in international theatrical exhibition operations, with a number of cinemas around the globe and a strong radio presence through Infinity Broadcasting Corporation, which operates 185 radio stations. Finally, Viacom's profits come from a mix of revenue sources. The primary source is advertising revenue from its media brands, particularly MTV and CBS; another source of revenue is sales of books and video rentals, and movie ticket purchases for its Paramount Productions.

News Corporation

History

In 2004 News Corp., the fourth largest global media company, announced that it was reincorporating in the US, confirming the status of the US as the most important multimedia market in the world. It also represented a significant loss to the image and future of Australia as a major player in the Information Age. As one of the largest vertically integrated media conglomerates on the planet, News Corp. gave three major reasons for the move. First, to expand the shareholder base, scope, and demand by becoming an American company. This allows News Corp. to be listed on major US indices which only list US stocks, and to open the company to the many pension funds that are limited to US stocks. Second, more than 75 percent of their revenue and profits come from US multimedia operations. Only a very small portion of their revenues come from Australian operations. Third, such a move will provide News Corp. with access to much larger capital markets. These markets may become crucial as News Corp. attempts to create a global satellite sports-entertainment network similar to CNN's all news network.

The largest shareholder of News Corporation is Australian-born Rupert Murdoch, a naturalized US citizen who resides in Europe. He is a media mogul unlike any other.[15] With News Corporation, Murdoch has created an international empire of media, technology, and sports franchises. Murdoch himself is conservative and hires senior management of the same persuasion. For example, his US Fox network is headed by Roger Alles, a well-known conservative Republican. His news crews have learned how to slant both foreign and domestic news so as to guarantee that it will be aired. In general, Fox lacks a culture of professionalism and objectivity does not dominate the handling of news. Rather, they prefer to go with an edge and antibalanced format as personified by Bill O'Reilly.

Murdoch has used sports teams as a vehicle to obtain large audiences for his networks, not only for the sports programming but for other broadcasting initiatives as well. Although Murdoch tends to be outspoken and come across as unique in the media world, other media corporations such as Time Warner and Disney also have numerous sports assets. For example, Time Warner owns the Atlanta Braves, and has a joint venture involving NASCAR races. Disney owns the Anaheim Angels baseball club, as well as the Anaheim Mighty Ducks hockey club. Disney has also successfully produced several television movies with a hockey theme aimed at teenagers. The interconnection of sports and television is simply a growing international phenomenon. Murdoch is also part owner of a new sports channel in Canada, CTV Sportsnet. The growing convergence of sports and television continues with almost monthly announcements of major corporate agreements. Part of the strategy is to control the sports franchise, but these companies also want an advantage in the media rights of the sports league. Murdoch is no stranger to either controversy or sports. His FOX network came out of nowhere to purchase the broadcasting rights of the National Football League. Although the FOX network was initially perceived as a distant fourth national network in the United States, it has become a very serious challenge to the Big Three – ABC, CBS, and NBC – with hit shows. Through a separate company Murdoch has a substantial sports cable following that competes directly with Disney's ESPN. In the United Kingdom, Murdoch is a major player with his BSkyB television satellite network, which experienced startup difficulty until it purchased the rights to broadcast Premier League soccer matches. Now BSkyB is a major player with more than 7 million subscribers in the United Kingdom. News Corporation's corporate strategy is to use soccer as the engine to sell satellite dishes and programming packages across Europe. Other European media-related sports and television marriages are easy to find. Italian media giant Silvio Berlusconi owns the AC Milan soccer team, and the international car-maker Fiat controls Juvventus. In France, the pay-TV channel Canal Plus owns the Paris Saint-Germain soccer team. In the Netherlands, Philips Electronics owns AJAX, Amsterdam's soccer team.

News Corporation is a global media firm with significant interests in television, film, books, newspapers, magazines, satellites, cable systems, and sports.[16] It is a diversified global communications corporation with operations and holdings in every core and semiperipheral country as well as most peripheral regions, excluding Africa, due to the vast range of its satellite networks. Figure 3.5 reflects News Corporation's vast and widespread holdings.

Finally, the Murdoch family, including Rupert's sons, owns about 30 percent of News Corporation. The firm currently makes about 25 percent of its sales from global businesses and 75 percent from US media businesses.

Television:	Newspapers:
STAR TV	*The Times*
DIRECTV (38%)	*News of the World*
Sky Latin America	*Herald Sun*
FOX Sports Net	*The Sun*
BSkyB	*New York Post*
FOX Broadcasting FX	*Independent*
FOXtel	*The Sunday Times*
FOX Family Channel Sky PerfecTV!	The Australian newspapers:
FOX News	*Times*
FOX Television	*The Daily Telegraph*
FOX Sports Latin	*The Courier-Mail*
Channel [V] Asia Stations America	Magazines and inserts:
The Health Network	*TV Guide*
Film:	*The Weekly Standard*
20th Century Fox	*News America*
FOX Searchlight	*SmartSource*
FOX Music	*Times Higher Education Supplement*
FOX 2000	*Marketing*
FOX Animation	*Times Literary Supplement*
FOX Home	*Maximum Golf*
FOX Studios Entertainment	Other:
Books:	Ansett Australia PLD Telekom
HarperCollins	Mushroom Records
HarperCollins UK	National Rugby League
HarperCollins Australia	Festival Records
ReganBooks	ChinaByte
Zondervan	NDS
	FOX Interactive
	Kesmal

Figure 3.5 Major News Corporation properties

This mix may change, perhaps dramatically, with global, particularly Far East, initiatives growing substantially. Murdoch's family situation could easily be confused with the script of one of his soap operas. Rupert Murdoch, now nearly 80 and with a much younger wife, appointed his eldest son, Lachlan, as deputy chief operating officer and heir apparent to become president of News Corporation after Rupert departs. Yet his other son, James, as head of BSkyB, thinks he is in the running as well. Not to mention the young wife.

British Sky Broadcasting Group

British Sky Broadcasting Group (BSkyB) is the United Kingdom's leading pay-TV provider. Since 1989 it has distributed television programming to customers in both the United Kingdom and Ireland. It is a News Corp. property with Rupert Murdoch as Chairman and his young son James as Chief Executive. The business press roundly criticized the unilateral appointment in 2003 by the senior Murdoch of his son as CEO.

BSkyB has over 7 million customers with direct-to-home satellite dish receivers, as well as an additional 7 million customers who receive their pay services through cable systems. BSkyB provides news, sports, and entertainment programs through 450 channels covering 9 sectors. They are entertainment, news, children's, movies, sports, music, radio, adult, and specialty offerings. For example, Sky Sports offers over 36,000 hours of sports programming per year over 5 satellite channels and is seeing a consistent growth in viewership. In August 2003 an episode of US Fox network program *The Simpsons* featuring UK Prime Minister Tony Blair reached over 1 million viewers on Sky One. Sky News continues to receive industry awards and now has foreign bureaus in Washington, India, Brussels, Moscow, China, Jerusalem, and South Africa.

BSkyB has pioneered the introduction of digital television to Europe. This service, known as Sky Digital, provides the technically clearest available picture quality, along with CD-quality sound. Sky Digital offers 10 documentary channels, 5 sports channels, and up to 5 different movies every hour, along with all BBC television channels. By 2005 this digital service had over 7 million subscribers.

Finally, a look at BSkyB's multichannel entertainment offerings is informative. Sky One now outdraws the five terrestrial networks with programs such as *Las Vegas, 24, Cold Case, Scrubs, Malcolm in the Middle,* and the globally popular *The Simpsons.* Sky Movies offers 450 movies per week on 11 different pay channels. Some of the movies attracting more than 10 million viewers a week are *Men in Black, Pirates of the Caribbean, My Big Fat Greek Wedding,* and *Bruce Almighty.* Some of the satellite channel offerings are Bravo, Paramount, E!, Hallmark, Hollywood TV, Bloomberg, CNN, Disney, Nickelodeon, MTV (with 5 channels), and VH1 (with 3 channels). As the preceding so amply illustrates, American media fare is embedded in foreign satellite services to a very large extent. Since many of these channels are pay channels, there must be an audience for them. ECT deals with the collective impact of these audiovisual products over time. They are having an effect ranging from British boys preferring to play basketball over soccer to teenagers dancing and dressing like American pop icons. In the case of BSkyB this Americanization phenomenon is further reinforced by Murdoch's ability to direct the placement of his vast US-oriented Fox television and movie studio productions on the UK and Irish satellite systems.

STAR TV (Asia)

In the mid-1990s, Rupert Murdoch's News Corporation acquired control of STAR TV, and in 1998 STAR TV acquired Hutchvision Hong Kong Ltd. Hutchvision Hong Kong was the first Hong Kong-based satellite television licensee; it started broadcasting satellite television services, known as the STAR network, in 1991. The STAR TV network offers both subscription and free-to-air television services, reaching more than 300 million people across Asia, India, and the Middle East in a multitude of markets, making STAR distinct among broadcasters. STAR TV is the dominant satellite broadcaster in Asia and has viewers in 53 other countries as well. In addition, STAR TV is the only broadcaster to offer such a broad range of programs to all of Asia and the Middle East, with coverage from East Africa to Japan. STAR TV transmits more than 45 programming services in 8 languages. It controls more than 10 channels in Hong Kong alone, all of them broadcasting 24 hours a day. Programs feature a mix of movies, news, music, sports, and general entertainment. STAR TV is a commercial network relying on advertising from more than 20 global brands.

The STAR TV channels offer the region's widest television choice, whether in music, news, sporting events, Asian and international dramas and films, or cultural and informational programs. Services carried on the STAR TV network include ESPN, FOX News, and National Geographic. Several other satellite television broadcasters uplink their signals from Hong Kong, including CNN and CNBC.

The National Geographic Channel (NGC) signed a deal to act as a local broadcaster and as STAR TV's representative in India in order to sell ad time on the channel. The tie-in allows NGC to tap into STAR TV's existing marketing resources in the country. As of 1998, NGC reached more than 12.5 million homes in Asia and 7.5 million subscriber homes in India.

STAR TV launched its pioneering venture into satellite broadcasting by initially transmitting just 5 analog TV channels. Soon it was experiencing significant household penetration across the continent, increasing connections by tens of millions a year. Today, close to 100 million households across Asia, the Middle East, and India tune into News Corporation's STAR TV. STAR TV's offerings include English-language channels such as MTV, Prime Sports, and the BBC World Service. ZEE TV, which is broadcast in Hindi, was added in 1992.

With a satellite footprint stretching from Turkey to Japan, the STAR TV network was developed to deliver Asian audiences to global businesses and advertisers. But STAR TV has been criticized for airing too much English, violence, and sex. Yet Murdoch is determined to push his STAR TV across Asia.

The countries that have been prime markets for STAR TV have been those ranked among the newly industrialized countries of Asia. This is an example of a core-based multimedia giant offering broadcasting channels in semiperipheral and peripheral nations. Except in India, Singapore, and Malaysia, where the governments have restricted viewer access, STAR TV has been a major success story.[17]

Increasing government deregulation and liberalization as well as technological advances in satellites and receiving dishes ensure a solid future for the broadcasting industry in Asia. In the immediate future, STAR TV plans to consolidate its position as Asia's number one satellite broadcaster. To maximize audience size, there are indications that STAR TV, as well as other foreign satellite channels, will increasingly move to provide local-language fare. Although audiences welcome the local-language programming, the net result is that larger STAR TV audiences are being built at the expense of local and frequently government-owned television networks. Most local stations are still noncommercial and lack the flair and broad scope of STAR TV's multiple channel system. Therefore, the impact of STAR TV, and to a lesser extent other networks such as the BBC and CNN, offer Asia and other nations a new commercial model that is a direct application of electronic colonialism. These advertising-supported networks need audiences to sell to their global brand sponsors in order for both the networks and the global products to succeed in these new vast markets.

Finally, a subsidiary, Sky Global Networks, incorporates the regional satellite services of BSkyB in Europe and Latin America as well as STAR TV in Asia. News Corporation's Asian focus is now rapidly shifting to concentrate on China. In addition to the STAR TV activities, News Corporation has a minority stake in Phoenix Satellite Television, which is based in Hong Kong and targeted at mainland China. This service carries movies as well as other programming. Minority stakes are also held in Chinese internet portals, Chinese websites, and joint ventures with China's *Peoples Daily Newspaper*. Murdoch's strategic plans involve substantial expansion across China. Coupled with the Summer Olympics, Wal-Marts, and Disney opening a theme park in Hong Kong, along with other aggressive media and internet activities, according to electronic colonialism theory, it will only be a matter of time before the Chinese population exhibits more Western values, ranging from speaking English, to wearing Western clothing, to Western media consumption, to internet usage, all of which ultimately could lead the nation to achieve core status and leave behind the mostly agrarian and totalitarian society of a few decades ago. This is why News Corporation, Disney, and others are making substantial investments in China.

DIRECTV Group

This satellite provider of digital entertainment services, founded in 1994, is now 34 percent owned by Fox Entertainment Group. DIRECTV is the largest pay satellite service in the US (Echostar DISH network is second), with almost 13 million subscribers. It also owns 80 percent of PanAmSat and has 1.5 million customers across 28 Latin American nations under DIRECTV Latin America. It offers several Spanish and Chinese channels and the Group is chaired by Rupert Murdoch.

Synopsis

The elder Murdoch controls all News Corp. properties on a daily basis and he makes sure that they follow his political leanings. His vast multimedia holdings have always been global in nature. His Fox holdings in the US are increasing in audience share and the decision to move the corporate headquarters from Australia to New York in 2004 further solidify the focus on the Fox sector of the company. With satellite systems in Europe (BSkyB), Asia (Star TV), and North America (DirecTV), Murdock may be well on his way to creating a global media infrastructure. The big unknown for the company will be which son succeeds him. This may be determined by whom his young wife, and one day widow, supports.

General Electric

General Electric (GE) was established in 1892 by Thomas Edison and now has several global product lines such as lighting, appliances, power sources, aircraft, medical systems, financial services, and NBC Universal. It operates in over 100 countries and employs over 150,000 people in the United States and about the same number worldwide.[18] The company has a US annual growth rate of 3 percent and a global growth rate of 6 percent. In 1986, GE purchased RCA, which owned NBC, and in the 1990s NBC became part of GE's global expansion strategy. In 1996, for example, NBC expanded to offer four overseas channels, two in Europe and two in Asia. CNBC and MSNBC are also available in homes and hotels in Asia and Europe, reaching over 150 million television sets. In 2004, combining

NBC Television Network	CANAL de Noticias
MSNBC	Telemundo
CNBC	Mun2
NBC International	Sci-fi
NBCi	Trio
NBC Europe	USA Network
CNBC Europe	Universal Pictures
CNBC Asia Pacific	Theme Parks
Paxson Communications	Focus Feature

Figure 3.6 Major NBC Universal properties

French-based Vivendi's Universal properties with NBC's holdings created NBC Universal. NBC holds 80 percent ownership, and Vivendi holds the rest. (See figure 3.6.)

History

Industrial giant GE owns the NBC television network, which serves 15 company-owned and operated stations and more than 200 US affiliates. NBC also operates the 24-hour cable channels CNBC and MSNBC. Although home to such hits as *Law and Order, Will and Grace, West Wing*, and *ER*, the network, like the others, is losing market share to cable channels and the internet.

NBC is a global media company with broadly diverse holdings that consist of the following elements: NBC television network, NBC-owned and operated stations, NBC Entertainment, NBC News, NBC Sports, CNBC, MSNBC, NBC Cable, NBC International, NBC Interactive, and MSNBC Desktop Video.

NBC has been setting industry standards in technology and programming for more than 70 years. It was the first network to broadcast in color, the first to broadcast in stereo, the first to present a made-for-TV movie, and the first to offer an early morning news program. Most recently, it was the first network to broadcast both online and digitally.

NBC's first major organizational change came in 1986 when GE acquired RCA and thereby became NBC's parent company. Then in 1993, NBC launched Canal de Noticias NBC, a 24-hour Spanish-language news service, across Latin America. In 1994, Canal de Noticias NBC debuted on cable stations in the United States. In 1996, NBC became primetime's number one network in every category, leading ABC and CBS. In 1999, NBC agreed to acquire a 32 percent stake in West Palm Beach, Florida-based Paxson Communications Corp. for $415 million. The agreement combines NBC's powerful brand name and broadcast group with Paxson, owner of the most television stations in the United States. NBC said the move provided a second national distribution outlet for NBC programming while giving Paxson additional resources to strengthen its broadcast group and PAX TV network. In 2004 GE made a dramatic and significant media move in acquiring an 80 percent stake in Universal television and movies. The renamed NBC Universal is now a much larger global stakeholder in the evolving global multimedia sector.

NBC Universal operates in four divisions: Network, Production, Film, and Theme Parks. The networks are now extensive and most are carried on cable and satellite channels around the world. NBC Universal television has 14 owned and operated stations along with 200 affiliates. They also control Telemundo, a large Spanish-language network, with 15 owned and operated stations and 32 affiliates. Telemundo is carried on nearly 450 cable systems. Telemundo Internacional is available in over 20 of the largest markets across Latin America.

The other NBC Universal networks are mun2, a Latino network aimed at MTV's teenage audience; Sci-Fi channel; Trio, a popular culture channel; and USA Network. Offshore, there is NBC Europe reaching 85 million households, and CNBC Asia Pacific reaching 30 million. In film, they have a major stakeholder in Universal Pictures. Under this new ownership the corporate strategy is aimed at global expansion. They also control Focus Feature, which is a worldwide film distribution company. Finally, in addition to Universal Studios theme parks in the US, they also have parks and resorts in Japan and Spain.

NBC also became the main broadcaster for the International Olympic Games. NBC broadcast the summer Olympics from Atlanta, Georgia, in 1996; from Sydney, Australia, in 2000; and from Athens, Greece, in 2004, marking the fifth straight summer Olympics broadcast by NBC. NBC Universal Sports will also broadcast the 2008 games in China. NBC also has the rights to the 2006 and 2008 Winter Games.

Bravo

Acquired by NBC in 2002, Bravo is an arts and culture network with over 80 million households across North America having access to it. A number of foreign satellite and cable systems also carry the upscale shows, such as the Montreal-based Cirque du Soleil.

CNBC

Two of the world's leading media companies, Dow Jones and NBC, came together in December 1997 to create CNBC, the Consumer News and Business Channel. This global alliance created a powerful combination of strengths: Dow Jones produces vital world business and financial news and information; NBC is one of the leading television networks in the United States. This move unites the worlds most recognized business news brands including the *Wall Street Journal*, CNBC, and Dow Jones. CNBC is available to 175 million households worldwide; it is watched by millions of people around the globe every day. As baby boomers start worrying about retirement, they focus on investing their money, and CNBC has the pertinent information to answer their questions.

Dow Jones has also partnered with NBC and Microsoft's internet venture activities, specifically MSNBC. MSNBC's online business section is now the CNBC business section, with Dow Jones receiving part of the revenue. Dow Jones has also become a third partner in the MSNBC Desktop Video service and is a partner in future online services being developed by NBC and Microsoft. Headquartered in the financial heart of Singapore, CNBC Asia works out of the world's first full-time virtual reality broadcast studio, giving it the ability to create computer-generated, custom-designed sets, and allowing it to take an innovative lead in the presentation of complex data. CNBC Asia Pacific has bureaus in Australia, Thailand, India, Japan, China, and Taiwan.

Finally, in 1999 NBC combined several of its internet properties into a single subsidiary known as NBCi. NBC is marketing this internet-based service as a global integrated media company. NBC's internet operations attract about 25 million users monthly, and they compete globally with Time Warner, Yahoo!, and the Disney Internet Group.

Synopsis

General Electric is an enormous global conglomerate with a broad range of products across a wide spectrum of industries. GE's broadcasting interests are fairly recent, having acquired NBC in 1986, but the network has never provided the financial returns of other GE units. For example, GE Financial Services accounts for nearly one-half of GE's revenues. In May 2004 NBC

Universal was formed with General Electric (80 percent) and Vivendi (20 percent) combining assets to create a giant global multimedia company. NBC is adding its networks to global cable and satellite channels and is making aggressive moves with internet sites for a greater global profile. Finally, with the various Telemundo networks, they plan to have a major media presence both at home and abroad in the growing Hispanic regions.

Dow Jones & Company

Dow Jones & Company is widely known for two assets, yet it also has significant global activities. Their flagship publication is the *Wall Street Journal* (WSJ), which was first published in 1889. Also, in 1896, they started the Dow Jones Industrial Average (DJIA), which today consists of 30 blue-chip US corporations, one-third of which reside in the information or media sectors. Examples of these companies are IBM, Microsoft, General Electric, which owns NBC, and the Walt Disney Company.

In terms of international assets, in 1946 Dow Jones started the prestigious *Far East Economic Review* and in 1976 they launched *The Asian Wall Street Journal*, followed in 1983 by *The Wall Street Journal Europe*. In 1994 they established *The Wall Street Journal Americas*, published in Spanish and Portuguese, and in 2004 *The Wall Street Journal India*. Dow Jones is also partnered with the *Financial Times* of London and the *Independent Media* to put out a Russian business daily called *Vedomosti* (*The Record*).

The various WSJ editions, both in the US and abroad, have an ultraconservative tone, slant, or bias. One could make the case that the WSJ is a development journalism enterprise on behalf of free enterprise. They promote an editorial mantra of hostility toward social issues or critics of business practices. For example, the WSJ has historically campaigned against universal healthcare, environment legislation, the United Nations, and affirmative-action programs. In terms of the Iraq war they provide coverage in unison with the Pentagon. Rather than seeking balance and objectivity in their stories, they stoop to ridicule, much like Bill O'Reilly of Fox News or Rush Limbaugh's radio rants. As an example, the WSJ editorial piece on November 18, 2004, states, "The al-Zarqawi TV network, also know as Al Jazeera, has broadcast the tape to the Arab world, and the US media have also played it up."[19] The videotape refers to NBC's Kevin Sites footage of a US Marine shooting a wounded Iraq civilian. Al Jazeera is an Arab network that has a wide audience in the Muslim world and it is covered in greater detail in a later chapter. The WSJ in similar fashion had earlier complained about other US and foreign media outlets focusing on the photos of the Abu Ghraib prisoners' abuse. For the WSJ this uncritical support for the US's military policy translates into easier access to senior Washington officials for a broad array of future stories. The basic point is that the ultraright tone of the WSJ properties panders to a global niche, which is an audience defined by wealth.

On the electronic side, in addition to its internet sites for various print properties, since 1997 Dow Jones has had a major global alliance with CNBC. Across both Europe and Asia, Dow Jones provides CNBC with business and news programming. As the global economy evolves and corporations become more global in scope and talent, the Dow Jones Company is well positioned to expand its business-oriented multimedia properties around the globe.

Synopsis

Dow Jones has selected an extremely important niche market, namely the business press worldwide. It has a pro-business and ultraconservative editorial slant. It tends to be against social issues or policies that are aimed at assisting the less fortunate in the world. Another oddity is that the largest communication conglomerate in the world, Time Warner, with 2003 gross income of $38 billion, is not on the DJIA, while smaller Disney, with income of $27 billion, is. Viacom is also larger than Disney, but does not appear on the DJIA. During this decade both Time Warner and Viacom will likely be added to the DJIA as industrial-era firms are removed and are replaced by additional information-based enterprises.

Gannett Company, Inc.

The Gannett Company is an international, diversified news and information company. It is the US's largest newspaper company in terms of circulation, owning 101 dailies, including *USA Today*. *USA Today* has a circulation of over 2.3 million and is available in over 60 nations worldwide. Columnist Peter Johnson provides excellent media analysis and coverage. Gannett has operations in England, Belgium, Germany, Italy, and China. In the United Kingdom it owns about 20 dailies and Newsquest plc, the latter controlling over 300 regional papers. Newsquest also has over 80 internet sites. Gannett also produces USATODAY.com, one of the major internet newspaper sites in the world.

Wal-Mart

This retail juggernaut now has over 1,500 stores in 9 nations. Wal-Mart International employs over 330,000 workers in Argentina, Brazil, Canada, China (34 stores), EU, Japan, Korea, and Mexico. Annual sales in these foreign nations are close to $50 billion and growing rapidly. They plan to open over 100 new stores in foreign nations annually.

In terms of multimedia, Wal-Mart has two sectors. First, retail store sales, and second, internet sales. It is a growing media seller in both categories. For example, their stores sell DVDs, CDs, VHS, and cassettes. They sell more DVDs than Blockbuster. They were the largest retailer of *Finding Nemo, Harry Potter*, and *Lord of the Rings*. On Walmart.com they offer two media products. First, music downloads at less than a dollar per song from any genre. Second, sales of DVDs, VHS movies, and other products with an audiovisual connection. Another example of their power is in consumer electronics. Sales of these units are second only to Best Buy (and more than Circuit City, Dell, and Target combined). When Wal-Mart sells the hardware, like a DVD or CD player, then they also sell the software as well. This connection gives them a major advantage over competitors who only sell or rent one or the other.

Wal-Mart is a new global stakeholder in terms of international communication, but because of their enormous purchasing power and number of global outlets they represent a future major player in this sector. They also bring with them market clout, controversy, anti-unionism and a strong US free-enterprise orientation. They are a serious and effective promoter of electronic colonialism wherever they go.

Conclusions

Globally there is an expansion of movie theaters, cable systems, satellite distribution systems, personal computers, music, CD, and video outlets. This infrastructure is fueling substantial expansion by global communication firms. In particular, US multinational communication corporations such as Disney, News Corp., GE, Time Warner, Dow Jones, Gannett, and Viacom are strategically repositioning themselves as global corporations rather than simply US communication firms. As their internet and other offshore assets grow they are being propelled into the global marketplace. In their corporate annual reports, as well as in other company documents reflecting strategic planning, globalization and their increasing role in that milieu is the dominant theme. At least for the next decade and perhaps beyond, continuing global offshore growth for these US-based communication companies will exceed any domestic corporate growth.

The growth and impact of US multimedia firms changed considerably in 2004. The addition of News Corp. from Australia, and Universal properties to NBC from France's Vivendi, represents an enormous net gain for the US media sector. At the same time it represents a net loss to two other core nations, Australia and France. In Australia's case, the advantage of having the common English language could further propel it to become even more of a communication colony of the US popular culture. Some Australian critics of the News Corp. move to New York city cited the cultural and employment issues in their futile opposition to the relocation. Australia and several other nations are likely to continue to lose their bright young talent to Hollywood and New York. The likes of Nicole Kidman, Mel Gibson, Russell Crowe, Crocodile Dundee, Helen Reddy, and Olivia Newton-John represent the talent drain that is only going to increase, as Australia becomes an even greater media outpost and electronic colony of US cultural goods and practices.

Because the United States is the leading core nation, these corporations have become aggressive in other core nations in both Europe[20] and Asia.[21] At the same time, they have expanded into the semiperipheral nations because these represent substantial new markets where there is strong demand for US products of all types, ranging from CDs and DVDs, to movies, to the internet. These semiperipheral nations also have the greatest number of potential new customers with discretionary disposable income. They represent a new customer base for all the major US communication empires.

A good example of global expansion is Disney's new theme park being developed in conjunction with Chinese authorities in Hong Kong. Clearly, Disney is positioning itself to use the Hong Kong site as a gateway into the immense Chinese market during the twenty-first century. A related expansion into China took place in the 1990s as Rupert Murdoch recognized that his Asian satellite system, STAR TV, could potentially attract a multitude of new customers across China and the entire Pacific Rim.

US media giants, with their advertising, products, and services, have inundated only a few peripheral nations. Most peripheral nations lack the necessary technical infrastructure, ability to provide security, or sufficient disposable income to make it economically worthwhile to establish major activities in these regions. At the same time, some of these peripheral nations are seeking to avoid contact with US popular and media culture as they attempt to protect and promote an indigenous culture, which is usually low technology, or because of religious beliefs, authoritarian governments, or antidemocratic leaders.

Finally, these global media firms must continue to grow if they want to remain competitive. Because the potential growth is greater offshore, they will continue to direct greater efforts toward, and place corporate executives in, global regions in order to produce the rate of return demanded by senior management and shareholders. This expansion occurs in unison with their advertising agencies. As such, the nations they operate in need to have a market-based economy for these firms to thrive, profit, and expand. Obviously, some of this expansion comes at the expense of indigenous production houses, or local advertising agencies. Because these US media conglomerates have enormous libraries of television and feature films that have already paid for themselves as first-run productions in the large US domestic market, they can compete aggressively internationally with an arsenal of video and audio products that collectively can swamp any foreign network or production house through sheer volume.

Notes

1   The emergence of global television has always had its critics. They focus primarily on the social, cultural, and political aspects of the global dissemination of popular shows. Most of the shows were American, with a few British shows doing well on a global scale. In the 1980s, the global success of *Dallas* became the rallying symbol for cultural nationalists in several nations. For a broad critique of this phenomenon, see Cynthia Schneider and Brian Wallis, eds., *Global Television* (Cambridge, MA: MIT Press, 1988) and Richard Gershon, *The Transnational Media Corporation* (Mahwah, NJ: Erlbaum, 1997).
2   Europe and most of Europe's former colonies refer to multimedia as audio-visual products. A prime example of this, including a broad, detailed description of the concerns and challenges, is contained in the European Commission's *Economic Implications of New Communications Technologies on the Audio-Visual Markets* (Brussels: European Communities, 1998).
3   W. A. Swanberg, *Luce and His Empire* (New York Scribner, 1972).
4   Gerald Levin, "The Legacy of Henry Luce: Values for the Digital Age," Speech to the Aspen Institute, Aug. 7, 1999, Aspen, CO, p. 2.
5   Ibid., p. 2.
6   Ibid., p. 4.
7   Nina Munk, *Fools Rush In: Steve Case, Jerry Levin, and the Unmasking of AOL Time Warner* (New York: Harper Business, 2004).
8   Ken Auletta, *Media Man* (New York: W. W. Norton, 2004).
9   Steven Watts, *The Magic Kingdom: Walt Disney and the American Way of Life* (Boston: Houghton Mifflin, 1998).
10 Bob Thomas, *Building a Company: Roy O. Disney and the Creation of an Entertainment Empire* (Boston: Hyperion, 1999).

11   The Chinese government's approval of a major Hollywood-based theme park occurred in the same year that China entered the World Trade Organization (WTO). The two events are not unrelated. China is attempting to reposition itself as a modern global player in the communication industry. By joining the WTO, it has agreed to open its telecommunications market, allow foreign firms to provide internet services, and increase the number of US feature films imported into China. Beijing, China, is the host city for the Summer Olympics in 2008. Clearly, these activities, along with Disney's activities in Hong Kong, reflect the acceptance of US business practices, information technologies, and popular culture. In return, China will no doubt attempt to export more of its goods and services into core nations, particularly the United States. At the same time, however, China has become market sensitive, it wants to participate and follow the rules and regulations, including dispute resolution mechanisms available through the Geneva-based WTO. Although China still cracks down on cybercafes and is repressive with dissidents, it nonetheless aims to move from semiperipheral status to core status by 2020. The European-based Reporters Without Borders lists China as one of the worst press-freedom nations on the planet. Finally, the Disney Corporation, along with other major US corporations, would not be making such major long-term investments in China if it thought these investments would either fail or be confiscated by the Chinese authorities. Although there is no written agreement not to do such things, clearly the Chinese in a broad range of activities are indicating that they want to participate in the global information society of the twenty-first century, eventually on an equal basis, as China seeks to become a core nation. But their repressive heritage and practices emerge against progressive media systems far too frequently.

12   James Stewart, *Disneywar: The Battle for the Magic Kingdom* (New York: Simon & Schuster, 2004). Two additional books which trace Disney's influence are Janet Wasko, *Understanding Disney: The Manufacture of Fantasy* (Malden, MA: Blackwell, 2001) and Janet Wasko, M. Phillips, and E. Meehan, eds., *Dazzled by Disney?* (London: Leicester Press, 2002).

13   Robert Slater, *The New GE: How Jack Welch Revived an American Institution* (Highstown, NJ: Irwin, 1992).

14   Tony Chiu, *CBS: The First 50 Years* (New York: General Publishing, 1999).

15   Rupert Murdoch's various dealings have come under criticism around the globe. One of the better summaries is contained in Russ Baker's piece in the *Columbia Journalism Review* of May/June 1998.

16   News Corporation's global media ventures have a major strategic asset that other global competitors frequently do not. News Corporation's control of STAR TV in Asia, BSkyB in Europe, as well as several other satellite and cable ventures allows these networks to draw from the extensive library of software produced by the various FOX production facilities. Through their control of 20th Century Fox studios, FOX Broadcasting, FOX News, FOX Family Channel, FOX Sports Net, and a service of 22 US-based FOX television stations, News Corporation media and systems managers around the globe

have a ready and lucrative arsenal. These FOX shows and channels provide an enormous competitive advantage to the Murdoch Group compared to the competition, which must attempt to outbid each other in order to purchase syndication game and drama shows, movies, or other programming materials.

17 For a further elaboration on access, cultural imperialism, and the rapidly changing Asian and Indian television environment, see Peter Shields and Sundeep Muppidi, "Integration, the Indian State and STAR TV: Policy and Theory Issues," *Gazette* 58 (1996), pp. 1–24; KiSung Kwak, "Structural and Cultural Aspects of the Regulation of Television Broadcasting in East Asia," *Gazette* 59 (1997), pp. 429–33; Amos Owen Thomas, "Regulating Access to Transnational Satellite Television," *Gazette* 61 (1999), pp. 243–54; and Robert Schmidt, "Murdoch Reaches for the Sky," *Brill's Content*, June 2001, pp. 75–9, 126–9.

18 Robert Campbell, *The Golden Years of Broadcasting: A Celebration of the First Fifty Years of Radio and TV on NBC* (New York: Scribner, 1976).

19 "Semper Fi," *Wall Street Journal*, Nov. 18, 2004, p. A18.

20 Reinhold Wagnleitner, "The Empire of the Fun, or Talkin' Soviet Union Blues: The Sound of Freedom and U.S. Cultural Hegemony in Europe," *Diplomatic History* 23(3) (Summer 1999), pp. 499–524.

21 Srinivas Melkote, Peter Shields, and Binod Agrawel, eds., *International Satellite Broadcasting in South Asia* (Lanham, MD: University Press of America, 1998).

Chapter 4

Non-US Stakeholders of Global Communication Systems

Introduction

Although some global media systems such as CNN, MTV, BBC, Disney, News Corporation, and the internet come to mind as high-profile stakeholders in the global media world, there are clearly other major players. This chapter details the major global media stakeholders outside the US and describes their various communication interests. Although the United States frequently elicits substantial criticism for exporting a Hollywood culture of sex and violence and for dominating television and theater screens around the world, some of the major global enterprises, such as Sony, Bertelsmann, VNU, and many others, are foreign-owned multimedia corporations.

For example, Japan's Sony Corporation controls Columbia Pictures; Germany's Bertelsmann has a stake in 600 companies in over 50 countries, including BMG Music, Random House, and Barnes & Noble; France's Matra Hachette publishes *Elle*, *Car and Driver*, and several other magazines; VNU owns the industry's important rating firm, Nielsen. These global media conglomerates and others are detailed in this chapter. (It should be noted that the British Broadcasting Corporation, the BBC, is covered in chapter 6 as a global competitor to CNN.)

Cultural Imperialism

In the 1960s and 1970s, critical scholars produced a body of literature on the subject of cultural imperialism.[1] These scholars condemn the US role in global media expansion. Some of this criticism found its way into the rhetoric of UNESCO in the 1980s and continues to be repeated by people promoting the MacBride agenda. The agenda seeks to reignite the support for NWICO (the New World Information and Communication Order), and promote a more equitable and balanced flow of media in the international arena. Without going into detail about the origins of cultural imperialism, it is worth noting that there is simply no monolithic US global media empire. Although there is a global media empire, the media corporations are from various nation-states, but they are all located in core nations. They work in different languages with different interests and strategies, rather than promoting a simplistic New York–Los Angeles plot to capture the minds of unsuspecting foreigners. From records and CDs, to movies, magazines, television, and the internet, there is a great global mix of ownership among the current major multimedia stakeholders. This globalization and consolidation of the communications industry is going to increase and expand over time. About the only common denominator of the several far-flung global stakeholders is the desire to make a profit by expanding their audience size or share. They seek more customers to generate greater profits in order to keep their respective senior management, owners, and shareholders happy.

Concern about the possible effects of the mass media on individuals and cultures has been a preoccupation of academics since the Second World War. Much of the research focused on the impact of the media on developed, core nations, particularly the United States, Canada, and Europe.[2] But a small number of critical scholars began to examine the impact of the media on the less-developed peripheral nations and look at issues such as power, domination, economic determinism, and other variables.[3] The "Made in America" label began to take on different meanings to different researchers. But it was Herbert I. Schiller[4] who focused in a theoretical way on issues such as global ownership, one-way flow of information, power, and the impact of advertising. He studied ways by which core-based industries were having a deleterious effect on indigenous media industries in peripheral countries, as well as how these industries were drawing economic resources, such as box office revenues, from both industrialized and nonindustrialized nations around the world for the financial benefit of Hollywood. In the 1970s, the literature on cultural imperialism began to look at other media systems as well, everything from records, tapes, and television, to advertising and children's paraphernalia, particularly Disney products. There was growing criticism and documentation of US media giants by a small cadre of critical scholars. But in 1988, many of these scholars were taken aback when Japan's Sony Corporation paid $5 billion to acquire Columbia Pictures. The Hollywood film landscape began to change dramatically as this merger was rapidly followed by other US industries being bought by foreign corporations as part of the expanding global economy. Many of these transactions and the foreign stakeholders involved are detailed later in this chapter. The significant point here is that although the theory of cultural imperialism was gaining credence as a negative model of global relationships, Sony's deal forced scholars to rethink the question of who owns what and for whom. The problem became a transnational issue rather than a purely Hollywood or "Made in America" issue, as critics had contended for decades. The literature and momentum of critical scholars became stale and lost their spark during the 1990s as major foreign media corporations changed the global media landscape. At one point in the 1970s, the United States dominated the global media system to the greatest extent before or since. Beginning in the 1980s, with the takeover of some Hollywood studios by foreign corporations; the move of German, French, and Canadian companies into global cultural industries; and the entrance of the then Australian-based News Corporation into television and satellite businesses in North America, Europe, and Asia, a highly competitive global media marketplace began to develop. It functions to maximize profits from various global profit centers with little regard for nationalistic concerns, language, or academic critics, except when they interfere with the economic goals of these far-flung media empires.

The following sections document the extensive penetration of Europe, Canada, Japan, and other countries into US markets by virtue of their investments in a broad range of cultural products that are made and/or consumed in the United States. A model example of this is News Corporation, formerly based and incorporated in Australia. It had 75 percent of its revenues and profits from operations in the US. Reincorporating in the US was a logical move for this corporation. In addition, these giant non-American multimedia entities have a substantial customer base on a global scale. All giant foreign media corporations are in direct and daily competition with US giants such as Time Warner, Viacom, and Disney.

The United States of Europe (USE)

Europe's television, movie, music, cable, and satellite industries are experiencing an unprecedented frenzy of consolidation. The 25 European Union nations are working more and more as collective rather than individual nations when it comes to international media. Thus, the concept of the United States of Europe (USE) is a valid construct.

Historically, the origins of the USE can be traced to the period immediately after the Second World War. In 1951 the European Coal and Steel Community was established under French leadership. The six members were Belgium, West Germany, Luxembourg, France, Italy, and the Nether-lands. The agreement reduced barriers hindering cooperation and encouraged joint ventures in the two strategic industries, coal and steel. The idea was such a great success that the six countries decided to expand the concept to other sectors. They did so, and by the 1957 Treaty of Rome created a "common market" free of trade barriers and tariffs. Institutions, laws, regula-tions, policies, strategic planning, and in 2002 a new currency, the Euro, were designed to create a single, seamless market leading to the USE. This standardization and consolidation also impacted their cultural industries, or as Europeans refer to them, audiovisual industries. Today the USE stands at 25 member nations with more nations seeking admission. In 2004 alone, 10 new members, mostly former Soviet-dominated countries, joined the union. One of the possible new entrants is Turkey, with a large Muslim population – this may alter the cultural mix across the USE. The current population of the USE is larger than that of the USA.

Considering that prior to 1980 almost all European television and cable systems were either strictly government controlled or government owned, this recent merger mania is new to the European communications industry. With deregulation in the 1980s, there was a substantial wave of privatiza-tion of radio, television, and cable systems across Europe as well as the addition of several new commercial channels. Now a third wave of activity is taking place in which transnational communication corporations are becoming larger and larger as they purchase smaller systems across Europe, start entirely new channels or networks, or buy foreign multimedia outlets, prompting some critics to call these countries collectively the "United States of Europe." (See figure 4.1.)

1. Bertelsmann (Germany)

2. Vivendi (France)

3. Matra Hachette (France)

4. Canal Plus (France)

5. Pathe (France)

6. Pearson (UK)

7. VNU (Netherlands)

8. Mediaset (Italy)

9. Alex Springer (Germany)

Figure 4.1   USE major communication stakeholders

The motivation for the third wave of activity is straightforward. John Tagliabue puts it this way: "What is causing this frenzy of reorganization? Mainly, the global economy, which is forcing Europe's relatively small players to join forces to cover the costs of switching to digital and pay per view TV and of marketing integrated bundles of television, telephone and Internet services."[5] These combined and larger media companies are in a better competitive position because they can offer either larger audiences to advertisers, or a larger number of cable subscribers to generate revenues necessary to upgrade cable systems so that they are internet-ready. A related phenomenon in the United States of Europe is that more commercial corporations are designing advertising and programs for a pan-European audience. Advertisers want to deal with major trans-European broadcasters for a single package rather than with small individual media outlets on a city-by-city or country-by-country basis.

The future media environment of the USE will ultimately resemble the US model of large national entities such as ABC, CBS, FOX, and NBC having a number of major regional affiliates. In Europe there will be major new conglomerates, created through the consolidation of smaller, national-based systems that are reaching out to a pan-European audience. Many European communication corporations, which are detailed in the following sections, realize quite clearly that they need to engage in pan-European merger activities or they will be purchased by some other major stakeholder, or be left behind altogether. If they do not expand, they will be left with smaller audiences and reduced revenues in an era when production costs and competition for both European and US television series and movies continue to escalate.

Seen through the lens of world-system theory, the following communication corporations are all based in core nations much like the United States. These nations exhibit similar traits that make them highly competitive such as a high gross national product (GNP), heavy deployment of information technologies, and a sophisticated labor force. These European core nations are also expanding as rapidly as possible into other core as well as semiperipheral nations. Geographically, they have an advantage because many of the semiperipheral nations are adjacent to the European community. Peripheral nations around the globe are in many cases former colonies of European nations. On the one hand, this may give the USE an advantage in marketing their communication products and systems to peripheral nations. On the other hand, deep-seated antagonism and a legacy of hostility between the colonies and their former European masters might prevent some peripheral nations from doing business with their former colonizers.

A final point is that, in the US, cultural industries are viewed as economic entities, but across Europe and elsewhere these same industries are viewed through a very different prism. They are not solely viewed as economic entities in terms of dollars or euros. The USE views cultural industries, or audiovisual industries, as part of their culture, history, and artistic heritage. Europeans are much more concerned about language, culture, employment opportunities in media industries, and preserving their history than considering media productions as being similar to economic output like cornflakes, lumber, or cars. Proof of this are the many public policies and significant financial subsidies that European entities promote and encourage. The USE is concerned about the cultural homogenization of media industries if they follow a US formula. The leadership for the cultural sector is assigned to various Ministers of Culture, which is a high-ranking cabinet post in almost all nations outside the United States. An example to illustrate this important point follows.

The EU provides specific grants to stimulate the development and distribution of European media productions. The goal is to increase quality and make available trans-European film and television programs across four genres or formats. These four are: fiction for television and cinema, documentaries, animation, and multimedia. The EU also underwrites writing workshops for various media and seminars about new media technologies. Since 2000 this program, entitled MEDIA PLUS, has a budget of over US$400 million. In addition, since only about 30 percent of films shown across the EU are European productions, the EU Minister for Education and Culture plans to provide over a number of years almost $1 billion in subsidies to expand the number of world-class films created across the enlarged EU. These productions are aimed at competing directly with Hollywood fare for global audiences and revenues over time.

Bertelsmann

The German-based Bertelsmann group of companies has a strong media presence in over 63 countries worldwide. It is the fourth largest media company globally (Time Warner, Viacom, and Disney are the first three). Carl Bertelsmann established the company in 1835 as a religious publishing house. Now its revenue is in the billions, and it has 6 major operating units worldwide. Bertelsmann remains a privately held company. The units consist of music, publishing, newspapers and magazines, broadcasting, printing, and a host of internet-related multimedia companies. Recently, new investments, particularly in internet and web-based activities, have been joint ventures with worldwide partners. For example, Bertelsmann's online book site is a partnership with Barnes & Noble, and many of its multimedia activities have been carried out in conjunction with the Axel Springer publishing house of Germany. Overall, Bertelsmann has invested in over 100 internet activities, but in 2004 it sold its interest in Barnes & Noble Online back to

Barnes & Noble Inc. at a substantial loss. This multimedia aspect of the corporate structure is relatively small; the music component, publishing, and book clubs dominate company revenues. Bertelsmann plans to be a major global player in a competitive market with future multimedia activities. Currently it makes 22 percent of global revenues for the US.

Bertelsmann Music Group (BMG) has branches in 5 continents and a 14 percent share of the world music market. BMG is the most international element of Bertelsmann's current media interests. One of BMG's labels is Arista Records, which represents music favorites such as Whitney Houston, Kenny G., and Toni Braxton. In addition to the latest hip-hop records by Arista, BMG Classics offers music lovers classical, jazz, New Age, and Broadway soundtracks. Bertelsmann also owns BMG Music Publishing. The company, which owns the rights to 700,000 songs, has offices in 27 countries and is among the world's chief music publishers. BMG Music Service offers US and Canadian internet users a music service club. Companies such as Time Life Music, Nestlé, and Kellogg's use BMG Special Products for their direct-marketing music activities and advertising incentives. Finally, RCA Victor and the Windham Hill Group are part of BMG. RCA Victor offers jazz, pop, crossover, Broadway, and movie soundtracks; Windham Hill Group in Beverly Hills offers instrumental music for singer/songwriters in the United States.

BMG Entertainment was the first of the major music corporations to present music on the internet not only by label but also by genre. Twang This! Country was another internet offering by BMG, which includes country labels.

In 2003, BMG merged with Sony Music, creating a 50/50 joint venture between Bertelsmann and Sony. Based on 2002 sales, the new merger would create a company controlling 25.2 percent of the global music market. The two conglomerates were initially concerned over approval by watchdogs at the European Union and in the United States, but heavy financial losses in the music industry contributed to the decision to approve the merger.

Bertelsmann holds two markets in Germany: artists and the New Media Laboratory, which falls under BMG Studios. Germany BMG Studios offers internet creations, animations, digital video processing, and classical sound recording. BMG also has a presence in Austria, Australia, Canada, Hong Kong, Japan, and the United Kingdom. BMG Ariola Austria is the market leader in Austria. Australia's most famous pop star, John Farnham, is a BMG artist. BMG Music Canada is the country and dance market leader. BMG Entertainment manages the entire music business in the Pacific Rim region from India to Australia out of Hong Kong. In 1987, Bertelsmann took the first step into the Asian market with the establishment of BMG Japan. Finally Bertelsmann owns Deconstruction Records, which concentrates on British dance music. With all of its offerings, the company decided to produce CDs under the name Sonopress. Sonopress has locations in

Europe, North and South America, Asia, and Africa. The CD company is among the leading CD manufacturers worldwide. Bertelsmann is also considering buying additional European labels.

Bertelsmann's interests in magazine and newspaper publishing are carried out through its Gruner + Jahr subsidiary, which publishes 120 magazines and newspapers in 14 countries. Bertelsmann holds a 75 percent stake in Gruner + Jahr, and is also the sole owner of Random House, the world's largest book publishing company.

Bertelsmann also has major interests in television, which are 50 percent owned by the RTL Group (formerly CLT-UFA), the largest TV/radio group in Europe. The RTL Group was formed through the 2001 merger of CLT-UFA, Pearson TV, and Audiofina. The company has television stations in Germany, France, the Benelux countries, Great Britain, Sweden, and the Czech Republic. RTL is Europe's largest broadcasting company, and Bertelsmann has a 90 percent share in the Luxembourg corporation; Audiofina controls the rest. In Germany alone, Bertelsmann owns 5 stations, which include RTL, RTL II, Vox, Super RTL (a joint venture with Disney), and RTL Shop, a home shopping channel. RTL is the most successful advertising-financed commercial TV station in Europe. In addition to its TV station, RTL Radio targets German-speaking listeners. The radio station has been synonymous with entertainment for the last 40 years. Finally, the VOX station began airing in 1993 and offers a national range of programs. RTL holds an 82.5 percent stake in this channel.

M6 is the television station Bertelsmann owns in France. Within 10 years, M6 developed into the most profitable advertising-financed private TV station in France. The RTL Group holds a 40 percent stake in M6. In addition to the television stations, Bertelsmann owns UFA Film & TV Production. This division is located in Potsdam-Babelsberg and produces 800 hours of television each year, making it one of Germany's largest production companies. To enhance its film and production interests, BMG Video holds labels with UFA and Atlas Pictures. Finally of Bertelsmann's television interests, UFA Sports in Hamburg is Europe's leading TV sports marketing company.

Most recently, Bertelsmann has focused on developing its multimedia capabilities. Bertelsmann New Media consists of online and portal gateways, the Game Channel, and Sport 1. The Game Channel is the second largest game-oriented internet channel. This interactive internet site allows people around the world to compete in "multilayer" games. The site offers a matchmaker service to find players around the globe who are at similar levels of skill. Bertelsmann and Axel Springer Publishing held a joint venture in Sport 1, an online service providing Germany's most important sports address on Europe's internet, but it was sold to Kirch, a regular partner of Axel Springer, in 2001. Kirch has since collapsed.

Germany's leading multimedia agency, Pixelpark, incorporates digital and brand communication in the business fields of e-commerce, e-finance, and e-marketing. Finally, Telemedia, another joint venture between Bertelsmann's New Media, the Axel Springer publishing house, and the WAZ publishing group, design and implement internet and intranet solutions in Germany. Bertelsmann has joint ventures with other publishing houses as well in order to spread the financial risk. Finally Bertelsmann, through its partial ownership of UFA Sports, has a long-term interest in Sampdoria, an Italian soccer club.

Vivendi

France's Vivendi Corporation was a major player in France and across Europe's audiovisual sector. The company was established in the nineteenth century starting with and continuing to have major interests in public utilities and construction. In 1997 it added communications to its corporate interests by purchasing a 30 percent stake in France's Havas. In 1998 the company changed its name from Générale des Eaux to Vivendi to reflect its new communications interests. Currently, Vivendi controls 18.5 percent of GE's NBC Universal. The latter's diverse properties are covered in the preceding chapter. Vivendi's global presence is strongest in former French colonies and operates in 71 nations.

Recently Vivendi sought to provide a single source for consumer and corporate telephone, cable, internet, and multimedia services. In 2000, Vivendi acquired the Seagram Company of Canada. The $55 billion merger of the two companies constituted the second largest merger in the world, second only to the merger of AOL and Time Warner. Just as AOL sought the content of Time Warner's vast holdings, so Vivendi was after Seagram's three major communication units: Universal Studios and Universal Pictures, as well as the Universal Music Group. Vivendi hoped to create the synergy needed to become a major global player in the rapidly evolving communications sector. It failed badly. Jean-Marie Messier, then the flamboyant president of Vivendi, was not only fired but is now being sued by his former employer, and he had to pay a substantial fine to the US Securities and Exchange Commission.

The French government is the quickest to play the culture card, but it let Vivendi abandon most of its substantial audiovisual properties. Now these properties, including music, television, feature films, and video games, are back under US control. France had a chance to be among the big stakeholders in communication corporations but now it will see greater American presence across their cultural sector. Even France's largest and most popular tourist destination is EuroDisney.

Hachette Filipacchi

A merger formed France's Matra Hachette in 1992, and the company is now known as Hachette Filipacchi. It is an extremely diversified conglomerate with major publishing and media interests as well as military-industrial activities. It produces the Dr. Seuss books, CD-ROM encyclopedias, and several consumer-oriented magazines published internationally, including *Elle*, *Car and Driver*, and *Photo*. Hachette Filipacchi also publishes the Grolier Encyclopedia, *Woman's Day*, *Metropolitan Home*, *Harlequin*, and *Popular Photography*. It is now the fourth-largest US magazine publisher overall and the largest foreign magazine publisher in the United States. Globally, Matra is the number one magazine publisher. The focus of its various magazines is primarily on advertising and then on circulation; ad pages constitute 65 percent of content, with editorial and story content making up 35 percent. *Elle* has 25 editions around the world. Hachette also publishes several newspapers in France. Hachette properties claim close to 50 million readers on a monthly basis. It became one of the first global marketers by promoting Elle Channel with Parisian cosmetic firm Estee Lauder's Clinique cosmetic brands. In addition, General Motors Corporation advertises in Hachette's 11 magazines published by Time Warner. Matra Hachette is visible on the internet. It has 20 sites on AOL and promotes its magazines extensively on websites. The corporation views itself as a global, highly diversified industrial and multimedia group. It is currently focused on new ventures in China and Russia. With almost 250 magazines in more than 30 nations, Hachette publishes more outside of than inside France. Hachette also owns Interdeco Global Advertising, the top advertising agency in France.

Canal Plus

Created in 1984, France's Canal Plus is the European leader of pay-TV, offering premium programming on several channels. After an initial launch in France, Canal Plus is now available in 16 European countries. Currently, it offers 21 channels and has 14 million subscribers across Europe. It has a strong focus on sports, particularly World Cup soccer, because it owns the Paris Saint-Germain soccer club, and it broadcasts European Grand Prix auto racing. Canal Plus also offers over 300 films annually and is the largest French producer or co-producer of French films for both theater and television. Recently it co-produced Roman Polanski's *The Pianist*.

Canal Plus promotes digital technology through Canal's interactive software technology. It is one of the best-known European suppliers of television decoder units for digital pay-TV reception, and plans to have terrestrial digital service available across France in 2005. Canal Plus, through its film division, StudioCanal, is seeking to bring together European film providers for both television and theater distribution in order to encourage the development of a unified, pan-European film industry. Its multimedia program library is Europe's second largest. As a corporation, it sees itself as the European alternative to Hollywood feature films, yet it is willing to work with US studios and has various co-production deals in Europe with Warner, Paramount, and Vivendi Universal studios. The current cost of producing blockbusters for a global audience is beyond the fiscal reach of most European film studios. Canal Plus is a subsidiary of Vivendi Universal, but financial and regulatory troubles have caused Vivendi to explore a breakup or sale of Canal Plus. It has sold several divisions of Canal Plus to outside companies following the fiscal mess created by Messier.

Pathé

Pathé is a major European entertainment and film production company located in France. It also owns movie theaters and is a major European player in both feature movies and television programming. Pathé has investments in other communication enterprises as well, owning part of France's Canal Plus, and AB Sports Channel. It also owns 22 percent of the French daily newspaper *Libération*. Pathé has extensive holdings of film rights and produces a small number of new feature films each year. Its high-profile films include *Lolita*, produced in 1998, *Chicken Run*, produced in 1999, and *Oliver Twist* and *Alexander* in 2004. Pathé has a partnership agreement with Olympique Lyonnais soccer club. It with partners operates 740 screens in France, Switzerland, and the Netherlands; they switched to the US model of multiscreen venues in the 1990s. Pathé also produces documentaries as well as programming for several European thematic channels. Through co-productions, Pathé is well positioned to be a major stakeholder in the expanding European audiovisual economy. Historically it has a corporate culture that avoids France's narrow, ethnocentric ethic of avoiding all things anglophone. Pathé shunned French nationalism and sought media opportunities and properties across Europe without regard for national boundaries or constraining linguistic tastes. Finally, a wealthy French family with a long history of media and sports interests privately owns Pathé.

Pearson

Pearson, based in the United Kingdom, is a global media company that controls several media properties. For example, it publishes the *Financial*

Times (*FT*), which competes directly with the *Wall Street Journal*. *FT* is aimed at the global business community and has been a successful newspaper since its introduction in 1888. *FT* has correspondents in 70 nations and their online edition, FT.com, has over 3 million monthly users around the globe. Pearson also owns 50 percent of the weekly global magazine *The Economist*. Through its TV production facilities, Pearson produces over 150 programs, including the hit popular culture show *Baywatch*, for global audiences. On the publishing side, the corporation has sought a niche in educational and reference publishing. Pearson owns Prentice-Hall, Addison Wesley, Longman, Allyn and Bacon, Scott Foresman, the Penguin Group, and Simon & Schuster's educational units. As part of its educational niche, Pearson also controls the largest number of websites directly related to major leading textbooks. Clearly demonstrating the strategic importance of the US marketplace to all non-American communication firms are Pearson's 2003 sales figures on a geographic basis. For their domestic market in the United Kingdom the company realized 12 percent of their total global sales, and by comparison the North American market accounted for 68 percent. In terms of profits, US–Canada sales provided a staggering 87 percent of Pearson's overall profits.

VNU

Netherlands-based VNU was founded in 1964 and is a global information and multimedia company with interests in over 100 countries. They are into publishing, television, films, music, home entertainment, tracking both audio and video retail sales, internet services and sites, and major media and audience rating services through Nielsen. Among VNU's 140 publications are *Billboard Magazine*, *The Hollywood Reporter*, *Ad Week*, *Brand Week*, and *Media Week*. Their North American interests provide the Dutch parent company with over 50 percent of its global revenues.

A major asset of VNU is the audience ratings firm Nielsen Media Research. This firm provides television, radio, and print measurement in over 40 countries. Through Nielsen Monitor Plus, a media buying and advertising information service, VNU measures over 85 percent of the globe's advertising expenditures. Nielsen/NetRating is the leading internet audience measurement and analysis service, including tracking online advertisements. This firm tracks more than 70 percent of the globe's internet traffic.

Finally, Nielsen Media Research provides detailed information of television viewership in the United States for over a million households. But some of its data collection methods and analysis have come under criticism in recent years.

In terms of ECT the Nielsen subsidiaries are prime examples of how core-based firms control much of the data about electronic and print media. The wealth of data, knowledge, and analysis provided by Nielsen to subscribers is enormous, across a vast range of commercial multimedia lines. The advertising giants, for example, are all based in core nations. They have clients in almost all semiperipheral nations and some peripheral ones as well. Yet the data and research provided to them by Nielsen serves a two-fold purpose. First, to strengthen and fine tune what and how they perform for their already-existing client base, and second, to recruit new clients by impressing them with their arsenal of data and services, of which Nielsen is just one part. For any totally new ad firm to emerge or for any semiperipheral-nation-based firm to become a major ad agency is almost an impossible task. This phenomenon and reality of the global role and scope of the existing ad agencies, in partnership with Nielsen, makes the quest for more customers for core media products an easier task, because the basic research and strategy works relatively well.

Mediaset

Mediaset controls the three largest private television channels in Italy. The majority owner is Italian prime minster Silvio Berlusconi; he is also president of the AC Milan soccer club. Mediaset is seeking international expansion for its vast library of soap operas and sitcoms. Beginning in 1997, Mediaset acquired Italian broadcasting rights for all NBC movies and miniseries. In 2004 it began a 24-hour commercial children's channel, named Boing, in partnership with Time Warner. It will also jointly produce major productions for the international market. Mediaset networks are delivered through cable and satellite, which facilitate further global expansion, particularly for the Italian-speaking market. Finally, Mediaset operates a pay-TV network called Happy Channel and controls the top Italian advertising agency, Publitalia.

Axel Springer

Germany's Axel Springer group is a major European newspaper and magazine publisher with other media interests including books, video, and the internet. Foreign newspaper as well as magazine publications are located in Austria, France, Spain, Switzerland, Poland, Hungary, Russia, and the Czech Republic. Axel Springer also has interests in Austrian radio stations and has a 51 percent stake in a Canadian animation studio.

The group has nearly 200 newspapers and magazines and is the largest German publisher in terms of circulation. In 2001 it was adversely affected by an investment loss when the German-based Kirch group went bankrupt. Across Germany media firms that are being sold are being directed to seek out German purchasers rather than outsiders like Murdoch's News Corp. Given the vast amount of consolidation across the media industry, it is becoming more difficult to maintain local ownership.

Telefonica SA (Spain)

The Spanish telecommunication giant also has a major television production facility based in the Netherlands, Endemol Holding Company. It produces over 25,000 hours of programming yearly and has some major global hits. Endemol operates across 23 European countries, where it is frequently the largest TV producer.

Some of the company's TV success stories are *Big Brother* (on CBS), *Fear Factor* (on NBC), and *Extreme Makeover* (on ABC), which they license to major television networks around the globe. From time to time, US multimedia firms seeking a solid television production foothold in the European Union have attempted to buy Endemol.

European Broadcasting Union (EBU)

The EBU is a significant transnational entity for public broadcasters across Europe, the Middle East, and North Africa. Given that almost all nations outside the US have had large and successful noncommercial, i.e. public-service, broadcasters since 1950, the EBU has been a crucial professional association of national, noncommercial broadcasters. Working in 52 countries, the EBU operates Eurovision and Euroradio networks. It also facilitates the exchange of programming and negotiates broadcasting rights for major sports events, such as soccer and the Olympics, and finally works to facilitate original co-productions among member broadcasters. In 2005 they issued the Madrid Declaration. The five main issues in the Declaration are:

1 the major role played by public-service broadcasters to further European integration;
2 a proactive approach on the part of the EBU and its members to support public service;
3 the need for public-service broadcasting to be at the forefront of new initiatives regarding digital terrestrial broadcasting;

4 comprehensive delivery of public-service content on the full spectrum of new digital platforms;
5 the crucial importance of guaranteed stable and long-term funding to allow the full implementation of public-service duties. (For the full text of the Declaration see: http://ebu.ch.)

Finally, the EBU will be busy monitoring the proposed actions of the World Trade Organization (WTO) as they impact the public broadcasting sectors. The EBU does not view broadcasting as a commercial commodity to be included in WTO's free trade undertakings. (The WTO is discussed in a later chapter.)

Other Foreign-Based Multimedia Corporations

European-based multimedia corporations are by no means the only non-US stakeholders in the global communication industry. The following sections detail the primary global communication stakeholders located in nations outside of Europe and the United States. (See figure 4.2.)

CanWest Global Communications Corp. (Canada)

One of the largest private broadcasters in Canada, CanWest Global, initially started in the 1970s as a third (behind the CBC and CTV networks) national television network, called Global Television. It has since expanded

1. CanWest Global Communications Corp. (Canada)
2. WETV (Canada)
3. Aboriginal People's Television (Canada)
4. Grupo Televisa (Mexico)
5. Globo Communications (Brazil)
6. Cisneros Group (Venezuela)
7. Sony (Japan)
8. Bollywood (India)

Figure 4.2 Non-USE major communication stakeholders

into cable as well as film and television production activities. It also publishes 11 major Canadian dailies. Beginning in the early 1990s, CanWest bought a 70 percent part interest in New Zealand's only private-sector broadcaster, TV3. In the late 1990s, New Zealand began operating a second privately owned network, TV4. And again, CanWest played a significant role. New Zealand's top-rated commercial radio network, RadioWorks, which includes 7 major urban radio stations and other FM stations, is partly owned (70 percent) by the CanWest network. In 2001 they acquired Radio Works New Zealand, the second largest radio group in that country. Global's radio interests now account for about half of New Zealand's radio advertising revenues.

During the 1990s, CanWest also acquired 56.5 percent ownership of Australia's Ten TV network, and started with United Kingdom's Granada Media, the private sector's first TV3 TV network in Ireland, with 45 percent ownership. CanWest has film interests in the US through its Seven Arts International Division and recently concluded an internet agreement with Minnesota-based Internet Broadcasting Systems (IBS). This joint venture will permit the expansion of an internet-based network of news and information sites across North America. Los Angeles, Minneapolis, Cleveland, and other cities have been targeted for joint venture internet developments, along with the expansion of the media outlet Channel 4,000, which is a TV website owned by IBS of Minneapolis. Finally CanWest's European interests are channeled through their London-based organization, CanWest Entertainment International. Future strategic plans for CanWest include further global expansion and buying print properties in North America.

WETV (Canada)

WETV is a global television network that takes both commercial and public broadcasting approaches. It seeks to combine public and private funding in order to provide a global market as an alternative television service. In part, its aim is to redress the underrepresentation of peripheral nations and to counterbalance the overexposure of core nations' programs on competing commercial television networks. Therefore, WETV provides global access for underrepresented countries and indigenous cultures in Asia, Africa, Latin America, and eastern Europe. Much of the programming is educational.

Canada's International Development Research Corporation supports the service. The mission of WETV is to promote sustainable development and further the expression of cultural diversity through its television network. Regular programming was initiated in October 1996. Today there are a significant number of partner broadcasters. Several international agencies with interests in economic development have assisted in the creation of WETV. The programming comes primarily from independent producers, development agencies, and various affiliated stations. In some circumstances, WETV undertakes the role of co-producer with independent producers located primarily in peripheral regions. Twelve minutes of advertising are set aside each hour, 6 minutes retained by the affiliate and 6 minutes retained by WETV. Startup funding came from a variety of sources, primarily Canadian, but early public funding came from the Netherlands, Norway, Sweden, and Switzerland. The United Nations has also been a program sponsor. A number of the programs are in Spanish, but the service is primarily in English. A sample of the 50 partner countries that signed affiliate agreements to carry WETV are Argentina, Brazil, Canada, Cuba, Jamaica, Mexico, Peru, Uganda, United States, and Zimbabwe; the number of affiliate agreements increases monthly. Over time WETV will likely obtain global penetration but remain a niche market, attracting limited but dedicated audiences around the globe.

In Canada, WETV launched a Green Channel in 2001, which focuses on environmental issues. It is also available globally through their internet site.

Aboriginal People's Television Network (Canada)

Aboriginal People's Television Network (APTN) was launched in 1999 as a means of promoting positive images and messages about aboriginals and aboriginal lifestyle. The new specialty channel is attempting to reverse the longstanding trend of negative mainstream media coverage of aboriginals. AFTN presents aboriginal programming from Canada, the United States, Australia, and New Zealand. The schedule includes children's, educational, and cultural programming as well as news, current affairs, and political programming. Most programming is produced, written, and staffed by media professionals of aboriginal ancestry.

Approximately 50 percent of the shows are in English, 25 percent in French, and 25 percent in a variety of aboriginal languages, primarily Inuit. APTN is a clear example of development communication. The goal of the network is to present pro-social and proactive messages on behalf of aboriginal communities as an alternative to the traditional mainstream TV networks, which are staffed almost entirely by nonaboriginal personnel.

Grupo Televisa (Mexico)

The roots of the Azcarraga family empire date back to the radio era. Emilio Azcarraga Milmo began his media career with the radio station XEW-AM in

Mexico City during the 1940s. The Azcarraga family subsequently owned the station. In 1972 the Azacarraga family formed the giant television network Televisa by combining two other television companies. Emilio Azcarraga Milmo died in Miami in April 1998, leaving Latin America's largest multimedia corporation, Grupo Televisa, to his son, Emilio Azcarraga Jean. The Azcarragas now control a sprawling operation that includes four network channels with 280 affiliate stations; a publishing company called Editorial Televisa; 3 record labels (Melody, Fonovisa, and Musivisa); 17 radio stations; one cable channel; one satellite system; a movie company, Estadio Azteca (a massive 120,000-seat stadium); 2 soccer teams; and a cellular phone company. In addition, they have investments in the US Spanish network Univision; the stateside cable channel Galavision; a Venezuelan television network; and the satellite company PanAmSat. Altogether, Grupo Televisa is the largest Spanish-language media conglomerate in the world.

Univision is the largest Spanish-language network in the United States. It was launched in 1961 and currently is experiencing substantial growth. As the US Hispanic population increases rapidly it has become the largest minority in the United States. Univision, which is 15 percent owned by Televisa, features telenovelas, soap operas that last for several months. The Univision network reaches the vast majority of US Hispanic households through 21 owned and operated stations, as well as through 27 broadcast affiliates. Grupo Televisa provides Univision with a large number of Spanish-language programs that appeal to the growing US Hispanic audience. Univision is a major, and sometimes the dominant, channel in US cities such as Miami and Los Angeles, and in several Texas and Arizona cities. Univision is also beginning to attract substantial advertising revenue from major US corporations because reaching the Hispanic audience is becoming more critical to increasing market share for media and consumer products alike.

Televisa has already rolled out new channels including Conexion Financiera, which broadcasts business news from studios in Mexico City, Buenos Aires, Madrid, and New York. In Spain the company is involved in a venture led by Telefonica de Espana to launch digital service.

About 60 percent of Grupo Televisa's revenue comes from television activities; the publishing division accounts for 20 percent. With the rapid growth of Spanish media in both the United States and Europe, the Azcarraga empire is growing, with hopes of competing with the Disney and Sony corporations.

Globo Communications (Brazil)

Globo is a multimedia giant with a television network, newspapers, magazines and books, radio, cable systems movies, internet, and records. In addition to owning Rio de Janeiro's largest circulation newspaper, *O Globo*, the Company's television interest attracts over 60 percent of the Brazilian audience and is the largest television network in Latin America. The company is privately owned by the Marinho family and accumulated enormous debts during the 1990s. They were able to restructure US$1.3 billion of their debt in late 2004 and avoid bankruptcy. Historically the Marinho elders have had a close relationship with the political masters of Brazil. In terms of exports Globo has limited sales since they work in Portuguese, with the exception being telenovelas which do well in parts of Europe.

Cisneros Group (Venezuela)

Established in 1929 in Caracas, Venezuela, this is now one of the world's largest multimedia firms in private hands. The chairman and CEO is family member Gustavo Cisneros, who directs its vast holding across the Americas. The company seeks to serve the 500 million Spanish and Portuguese markets across Europe and the Americas with high-quality audio and video entertainment. The flagship television station is Venevision, the largest in Venezuela. The Group also has a 20 percent interest in several Univision properties, such as television, radio, music, and the internet. In addition, it offers Galavision, 11 different genres of pay-TV, an interest in AOL Latin America, and for the US market, Venevision International. This company, based in Miami, provides Cisneros products across 5 continents, involving 20 languages in over 100 countries. Finally, in 2001 an alliance of Venevision, Televisa, and Univision formed as a global multimedia strategy to compete more effectively in the growing global Spanish-speaking markets. One of their new ventures is TeleFuture Network.

Sony (Japan)

Originally established in 1946 under the name Tokyo Telecommunications Engineering Corporation, Sony Corporation got its new name in 1958. Company founders were determined to create new markets with communication technology. The company produced the first Japanese tape recorder in 1950, and by 1955, after receiving a transistor technology license from Western Electric, launched the first transistor radio. The company then produced the first Sony trademark product: a pocket-sized radio.

In 1960, Akio Morita (1921–99), one of Sony's founders, moved to New York to oversee major US expansion. During this time, Sony launched the first home video, a solid-state condenser microphone, and an integrated circuit-based radio. Another decade of explosive growth was launched by Sony's 1968 introduction of the Trinitron color television tube. The VCR and the Walkman were other early Sony successes. Competition, especially from other Asian countries, was affecting the Sony Corporation by the 1980s. For this reason, Sony, under Morita's leadership as chairman since 1976, used its technology to diversify beyond consumer electronics. In 1980, Sony introduced Japan's first 32-bit workstation and became a major producer of computer chips and floppy-disk drives. Sony expanded its US media empire by acquiring CBS Records from CBS for $2 billion and Columbia Pictures from Coca-Cola for $4.9 billion, both in 1988. Sony was now in the US entertainment industry in a big way. In 1992, Sony allied with Sega to develop CD video games, and with Microsoft to make electronic audio-, video-, and textbooks.

Sony Corporation is headquartered in Tokyo, Japan; the sister company in the United States is called Sony Corporation of America. The company employs 163,000 people worldwide. Sony's major products include audio and video equipment, televisions, information, communications, and electronic components. Some of the products produced for the audio division includes CD players, headphone stereos, hi-fi components, radio-cassette portable stereos, radios, car stereos, and digital audiotape. The video division produces VHS and DV-format VCRs, DVD video players, video CD players, digital still cameras, and videotapes. The television division produces color TVs, projection TVs, flat display panels, and large color video display systems. Also, computer displays, personal computers, internet terminals, telephones, and car navigation systems are all Sony products.

In 1998, Sony invested in the US Hispanic broadcast network Telemundo, which is the second largest Spanish-language network in the United States, attracting about 25 percent of the Hispanic audience. The other 75 percent is the audience of Univision, which is partially owned by Mexico's Televisa. The US Hispanic market is estimated to be 30 million and growing rapidly. Telemundo is central to Sony's worldwide Spanish-language television strategy. Sony produces over 500 hours of Spanish-language programming for 7 international channels and plans to increase the network's programming budget in order to boost Telemundo's ratings. Given the rapid increase in Hispanic audiences across the United States, Sony hopes to use Telemundo to increase advertising revenues by producing high-profile telenovelas in primetime. Telemundo is also promoting Spanish artists under contract to Sony Music. Telemundo is based in the largely Latino Miami, Florida, and owns and operates 7 television stations in the United States. Telemundo experienced financial difficulties in the early 1990s and is looking to its new owner, Sony Corporation, to assist it in becoming a major contender for audience share against the strong competition of

Univision. Sony also has two other Spanish networks, which cover most of Latin America: Action Channel and Sony Entertainment Television. Both use Sony's Columbia Pictures productions throughout their schedules.

Sony's music division offers recordings from acts ranging from Michael Bolton to Rage Against the Machine. Sony's film and television offerings include the film *As Good As It Gets*, starring Oscar winners Helen Hunt and Jack Nicholson, and the popular TV game show *Wheel of Fortune*.

Sony is planning for the future. The company is rededicating itself to producing quality audiovisual products including digital televisions, internet-ready televisions, CD-ROMs, and digital satellites. Sony is also making advances in video cameras. New technologies, including NightShot, make it easier to tape at night, and Super SteadyShot will enable the user to move more freely and not have to worry that shaking will spoil the picture.

Finally, Sony is embarking on a new venture focusing on multiplex theaters, retail stores, and food courts, all in urban settings. This move represents Sony's attempt to demonstrate that it can combine multimedia entertainment and more broad-scale retail activities in order to create the urban shopping environment of the twenty-first century. Three new Sony entertainment complexes are located in San Francisco, Tokyo, and Berlin. The San Francisco version is an $85 million complex covering more than 350,000 square feet. These ventures will position Sony to compete with Disney and NBC Universal's entertainment theme parks. Sony's entertainment complexes have the added dimension of a plethora of retail shops and upscale dining establishments. Sony is attempting to apply its cutting-edge technologies and entertainment systems to a much broader urban landscape in order to attract millions of visitors with a combined substantial annual disposable income.

Bollywood: India's Film Industry

The cinema of the semiperipheral nation of India rates specific mention. It began in 1896 with a film produced by the French brothers Lumière. Then in 1913 the first Indian-made silent feature film was produced. From these humble origins the film industry in India is now producing over 800 films per year. The vast film industry has been nicknamed "Bollywood," a combination of Hollywood and Bombay. The films are primarily Hindi productions with a number of regional centers producing other films in their own languages.

Bollywood is a major focus of India's popular culture both at home and abroad. The commercial films are shown on the Indian subcontinent, across the Middle East, Africa, Asia, and North America to the large number of Indian expatriates in these regions. The genres of musicals, romance, comedy, and melodramatic themes dominate. A typical budget for a feature-length movie with export expectations is still only US$2 million as compared with Hollywood stars commanding more than $10 million each for a single movie. Also Indian censors are very active and restrict many plots with a sexual caché. Across India more than 6 million workers are employed in the cinema sector and leading stars are national heroes. The growth of cable channels and DVDs is providing additional outlets for Bollywood productions and increased revenue growth. Though a niche cinematic industry, it has survived surprisingly well in the face of major core-nation competition.

Conclusions

This review of global broadcasters illustrates two important points, which will be developed in some detail here. The first is the connection between sports and the mass media. This partnering is particularly common in Europe where many major broadcasting conglomerates also own, in part or in whole, major European soccer teams. US media firms also own several sports teams. The second facet is the substantial and ever-increasing role that non-US media stakeholders are playing in global communication.

The sports connection

The connection between sports and the mass media has had a long and checkered career. For example, attempts to link the International Olympic Movement (IOC) and the summer and winter Olympic Games with the world television audience were tenuous during the 1950s and 1960s. It was not until the 1970s that the value of media rights for the Olympic Games escalated dramatically because of bidding wars among ABC, NBC, and CBS. In the 1990s, the gray area between amateur and professional sports became even shadier when for the first time professional basketball and hockey players participated in the Olympic Games. Today the Olympics enjoy substantial revenue from a combination of media and marketing funds that were created as part of the selling package for host cities. Host cities incur enormous local expenses but now recoup those expenses, plus tourism dollars, thanks to the huge sums paid almost exclusively by US television networks. Major US firms purchasing marketing rights supplement these dollars. It should come as no surprise that sponsorship of the Olympics makes sense, and that this sports connection should work for corporations with other sports as well. Even now, the National Football League holds exhibition games in Europe and the National Hockey League holds exhibition games in Asia as part of their attempts to go global. European football, known in the United States as soccer, has limited exposure in the United States except during the World Cup. The 1999 US women's World Cup victory shown live on television had a dramatic influence on soccer and media exposure in North America. In the future, global sports leagues will emerge, and global broadcasting will parallel that movement. Current media outlets such as News Corporation, Disney, AOL Time Warner, and others may aggressively purchase international sports teams in order to influence or obtain international sports broadcasting rights, primarily for teams that draw enormous global audiences that are ripe for global products such as Coca-Cola, American Express, McDonald's, Kodak, IBM, and UPS.

It appears that Murdoch's News Corporation strategy concerning sports may be changing in Europe. Previously, he had announced large-scale attempts to purchase major media systems, which frequently ran into regulatory trouble as the culturally sensitive Europeans looked with disfavor on the Australian-born media giant. More recently, he has been acquiring part ownership in nonmajor media outlets across Europe. For example, in 1999 he acquired 35 percent of an Italian digital pay-TV service known as Stream. Murdoch, along with other partners, is now acquiring the rights to broadcast Italian soccer games. In Germany, News Corporation bought 66 percent of the niche channel entitled TM3. This relatively obscure channel outbid Germany's number one commercial TV channel for all domestic broadcasting rights to Europe's major soccer league for 4 years.

Global stakeholders

These descriptions of transnational media conglomerates reflect a basic point – namely, that global communication systems are only partly American in shape, content, and ownership. Many powerful non-US global corporations are extremely active in the global communication marketplace. Even though these non-US firms compete with Hollywood and New York, they do so while sharing the same commercial values. The goal of these global media corporations is to maximize profits for owners and shareholders, much like their US counterparts; they entered the global arena to increase market share. They are all based in core nations. All global media firms rely heavily on foreign customers, whether they are in other core nations or in semi-peripheral or peripheral zones. These non-US firms need to have a significant presence in the US market to be profitable as well as to be considered major global players. They have taken advantage of the significant structural changes in the 1990s that encouraged privatization and deregulation at the same time that satellite technology, cable systems, and the internet were expanding rapidly. In Europe and in eastern Europe, where government-controlled and government-owned media became a phenomenon of a previous era, aggressive corporations quickly sought either to extend their traditional interests in the mass media, beginning with print products, or move into new areas and make strategic decisions to diversify previously nonmedia corporations. The outcomes are similar. All major global multimedia corporations are seeking to maximize profits in order to increase or improve the rate of return for their shareholders. They do this through a combination of expanding current markets and adding new market share through acquisitions or joint ventures. Ultimately, they seek the expansion of electronic colonialism. Just as US global media firms seek foreign customers in Asia and Europe, so Asian and European firms are aggressively pursuing customers in North America. They do so by producing shows and other media products that will attract a substantial customer base along with healthy advertising revenues. Bertelsmann and Sony are prime examples. Sony Pictures Classics spent over $10 million to market a single film, *Crouching Tiger, Hidden Dragon*. But the reality for most foreign firms in the feature film business is that the costs have moved the bar far beyond their reach. One example, that of female movie stars, speaks volumes. Julia Roberts and Cameron Diaz command between $20 to $30 million each per movie. For somewhere between $10 and $20 million producers have their pick of Halle Berry, Drew Barrymore, Nicole Kidman, Reese Witherspoon, Sandra Bullock, Renee Zellweger, or Angelina Jolie. The vast majority of foreign-produced feature films do not have total budgets in this league, let alone for a single star.

Clearly, customers with disposable income are free to make choices among a plethora of books and magazines, movies and television channels, records, tapes, internet sites, and other communication products around the globe. Most are unaware of who owns the content, which controls the delivery system, or how important advertising is in terms of revenue for these global empires. Few could identify, or would care, which firm actually owns the product they are viewing, listening to, or reading.

Early in the twenty-first century it is likely that the biggest global communication firms will be conducting most of their business abroad, or capturing more customers in foreign markets, and will have less to do with the nation-state their corporation was established in. A global mindset, global advertising, and global strategic planning will reflect the successful communication management of tomorrow. Business without borders will be the norm rather than the exception for global multimedia corporations. Like the internet, global communication systems and products will transcend national boundaries.

A new policy issue is looming on the horizon, which could impact the non-American multimedia stakeholders. Namely, the World Trade Organization (WTO) as part of its new round of negotiations is looking to include the audiovisual sector in new multilateral talks.[6] The WTO as part of its broad tariff reduction goal may include government subsidies as well. For many nations, particularly the USE, this could result in the ending of government grants or programs that seek to bolster their film and television industries. This important and looming policy issue is discussed in chapter 11.

Notes

1 See, for example, Juan E. Conradi, "Cultural Dependence and the Sociology of Knowledge: The Latin American Case," *International Journal of Contemporary Sociology* 8(1) (1971), pp. 35–55; Kaarle Nordenstreng and Tapio Varis, *Television Traffic: A One-Way Street?* (Paris: UNESCO, 1974); and Thomas Guback, *The International Film Industry* (Bloomington: Indiana University Press, 1969).

2 See, for example, Ben Bagdikian, *The Media Monopoly* (Boston: Beacon Press, 1992); Jeremy Tunstall, *The Media Are American* (New York: Columbia University Press, 1977); Thomas McPhail and Brenda McPhail, *Communication: The Canadian Experience* (Toronto: Copp Clark Pitman, 1990); and Anthony Smith, *The Geopolitics of Information: How Western Culture Dominates the World* (New York: Oxford University Press, 1980).

3 See, for example, Andrew A. Moemeka, ed., *Communicating for Development* (Albany: State University of New York Press, 1994); Oliver Boyd-Barnett, *The International News Agencies* (London: Constable, 1980); Tsan Kuo Chang, "All Countries Not Created Equal to Be News," *Communication Research* 25(5) (Oct. 1998), pp. 528–63; and Rob Kroes, "American Empire and Cultural Imperialism: A View from the Receiving End," *Diplomatic History* 23 (1999), pp. 463–78.

4 Herbert I. Schiller, *Communication and Cultural Domination* (White Plains, NY: International Arts & Sciences Press, 1978); and J. Tomlinson, *Cultural Imperialism: A Critical Introduction* (London: Pinter, 1991).

5 John Tagliabue, "A Media World to Conquer," *New York Times*, July 7, 1999, p. 5.

6 Caroline Pauwels and Jan Loisen, "The WTO and the Audiovisual Sector," *European Journal of Communication* 18 (2003), pp. 291–314.

Chapter 5

Global Issues, Music, and MTV

Introduction

In the twenty-first century, communication, media, and information exports will become the primary engine of the global economy for the United States. Since the end of the Second World War, US aerospace industries have provided the primary export product, with sales of both commercial and military aircraft, to various nations around the world. These sales greatly assisted the US balance of payments as well as domestic employment. But with the end of the Cold War and in the aftermath of 9/11 the global demand for aircraft has subsided. In addition, the passenger airline manufacturing business has become a global duopoly of Boeing Aircraft and its European competitor, Airbus. As a result, makers of US cultural products ranging from movies and TV programs to music and computer software are overtaking aerospace as the primary US employers and exporters. A good example of this export phenomenon is Viacom's Music Television (MTV), which is available in well over 100 countries with a potential audience of 400 million households.

According to the US Department of Commerce, the sale of feature films, TV shows, and home video rentals to foreign markets increased significantly during the 1990s. It is projected that global revenues will exceed $20 billion by 2006. The same report estimates that the US music industry accounts for 50 percent of global sales with revenues of $8 billion annually.[1]

When imported products consisted of military aircraft or jumbo jets, there was little widespread concern among foreign populations. But when the imported products began to consist of mass-media outpourings with cultural as well as economic implications, animosity began to grow toward the prevalence of core nations' cultural artifacts and economic values. Clearly, not everyone or every nation welcomes the globalization of the mass media. Many peripheral nations and some industrialized nations, particularly Canada, Ireland, and France, are concerned about the dominance of US global media exports.[2] David Rothkopf explains the issues:

> Globalization has economic roots and political consequences, but it also has brought into focus the power of culture in this global environment – the power to bind and to divide in a time when the tensions between integration and separation tug at every issue that is relevant to international relations.
>
> The impact of globalization on culture and the impact of culture on globalization merit discussion. The homogenizing influences of globalization that are most often condemned by the new nationalists and by cultural romanticists are actually positive; globalization promotes integration and the removal not only of cultural barriers but of many of the negative dimensions of culture. Globalization is a vital step toward both a more stable world and better lives for the people in it. Furthermore, these issues have serious implications for American foreign policy. For the United States, a central objective of an Information Age foreign policy must be to win the battle of the world's information flows, dominating the airwaves as Great Britain once ruled the seas.[3]

The world's information and media flows have been enhanced by the widespread surge in sales of televisions, DVDs, CD players, satellite dishes, cable, and, in some cases, personal computers. In addition, there have been infrastructure advancements such as the growth of Blockbuster Entertainment Corporation's video chain with more than 2,000 outlets in 26 foreign countries, or Tower Records, which has over 70 stores in over 15 countries. On the print side, the amount of US content exported around the world is significant. *Reader's Digest*, for example, is produced in 19 languages with 48 international editions. It has a combined global circulation of 23 million, about 11 million of which is US based. Even *Cosmopolitan*, a niche magazine for women, has global sales of close to 5 million copies, with 40 foreign editions in 25 languages.

US media companies frequently enjoy an economic advantage denied to almost all of their offshore competitors. The domestic US audience is not only large and wealthy, but it also has a substantial and varied taste for entertainment and media products of all types. This continent-wide market provides the economic resources necessary to support a global culture. In addition, the latest mass-media technologies frequently are introduced within the US marketplace, thus allowing US producers to experiment with and refine technical and marketing strategies before moving offshore to an ever-expanding group of global customers. These customers are in other core nations as well as in all the semiperipheral and some of the peripheral nations.

This chapter reviews communication exports and the globalization of the media marketplace. The export market for US-produced television programming and the international music industry is examined in detail. Particular attention is given to MTV, a network that personifies the marriage of global television with leading musicians, and a global youth culture.

Global Television

As noted earlier, foreign television networks consume large quantities of US television shows via syndication. Particularly attractive are US-made situation comedies and dramas with high production values.[4] Major series such as *Dallas, Columbo, Star Trek, Baywatch, Seinfeld, ER, The Simpsons, Cosby, Friends, Sex and the City*, and others dominate many foreign television schedules. For example, it is estimated that an audience in excess of a billion viewers viewed *Baywatch* in 148 nations. *Baywatch* began in 1989 and lasted 10 years with 210 episodes available for syndication. *The Simpsons* is available in over 70 nations and is the longest-running animated comedy.

However, in the 1990s an interesting shift occurred. The major networks replaced these expensive dramas and sitcoms with programs based on reality shows or the news magazine format (similar to CBS's *60 Minutes*). Today, the genre includes *20/20, PrimeTime Thursday, Nightline, 60 Minutes II*, and *Dateline NBC*. One of the consequences of this trend is a steep increase in the prices of the fewer remaining successful sitcoms, such as *The Simpsons, Seinfeld, Friends, Everyone Loves Raymond*, or *Frasier*, available for syndication.

Cost escalations

Among the reasons why networks are cutting back their production of primetime drama is the high cost of such programming. The cost of primetime episodes now averages about US$1.5 million an hour, about double the cost of an equivalent episode a decade ago. Some series are substantially more expensive: each installment of *ER* costs $13 million; Tim Allen of *Home Improvement* personally received $1.25 million per episode; and even the *The X-Files*, which was for a time filmed in Vancouver, Canada, to keep costs down, costed $2.5 million per episode. Each of the six leading actors on *Friends* received $1 million per half-hour episode. And they walked away from that successful show. With high-profile stars demanding larger salaries and with competition for experienced writers and cast, production costs are increasing dramatically. In comparison, news programming costs about $500,000 an hour. Even "reality" shows such as *America's Most Wanted*, *Survivor*, *Cops*, *Candid Camera*, *You're Fired*, or Cosby's *Kids Say the Darndest Things* are relatively inexpensive compared to the costs of leading dramas, comedy, or broadcasting rights for major sports programming.

Audience fragmentation

As costs escalate, US networks also must face the reality of a fragmenting audience. CBS, NBC, and ABC dominated the television market from the inception of the medium until the 1980s, when the FOX network joined them. In June 1998, however, these four networks were for the first time outwatched in primetime by audiences viewing cable options. During the 1990s, viewers deserted the major networks to tune into what are often called "narrowcasting" or niche channels. The rapid growth of alternative cable options, including both specialty channels (ESPN, MTV, A&E, CNN, MSNBC) and super channels such as WGN of TBS, had a significant cumulative impact on the audiences for the major television networks. The major networks have been reduced to less than 50 percent of the total primetime audience. They have been forced to scramble to maintain an audience share sufficient to maintain high advertising rates.[5]

Clearly, one of the factors making the new media offerings so attractive is their ability to target specific or niche audiences. Another is their programming flexibility, which permits them to address unique high-interest events. Take, for example, the infamous white Ford Bronco low-speed chase and the subsequent trial of former football star O. J. Simpson. This case, involving a well-known personality and a lengthy and sordid trial about sex and murder, captivated enormous audiences in North America and abroad. As the dominant news story of its time, it provided audiences with niche news and public affairs networks, with thousands of hours of programming over several months that not only filled their schedules but also attracted a new and larger audience. While the new players focused on the trial, the Big Four networks found themselves in a no-win situation. Leery about abandoning their traditional audiences by preempting afternoon soap operas or primetime sitcoms, they limited their coverage to the traditional newscasts. Although these networks retained a portion of their audience, many viewers were motivated to tune in to Court TV or other all-news alternatives they had never watched before. All-news networks cover every detail of these major stories, whereas the Big Four networks are forced to select when and how to preempt their schedules. The media's handling of the hearings before the 9/11 Commission is a case in point.

Clearly, technology is responsible for this proliferation of media options and the continued fragmentation of the viewing audience. The number of cable channels is expanding more rapidly than anticipated. With the advent of digital television, viewers will have access to over a hundred channels. Even if only a small number of individuals watch these channels, such as the History Channel, the Spanish Channel, or the Golf Channel, the total impact on the networks in the long run will be staggering. In the final analysis, the Big Four networks are not only losing audiences, but they are also losing revenues, thus limiting their ability to experiment with the same number of sitcoms as the early days of television, when they collectively controlled the entire audience base. This reduction in the number of successful sitcoms means that fewer are available for foreign syndication, and thus their price tags have increased substantially. Although this may reduce the US presence on foreign television screens, a simultaneous increase in the viewing of CNN – particularly when global news stories break, such as the Persian Gulf War, the death of Princess Diana, or international terrorism – is likely to ensure that foreign media continue to carry extensive US programming options. (CNN is covered in detail in chapter 6.)

As costs escalate, audience size shrinks, and advertising revenues decrease, the major US television networks are reengineering their positions and strategies, not only with respect to each other, but also with respect to the myriad cable channels now available. As more broadcast, cable, DVDs, and internet options become available to viewers, General Electric's NBC, Viacom's CBS Corporation, and Walt Disney's ABC network are cutting staff. These decisions reflect the reality of escalating programming costs and decreasing viewership. Of the original Big Three networks, NBC is well situated, primarily because it responded to the cable challenge by introducing its own specialty channels – MSNBC and CNBC – as a means of competing for the advertising revenue available to these niche markets. NBC also established channels in Europe and Asia. Yet many analysts suggest that these efforts are insufficient and predict that major industry restructuring, including mergers, will continue in the future.

New international realities

Despite the problems, foreign markets are still lucrative for US producers. The proliferation of media options is increasingly an international phenomenon, and this creates new opportunities for US program sales abroad. As technology has led to increased media choices, so also governmental media and regulatory policies have had to adapt. Historically, much of broadcasting, originally radio and then television, in the industrialized countries outside the United States was dominated by public, government-supported systems. The British Broadcasting Corporation (BBC) served as the model for many national media networks, particularly in British colonies. For many years, for example, most European viewers had access to only one or two public television channels, which were publicly financed and carried no advertising. Neither private networks, cable, nor satellite services were available or licensed. This situation changed substantially in the late 1980s when deregulation, liberalization, and commercialization took hold around the globe.

In an era when broadcasting options were limited to one or two public media outlets, regulation was significant. In fact, the rationale for public, as opposed to private, broadcasting relied on the notion that the electronic mass media were social institutions with certain public accountability goals. These media were assigned responsibility for providing educational broadcasting, promoting democracy and human rights, and providing balanced programming. With the introduction of private broadcasting outlets, government regulation was reduced in favor of market forces. Today, this duopoly between public and private broadcasting systems co-exists in most industrialized nations. As a result, the viewing and listening public now has substantially more media choices, and US producers have larger markets for their products. Not surprisingly, a growing number of the foreign options have a distinct made-in-America flavor.

Modeling: creating indigenous programs with US cultural values

Most foreign nations, with significantly smaller audience bases, are unable to compete with the expensive, high-quality production values of US dramatic television programming. In order to fill the available broadcast schedule and maximize their revenues, they purchase US syndicated programming. Consequently, many nations, industrialized and less developed alike, experience significant erosion of their own cultures. But the issue does not end with the direct importation of US programming.

Recently, a more insidious practice has further threatened national cultures. As mentioned earlier, the US networks have recently introduced lower-cost reality-based programs or game shows. Although these programs are attractive to US audiences, they do not export well. Because their themes tend to be parochial and time sensitive, their chances for foreign syndication and release are marginal. Instead, foreign producers tend to copy the news magazine or reality show format and insert local content, announcers, or venues. In Australia, for example, which imports significant numbers of US feature films and television productions for domestic consumption, home-grown productions increasingly look very much like US programming. A few examples illustrate the point. Australia has its own version of NBC's *Today Show*; an equivalent of the Newlywed Game called *A Current Affair*; a clone of MTV's *Real World* entitled *A House from Hell*; its own *Wheel of Fortune*, *Funniest Home Videos*, and *60 Minutes*. Thus, even when there is indigenous production capacity, the US influence is visible on foreign television throughout the industrial world, particularly in English-speaking countries. Great Britain, Canada, Ireland, and New Zealand, also major consumers of US television and feature films, model many local productions after US counterparts.

The tendency to produce adaptations of US models has both cultural and programmatic implications.[6] Of significant concern is the different manner in which the United States and other nations view cultural industries. The US rationale for promoting television, feature films, DVDs, records, CDs, and other cultural products is based on the notion that the marketplace will determine winners and losers. Sometimes the winners, such as the movie *Titanic* or *My Big Fat Greek Wedding*, reap enormous rewards for their producers. Other films are duds and force their parent studios into bankruptcy. This is the price investors are willing to pay to ensure that the marketplace rules. This attitude contrasts dramatically with the perception of almost all other nations, which view cultural industries from a non-economic perspective. For them, films, DVDs, radio, music, CDs, and other media products are an expression of their historical roots, current culture, and future destiny. In order to ensure an indigenous media presence, many of these countries subsidize their national radio and television networks, feature-film industry, and other cultural sectors.

France provides an outstanding example of the extent to which a country is willing to use tax revenues to subsidize media productions and products to compete directly with US cultural industries. Primarily, although not solely, due to language constraints, domestic French productions tend to fare poorly in the open global market. Recently, the government helped finance the film *Asterix* – at a cost of $50 million, the most expensive French film ever made – in an attempt to recapture part of the French domestic market. Currently, French films garner less than 50 percent of the French market. In 1998, French films captured only 27 percent of their national market, due in large part to the tremendous success of a single film: *Titanic*.

The French and other European markets are facing an additional threat – the growth of the US-style multiplex cinema. Although the cineplex has increased the number of screens and cinema attendance, it has failed to create an increase in audiences for European films. Rather, it has promoted the further penetration of US movies in foreign markets, and US box office receipts continue to escalate. Today, Hollywood, whose collective revenues in 2003 amounted to $16.6 billion, reaps about half of its profits from offshore audiences, compared with only 25 percent in the early 1980s. Given this shift in profit figures, Hollywood producers are now spending significant sums to market major blockbusters internationally. These multimillion-dollar marketing budgets alone dwarf the amounts available to produce entire films by independent competitors around the globe.[7] Finally, these same Hollywood production houses have added DVDs to their revenue stream with some foreign sales of DVDs exceeding domestic (US) DVD sales.

Global media marketplace

The global media marketplace is perceived as being under the control of the United States, which exports its culture through television shows, movies, music, McDonald's, sportswear, and shopping malls. However, Rod Carveth, who agrees that the economy is becoming globally integrated, suggests that the US may be losing its competitive advantage.[8] According to Carveth and others, the US needs to change its strategy if it wants to regain its predominant position in the global media industry. These analysts contend that a number of developments, such as global media mergers and acquisitions; legal and cultural import barriers in the European Union (EU), Canada, and Japan; as well as strategic miscalculations by US media firms, have eroded the country's competitive advantage.[9] In order to reassert itself, strategists suggest that the United States must adopt a cooperative rather than a competitive strategy in international media.

For years the United States maintained an international advantage because of its superior talent, and technical, marketing, and capital resources. The domestic industry also benefited from the export of its products to foreign markets. Throughout this period, US superiority in electronic media was evident, and the United States failed to anticipate any competition from foreign markets.

As an early leader in the electronics industry, the United States was unprepared when it began to lose its competitive advantage to Japanese and European manufacturers. During the 1980s, major US consumer electronics manufacturers such as RCA abandoned the industry. Although research and development fell off in the United States, it blossomed internationally, particularly in Germany, Japan, and France, where substantial strides were made. The US international media presence was further weakened when many countries, including Canada,[10] began to impose restrictions on US media exports as they simultaneously began to subsidize their own media productions, thus creating more programming to compete with US media products. In addition, when 12 European nations joined to form the European Union in the 1950s, they began to open up the former Soviet Union and eastern European countries to freer trade with Europe and Japan. European media companies such as Bertelsmann, Hachette, Canal Plus, and Pathé began to compete in the global marketplace. Moreover, they were prepared to meet the increasing demand for European-produced programming that reflected the unique identities of Europeans.

Another factor that weakened US domination was a series of mergers or acquisitions through which foreign corporations gained control of US media undertakings. The trend of merger and acquisition activity began when Australian-born media baron Rupert Murdoch and his company News Corporation acquired newspapers such as the *New York Post*, the *Chicago Sun-Times*, and the *Boston Herald*. Another player was Robert Maxwell of the United Kingdom who purchased Macmillan publishing and Saatchi & Saatchi (United Kingdom), the successful international advertising conglomerate. Perhaps the most high-profile acquisition of a media company was that of Columbia Pictures by Japan's Sony Corporation, but others included Hachette's (France) purchase of the Diamond's magazine chain, the sale of A&M Records to Philips (Netherlands), Bertelsmann's (Germany) acquisition of RCA/Ariolas Records, and VNU's (Netherlands) takeover of the Nielson rating company. Non-US companies have consolidated as well, in order to strengthen their combined market share. In 2003, Sony and Bertelsmann merged their music divisions to create a music industry giant.

In all of these cases, the players were motivated by an appreciation of the manner in which the mergers would permit the companies to combine their strengths to achieve savings in production, distribution, and exhibition of media products. They anticipated some type of positive synergy. Moreover, these foreign companies wanted to gain access to the vital US market.

Given the changing global media marketplace and barriers preventing the United States from becoming an international broadcaster, Carveth and others contend that it is important for US firms to merge with and/or acquire international companies if the country wants to regain its international competitive edge. The United States needs to jump on the merger and acquisition bandwagon. Virtually every other nation in the world, including those in the European Union, lack sufficient domestic programming to meet their future media goals.[11] The best strategy for ensuring US access to these markets is for domestic companies to form alliances with international players. The resulting co-productions will open new markets. In 1990, for example, NBC and London-based Yorkshire Television formed a joint venture called Tango Productions, which enabled NBC to avoid or at least minimize the import regulations of the EU when selling its media products. Other joint ventures have developed between US and non-US firms. Clear Channel Communications of San Antonio, Texas, now holds interests in several global firms, including a 50 percent stake in the Australian Radio Network (ARN), to go along with approximately 1,200 US radio stations.

The International Music Industry

In the early 2000s, global music sales were over $40 billion. The three leading regions in terms of sales are the US, Europe, and Japan. English is by far the dominant language for the artists, with one notable exception. The exception is the growing niche market for Spanish music and this is primarily due to one artist: Ricky Martin. The global industry is in a state of flux for two reasons. First, there is a series of potential acquisitions as the industry consolidates on a global basis, and second, how to deal with both legal and illegal downloading of music from the internet.[12] More is said about this aspect in chapter 12, dealing with the impact of the internet.

In examining the music industry, it is important to recognize that most of the relevant information is collected and maintained by Billboard using SoundScan data. SoundScan data collects point-of-sale information on all music formats and configurations sold at about 70 percent of the US retail outlets, and then projects sales for the entire US marketplace. Those data provide a wealth of knowledge about the industry.

The international music industry was, until recently, dominated by five major global players, all from core nations: Vivendi Universal Music Group (France), Sony Music (Japan), EMI Group (United Kingdom), Warner (US), and Bertelsmann (Germany). In 2003, however, Sony Music merged with Bertelsmann's BMG, cutting the number of majors to four. Of the top four, now only one is American owned. (See figure 5.1.)

All recording artists, except for those represented by the US's Warner Music Group, must rely on foreign markets to recoup their companies'

1. Vivendi Universal Music Group (France)

2. Sony/BMG Music Entertainment (Japan/Germany)

3. EMI Group (UK)

4. Warner Music Group (US)

Figure 5.1 Big Four music industry

investments in the first album, which now require the additional expense of video production as part of the initial promotion package. It is estimated that first video album costs now exceed $1 million.

The four major players control every aspect of the supply chain from copyright on the music through the distribution cycle to the consumer. All four corporations have extensive sales outlets in all core nations, all semi-peripheral nations, and now many peripheral nations. The dominant artistic language is English, giving a substantial advantage to British and North American artists and bands. Finally, as discussed elsewhere, MTV's global television niche for the teenage market has also served to promote the global expansion of the music industry.

Although there are several independent labels, and some occasionally do well with individual records such as Disney soundtracks for movies such as *Pocahontas* or *The Lion King*, the bulk of the global sales, approaching 75 percent, are controlled by the Big Four. Further details concerning their activities and artists are discussed in the following section, along with the role of MTV in the global music scene.

Vivendi Universal Music Group (France)

The largest global music company is Universal Music Group (UMG). UMG has ventures in 71 countries, over 10,700 employees, and almost 25 percent of the world's market for music of all types. It also controls the third largest music-publishing group. Some of UMG's artists include ABBA, Brian Adams, Elton John, Vince Gill, Guns N' Roses, U2, Enrique Iglesias, Sheryl Crow, and Shania Twain. UMG's record labels include MCA, Universal, Dream-Works, Mercury, Motown, Decca, Philips, and others. It also has almost half of the global sales in the classical music genre.

Until 2000 UMG was a division of Seagram's of Canada. It is also aggressive in providing online music. A major factor in UMG's size and success was the acquisition of PolyGram Records in 1998 by the Seagram group. PolyGram was a major European-based music giant that traced its origin to Siemens Corp., established in 1898. Mergers and acquisitions have been the hallmark of the music recording industry as illustrated by the size and activities of the five major record conglomerates. In November 2000, UMG agreed to purchase a portion of MP3.com, an internet site that uses a data-compression technology to offer a massive number of songs to end-users. The firm has been sued for copyright violations and is now seeking peace with the recording industry. In 2003, UMG sold MP3.com to CNET. MP3.com was relaunched in 2004 as a portal site, after its archives were destroyed due to the threat of legal liability.

Sony BMG Music Entertainment (Japan/Germany)

The second largest music conglomerate is the Sony BMG Music Entertainment Group, the product of a merger between the music divisions of Sony Corporation of Japan and Bertelsmann of Germany. The newly merged company controls approximately 25 percent of the global music market, and is close to surpassing Universal as the largest global music company. Sony got into the record business when it acquired CBS Records Group in 1988. Sony's music labels include Columbia, Epic, Nashville, Sony Classical, Legacy, and others. It has major recording artists under contract such as Celine Dion, Mariah Carey, Will Smith, Ice Cube, Barbra Streisand, Charlotte Church, and Bob Dylan. Sony jointly owns the Columbia House record club with Warner Music. Sony has always geared its musical interests to a global, as well as English-language, platform. This global reach reflects its corporate desire to be a Japanese-based corporation with the bulk of its corporate activities carried out in other core nations, as well as semiperipheral and peripheral nations.

Before its merger with Sony, the Bertelsmann Music Group (BMG) was the fifth-largest music conglomerate. Bertelsmann is an enormous, privately owned, European-based multimedia conglomerate. BMG brings to the merger over two hundred record labels including Arista, RCA Victor, and Ariola. Some of BMG's better-known artists are Whitney Houston, Carlos Santana, Elvis Presley, Frank Sinatra, Duke Ellington, David Bowie, the Chieftains, and Barry Manilow. Sixty of BMG's artists have sold over a million albums. BMG has a major online presence, a large music-publishing group, the world's largest music club, and a joint venture with UMG to sell music through their website GetMusic. Through the manufacturer Sonopress, BMG is the world's second-largest producer of CDs.

In October 2000, Bertelsmann formed an alliance with Napster Inc. Their plan was to charge users for music files and pay royalties to artists through their recording companies. This deal was never consummated due to Napster's legal troubles. Napster has since made an internet-distribution deal with Universal instead.

EMI Group (UK)

The third-largest music group is EMI, which includes the major labels EMI, Capitol, and Virgin Records. Some of EMI's most popular artists are Garth Brooks, the Spice Girls, the Beatles, Norah Jones, Keith Urban, and the Rolling Stones. EMI is also the world's largest publisher of sheet music, controlling over one million copyrights. It also has internet interests that offer digital downloads and other e-commerce services.

In October 1999, EMI's merger with Time Warner was abandoned. The $20 billion joint venture would have created the largest music group in the world and provided Warner Music with much greater European sales, which it needs. The European Union's (EU) Merger Task Force opposed the merger. Mario Monti, the former EU competition commissioner, threatened to hold up the merger of AOL and Time Warner unless Time Warner agreed to walk away from the EMI takeover. Some critics speculated that the EU merger officials had an anti-North American agenda in denying the Time Warner deal, considering that the overall music industry is going through a wave of mergers. In 2004 EMI acquired Mute and still continues to add other sheet music properties.

Warner Music Group (US)

When Time Inc. took over Warner Bros. in the late 1980s, it also acquired the Warner Music Group. As discussed, Time Warner tried to purchase EMI Music of the United Kingdom, which would have allowed it to control one-third of the global market. The record labels controlled by Warner Bros. are Warner Music International, Elektra, Atlantic, Maverick, Reprise, and Rhino. Some of its 1,000 artists are the Red Hot Chili Peppers, Madonna, Eric Clapton, Faith Hill, and Sammy Davis Jr. In addition to being available at record stores around the globe, Warner Bros. artists' music is also available through Warner's online site or through over 150 Warner Bros. stores located in core nations as well as Mexico, the Middle East, and the Pacific Rim. Warner also is a major music publisher. In 1999 Warner Music had 38 out of the top 200 bestselling US albums. More than half its revenue came from outside the United States, but it is still seeking a larger share of the EU market.

In November 2003, Warner Music was sold for $2.6 billion to a group of investors led by Edgar Bronfman Jr., thus creating the only privately held music company among the big four. Bronfman, formerly a Vivendi executive and former CEO of the Seagram Co., won a bidding war against EMI to buy Warner Music. Had Warner Music been sold instead to EMI, there would not have been a single US corporation among the Big Four. Bronfman, a third-generation Seagram heir, is a native of Canada, but Warner Music remains based in New York.

Synopsis

The four global music groups have extensive corporate activities in many nations. The bulk of the artists, whether contemporary, alternative, rap, classical, country, or rock, are English-speaking artists. The Big Four music producers also control as much of the production process as possible, from finding new talent to web-based purchases. The giant music producers have corporate roots in the United States, Japan, and Europe. They have become industry leaders through a series of mergers and acquisitions, which are likely to continue in the future despite the anti-US bias of the EU's merger commission.

A second significant conclusion is that all the major record companies have established significant web-based marketing, retail, and promotion sites for their artists. Yet, as digital distribution systems become available through the internet, some speculate about the long-term consequences for the global recording industry. In response, some recording companies and groups have initiated legal action against the rapidly expanding internet sites that provide nonroyalty copies in digital format to internet clients. Future internet online music business is estimated to be worth billions of dollars. The issue is whether consumers will purchase or simply download the necessary software to create audio files, which are technically equivalent to CDs. Several firms are offering MP3 solutions, which permit high-quality digital audio to be recorded and downloaded by home servers. MP3 is the industry term for the new data compression system that allows the pirating of music over the internet, an activity that could clearly undermine and change, perhaps forever, the economics of the global recording industry. The movement toward a free virtual jukebox has been altered, as both UMG and BMG have become shareholders in MP3 format firms. Now they have established a fee structure. Although the internet is discussed elsewhere in this book, it is worth noting here that not a single electronic medium is not susceptible to change as a result of the internet environment.

Finally, it is worth noting that a number of high-profile individual artists have been trying to get out of their lifetime recording contracts. They sign these agreements when they are virtually unknown, and the contracts are heavily weighted in favor of the recording studios.

MTV: The Dominant Global Music Connection

Music recordings are a powerful entertainment medium in their own right. When offered in conjunction with the excitement of video, their appeal is even stronger. Not surprisingly, young people are tuning in to Viacom's

Music Television (MTV) channels around the world. MTV reaches over 340 million viewers in 140 countries, particularly in Europe and Asia, and currently is the world's largest television network, broadcast in one-third of the world's TV-viewing households. Viewed primarily by preteens, teens, and young adults, MTV is an impressive global youth television phenomenon. Comprised of 100 affiliated international networks including MTV Latino, MTV Brazil, MTV Europe, MTV Mandarin, MTV Asia, MTV India, MTV Australia, MTV New Zealand, and MTV Africa, the MTV network already has the ability to reach a large proportion of the world's youth each day. Moreover, new MTV networks are under consideration. MTV has signed a licensing deal with Russia, anticipating that the country's youth are now ready to tune in to a 24-hour music television network. MTV Russia will likely reach more than 10 million households and feature musicians such as Madonna, U2, Prince, Nirvana, and the Spice Girls, as well as local Russian groups. Over 80 percent of MTV's total audience is now outside the United States.

MTV was the first 24-hour, 7-day-a-week music video network. It is supported by advertising and constitutes a basic service on most cable networks. Targeted at the 12- to 34-year-old age group, MTV's international satellite-delivered music programming reaches millions daily around the globe. Owned by Viacom, MTV operates several cable television programming services – Music Television, MTV2, VH1, Nickelodeon/Nick at Nite, Country Music Television (CMT), TNN, and TV Land (see figure 5.2). MTV is also experimenting with the internet and its own websites in order to examine the possibilities of providing music in online ventures.

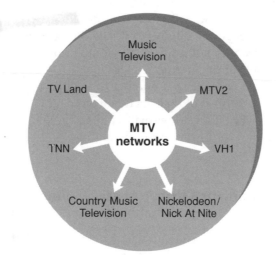

Figure 5.2 MTV's global youth culture

Although there are an estimated 80,000 websites devoted to music, many of which have become digital shrines to major recording artists, MTV.com is the most popular music website in the world. MTV has an internet subsidiary called MTV Group, which controls all MTV websites. And the number of websites is enormous. The internet properties are MTV.com, VH1.com, SonicNet.com, various international websites, chatrooms, news, streaming audio, and MTV merchandise.

Because music tastes are highly localized, MTV's global airtime is filled with locally produced programming and American shows. Despite that fact, teens around the world basically are listening to and viewing the same music videos. For example, in 1996, Madonna, Queen, and the Rolling Stones topped the charts of MTV Latino. Although MTV Europe reserves 30 percent of its broadcast hours for indigenous European groups, Michael Jackson and Tina Turner were among MTV Europe's top five artists. In 2001, MTV Japan went on the air as a 24-hour Japanese-language service. Of course, it goes without saying that musical groups who fail to produce a video to accompany their recording releases are simply excluded from MTV's playtime. Just as CNN has altered the global news business forever, so MTV has altered the global music trade.

Given MTV's popularity, advertising is another issue that bears attention. According to Jay Pettegrew and Roy Shukar,[13] MTV worldwide is one large, continuous, commercial advertising network. Not only are the music videos "commercials" designed to enhance the sale of albums, but advertising for other products also surrounds them, and many artists openly promote commercial products within the music videos themselves. Many critics assert that MTV is a commercial propaganda outlet specifically aimed at impressionable teenagers.

Clearly, MTV promotes Western popular culture worldwide. Any reciprocal play is limited by the nature of MTV's North American broadcasting schedule. Moreover, the Westernization of global culture is further enhanced by the basic fact that much of MTV programming and most music videos are produced in English. Even MTV Asia's interactive chatline, which requires internet access, functions in English. Concerns about the pervasive commercialism and cultural imperialism of MTV programming worldwide is growing. After examining MTV's impact in Asia, Stacey Sowards concludes:

> While MTV Asia has made appropriate, culturally aware marketing decisions that has allowed it to establish a firm base in Asia, the programming is still largely a manifestation of American culture. The differences in comparison to MTV in the United States are surface structural changes at best. There are several programs that are Asia specific; however, many of them are not, but are simply exported from the United States in the same way that *Dallas* and

Baywatch are. More than 50% of MTV Asia's programs are imported directly from MTV in the United States. Additionally, American popular culture is ubiquitous throughout programs; even those that attempt to include Asian cultures. The programs that incorporate Asian cultures reflect American culture, through the way the VJs speak, the music that is aired, and the image that is portrayed. Even the use of Asian VJs fails to avoid the hegemonic nature of MTV Asia, since they also speak English, and attempt to represent American cultures and ideology through fashion and music selection. In fact, the American essence of MTV Asia is probably what attracts such a large Asian viewership. Additionally, MTV Asia also has the effect of Americanizing Asian music, as seen by Asian musicians whose key influences are American bands. Furthermore, to be able to watch MTV Asia, one must have access to a satellite dish, excluding most of Southeast Asia, except those that have enough money, usually the elites.[14]

More recently the MTV network incorporated political coverage of elections into a segment called "Choose or Lose," which called on young people to "vote loud." Viewers age 18 to 24 accounted for nearly 20 percent of the voters in the US. Presidential contenders and companies such as AT&T and Ford Motor Company now recognize the potential of MTV's campaign coverage to bring their messages into the homes of the twenty-somethings. By focusing on the "three Es" – education, economy, and environment – "Choose or Lose" became the primary broker for 30 million young voters who were MTV viewers, while simultaneously providing a venue for candidates and major companies that wanted to target younger audiences for their commercials.

MTV and electronic colonialism

One clear example of the application of the theory of electronic colonialism is found in music television, globally known as MTV. MTV has attempted to colonize not a broad range of viewers and listeners, but rather a select niche, namely the youth culture. MTV wants the minds of this global youth culture to follow them and buy the products which surround the music videos as commercials. Demographically this is an important group, particularly for advertisers of youth-oriented products, which range from clothes to cultural products such as films, records, CDs, DVDs, and iPods. MTV seeks on a global scale to influence the attitudes, preferences, and purchasing behaviors of teenagers around the globe. MTV promotes a mainstream diet of primarily British and American artists, plus non-Anglo musicians who need to mimic the format of individual artists or bands that are mainstream in either the United States or Europe. MTV does this in order to continue expanding its reach and influence on the attitudes of the teenage set in as many nations as possible. MTV is not solely concerned with music or the issues and themes surrounding the music industry; its goal is to positively influence the global teenage audience into accepting commercial habits and products that are predominantly from core nations. In this market-orientated process MTV will produce a handsome profit for its parent, Viacom.

In order to further colonize and capitalize on the global youth culture, MTV has turned to the internet. MTV's own internet service, MTVi Group, seeks young customers with credit cards who can download music materials from the internet for a fee. MTV is banking on the notion that around the globe there are a number of teenagers with sufficient disposable income to purchase music and merchandise over the internet. After years of relentless consumerism on MTV, management hopes it will ultimately pay off through internet-based purchases.

Through electronic colonialism, MTV has managed to marginalize many indigenous artists and indigenous genres of music, from aboriginal music in Australia, to African music, to nontraditional Indian music.[15] MTV gives little time or exposure to these alternative genres. As Jack Banks, in his article, "MTV and the Globalization of Popular Culture," notes, MTV has become so influential that both Hollywood film studios and the global record conglomerates now not only use MTV as a major advertising vehicle to reach the teenage audience, but they are also coordinating on a global scale the release of new films or new videos on a preferential basis through MTV's global network.[16]

MTV was one of the first cultural-industry giants to recognize the expanding global economy and become part of it. Individual artists around the globe will lament their marginalization due to MTV, but, as Banks further notes, "Clearly MTV and music video are influencing the emerging global economy as well as the contours of a global popular culture – what remains uncertain is the role played by MTV in molding a global consensus about the shape of this economy and culture."[17] Given the expanding global strategic plan of Viacom, MTV's parent company, MTV has come to represent the music video juggernaut. That is, if you are a musician who is part of it, you reach a global audience and become rich and world famous virtually overnight; but if you are not part of MTV, your chances of succeeding as a music video artist in any significant way are reduced substantially.

A final important point about MTV is that it also has a social conscience. It puts on creative programming to encourage teenagers to get out and vote and it also promotes global awareness of social problems. It takes a liberal agenda to its finely tuned audience segment. Take the example of the genocide in Darfur in the Sudan. The US administration has ignored it just as many others have. Not MTV. They speak out against this widespread slaughter with compelling programs. As Nicholas Kristof writes in the *New York Times*, "Indeed, MTV is raising the issue more openly and powerfully than our White House. (Its mtvU channel is also covering Darfur more aggressively than most TV networks.) It should be a national embarrassment that MTV is more outspoken about genocide than our president."[18] Media analysts can only wonder what the outcome would have been if Time Warner's CNN had applied its influential resources to the same region and tragedy as Viacom's MTV did.

Conclusions

The global media market is in a state of constant change. Much of the change is fueled by technologies and business practices of core nations. The expansion of cable and satellite delivery systems has provided significant growth internationally for television audiences. These audiences are familiar with US television shows and, as the number of television channels expands through global privatization and deregulation, there will be a host of new customers and viewers for Hollywood sitcoms, TV movies, music videos, and network syndicated shows. Concomitantly, this expanding foreign market has facilitated the growth of cultural industries in the United States. It has significantly increased their role and influence within the US economy. Their future role also looks bright, as there is an almost insatiable demand for made-in-America television, music, and movie productions.

One particular medium that has done exceptionally well both domestically and globally is MTV. The marriage of music and video, with musicians from core nations, has permitted the rapid expansion of this major music television network. The only cloud on the horizon is the emergence of the internet and the strong possibility of CD-quality music being downloaded from internet sites. This phenomenon could allow listeners to bypass local music outlets, thereby affecting how the product of international music stars is packaged, distributed, and priced in the near future. However, the industry has been fairly successful in recent attempts to protect copyrights (and therefore, to protect profits) against the threat posed by internet file sharing.

Finally, although the literature and thrust of cultural imperialism has lost its spark, there are still a number of vocal critics. Much of the criticism is aimed at US-based industries, particularly Hollywood, but also to a lesser extent television shows with large global export markets, such as *Baywatch* or *The Simpsons*, or the MTV network. What is interesting is that foreign-owned and -controlled communication giants such as Bertelsmann and Sony have managed to avoid the storm of criticism directed at Hollywood in general and Disney, Viacom, and Time Warner in particular. Yet at the same time, these foreign firms have enjoyed, from a fiscal perspective, the growing market for cultural products around the globe. These foreign firms have recognized the increased importance of US cultural industries, particularly the profitability associated with successful global sales, but they have somehow managed to dodge the hostile criticism that continues to emanate from critical-school theorists in Europe, Latin America, and North America. The ubiquity of music and other mass culture products is spread globally but produced by a few core nations, yet the shrill rhetoric of concern and protest is aimed mainly at one core nation: the United States.

Notes

1 *Entertainment and the Electronic Media* (New York and Washington, DC: McGraw-Hill and US Department of Commerce, 1999), pp. 321–9. For a detailed decade-by-decade analysis of US television sales abroad, see Kerry Segrave, *American Television Abroad: Hollywood's Attempt to Dominate World Television* (Jefferson, NC: McFarland, 1998).

2 Some nations have gone to great lengths to thwart the intrusion of Western popular culture. The overthrow of the Shah of Iran was motivated in large part by distaste for the Western values, media, and culture he was promoting in Iran. In Afghanistan under the Taliban the leaders took drastic measures by ordering the removal of all televisions, VCRs, and satellite receivers from the country. Canada has taken a less draconian approach. For decades that country has attempted to reduce the influence of US mass media through the promulgation of Canadian content rules that require the media to produce and distribute Canadian material. The French-speaking province of Quebec has gone even further to protect its cultural heritage by instituting a provincial language policy that requires the use of French as the predominant language of business and culture in the province. Language "police" oversee the use of French in all commercial enterprises, going so far as to demand that the French lettering on signs be twice as large as their English counterparts.

3 David Rothkopf, "In Praise of Cultural Imperialism," *Foreign Policy* 107 (1997), p. 39.

4 As a general rule, TV sitcoms or dramas need to have at least a three-year run to be successfully syndicated. This provides approximately 66 episodes that can then be sold as a package for either the domestic rerun market or international syndication. Clearly, shows with successful runs of five or more years in syndication enjoy substantial secondary revenue streams in addition to their lucrative initial showings. Now, with DVDs, the ownership rights for some shows or movies are a license to print money.

5   Because of high costs, the number of foreign network news bureaus also has been reduced. For example, CBS foreign news bureaus, which once numbered 12, now operate in only 4 cities – London, Moscow, Tokyo, and Tel Aviv. Yet they continue to hire brilliant foreign journalists, such as Sheila MacVicker in Europe.

6   The use of US media models and strategies is not limited to the mimicking of cultural industries but extends even into the field of politics: Britain's prime minister, Tony Blair, hired media consultants to model his political campaign, emulating the successful style of former US President Clinton. More recently, Chancellor Schroeder of Germany also employed made-in-America campaign techniques including the extensive use of sophisticated polling in order to conduct his successful election campaign.

US political consultants now have branch offices located throughout Europe, Latin America, and elsewhere. They offer assistance to political candidates who wish to utilize the successful media strategies and tactics developed over the last three decades in the United States. This breadth of experience gives these US political media consultants a global market advantage.

This trend is not without its critics. During the 1999 Israeli election campaign, a Washington-based pollster's role became a controversial part of the Labor Party's campaign. In Sweden the Social Democratic Party's hiring of a high-profile US consultant became an issue in the campaign. Clearly, just as there are critics of the Americanization of television and popular culture, so too there are vocal opponents of the Americanization of the political process, particularly during national election campaigns. Much of the US consultants' advice is about how to use and appear on television, as well as how to run negative commercials about their opponents. But in the final analysis this phenomenon is just another niche example of the pervasiveness of electronic colonialism theory.

7   Additional details about the plight of the European movie industry are contained in *The Economist*, Feb. 6, 1999, p. 68. For a more in-depth analysis, see *European Audiovisual Conference: Challenges and Opportunities of the Digital Age* (Brussels: European Commission, 1997).

8   Rod Carveth, "The Reconstruction of the Global Media Marketplace," *Communication Research* 19(6) (1992), p. 705.

9   Alison Alexander, James Ovens, and Rod Carveth, eds., *Media Economics: Theory and Practice* (Mahwah, NJ: Lawrence Erlbaum, 1998).

10 Thomas McPhail and Brenda McPhail, *Communication: The Canadian Experience* (Toronto: Copp Clark Pitman, 1990).

11 R. Carvelh, J. Ovens, A. Alexander, and J. Fletcher, "The Economics of International Media," in *Media Economics: Theory and Practice*, eds. A. Alexander, J. Ovens, and R. Carveth (Mahwah, NJ: Lawrence Erlbaum, 1998), pp. 223–45.

12 A look at the turmoil caused by the internet is also detailed in *The Economist*, June 16, 2001, pp. 6–17.

13 Jay Pettegrew, "A Post-M Moment: Commercial Culture and the Founding of MTV," in *Gender, Race, and Class in Media*, eds. G. Dines and J. Hunez

(Thousand Oaks, CA: Sage, 1995), pp. 488–98; and Roy Shukar, *Understanding Popular Music* (London: Routledge, 1994).

14   Stacey Sowards, "MTV Asia: Cultural Imperialism in Southeast Asia," paper presented at the National Communication Association Annual Conference, New York, Fall, 1998.

15   Tony Mitchell, "Treaty Now! Indigenous Music and Music Television in Australia," *Media, Culture & Society* 15(2) (1993), pp. 299–308.

16   Jack Banks, "MTV and the Globalization of Popular Culture," *Gazette* 51(1) (1997), p. 51. For a detailed analysis of music videos, see Jack Banks, *Monopoly Television: MTV's Quest to Control the Music* (Boulder, CO: Westview Press, 1996).

17   Banks, "MTV," p. 59.

18   Nicholas Kristof, "Mr. Bush, Take a Look at MTV," *New York Times*, April 17, 2005, p. WK 15.

Chapter 6

CNN International: Role, Impact, and Global Competitors

Introduction

Memories from major global breaking news stories – such as the coverage of China's Tiananmen Square protest, both Gulf Wars, the death of Princess Diana in Paris, the tragedies in Moscow, the Asian tsunami, and in the US, the Columbine High School shooting, the O. J. Simpson, Kobe Bryant, Martha Stewart, Scott Peterson, and Michael Jackson legal difficulties – are reminders that the press is onsite to bring the viewing public up-to-the-minute news stories. Newsgathering in the United States is plentiful and apparent on ABC, CBS, FOX, NBC, and other news outlets. In addition, there are now three US all-news channels: CNN, MSNBC, and FOX News.

Major US, European, and Asian television broadcasters have been covering international events since the 1950s. Foreign broadcasters such as the British Broadcasting Corporation (BBC) and Germany's Deutsche Welle, along with many international bureaus of major television networks, have been covering global events on their evening newscasts for decades. What is different now is that the Cable News Network (CNN) changed the global media format in a dramatic way. Viewing went from a format based on 30- or 60-minute primetime newscasts to a 24-hour format that focused on news and public affairs programming from both national and global perspectives. CNN and other all-news networks thrive on controversy, breaking news stories, and stories that go on for days, or even weeks, such as the tsunami of December 2004. Another example is the 2000 Florida election recount saga which saw CNN's audience rating increase six-fold, while 4-year-old MSNBC experienced its highest ratings ever. CNN has attracted competition because it proved there was a niche market for all-news television. CNN is a media property of Time Warner and has been losing market share, particularly to FOX News. More is said about this phenomenon later.

News crosses domestic and international boundaries. International communication and new technologies have had a profound effect on news institutions, news sources, newsgathering techniques, and audiences almost everywhere. The global media trend grew throughout the twentieth century along with the global economy. This was made possible by radio, wire services, magazines, newspapers, satellites, videophones and the advent of global all-news networks in the 1980s. As more countries opened their borders to imported signals, both news and entertainment took on greater importance as media firms of all varieties sought larger audiences. These larger audiences were often from other core nations, as well as from semiperipheral nations, and occasionally peripheral nations. Media firms sought out these larger audiences in order to increase advertising revenue for the commercial-based global television networks. From the electronic colonialism perspective, the potential impact of the advertising on consumer behavior was frequently a greater concern than the programs themselves. The implications of global advertising and the relationship to world-system and electronic colonialism theories are detailed in chapter 9.

Along with international news coverage comes growing competition. By the 1980s, the world had developed a huge appetite for television programming of all kinds, including news and information. Interestingly, in the early 1980s it was Ted Turner who took the bold initiative to establish the first 24-hour all-news network. It was based in Atlanta, Georgia. He saw a need and stepped in with his Turner Broadcasting Company. On June 1, 1980, Turner introduced the Cable News Network, otherwise known as CNN. In addition to CNN, in 1981 Turner launched CNN Headline News, and in 1985, the Cable News Network International (CNNI), in reaction to increasing competition. CNNI's goals were to expand internationally oriented programming, upgrade satellite carriage, expand its newsgathering capabilities, and become the primary global television network for news. Ted Turner deserves credit for his tenacity, vision, and deep pockets in terms of realizing that there was a market out there for 24-hour news.

Without a doubt, CNN is the godfather of global television news reporting to audiences around the world. Millions in over 200 nations now see the 24-hour all-news format. Historically, the markets for Britain's *The Economist* or the *International Herald Tribune* were early indications that there was a niche market for the international news sector. What CNN managed to do was to make the development of the niche television news market a global phenomenon. As the global economy evolves and expands, people are defining themselves in terms of television viewing as regional or world citizens. They are concerned about world events as well as local, regional, and national events. Turner understood this desire for global information. He had the crucial financial resources to keep CNN on air during its early years. It was not until the mid-1980s that CNN was breaking even, let alone making a profit.

Before CNN, the prestigious French newspaper, *Le Monde* (The World), had the definition and concept right. The trouble was it never had the distribution system (or possibly the language factor) to become a world newspaper. Originally, radio faced similar barriers, with one major exception – the BBC World Service. Although there were other world radio services, none had the network clout or the international respectability of the BBC World Service. In terms of television, originally only nation-states, for the most part, developed and licensed television networks. Many were frequently just an extension of their national radio networks. They were delivered by way of limited terrestrial microwave networks or via telephone lines within a nation's borders. No transnational television systems were created until the reality of CNN's success forced other nations, particularly within the European Union, to consider competing services, such as EuroNews. Satellites were the major technical force behind CNN's success.

CNN's success

CNN was so successful that it attracted competition. Currently, two of CNN's main competitors in Europe and Asia are Rupert Murdoch's satellite channels, including BSkyB, and the BBC. In 1994 the BBC launched a 24-hour television news service, starting in Asia. Although the BBC had previously run a limited European service, the Asian initiative made it a full-fledged competitor of CNN. Another CNN competitor is the EU's EuroNews, a recent effort to present foreign news and analysis from a pan-European perspective. The French government has announced plans for a satellite-based French equivalent of CNN in order to bring a French public-policy perspective to international issues. It will be a joint venture of the public and private French television networks and be known as the International Information Channel (CII). The new channel received $40 million in startup funds from the French government and is expected to launch in early 2006. CII represents the French challenge to the CNN editorial stance on world events, much as Al Jazeera and Al Arabiya represent the Arabic challenge to and viewpoint in contrast to CNN as well as the BBC. CII has no plans to actually broadcast in France – thus it is obvious that its foremost goal is to provide a French viewpoint to the rest of the world.

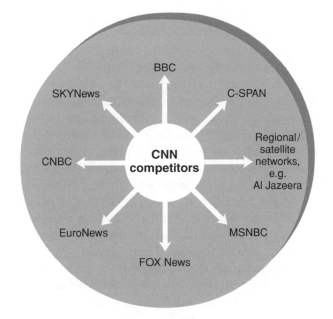

Figure 6.1 CNN's foreign and domestic competitors

Because of CNN's national and international successes, in addition to attracting global competition, CNN has managed to attract US-based competition as well. Two new 24 hour all-news networks – MSNBC and FOX News – now provide domestic competition for CNN and its headline news networks (see figure 6.1).[1]

This chapter details CNN's major international media role from its inception to current activities. It also deals with other major global media organizations such as the BBC, Voice of America, Radio Marti, and Deutsche Welle.

CNN

International news and information gathering changed because of Ted Turner's Cable News Network (CNN). A new era of reporting was born as domestic boundaries became obsolete in an era of satellite and cable. Although several countries and companies were entering the global information marketplace, no one news source was to be as successful as Turner Broadcasting and its crown jewel, CNN.

CNN, a division of Turner Broadcasting Systems, is the world's international news leader. In October 1996, Time Warner acquired Turner

Broadcasting for US$6.54 billion, and Ted Turner became vice president of Time Warner and its largest shareholder. He has since resigned and lost a fortune, as the later merger with AOL has been a fiscal disaster. The CNN merger created an unparalleled media giant with the ability to bring the most thorough, immediate, and live coverage of the world's news to a worldwide audience. In the pursuit of timely, unbiased, and indepth news reporting, CNN pioneered innovative techniques and broke new ground for the television news industry. The high-energy environment at CNN and its sister networks is home to over 4,000 employees worldwide. Currently, CNN has 31 bureaus worldwide. It has also reached several milestones. Besides launching CNN Headline News and CNNI, CNN has also branched out into CNN Radio. This division provides all-news programming to nearly 500 radio stations nationwide. In 1988 the division introduced Noticiero CNNI, which produces 6 hours of Spanish news for distribution on CNNI in the United States and throughout Latin America. And in 1995, CNN was launched into cyberspace. CNN Interactive is the world's leading inter-active news service. Its staff of world-class journalists and technologists are dedicated to providing 24-hour-a-day access to accurate and reliable news and information from any location.

As a unit of parent Time Warner CNN has not faired well. A series of senior management changes and missteps at Time Warner have adversely impacted CNN. Only the shrewd hand of CNN's Executive Vice President, Eason Jordan, kept the global network as a major force among all news networks. He was sacked in 2005.

First Live Broadcast

CNN's first live broadcast involved the high-profile black civil rights leader and well-known Democrat, Vernon Jordan. On May 29, 1980, Jordan was shot in Fort Wayne, Indiana. President Jimmy Carter visited him in the hospital. CNN distributed the story live during the day before the other major networks had a chance because traditional networks held back such breaking stories for their major evening newscasts. The networks were scooped during the day and were to repeat this lesson frequently as CNN broke stories at any time.

Tiananmen Square

Another major news opportunity in the late 1980s had drastic and unex-pected consequences for CNN. In May 1989, President Gorbachev of Russia was making an official visit to China. Because this was the first summit meeting since 1958 between the leaders of the two largest communist nations, all major US networks were provided permission to broadcast from China. CNN, with anchor Bernard Shaw, received permission to establish a temporary outdoor studio in Beijing, close to the Sheraton Hotel. CNN set up a portable satellite earth station in order to transmit its signal to its headquarters in Atlanta, Georgia. After six days, President Gorbachev left China, but CNN still had permission from the Chinese authorities to transmit for another day. By coincidence, the Tiananmen Square confrontation occurred within the next 24 hours. The Chinese authorities were devastated by the global coverage provided by CNN. US President Bush, who was at his vacation home in Kennebunkport, Maine, openly stated that he was watching the events unfold, live on CNN, and that all he knew was what CNN was showing – just like the rest of the world. The drama escalated as the Tiananmen Square demonstrators continued to defy Chinese troops and tanks. A separate drama began to emerge as Chinese authorities attempted to cut off the live CNN coverage. The CNN crew refused to disconnect their equipment, and the entire incident and confrontation was broadcast live. The Chinese authorities were outraged, but CNN would not cease live coverage until it received an official letter from the Chinese Ministry of Telecommunications revoking the original 7-day transmission agreement. A kind of double coverage ensued when ABC began covering CNN's situation along with its own coverage of the confrontation. During CNN's coverage, Bernard Shaw explained how the network managed to break its live news:

If you're wondering how CNN has been able to bring you this extraordinary story . . . we brought in our own flyaway gear, about eighteen oversized suitcases with our satellite gear . . . We unpacked our transmission equipment and our dish. So whatever you've seen in the way of pictures and, indeed, in the way of words, came from our microwave units at Tiananmen Square bounced right here to the hotel, through our control room on one of the upper floors – I won't mention the floor for protective reasons – back down through cables up on the CNN satellite dish, up on the satellite, and to you across the world . . . And I have to say this, for those cable stations that want to cut away, and I can't believe that any of you would want to cut away, you're gonna risk the anger and angst of all your viewers if you do . . . We have about two and a half minutes left on the satellite.[2]

The letter from the Chinese Ministry of Telecommunications finally arrived; it was delivered live and within minutes CNN coverage stopped. The drama and the replays out of Atlanta placed CNN in a new light. It was now truly the global news network it had always claimed to be. But it needed another major global story in order to demonstrate that it had the flexibility, equipment, and personnel to deliver live news coverage that was either comparable or superior to that of the major US and European networks. The Persian Gulf War provided that vindication.

Persian Gulf War I

CNN was well prepared to be the media outlet for live coverage of the 1991 Gulf crisis. CNN carried not only the bombings but also Saddam Hussein's meeting with British hostages. And when Jordan's King Hussein wanted to deliver a message about the Gulf crisis, he delivered it live on CNN. World leaders began to communicate about the Gulf crisis through CNN; world leaders in North America, Europe, and the Middle East knew the status of the war because they were simultaneously glued to CNN's live coverage. It also created a media superstar in CNN reporter Peter Arnett. Previously, both Ted Turner and CNN executives had courted Middle Eastern governments and television officials, and now that groundwork was paying off. CNN was granted permission to broadcast live from Baghdad. The other US networks watched in envy as CNN produced the only global live coverage from the war zone, frequently from behind enemy lines. Bernard Shaw joined the CNN crew in order to provide 24-hour coverage. Despite warnings from the White House to vacate the region, CNN reporters and production crew decided to stay. When the first bombing began on January 16, 1991, all major US and European networks had crews in the Middle East. But 4 days after the war began, of the hundreds of journalists and crewmembers, only 17 remained. Nine of these were from CNN. Following Operation Desert Storm, CNN, and particularly Peter Arnett, were criticized for being too lenient by permitting Iraqi officials too much airtime during the war. American officials wanted a cheerleading tone. Given the foibles of live coverage, some mistakes were inevitable, but internationally CNN became the new global medium for breaking world news. It was considered objective and became the "gold standard."

The 1991 Persian Gulf War presented opportunity as well as challenge for CNN. The challenges were twofold. First, was the US public willing to support a military action against a foreign country, particularly after the Vietnam War debacle? Second, would CNN news crews, including production staff, be permitted, as well as technically equipped, to send live signals from Baghdad, the capital of Iraq? The opportunity was straightforward: CNN would be able to broadcast live a major international conflict not only for its vast US audience, but also for a substantial number of viewers around the globe. What made the Gulf War all the more pivotal for CNN's success was the fact that it was not just the first but also one of the few broadcasting outlets permitted by both Iraqi and US military authorities to continue shooting video. European, Canadian, and Asian broadcasting counterparts were denied access to frontline footage. The Gulf War turned out to be another defining moment in CNN's history. Even the leaders of the two nations engaged in the conflict – the United States and Iraq – openly conceded that they were following the progress of the war on CNN. CNN was interpreting the war for the world. This war was CNN's war. This fact bothered many foreign broadcasters, public policy experts, and politicians in other nations since they were reduced to viewing events and interpreting history in English and at least a step behind CNN. As a result, after the war several governments, particularly European, established competitor or alternative television services, so that when major international events occurred, they would have their own broadcasters, analysts, and footage to serve their national interests and present their perspectives, rather than having to rely on a foreign broadcaster, such as CNN. These competitor networks included EuroNews as well as the expansion of the BBC World Television Service, both of which are covered in greater detail later in this chapter. The Persian Gulf War heightened the context in which the news media covered and defined international news and information stories. Philip Taylor summarizes the significance of CNN's new role as a result of the first Gulf War:

> Throughout the autumn and winter of 1990, thanks to the role which Cable News Network (CNN) had defined for itself as an instant electronic interlocutor between Baghdad and Washington, it became clear that television would play a particularly prominent role in any conflict, with Saddam and Bush frequently exchanging verbal blows via the ten-year-old television network once lampooned by rivals as the "Chicken Noodle News."
>
> But it was already apparent that, by providing a public forum to the traditionally secretive world of diplomacy, CNN was quite simply changing the rules of international politics and that, as a consequence, it was also likely to alter the way in which modern warfare would be projected onto the world's television screens.[3]

The reporter known for his unprecedented coverage of the Persian Gulf War was CNN's Peter Arnett; his war coverage made him one of the world's most visible reporters. Arnett's success in Baghdad is cited as his most significant accomplishment simply because his coverage of the war was broadcast on live television. CNN positioned Peter Arnett as the archetypal journalist: the reporter who met newly defined professional challenges despite great personal risk and hardship. By staying behind enemy lines to report the story, he exemplified the reporter's responsibilities in an age of live, satellite-fed communications.

Although some loved Arnett, he was criticized as well. Some of the criticism focused on Arnett's supposed lack of loyalty to the United States, which is how some people interpreted his insistence on staying behind enemy lines. When Arnett reported that the allies had bombed a plant producing infant formula rather than biological weapons, as the US military insisted, public fears intensified that his dispatches were being used for propaganda purposes. At one point, US lawmakers pressed for control over his broadcasts.

CNN's news coverage of the first Persian Gulf War again highlighted the network's unprecedented coverage in the international marketplace. But CNN wants to remain the "first choice" provider or "gold standard" of international news and information coverage.

On an average day, CNN has a domestic audience of more than a million households. When major news events break, however, whether in China, Asia, or the Middle East, the ratings go through the roof. CNN captures the vast share of the global television news audience. Interestingly, CNN did not send Peter Arnett to Kosovo, and his fame and position quickly sank at the network. He never recovered from his association with the 1998 Tailwind controversy (discussed later in this chapter), and was dismissed by CNN in 1999.

Cable News Network's presence is felt in every part of the world. CNN has become synonymous with news from every corner of the world. CNN's founder Ted Turner transformed his Atlanta-based company into a creditable international news service with the help of renowned journalists. CNN has launched a new era of global news and information coverage using aggressive strategies ranging from covering news whenever and wherever it happens, to breaking the news first, and providing live coverage from the scene. All of these strategies have made Turner's company the leader in shaping international events.[4]

A brief history of CNN is in order here. Turner dedicated the network to around-the-clock news operations in the early 1980s. Satellites were used to deliver CNN to cable operators, but only about 20 percent of US TV viewing households received cable television. Turner needed more viewers if his new venture was to succeed. To increase cable access, he introduced ESPN, HBO, Nickelodeon, Arts & Entertainment (A&E), USA, Disney, Showtime, and CSPAN to attract a larger cable-viewing audience (see figure 6.2). By 1985, Turner's original news channel was reaching more than 33 million households, 4 out of 5 US homes with cable, and nearly 40 percent of all US homes with televisions. Headline News alone had 18 million subscribers. These numbers were vital to CNN's economic success because larger audiences meant greater advertising revenues, and by this time CNN was attracting national advertising accounts. By the mid-1980s, Turner wanted to attract an even larger audience, so he turned to the global market for growth. As international trade and shifts in the world markets became

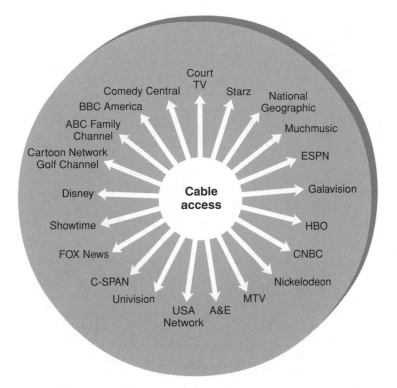

Court TV
Comedy Central
BBC America
ABC Family Channel
Cartoon Network
Golf Channel
Disney
Showtime
FOX News
C-SPAN
Univision
USA Network
A&E
MTV
Nickelodeon
CNBC
HBO
Galavision
ESPN
Muchmusic
National Geographic
Starz

Cable access

Figure 6.2 Examples of cable networks which started or expanded after the introduction of CNN

more relevant to the US economy, these activities created demands for more up-to-date global information. CNN also became a model niche cable channel that others began to mimic.

CNN's family of networks has grown to nearly a dozen news channels and a wholesale news service (CNN Newsource) that sells video news to approximately 700 broadcast affiliates worldwide. With Turner's array of 24-hour networks and services, today CNN is a major player in domestic and international programming. Some of CNN's networks consist of the following: CNN, CNN Headline News, CNN Radio, CNN International (CNNI), CNN World Report news exchange, CNN Newsource, CNN Airport Network, CNN Interactive, CNN Money, and CNN en Español. CNN now has webpages in the following languages: English, Arabic, Spanish, Turkish, Portuguese, and Korean. In 1999, CNN launched a Spanish-language channel in Spain. This service was the first CNN local language news channel completely controlled, staffed, and operated outside of its US corporate headquarters in Atlanta.

In a move that enhanced Turner's presence in global markets, state media monopolies around the world began to allow modest competition. Countries such as India, Japan, Hong Kong, Russia, and South Africa wanted news services in addition to the local coverage that was brought to them by their state (public) broadcasters. Turner moved quickly to reach these new audiences by distributing CNN internationally. CNN now employs a satellite system that covers 6 continents; it reaches over 200 countries with potential access to half a billion people every day, and has a global team of almost 4,000 people. Even in countries where CNN is unavailable to ordinary people, because of limited cable or satellite systems or because of political censorship, CNN International has become the prevailing choice of viewers in major hotels, government offices, and presidential palaces. CNN's newsgathering has increased its number of international news bureaus to 21. A remarkable aspect of CNN's expansion in the 1990s was that it mostly occurred while other US networks were slashing the budgets and number of their foreign bureaus. Clearly this expansion strategy changed after the Time Warner takeover.

CNN has built much of its reputation as a creditable news source from such news coverage stories as the student protest in Tiananmen Square in Beijing, the bombing of Baghdad, the burning of the parliament building in Moscow, and the Indian Ocean tsunami coverage. Because of CNN's extensive coverage of such important international news stories, it is now doing business in China, Baghdad, and Russia. In 1997, CNN opened a bureau in Cuba, even though it was required to obtain US government approval first. To date, no other US network has opened a bureau in Cuba because they refuse to obtain the required US license to report from that nation. One reason CNN has had such a rapid rise is its innovative use of communication technologies to reach larger audiences. Satellites gave CNN a national audience in 1980, and since then satellites have enabled Turner to be the first international broadcaster to link the globe using a mixture of Intelsat, Intersputnik, PanAmSat, and regional satellite signals when existing land-based systems could never have done the job.

The strong relationships CNN has built with networks, news agencies and broadcasting unions worldwide, and with freelancers have enabled it to bring news and information coverage to households around the world. Much of its coverage is found in CNN's World Report program.

World Report

What has CNN World Report brought to the newsgathering table? Beginning in 1987, CNN World Report has been an internationally distributed news program consisting of news items contributed by foreign broadcasters. Since its birth in 1987, World Report has been an outlet for news organizations of any political persuasion to report news about their countries from their own perspective. As of 2004, over 240 stations representing 143 countries participated in the World Report. This suggests that CNN World Report continues to serve the needs of world broadcasters. Some 200,000 news items have been aired from public and private stations such as CCTV in China, Cubavision in Cuba, CyBC Bayrak TV in Cyprus, MTVMultivision in Mexico, TV Asahi in Japan, RNTV-Radio in the Netherlands Television, SABC in South Africa, and ZBC in Zimbabwe.

World Report has had a considerable effect on CNN and its coverage of high-profile, controversial news and information stories. According to Ted Turner:

> We never would have been allowed to stay in Iraq during the Iraqi war if it hadn't been for the World Report. We've gotten a lot of access as a result of our making a real effort to having people from other countries and other news organizations feel comfortable about us. We've got a lot of access to world leaders and so forth, and then, allowed to be behind the lines and allowed to stay in circumstances where other news organizations weren't allowed to. Partly that was the case that we'd been allowed because so many world leaders were watching us when there's a conflict anywhere in the world, or anything controversial, where people, where leaders need to get their point across. Like Saddam Hussein did. At least we gave him some access that they otherwise wouldn't have gotten if CNN wasn't there, because basically we believe that everyone has a right to be heard.[5]

Turner Broadcasting Company's international success is also its curse. CNN's managers know they are no longer playing in a field of one. Imitators will strive to equal or surpass the US news company's global reach. But CNN's ability to watch its competitors and stay one step ahead will leave little room for a takeover. Competition is healthy for CNN because it keeps forcing the network to reexamine fundamental strategies of global versus niche programming. For example, in 1997 a senior executive left ABC to become CNN president. He tried to reposition CNN to become a more broadly based information channel rather than merely a breaking news channel. He was sacked in 2000. His successor was also replaced in 2004.

Today, executives at CNN state that their goal is to get people around the world to watch CNN. This means being more international in scope and more local from the standpoint of viewers in other parts of the world. To meet the information needs of the global market, CNN generates news programs that are compelling and relevant to a global audience. It also means that CNN reports on important events whenever and wherever they happen. In so doing, the network is trying to expand its role as a global communicator, the channel for diplomats and generals – even angry crowds in streets and town squares – with the potential to shape public life in every corner of the planet.[6] As mentioned, however, CNN's success has attracted competition. Some of its chief competitors, along with one of CNN's less stellar moments, are discussed in the following sections.

CNN's erroneous report

In June 1998, CNN, along with *Time* magazine, alleged that the US Department of Defense engaged in damaging activities at one point during the Vietnam War. Specifically, the CNN/*Time* allegations concerning Operation Tailwind asserted that the US Army hunted down and killed US defectors, and that as part of this operation, the nerve gas sarin was used. Major wire services and other media outlets picked up the story. A thorough review of Operation Tailwind was undertaken by the US State Department, led by then Secretary of Defense William Cohen, who in July 1998 asserted that investigators had found absolutely no evidence to support the allegations. Shortly thereafter CNN retracted the nerve gas story and dismissed CNN staffers associated with the story. One notable exception was Peter Arnett, who was associated with the false story. He managed to keep his position at CNN, due in large part to his stature as the most successful reporter for CNN during the Persian Gulf War. But in 1999, he was not assigned to cover the Kosovo conflict, and he was eventually dismissed by CNN for complaining to the press. Many consider that this reporting fiasco will have long-term negative consequences for CNN's credibility as an all-news network, as well as for its investigative reporting standards.

Kosovo and CNN

The Kosovo war, in the former Yugoslavia, in the spring of 1999 was different from the Persian Gulf War in several respects. From a military perspective, there were three major differences in the US position. First, the United States was not involved to protect traditional interests, such as oil in the Middle East, or to stop the advance of communism, as in Vietnam. Rather, it was a humanitarian war fought to stop the ethnic cleansing of Albanians by the Serbian Army. A second major difference was that Kosovo was NATO's war; the United States participated as only one of 19 NATO countries. Great Britain also participated and became very outspoken during military press briefings carried by the BBC. NATO had its own press spokesperson, Jamie Shea, based at NATO headquarters in Brussels, and US military spokespersons provided daily briefings as well. There were other military briefings by spokespersons from Italy, Greece, Germany, and other NATO nations. CNN was able to give extensive coverage from multiple perspectives. In addition to CNN, all other major US networks and many European networks covered the Kosovo conflict. What became interesting was that no single voice spoke from NATO's perspective. Rather, there were at least three major spokespeople from the United States, the United Kingdom, and NATO. From time to time, they gave different versions or different information about what had happened in the previous 24 hours. The major US and European networks quickly took advantage of any discrepancies. Many US networks had also hired retired military as analysts who provided endless details of the action and commented on what should be happening. Frequently, the commentary put the US State Department on the defensive, or caused the US Secretary of Defense to issue clarification statements.

The third major difference involved NATO's list of legitimate military targets. The traditional targets were power stations, bridges, military barracks, and airfields, but during the Kosovo conflict a new category was added – media outlets. Air raids were directed at Serbian television buildings, radio stations, and press buildings. These attacks on the Serbian media outlets as part of the air war reflected NATO's concerns about winning the public relations war as well as seeking an end to ethnic cleansing.

Following months of air raids, other aspects of the media environment became evident. First, Serbian President Slobodan Milosevic had a stranglehold on the Serbian media and used it as a propaganda machine. At the beginning of the air raids, the Milosevic government expelled all foreign journalists and closed down Belgrade's independent press. As a result, Western journalists, who now had to seek alternative working sites in neighboring countries, began to rely extensively on CNN's broadcast of the Kosovo war because CNN was one of the few Western media companies allowed back into Belgrade. This reliance on CNN escalated with the accidental bombing of the Chinese embassy in Belgrade, and with the accidental bombing of Kosovo refugees by NATO. This allowed CNN to set the media agenda because many reporters miles away from the air raids had to file stories about the daily bombings. Finally, the British press took considerable delight in the acerbic statements of Prime Minister Tony Blair and his Defence Secretary, George Robertson. They began to describe Milosevic in extremely negative terms, ultimately comparing the entire Serbian ethnic cleansing of the Albanians as akin to Hitler's genocide of the Jews during the Holocaust. The British tabloid media played up this excessive rhetoric, causing Blair to appear even more hawkish on the Yugoslavian war than US President Clinton.

Finally, NATO appeared to lack an overall communication strategy, and during daily press briefings appeared disorganized from time to time and uncertain about what was actually happening. Future NATO-sponsored military activities will likely see a significant improvement in media relations. The Kosovo war presented NATO with many challenges and taught that organization some lessons about media attention and the media's constant demand for up-to-date and accurate information rather than military propaganda.

With the merger of AOL and Time Warner, CNN faced a new reality and a different set of new bosses. CNN's founder, Ted Turner, left the company in 2003. In 2001 CNN laid off almost 10 percent of its employees when it let 400 employees go. During the same era CNN failed to replace President Rich Kaplan, who was dismissed in 2000. They have also been losing market share to MSNBC, FOX News, internet news sites, and competing international services, such as BBC World TV. John Cook, in his piece "CNN's Free Fall," writes about the lack of strategic planning, downsizing, and new ownership in this way: "the changes have fostered discontent and disillusionment among the rank and file, many of whom were perfectly content with the old CNN."[7] Cook also makes the point about a new, major shift away from the former model of news being the central focus, to a personality-centered schedule focused around stars, such as Christiane Amanpour, Wolf Blitzer, Brian Nelson, and Jeff Greenfield.[8] As of early 2005, CNN's lineup has added to its cast of star personalities with Paula Zahn, Aaron Brown, and Anderson Cooper. This repositioning of CNN, along with new ownership focusing on the bottom line, means that the Ted Turner stamp, creativity, media acumen, and era have come to an ignominious end.

The CNN effect

The CNN effect or factor refers to the process by which the coverage of a foreign event by CNN causes that event to be a primary concern for its audience, which in turn forces the federal government to act.[9] What CNN chooses to focus on becomes a major public policy issue, or headache, for the US State Department. CNN has such an impact that it cannot be ignored in Washington. It has the effect of being an outside agenda-setting voice for US foreign policy. This factor is extended when other networks begin to match CNN's focus on a foreign news event. When other networks begin to match CNN's coverage then the matter becomes an issue for a series of core governments. Others also argue with regard to what CNN fails to cover, that an increasing problem with budget cuts means that there is no public outcry for action and thus little assistance or policy attention played.[10] The US and British administrations were forced to respond to the Somalia crisis because CNN would not drop their coverage; whereas in Sudan a civil war has raged for years with no core-nation response, since CNN has chosen not to focus on their plight. Even former US Secretary of State Colin Powell admitted that he has to keep abreast of what CNN is covering abroad. Powell, to his credit, when he was a military leader used to audition media relations personnel for the Army, since he realized their significant impact on viewers' reaction to events when CNN and others interviewed them.[11] Finally, in 2005, Florida Governor Jeb Bush, traveling in Asia reviewing the tsunami damage, lamented that as soon as CNN leaves, where will be the aid workers and public pressure to assist in the lengthy repairs and costs?

In terms of foreign affairs, if it is not on CNN, it does not exist. It does not matter if it is the US Secretary of State, the British Minister of Foreign Affairs, the head of the United Nations, or a Japanese ambassador: if CNN does not pick up the story it disappears. The ability of CNN to set the global agenda is new to the role of the global media. When it ignores an issue, the issue languishes and fails to make the radar of editors around the world, with few exceptions.

The phenomenon of the CNN effect, agenda-setting, or factor may be short lived for CNN as they lose market share. Yet at the same time the media's public-policy role will likely even increase as other networks, as well as the internet with its bloggers, pick up the role of focusing greater attention on foreign policy, global issues, and aid. At other times, when CNN focuses on an issue, such as Abu Ghraib and other scandals and torture violations, the governments of the US and UK are forced into a damage control mode. Their spin masters are mere amateurs when taking on the impact and influence of the major media outlets, particularly CNN.

How CNN was out-Foxed but not out-classed

CNN was the global media king in 1991 with its strong coverage of the first Gulf War, but less than a decade later FOX News overtook it. It did so based on brash personalities like Bill O'Reilly, being in the right place at the right time,[12] and being an unabashed supporter of the Wars in Afghanistan and Iraq, and basically all things Republican.

In the early 2000s, CNN was overtaken in the US domestic all-news market by News Corp.'s FOX News. CNN continued to attract the largest global news audience (BBC World Television is second), but in the crucial and enormous home market it was knocked to second place. Quickly this also translated into lower advertising rates, and at parent Time Warner, which was bleeding due to AOL's failure to turn a profit, CNN lost its jewel status. Several management changes at CNN mandated by Time Warner also failed to stop the ratings slide. With FOX News proudly catering successfully to a right-of-center audience, this has left CNN with an identity crisis as to what and how to attract back its own departed audience. This problem is exacerbated by the high costs of covering a War in Iraq or a tsunami in Asia and the desire of Time Warner to reduce CNN's overall costs.

To put CNN's problem in perspective, consider the results of the 2004 US presidential election. Basically, CNN has tried to be an objective and middle-of-the-road network, and under Ted Turner's leadership this formula worked very well. (It is worth noting that since the merger of AOL and Time Warner in 2001, Turner has lost billions in Time Warner stock and he is no longer with the company.) But the overall US audience shifted as reflected in the federal election breakdown. The right wing of the political spectrum, as represented by the Republicans, won 51 percent of the popular vote, and the liberal wing won 49 percent, most of which were votes going to the Democrats. The problem is that CNN had claimed the center of the electorate – where fewer Americans sit. The media audience either perceived themselves as conservative and viewed FOX News, or as liberal and viewed a range of media outlets, including the internet. The end result was that CNN was positioned in a declining realm as the middle audience collapsed and moved mainly to the right or a fair amount to the left. In essence, the CNN network is now going through a type of identity crisis in terms of what it wants to be and where it wants to place itself with reference to its competitors.[13] The polarizing effect of the elections hit CNN's strategic position hard. Meanwhile Rupert Murdoch's FOX News delighted in its newfound audience niche and increasing ad rates. This has left CNN in an audience quagmire with few repositioning options – unless they make a direct frontal attack on FOX News by shifting their editorial slant to the right and thus risk losing the audience that they have now.

Gulf War II: embedded journalists

War coverage took a different tack during the second Gulf War in Iraq. The US military, which had a legacy of hostility toward the media, decided to embed journalists in combat units across Iraq and six war ships in the area. Given that the US military had blamed the media for the loss of public support for the Vietnam War, the 1983 invasion of Grenada and the 1989 war in Panama saw heavy control of the press, and the 1991 first Gulf War was primarily limited to CNN's coverage. It did come as a surprise that the US military would allow 775 journalists, photographers, and camera crews to cover the Iraq War in 2003. Embedding affects the tone and nature of the overall coverage. From the boot camp to the front lines, embeds quickly took on an air of camaraderie. They had to follow military guidelines and use military transportation. Overall the tone and slant of the stories and film footage was to the benefit of the US, and to some extent, the British military's coverage back home. For example, an empirical study of the coverage by embeds revealed "that embedded coverage of 'Iraqi Freedom' was more favorable in overall tone toward the military and in depiction of individual troops."[14] The authors conclude with a warning concerning the craft of objective journalism when they state: "However, for the journalism establishment, embedding embodies a 'professionally treacherous' reef. Journalists get to cover combat operations close up, giving them the access to combat operations that they want. But, in the process, they lose perspective and, thus, sacrifice the idealized standard of reporter objectivity."[15]

This response by the embeds was not totally unexpected by the Pentagon, or they would not have done it. Many independent or unilateral journalists, likely to be more critical of the war effort and the lack of weapons of mass destruction, were kept out of Iraq by the US military and were forced to watch the war, likely on CNN, from neighboring Kuwait.

Finally, CNN was treated like any other network and had several embeds along with all competing networks. CNN's virtual monopoly coverage of the first Gulf War had evaporated with the new embed policy. In addition, the use of the internet by reporters as well as soldiers also managed to outrun or scoop traditional media. The new phenomenon of weblogging (blogging) is covered in the internet chapter.

British Broadcasting Corporation (BBC)

Introduction

The BBC is significant for two major reasons. The first is that it operates a global television service in competition with CNN and a host of other regional networks. Second, the BBC as the early public-service, noncommercial British radio network was exported around the world as a media model to a vast number of British colonies. As a direct result noncommercial, government-controlled broadcasting in the public interest was what millions listened to and then watched with the introduction of television. The commercial model with advertising did not come to many nations until after the Second World War. And even then it was introduced slowly and frequently with oppressive regulations, many favoring the public broadcasters.

Radio

The BBC was founded in 1922; it went on the air in 1923 as a private radio corporation but quickly floundered. By early 1927, it had become a public corporation as the British government moved in to save the new medium. Since then, BBC radio has never sought advertising revenue, depending instead on two external sources of income. The first came directly from the British government in the form of an annual grant. The second came from license fees associated with all radio receivers. This licensing fee procedure was replicated with the introduction of television in the United Kingdom and is still in effect today.[16]

From its earliest days, the BBC was committed to public-service broadcasting. Lord John Reith, an early general manager of the BBC, describes its mission this way:

> Broadcasting must be conducted, in the future, as it has in the past, as a Public Service with definite standards. The Service must not be used for entertainment purposes alone . . . To exploit so great and universal an agent in the pursuit of entertainment alone would have been not only an abdication of responsibility and a prostitution of power, but also an insult to the intelligence of the public it serves.[17]

This focus on quality programming became a central tenet of the BBC. Soon the BBC became a model for other nations as radio began to expand around the world. Many of these nations were part of the former extensive network of colonies known as the British Commonwealth. The British not only exported their civil service, English language, and monarchy, but they also exported the public-service broadcasting ethic and model of the BBC. As early as 1927, the BBC began experimenting with short-wave radio in order to broadcast to Britain's far-flung and numerous colonies around the globe. By 1932 the BBC started a regular Empire Service by means of short wave. On Christmas Day that year, King George V became the first ruling monarch to broadcast live on radio his greeting to his subjects throughout the world.

The BBC got a major international boost and acquired an extensive audience through its high-quality reporting during the Second World War. The BBC became the international voice of the War and had no global rival. It also amassed substantial political power and influence; for years after the Second World War, it was able to severely limit the growth of commercial broadcasting and competition in the United Kingdom.

Television

The BBC started the world's first public television service on November 2, 1936. It was transmitted from Alexandra Palace to fewer than 400 television sets. Before the Second World War, television did not catch on quickly, due mainly to the lack of programs, the limited range of transmission, and the high cost of television receivers. Because television receivers were expensive, as was the license fee, only wealthy people could afford them. Therefore, programming was aimed at the elite, wealthier audience.

On September 1, 1939, television was shut off – the Second World War had begun. Without television, the BBC concentrated on radio and quality reporting of war activities. It also started airing a nightly War Report after the regular evening news. By the end of war, the BBC had gained a great global reputation as a high-quality and objective news broadcaster. And on June 8, 1946, BBC television was started up again to cover the Victory parade. The war was finally over.

From 1936 to 1955, there was only one television channel, BBC TV, later known as BBC1. But on September 22, 1955, for the first time the BBC faced some competition with the introduction of the Independent Television, or ITV. ITV ended the BBC monopoly and introduced a new and completely different style of television. ITV also gave viewers, for the first time, a choice.

One major difference between ITV and BBC TV was that ITV was funded and sponsored by outside advertisers. Also, unlike BBC TV, which used cinema newsreels and still pictures to broadcast the news, ITV used a less formal style of reporting imported from the US evening television newscasts. ITV quickly developed a substantial following.

Further choice in television channels opened up with the arrival of BBC2 in 1964. This allowed the BBC to air popular programs on BBC1, and more specialized, indepth programs on BBC2. Another technical move that helped promote BBC2 was the fact that in 1967 it was the first channel to start a color service. Because color televisions were expensive, many British people could not afford them. Also, the first color programs were few and far between. Other early disadvantages of color televisions were that they were bulky, unreliable, and had poor color quality. However after a few years, most of the problems were worked out, and on May 16, 1969, BBC1 and ITV were given permission to begin working on their own color services. By the mid-1970s, color televisions were smaller, cheaper, and more reliable, and color programming was now the norm.

In the early 1980s, Conservative Prime Minister Margaret Thatcher established a committee to investigate the possibility of seeking advertising revenue for the BBC. Despite the investigation and scare to BBC admirers, the commitment to high-quality, noncommercial programming remained intact.

Thanks to the threat during the Thatcher years of being partially privatized or driven by commercial interests, in the 1990s the BBC began to investigate other possible avenues of income. As a result, a new digital broadcasting service was established to compete with Rupert Murdoch's BSkyB. The BBC also began to market a foreign service that is now available on cable in North America and elsewhere. The BBC's online homepage is one of the most frequently accessed websites in the UK. Currently the United Kingdom also has the BBC equivalent of CNN, shaped in part by the Persian Gulf War, when CNN covered the war and the BBC and other European media were forced to play catch-up. The BBC's 24-hour all-news channel – News 24 – has been an early success.

In November 1991, the BBC launched the World Service Television, otherwise known as BBC WSTV, a public-service channel funded by the British Foreign Office that uses satellite technology to reach an extensive foreign audience. BBC World Service is an international news and information television channel broadcast in English 24 hours a day for a global audience. It provides news, business, and weather, as well as the best of the BBC's current-affairs, documentary, and lifestyle programming. The companion BBC World Service Radio has an estimated global audience of over 30 million listeners and is broadcast in 43 languages.

In the late 1990s, the BBC started a second international channel, BBC Prime. This global entertainment channel covers a broad range of programming. BBC Prime is available in most core, semiperipheral, and peripheral regions. Programs dealing with classics, cult comedy, and music do particularly well.

BBC broadcasts have been honed and refined over the years and are now the envy of many of the world's major broadcasters. It has set the world standard by which others are judged. BBC World Services operations are not easily duplicated, because its quality standards are unique. But with the advance of competition, particularly CNN, as well as other satellite and internet services, some are questioning the role and expense of BBC's World Services.

The BBC is currently facing a problem related to economics and the future of government funding. Because the BBC now attracts less than 50 percent of the domestic audience, there is growing concern that the traditional support for the license-fee funding concept may decline. Although the BBC has a loyal core of supporters, others strongly support the notion that commercial stations, advertising, market share, and ratings should determine the future of broadcasting. Critics claim that the traditions of public support, public service, and subsidizing media are vestiges of a bygone era. Many now want the future of the BBC and other broadcast services to be determined by open market forces rather than by officials behind closed government doors.

Royal Charter, 2006–16

Like all major broadcasters the BBC is facing a changing landscape. But since 1927 a unique aspect of the BBC is that it operates under the authority of a British Royal Charter. The Charter spells out in detail its public-service mandate. The current 10-year Charter ends on December 31, 2006. This is providing both supporters and critics of the BBC with an excellent opportunity to comment on what the BBC should and should not be doing, as well as to how it should carry out its mandate in the near future. The British government has promised a major policy document, known as a "Green Paper," to be published by 2005. The Green Paper will lay out the policy options concerning the future of the BBC, including global media services, the internet, and the contentious commercial activities run by BBC Enterprises. A significant part of BBC Enterprises' services includes BBC America and the selling of Teletubbies paraphernalia. The issue of the balance between resource allocations to national versus international services will also come under close scrutiny.

The BBC is facing the reality, as are other broadcasters, that digital communication has brought convergence and more channels. Today the BBC confronts more commercial competition, both domestic and foreign, the evolution of the internet, and new satellite channels. This will all be open for public discussion and debate.

The Royal Charter and Agreement will outline the terms and scope of funding as well as the operational areas in which the BBC provides service, on either a noncommercial or commercial basis. Currently there are three major sources of revenue of the BBC, with the license fee bringing in over $5 billion, with somewhat controversial commercial activities bringing in over $1 billion and growing, and finally almost a half billion dollars from government grants. All this for a radio network capturing about half the total British audience and less than 40 percent of the national television audience.

The critics of the BBC maintain two major complaints about its operations. The first is that the mandated funding through license fees is being used as cross-subsidies for other multimedia activities. Some of these are the children's channels, CBBC and Cbeebies, which both Viacom and Disney objected to, various BBC internet sites, and the successful BBC Enterprises' commercial activities. In conjunction with this complaint, there are two radical solutions offered. First, do away with the license fees altogether and make all services commercial; or second, stick to only noncommercial activities and sell off the commercial ventures.

The second major complaint is about standards and quality. In 2004 the Hutton Report strongly criticized the news and public affairs divisions for lacking proper oversight concerning a controversial story about Iraq. The chairman and chief executive of the BBC resigned over the matter. Others condemn the television side for debasing its shows by chasing high audience ratings as they mimic US networks and go for mindless reality shows. These critics want higher-quality shows that reflect world-class production standards, scripts, and on-air talent.

In the midst of the broad range of issues that will inform the public debate, including the British House of Commons, is another matter potentially involving all public broadcasters, namely the desire of the World Trade Organization (WTO) to include cultural industries under their tariff concerns. More is outlined about this issue in the chapter discussing the WTO, but one example illustrates the possible significance of the WTO's plans to the BBC. The current financing of the BBC involves an annual license fee levied on all radio and television receivers. This is a huge subsidy to the BBC. The WTO does not allow subsidies in its rules, since they distort the commercial, market-based playing field. Thus the BBC could find itself facing a financial crisis if the WTO pushes the matter.

Deutsche Welle

Deutsche Welle is the German short-wave system designed to broadcast worldwide radio and television. Information is provided 24 hours a day, including up-to-date information on German and European domestic and foreign issues, as well as economic and financial trends focusing on the Frankfurt stock exchange and the new monetary unit, the euro. Deutsche Welle TV offers 24-hour, commercial-free service, which includes news, sports, and cultural affairs programming. It provides about half its programming in German and the other half primarily in English, with a few hours in Spanish. Deutsche Welle Radio has two distinct channels: a German-language channel and an international language channel, which includes English, French, Spanish, Italian, and Greek.

Deutsche Welle began with short-wave radio transmissions in May 1953, and it is financed mainly with German government funds. Currently it utilizes short-wave, satellite, and microwave rebroadcast facilities. In April 1992, Deutsche Welle TV began transmission and was then on the air 14 hours a day. Deutsche Welle TV is now carried by cable systems throughout Europe and is rebroadcast in many parts of the world. More recently Deutsche Welle set up internet services in order to compete in the public affairs arena with the BBC and Voice of America. Since its inception, Deutsche Welle has received substantial German government support. But with the end of the cold war and the reunification of Germany, political support and federal government funding is in jeopardy.

EuroNews

In 1993 the European Union established its own transnational news network, known as EuroNews. It is headquartered in France and broadcasts television news in seven languages. The impetus to create this trans-European television news network was almost a direct result of CNN's coverage of the 1991 Persian Gulf War. The European networks were either nowhere to be found in Baghdad at the beginning of the war, or as the war progressed found themselves increasingly relying on CNN's coverage in order to follow the action. As a result, 18 European public broadcasters, including France, Italy Germany, Spain, Belgium, and Greece, put up substantial funding to establish EuroNews. In addition to government subsidies, EuroNews accepts commercial advertising. A noticeably absent member of EuroNews is the UK. Like CNN, the BBC is in direct competition for the EuroNews audience.

EuroNews currently is second to CNN in terms of viewing audience across Europe, and the BBC World Television Service is a distant third. Across Europe more than 90 million homes and over 100,000 hotels have access to EuroNews. Overall, EuroNews is viewed in 43 nations and has over 5 million viewers daily. The goal of EuroNews is to provide a European perspective on world, regional, and local affairs. Programs are being produced for Europeans by Europeans. The differences between US foreign policy and that of the EU have made the channel a vital part of the news and public affairs media across Europe. Currently, EuroNews has expanded to Russia and several eastern European nations. It is also available throughout most of the Middle East. EuroNews broadcasts 20 hours a day in the following languages: English, French, German, Spanish, Portuguese, Russian, and Italian. In addition to news and public affairs, it focuses on the European arts, culture, science, and technology. The main focus of all EuroNews programming is the implication of decisions, along with political and economic developments, from a trans-European perspective. No single country dominates coverage. There has been one negative fallout since the start in 1993. As various governments support EuroNews with public funds, the broadcasting funds allocated for EuroNews are indirectly coming from funds that traditionally would have been dedicated to national public television networks. EuroNews is trying to blunt this criticism by relying, year by year, more on advertising revenue in order to become more independent from public revenues from member countries.

Channel News Asia (CNA)

A new Asian-based news channel, CNA, began service in 2000. Similar to EuroNews, which is attempting to bring a European perspective to European and global events, so CNA is seeking to bring an Asian view to the Asian region, as well as global news events. It is based out of Singapore and has close government ties. CNA is seeking to compete with the major global news services such as CNN International, the BBC, and CNBC Asia. With an all-Asian staff, it has 10 bureaus and about 150 journalists across Asia, more than the three English-language all-news networks combined. Like the BBC, CNA is attempting to serve a market of about 16 million households, whereas CNN International is the clear regional leader, with about 30 million subscribers. CNA is trying to appeal to the Asian demographic in hopes of attracting viewers from across the most populated region in the world by focusing on news by Asians and from an Asian editorial perspective. Some journalists and media critics are concerned about the undetermined role of the authoritarian Singapore government on the status of CNA independence.

US Department of State and IBB

The US federal government created the United States Information Agency (USIA) during the First World War. Its initial purpose was to coordinate federal international information and counter negative foreign propaganda. USIA became an independent agency in 1953 and expanded its activities to include a broad range of international information, education initiatives, cultural exchanges, and media relations. In 1998, under the Foreign Affairs Reform and Restructuring Act, USIA was essentially divided into two sections. Much of the public diplomacy and foreign exchange activities were relocated in the State Department. The International Broadcasting Bureau (IBB) became a freestanding, separate agency at the same time to oversee all US, nonmilitary, international broadcasting services. In 1999, the USIA was disbanded altogether.

The activities transferred to the State Department currently include longstanding programs that have an impact on media systems and journalists in other nations. For example, the College and University Affiliations Program (CUAP) seeks to establish relations between US universities and their foreign counterparts. Examples of programs include a Palestinian media center, a grant to a Jordanian university to develop distance learning, and a grant to the University of Chile to establish an environmental science research agenda. The US State Department also funded the Aegean Young Journalists program, which brings together Greek and Turkish journalists. Many of the programs and partnerships funded have similar activities such as workshops, study tours, internships, and a US-based study tour. Another initiative is the Citizen Exchange Program (CEP), which brings both journalism professors and journalists from semiperipheral and peripheral nations to the United States for workshops and information exchanges. A goal of this program is to instill in delegates free-press values so that as their media systems are privatized or created, they will reflect the journalistic values and practices of an open and democratic society. Through the IBB, the US federal government has substantial involvement in international broadcasting. Three major units are involved in the global transmission of news, information, and public affairs programming, focusing primarily on Washington's foreign affairs and foreign policy initiatives and goals. The four major units are (1) Voice of America, (2) WORLDNET Television and Film Service, (3) Radio and TV Marti, and (4) Radio Sawa. In 1994, a new International Broadcasting Act was adopted and signed by President Clinton. The new legislation established a Broadcasting Board of Governors (BBG), which oversees IBB's activities. In addition to the three major services, the BBG also oversees aspects of federally funded broadcasting services related to Radio Free Europe, Radio Liberty, and Radio Free Asia. All of these services receive annual grants from the US federal government and strict policy guidance from the US Secretary of State.

The end of the Cold War era has seen a noticeable shift in and questioning of the role of these federally funded global broadcasting services. In their initial years, these services were designed as US propaganda voices through which to present – in local languages around the world – the US foreign policy position, the ideology of fighting communism, and US political and economic values. Now there is a greater emphasis on promoting US commercial and export interests abroad instead of the hardline and hysterical political rhetoric of the Cold War era.

Voice of America (VOA)

Voice of America (VOA) was founded in 1942 and was heavily funded by Congress during the Cold War. The first three decades focused on fighting communism and combating the global spread of Marxism. Now, in the absence of a global Cold War environment, the VOA is attempting to reposition itself. It is the international radio and television service of IBB and has a global audience of about 100 million people. It broadcasts on short-wave, medium-wave, and satellite transmissions in English and in 43 foreign languages. VOA programs over 1,000 hours a week and uses its own VOA correspondents at 23 news bureaus around the world, as well as using freelance reporters. VOA provides news, information, and cultural programming around the globe. Some of the programs promote the benefits of democracy, the free press and free markets, human rights, and the American way of life, politics, and business. All programming originates from Washington, DC, headquarters, but under the 1948 Smith–Mundt Act, VOA is prohibited from broadcasting inside the United States.

In the fall of 1994, VOA began television programming. Shortly thereafter it experienced a 20 percent budget cut and began accepting corporate underwriting to improve its budget. VOA TV simulcasts in six foreign languages, including Spanish and Chinese.

A noticeable distinction between the VOA and the BBC is that the former emphasizes a US orientation and a White House viewpoint, whereas the latter focuses on world news and global trends, with minimum attention to solely British news or to the British prime minister's agenda. Internationally, the VOA is viewed as a propaganda arm of the US government, whereas BBC programming is perceived as independent, objective, and more credible.

Worldnet Television and Film Service

Worldnet was launched in 1983 and is transmitted by satellite from television studios in Washington, DC. The programming is directed to US embassies and other broadcasters around the world. It programs 24 hours a day in English, but other programs are available in a number of world languages such as Russian, French, Spanish, and Chinese. Worldnet programs range from public affairs forums, to science discussion, to international call-in programs. Worldnet also transmits some public broadcasting programs, such as PBS's *The NewsHour*.

Office of Cuba Broadcasting

In 1983 the US Congress approved the establishment of Radio Marti under the provision that it would adhere to the Voice of America's regulations. In addition, the Reagan administration and the Cuban American National Foundation agreed that the station would be based in Washington, DC, to make clear that this was the official voice of the US government, not an outlet of fanatic Cuban exile organizations. Given these provisions, Radio Marti went on the air in May 1985. TV Marti first broadcast in March 1990. In 1998, under legislation passed by Congress and previously signed by President Clinton in April 1996, Radio and TV Marti headquarters and operations completed a move from Washington, DC, to Miami, Florida.

Under the VOA, Radio Marti's programs are to be produced in accordance with the following VOA regulations (US Public Law 94.30). The VOA charter states:

> The long-range interests of the United States are served by communicating directly with the people of the world by radio. To be effective, the Voice of America (the broadcasting Service of the United States Information Agency) must win the attention and respect of listeners. These principles will therefore Govern Voice of America (V.O.A.) Broadcasts.
>
> Following are the three policies stated:
>
> 1. V.O.A. will serve as a consistently reliable and authoritative source of news. V.O.A. news will be accurate, objective, and comprehensive.
>
> 2. V.O.A. will represent America, not any single segment of American society, and will therefore present a balanced and comprehensive projection of significant American thought and institutions.
>
> 3. V.O.A. will present the policies of the United States clearly and effectively, and will also present responsible discussion and opinion on those policies.[18]

The provisions stated by Voice of America are designed to ensure accuracy, objectivity, and balance in their content.

Radio Marti broadcasts 7 days a week, 24 hours a day, on medium wave (AM) and short wave. Its broadcast includes news, music, and a variety of feature and news analysis programs. With a staff of over 100 employees, Radio Marti's $13 million annual budget provides news, talk radio, and information programs. News and news-related programming make up half of Radio Marti's daily schedule. Radio Marti's goal is to fill the information gap caused by more than four decades of Cuban government censorship. There is a one-hour noon newscast, which includes a live interview/discussion segment with experts or individuals in Cuba and correspondents around the world. In addition, there is a half-hour newscast at 4:00 p.m., as well as live coverage of special events in the United States and around the world that stress the importance of Cuba. Topics covered with relevance to Cuba include congressional hearings and speeches by Latin American heads of state at major regional and hemispheric events. Despite complaints from the Cuban media, Radio Marti's programs offer listeners a Cuban American perspective on current events. In addition, the broadcasts offer feature and special programs with a wide range of information and entertainment. Some of the programs include roundtable discussions; commentaries by experts on political, economic, social, religious, and human rights issues; testimonies from former political prisoners and from human rights and labor sectors.

Despite efforts by Cuban President Castro to jam the transmission of Radio Marti, Cubans listen in significant numbers. It was for this reason that TV Marti was established: to provide Cuban viewers with programming available in other countries and in the western hemisphere. In addition, TV Marti provides – in Spanish – news, features on life in the United States and other nations, entertainment, and sports. It also provides commentary and other information about events in Cuba and elsewhere in order to promote the cause of freedom in and for Cuba. TV Marti is on the air only for about five hours a day. With a large staff and a fiscal year budget of millions, TV Marti has been a growing organization. Its technical operations are mounted aboard a balloon tethered 10,000 feet above Cudjoe Key, Florida; programming originates in studios in Washington, DC, and is transmitted to the Florida Keys via satellite. The signal is then relayed to a transmitter and a highly directional antenna mounted aboard an aerostat for broadcast to Cuba. TV Marti's transmission system delivers a clear television signal to the Havana area. Although jamming efforts by the Cuban government make it difficult to receive the signal in the center city of Havana, mobile monitoring indicates that international reception is possible in some outlying areas of the city and other more remote parts of the Havana province.

There is a downside to the unique manner in which TV Marti is transmitted. As mentioned, TV Marti's signals are transmitted from a balloon tethered above the Florida Keys. Also aboard is radar to track drug flights from Latin America. When TV Marti goes on, the radar goes off. Some critics contend that drug smugglers know the transmitting schedule and thus the best time to avoid detection. Finally, Radio and TV Marti have experienced internal management problems. Ultraconservatives dominate management, fanatical Cuban exiles living in the Miami area, and several journalists have complained and ultimately left because of editorial interference with their stories and assignments. Radio and TV Marti's research section was closed in 1997, and they have experienced declining audiences in Cuba.

Postscript

In the 1990s, the US Department of the Treasury issued a ruling requiring US media companies and journalists to obtain a license to broadcast, report, or open a bureau in Cuba. For the most part, major US media enterprises objected strenuously and refused to apply for a bureau license. Notable exceptions were CNN and the Associated Press. They and a few others are the only major US broadcasters with licenses and bureaus in Cuba. Others are applying. Failure to obtain a license from the Treasury can result in substantial fines for both the news network as well as individual journalists.

What is interesting is that the often-repeated formal position of the US government in international communication debates was to strongly oppose any licensing requirement by any government affecting the media. During the NWICO debates of the 1980s, the US government took the strongest position in opposition to licensing. It denounced calls for government responsibility for, influence over, or control of the mass media. Clearly, however, in the cases of CNN and AP, as well as in its various activities with Radio and TV Marti, the US government is deeply involved in practices that it rhetorically and administratively abhorred during the intense NWICO debates. To foreign critics it makes the US Federal government look duplicitous when dealing with the free press. Finally, in 2005 the outing of conservative media commentator Armstrong Williams as a well-paid covert propagandist for the US government did not help its global media image.

Conclusions

The last decade of the twentieth century witnessed two significant and long-term changes in global communication. The first was the rise of CNN, which began as a small UHF station in Atlanta, Georgia, and became the predominant global network for breaking news. CNN's effectiveness and expansion were aided substantially by the introduction of small satellite earth stations capable of linking virtually instantaneously CNN's corporate broadcasting center with journalists in any part of the world. Whether the breaking news was occurring in a major urban center such as Paris or Beijing, or in remote deserts or isolated areas such as rural Afghanistan, Iraq, or Kosovo, with a technician and a single reporter, CNN was able to broadcast live many breaking stories.

CNN's success also created a problem. As its role, influence, and ability to broadcast major events increased, other nations became concerned that their own governments' policies, including foreign policy, were being ignored or marginalized while CNN broadcast a primarily US perspective on international events. As a result, some nations started to develop alternatives to CNN. One of the most notable is the BBC. Although currently limited in reach, over time the BBC could become a major global broadcaster in the international television news arena as it once dominated the global radio networks. EuroNews is another good example of a network created to present a European perspective on European and world news for Europeans. That is also the expectation of the French as they launch CII.

Many radio services, particularly those offshore, were based on short-wave radio technology, which, thanks in particular to the internet, is becoming obsolete. A more pressing issue is that of continuing financial support for these primarily government-funded global media services. With the end of the Cold War and the lessening of the fear of nuclear attack, there is a corresponding reduction in governments' desire to fund global radio networks. All short-wave global networks are feeling the stress of decreasing support, both politically and financially. For example, the Canadian Broadcasting Corporation's foreign short-wave service, Radio Canada International (RCI), was eliminated during the 1990s as part of budget cuts. Part of RCI's budget was redirected to promote Canadian exports abroad. Other services have not fared as badly, but all are experiencing declining rather than expanding budgets. Some of these services, particularly the BBC and Voice of America, are shifting attention to the possibility of using the internet as a way of extending their audience reach and justifying government funding. Many are also soliciting external corporate advertising or corporate underwriting for select programming.

A final point is that the major global news networks are based in core nations – CNN in the United States, the BBC in the United Kingdom, and Deutsche Welle in Germany. These core-based global television news systems are designed for major export markets around the world because the majority of the services are commercially based and seek to extend their commercial viability by attracting larger audiences with the appropriate demographics for their advertisers. So these global systems have two basic audiences, one within the nations where the corporations are based and the other literally scattered around the world. Some are in remote villages and others are in major urban centers with potential audiences in the millions. With the expansion of both cable systems and satellite technology, the potential for niche, particularly news, networks was recognized early by major innovators and is now being mimicked by broadcasters on a global scale. But all global news networks present a core-nation perspective on the news they cover, and they all cover news in peripheral regions only rarely and even then with a bad news, coup, disaster, or earthquake focus.

Notes

1   Although the focus of this book is on global media, MSNBC and FOX News are relevant models for potential global expansion. They also provide considerable international coverage of leading stories, many connected with the global war on terrorism.

MSNBC, launched in July 1996, combines three technologies – broadcast, cable, and the internet – in order to provide 24-hour news from around the world. It is jointly owned by Microsoft and General Electric's NBC Universal and primarily combines the national and international news resources of the NBC system along with the financial, business, and technology resources of Microsoft.

Rupert Murdoch's News Corporation, on the other hand, owns FOX News Channel. It went on the air in October 1996 and provides 24-hour, all-news global coverage, in direct competition with both MSNBC as well as Time Warner's CNN.

An interesting phenomenon emerged during the NATO bombing of Yugoslavia in 1999. These three all-news networks clearly have an insatiable appetite for news coverage 24 hours a day. This now also includes extensive commentary on global events themselves, in addition to broad coverage of news conferences, video of bombing attacks, interviews with refugees, and so on. A new phenomenon during the Kosovo air strikes by NATO involved the significant new dimension of retired military personnel appearing again and again on all three networks to comment, mostly negatively, about NATO's actions and strategies. As a result, not only did President Clinton have to contend with political opposition to his military strategy in Washington, but also now he had a new wave of critics – that is, an endless cadre of retired generals who were, from time to time, reaching substantial audiences through the all-news networks. This translated, in terms of public opinion, into a larger and more skeptical US public concerning the United States' role in NATO, as well as its military interests in Yugoslavia.

In general, CNN has been able to attract more domestic viewers than either of its competitors, but there is one notable exception. In June 1999, MSNBC opted to pay the BBC for three hours of live coverage of the British royal wedding of Prince Edward and Sophie Rhys-Jones. For the first time in its brief broadcasting history, MSNBC beat CNN in total households that single day by featuring live a British royal wedding.

2 Hank Whittemore, *CNN: The Inside Story* (Toronto: Little, Brown, 1990), pp. 295–6.
3 Philip Taylor, *War and the Media: Propaganda and Persuasion in the Gulf War* (Manchester, UK: Manchester University Press, 1998), p. 7.
4 Don M. Flournoy and Robert K. Stewart, *CNN: Making News in the Global Market* (Luton, UK: John Libbey Media, 1997), p. ix.
5 Ibid., p. 34.
6 Ibid., pp. 208–9. Additional details about CNN may be found in Piers Robinson, *The CNN Effect: The Myth of News Media, Foreign Policy and Intervention* (London: Routledge, 2002); Royce Ammon, *Global Television and the Shaping of World Politics* (Jefferson, NC: McFarland & Company, 2001); and S. Kull, C. Ramsay, and E. Lewis, "Misperceptions, the Media, and the Iraq War," *Political Science Quarterly* 118(4) (Dec. 2003), pp. 569–98.
7 John Cook, "CNN's Free Fall," *Brill's Content*, April 2001, p. 68.
8 Ibid., p. 122.

9   Robinson, *The CNN Effect*.

10 V. Hawkins, "The Other Side of the CNN Factor: The Media and Conflict," *Journalism Studies* 3(2) (May 2002), pp. 225–40.

11 Margaret Belknap, *The CNN Effect: Strategic Enabler or Operational Risk?* (Pennsylvania: US Army War College, 2001).

12 Scott Collins, *Crazy Like a Fox: The Inside Story of How Fox News Beat CNN* (New York: Portfolio Press, 2004).

13 Jason Zengerle, "Fiddling With the Reception," *The New York Times Magazine*, Aug. 17, 2003.

14 Michael Pfau et al., "Embedding Journalists in Military Combat Units: Impact on Newspaper Story Frames and Tone," *Journalism and Mass Communication Quarterly* 81(1) (Spring 2004), p. 83.

15 Ibid., p. 84.

16 Asa Briggs, *The BBC: The First Fifty Years* (New York: Oxford University Press, 1985).

17 R. H. Coase, *British Broadcasting* (London: University of London Press, 1950), p. 46.

18 www.voa.gov

Chapter 7

The Roles of Global News Agencies

Introduction

This chapter covers global wire services, which are major components of the global communication system. These wire services bring to international communication different sets of stakeholders, yet each service has a significant role in the daily activities of multinational media enterprises. They are also being driven to expand globally by industry pressure to achieve broader scale and scope. Since the Second World War, the debate surrounding international communication has in large part focused on the international wire services. During the 1960s, the global wire services became the first and frequent targets of peripheral nations and other critics. During the NWICO debates of the 1970s, most of the issues involved some aspect of wire service behavior, location (they are all based in core nations), or corporate structure.[1]

Frequently, two general problem areas were cited in discussions of core-based global wire services. First, the wire services focused on covering news that was mainly relevant to colonial powers or dealt with regions where core-headquartered corporations had branch plants. The three major global services, Reuters, Associated Press, and Agence France Presse, are based in London, New York, and Paris respectively. The second major issue was that coverage of peripheral nations focused on negative news such as civil strife, natural disasters, or sensational and bizarre events. The wire services reported little if any good news about the poorest regions in Africa, Latin America, or Asia.

Two general groups of researchers attempted to document the wire services' one-way news flow and the imbalance in both East–West and

1. Reuters	5. Bloomberg
2. The Associated Press	6. Dow Jones & Company
3. United Press International (UPI)	7. Xinhua
4. Agence France Presse	8. Inter Press Services

Figure 7.1 Global news agencies

North–South coverage. One group sought funding and a voice from UNESCO, and by the late 1970s its rhetoric and demands had become shrill. The other group consisted of various pockets of scholars in the United States, Europe, the Nordic countries, Latin America, and elsewhere who conducted separate research, frequently using content analysis of a specific medium, usually print. In the final analysis, almost all of the research was critical of the wire services. Researchers frequently studied the print press to document what were perceived as structural problems in the core-based and -controlled wire services. With the demise of the Cold War, East–West tensions have evaporated for the most part, but certain structural criticisms remain concerning North–South news coverage.

The major global news agencies are detailed in this chapter. (See figure 7.1.) Reuters and the Associated Press are not only the giants but they also control vast television news reporting and internet interests around the globe, in addition to their historical interest in print-based journalism.

Reuters

Reuters wire service dates back to October 1851, when Paul Julius Reuter, a German immigrant, opened an office in London. Reuters transmitted stock-market quotations between London and Paris and focused on business news. The agency soon became known as a news source and eventually extended its services to the entire British press as well as the press in other European countries. Reuters expanded its services and began transmitting general and economic news from all around the world. Reuters' successful news service was booming. In 1865, Reuters was the first wire service company in Europe to transmit the news about President Lincoln's assassination in the United States.

Through technological advances such as the telegraph and undersea cable facilities, Reuters news services expanded beyond Europe to include the Far East by 1872 and South America by 1874. In 1883, Reuters began to use a "column printer" to transmit messages electronically to London newspapers. This format allowed editors to simply cut and paste stories from the Reuters feed. The use of radio further expanded the wire service in the 1920s, allowing Reuters to transmit news internationally. In 1927, Reuters introduced the teleprinter to distribute news to London newspapers. And in 1939, the company moved its corporate headquarters to its current location at 85 Fleet Street, London.[2]

Reuters' continued success and modernizing of services continued into the latter half of the twentieth century. It expanded in 1964 with the Stockmaster service, which transmitted financial data internationally. In 1973, the company launched the Reuters Monitor, which transmitted news and foreign exchange prices. Following a dramatic increase in profitability, Reuters was floated as a public company in 1984 on the London Stock Exchange and on Nasdaq in the United States.

In 1960, Reuters began to buy shares in Visnews, a global television news film agency. Reuters continued buying shares of Visnews until 1992, when the former bought out Visnews completely and renamed the company Reuters Television (RTV). RTV is the world's leading supplier of international news material for television, reaching 1.5 billion people daily and delivering material directly to media customers by satellites or terrestrial, land-based systems. Customers include broadcasters and newspapers around the world, but the news is tailored specially for financial markets. Broadcasters are supplied with fast, reliable news video ranging from big breaking stories to human interest, from sports to business. RTV service is the oldest comprehensive real-time news and information service that covers breaking news around the globe. It is ideal for those who want to know what is happening around the world because it often includes secondary stories not widely reported in the United States; these stories are broadcast extensively in other nations, however. Reuters' only major competition in supplying news to broadcasters started in 1994 with Associated Press Television News (APTN), which was established when AP bought out World Television News.

Reuters' corporate position as an international market leader is based on its four strengths: (1) a worldwide information and news reporting network known for speed, accuracy, integrity, and impartiality; (2) a constantly developing communications network and a product line distinguishable by its breadth and quality; (3) comprehensive financial databases for both real-time and historical information; and (4) a proven reputation for reliability and continuous technological innovation. Reuters offers its clients financial, media, and professional products and services. The financial products consist of datafeeds to financial markets and the software tools to analyze data. Under the financial umbrella are transaction products, which enable traders to deal in the foreign exchange, futures, options, and securities markets.

The media division delivers news in all facets of multimedia, which include television images, still pictures, sound, and graphics. Reuters' professional product division packages the news in electronic briefings for corporate executives in insurance, advertising, transportation, healthcare, and other corporate and professional sectors.

In addition to Reuters' financial, media, and professional services, the company also has several subsidiaries, including Instinet Corporation and TIBCO Software Inc. Instinet, founded in 1969 and acquired by Reuters in 1987, remains the premier provider of agency brokerage services worldwide. This division has offices in 8 key financial centers and provides its equity transaction capabilities and research services to clients in over 30 countries. Through affiliates, Instinet is a member of 16 exchanges in North America, Europe, and Asia. Clients use Instinet to improve their performance by reducing trading costs. In addition, clients using Instinet's global brokerage services have access to the best pools of liquidity. Using the real-time trading system, Instinet offers investment professionals a set of brokerage solutions to help them achieve better analysis, decision-making, and execution. In late 2004, Reuters began exploring a possible sale of Instinet.

TIBCO Software was acquired by Reuters in 1994 and is based in Palo Alto in California's Silicon Valley. This Reuters division offers information application and integration technologies on a variety of systems in order to share information used in finance, manufacturing, construction, and other industries. The Information Bus (TIB) technology is the global standard for integrating systems and software into a single event-driven enterprise. Event-driven clients who utilize TIB are better equipped for the international marketplace and can respond quickly to markets and customers. In addition, TIBCO develops innovative solutions for the financial industry. TIB's solutions are based on its patented "publish/subscribe" technology, which selects information on networks according to preset individual requirements and sends the data to the user as it is updated. In 2004, to pay down heavy debts, Reuters sold part of its stake in TIBCO for about $500 million. It now holds a 13.5 percent stake in TIBCO.

Today, Reuters supplies the global financial markets and the news media with the widest range of information and news products including real-time financial data; collective investment data; numerical, textual, historical, and graphical databases; and news, graphics, news video and news pictures. Approximately half a million users located in close to 60,000 organizations access Reuters information and news worldwide. Data are provided for over 400,000 shares, bonds, and financial instruments as well as for 40,000 companies. Reuters owns a stake in DataMonitor, Europe's largest provider of market analysis, and has a majority stake in the US-based TowerGroup, which provides internet financial services. In addition, Reuters is the world's largest news and television agency, with 2,035 journalists, photographers, and camera operators in 169 bureaus serving 163 countries. News is gathered and edited for both business and media clients in 25 languages. Approximately 10,000 stories made up of 1.5 to 2 million words are published daily. Because the national news agencies that distribute Reuters are permitted to resell the service, it is difficult to determine the precise number of subscribers to Reuters' service. Reuters is part-owner of the British Independent Television News (ITN) network and Worldwide Television News (WTN). Reuters also provides news and information to over 140 internet sites and reaches an estimated 10.9 million viewers a month. Reuters' services are delivered to clients over the world's most extensive satellite and cable communication networks.

Recently Reuters established a center in Bangalore, India. This new center is for outsourcing tasks usually performed in London or Washington. The Reuters editorial reference service unit from London and the daily news diary unit from Washington are being relocated to India to save money. Senior journalists within Reuters are concerned that outsourcing will move up the "food chain" over time and that the quality of editing as well as reporting on businesses will falter. Several current Reuters journalists are concerned about the future impact of the outsourcing practice.

Synopsis

Reuters established the first international wire service business. It had the major advantage of following the growth and spread of the British Empire around the world. It has continued to be the preeminent financial- and business-oriented global wire service, but when new markets emerge, Reuters also covers general or breaking news stories around the world, thanks to its enormous staff. Today it is a global media and financial conglomerate. Reuters was one of the first media firms to recognize the significance of the internet and to develop a broad range of internet services and sites. Finally, RTV is one of the two major global television news feeds, serving almost all major networks in Europe, North America, and elsewhere. Along with Associated Press, Reuters is the dominant global wire and video provider for almost all broadcasters and publishers.

The Associated Press

The Associated Press (AP) is another wire service with roots that date back to the mid-1800s. In May 1848, officials representing six New York City newspapers sat around a table at the *New York Sun*'s office discussing the high cost of collecting news, particularly from Europe, by telegraph. The newly invented telegraph made transmission of news possible by wire, but costs were so high that they strained the resources of any single paper. David Hale of the *Journal of Commerce* argued that only a joint effort among New York's papers could make the telegraph affordable and effectively prevent telegraph companies from economically constraining newsgathering. Although reluctant at first, the six highly competitive newspapers agreed to a historic cooperative plan, and AP was born.[3] AP was from the start a news cooperative and continues that unique ownership structure today. Over 1,550 member newspapers now own and control the not-for-profit cooperative.

One year after AP was established, Boston newspapers joined the New York founders of AP Regional. Newspaper groups soon followed – Western Associated Press, Southern Associated Press, Philadelphia Press, and several others. Washington and foreign news were staples from the start. In 1849, Daniel Craig established the Associated Press's foreign bureau in Halifax, Nova Scotia, the first North American port of call for Cunard's ocean liners. Headline news arrived from Europe with each incoming vessel and was telegraphed to New York. This was the practice until the establishment of the transatlantic cable in 1856, which made the Halifax port outmoded for news.

Today, AP's World Service distributes news and photos to 8,500 international subscribers and translates the report into 5 languages. In the United States, AP's board now consists of 18 newspapers. Other subscribers to the Associated Press are 5,700 US radio and television stations, plus 8,500 foreign newspaper, radio, and television operations. AP distributes information to 121 countries and has a full-time news and photo staff of about 1,100 domestically and 500 abroad. Approximately 8,500 international subscribers are clients for AP news and photos. It has won 28 Pulitzer Prizes for photography, the most for any news company.

AP expanded its services with a supplement called AP-DJ, a specialized financial and economic news service distributed abroad by a partnership of AP and Dow Jones & Company (DJ). Operating with the full economic coverage of AP and Dow Jones, supplemented by its own editorial and administrative staff, AP-DJ is distributed to private subscribers and the media in 43 countries. To meet the growing demand for sports coverage, in 1946 AP established the first news agency wire service dedicated entirely to sports. AP also published and circulated an annual AP sports almanac. Today, the sports wire and all other AP wires move at 9,600 words a minute.

In 1941 radio had become one of the most important means of communication in the United States, and AP was the broadcast pioneer. Between 1933 and 1941, AP's broadcast division had supplied news to radio stations owned by newspaper members only when the news was of major importance. But AP changed that by launching a separate radio broadcast wire called Circuit 7760, the first news organization to operate a broadcast news circuit 24 hours a day, 7 days a week. Just one year after Circuit 7760 was launched, AP's broadcast wire was serving more than 200 stations in 120 cities. AP continued to gain broadcast members, and in the 1940s the AP Radio network was launched. It provided hourly newscasts, sportscasts, and business programs to member radio stations and eventually became the first radio network in the world to be delivered by way of satellite. By 1979 the first news wire designed specifically for television stations was introduced.

AP's global video news was called APTN, after the purchase of WIN. It is currently Reuters' only major competitor. APTN has full-time video newsgathering facilities in 70 bureaus and has more than 300 clients, including ABC, NBC, CNN, CBS, FOX News channels, and Univision. APTN's primary service provides top international news stories as well as regional coverage in North America, Latin America, Asia, and Europe. By the mid-1990s, APTN provided video of the day's top news stories by satellite to broadcast organizations worldwide. APTN emphasizes enterprise journalism and the practice of telling the entire story in narrative form at critical moments in different international time zones.

Also by 1994, AP had launched AP All News Radio (ANR), a 24-hour-a-day radio newscast. ANR makes it possible for stations in all market sizes to carry the popular and profitable all-news format. Today, more than 50 radio stations are ANR affiliates, and they can easily insert local news and advertising into the ANR format. And finally APTV joined with Trans World International (TWI) in 1996 to launch SNTV, a sports news video agency. The partnership has claimed market leadership, drawing on the strengths of the world's largest newsgathering organization and the world's largest independent supplier of sports programming. SNTV currently serves over 300 broadcasters worldwide.

Because of the ever-changing newspaper and broadcast industry, AP remains a leader because of its new businesses and technological developments. Several new initiatives have enabled AP to support and enhance its worldwide newsgathering. For example, the agency sells packaged news to nonmembers such as governments and corporations. AP's Information Services Department sells to these clients AP Online, a group of subject-specific news wires tailored to each client's industry, public policy, or news needs. AP also sells photos to nonmembers through AP's Wide World subsidiary. AP Telecommunication is another subsidiary, which provides members and nonmembers data and network communication technologies. AP's AdSEND group speeds advertisements from agencies and retailers to newspapers as needed. In response to the widespread use of the internet, AP formed the

Multimedia Services Department for AP members to use on their homepages. In 1991, AP developed the AP Leaf Picture Desk so that nearly every newspaper in the United States could receive photos into a personal computer for editing and production. Also in 1991, AP's Graphics Bank became the first online graphics archive for television, using standard telephone lines. In 1994, AP introduced the first digital camera for photojournalists, called the AP News Camera 200. The Associated Press's news business developments are proving successful, and so is the agency's application of technological advances.

DataStream is AP's premier news service, which delivers an entire report of world, national, state, and sports news. Limited DataStream is tailored for midsize dailies that desire a complete news report but may have fewer resources on copy and wire desks. Limited DataStream with expanded sports provides enhanced sports content. AP Basic is tailored for smaller newspapers that emphasize local coverage but still need a high-speed wire with AP's depth and breadth of world, national, and state news. Dial-in Report is for very small newspapers that need a minimum of copy. Latin coverage, or the LatAm wire, provides coverage in Spanish of Mexico and other Latin American countries. AP's western regional service or West Wire, has a staff in 13 Western states that focuses on stories of high interest in the West.

AP's broadcast services include radio programming. Newsweek On Air and ENPS Newsweek On Air is a weekly one-hour syndicated radio program co-produced by the Associated Press and *Newsweek*. The program features the week's biggest news stories through interviews with newsmakers and *Newsweek* correspondents. ENPS is an electronic news production system, which will soon be the largest broadcast newsroom computer system in the world, linking radio and television journalists, production areas, and archives in more than 100 locations.

Synopsis

AP has integrated several major technical innovations into its various services, along with a broad array of wire-service-based news, photos, audio, and video feeds, including internet online services to clients around the globe. It is estimated that more than a billion people each day read, hear, see, or watch AP news or photos. AP has become North America's premier wire-service corporation. Its rise was accentuated by the financial problems faced by its one-time competitor, United Press International (UPI). With UPI floundering, AP's main global rival is Reuters, which offers competing services for almost every AP line from news to the internet. An issue of importance for the future of AP is the fact that some of the 1,550 US member newspaper owners are facing competition from other external media outlets, which are now purchasing some of AP's internet products. This strain on the cooperative may over time lead to ownership changes.

United Press International

The history of United Press International (UPI) goes back over 90 years. E. W. Scripps founded the United Press in 1907 to cover news from around the world. In 1935, United Press became the first major US news service to supply news to radio stations. In 1958, United Press merged with William Randolph Hearst's International News Service to become United Press International, or UPI. At that time, UPI was an aggressive and prestigious news service competing directly with AP. During the 1960s UPI had over 6,000 employees and more than 5,000 news subscribers. UPI began the first global wire-service radio network, providing radio stations with voice reports from correspondents around the globe. Several years later in the 1980s, the news service was the first in the industry to let subscribers choose and receive copy by topic and subtopic, rather than by a broad category only. At one point, UPI had over 1,200 radio clients. By 1995 the company completed a system for global satellite transmission that virtually eliminated the need to send news over telephone landlines. But management, ownership, and client problems forced UPI to cut back services. UPI's domestic news bureaus closed offices across the United States. The Washington DC bureau chief was Helen Thomas, UPI's longest-serving employee and a fixture at White House press conferences.

In 1999, UPI sold its broadcast news business to its one-time rival, AP, which picked up all US-based UPI radio and television clients. UPI is still struggling financially as it seeks a new electronic identity through internet activities; it now has fewer than 100 employees, based mainly in Washington DC, although it does have 6 other offices in Europe, Asia, South America, and the Middle East.

UPI was privately owned by a group of Saudi Arabian investors, but in 2000 it was sold to News World Communications (NWC), which is operated by the ultraconservative Unification Church. The sale prompted Helen Thomas to resign from UPI after 57 years. Since her resignation, more clients have declined to use UPI. The Unification Church, NWC's parent, was founded and is still run by the Reverend Sun Myung Moon. Reverend Moon specializes in sensational journalism with an extremely conservative slant. NWC publishes 20 newspapers worldwide, including *The Washington Times*. Rev. Moon is a wildly grandiose figure who for several decades has publicly proclaimed that he is the second coming of the Christian messiah. He also enjoys conducting mass marriages of his "moonie" followers.

Agence France Presse

Agence France Presse (AFP) is the world's third largest wire service, after Reuters and AP. AFP is the world's oldest news agency, dating from 1835, and is one of the world's largest wire services providing full-text articles to its clients. AFP covers politics, economic affairs, diplomacy, culture, science, international, national, business, and sports news written by journalists and correspondents in Europe, the Middle East, North America, South America, and Africa.[4] Many of the bureaus are still based in former colonies of France or in cities where Reuters and AP have competing bureaus.

AFP has bureaus in 110 countries and operates in 165, and it employs 1,200 staff journalists and photographers, along with 2,000 stringers, reporting out of almost every country in the world. Of these correspondents, 102 are stationed in peripheral nations (22 in Latin America and Mexico and 80 in Africa and Asia). AFP's coverage is not a lucrative proposition, but the agency's operations are subsidized by the income from the many official French government and embassy subscriptions. The English-language service is distributed worldwide and includes reports, roundups, analyses, and news. Subscribers to AFP include 7,000 newspapers and 2,500 radio and television stations.

Starting in January 1997, the AFP news feed was integrated into Bloomberg's multipanel information screen, produced in London on the European Canal Satellite. The Canal Satellite is an all-digital French direct broadcast channel on several different cable services. The agency also distributes selected news stories from AP. AFP runs the fastest-reaching network of any other news service, providing unmatched depth and breadth of coverage from regions where the other services are weak or absent. AFP is recognized as the premier supplier of information from Asia, Africa, and Arab-speaking nations.

Over the years, AFP has proved itself a leader in journalistic enterprise. For example, it was the first to announce the deaths of Stalin, Pope John Paul I, and Indira Gandhi. AFP has earned many compliments and awards for its continued coverage of some of the world's biggest stories including the 1999 war in the former Yugoslavia and the conflict in Chechnya.

Today, the agency continues to expand worldwide, reaching thousands of subscribers (radio, television, newspapers, companies) from its main headquarters in Paris and regional centers in Washington DC, Hong Kong,

Nicosia, and Montevideo. All share the same goal – to guarantee a top-quality international service tailored to the specific needs of clients in each region. They also do more reporting from peripheral nations than any other global service.

Bloomberg

Bloomberg was established in New York in October 1981 by Michael Bloomberg when he formed Innovative Market Systems, which in 1986 became known as Bloomberg LP.[5] After 15 years with the investment firm Salomon Brothers, Bloomberg identified the need for a business press suited to around-the-clock global financial information. He started from New York, but by 1987 was opening world offices, first in London, then in Australia in 1989, and the business has continued to grow worldwide since then. Bloomberg news is available in five languages: English, French, Spanish, German, and Japanese; it provides services to over 260,000 users in over 125 countries. The focus of its coverage is in economics, business, financial markets, technology, and global stock-markets and trends.

The first Bloomberg television product, launched in 1994, was called Bloomberg Business News, followed by Bloomberg Information TV, and finally European Bloomberg Information TV. Bloomberg Television is a 24-hour financial news channel that reports the economic and political news that affects markets. Its unique TV Data Screen provides financial data and breaking news headlines at all times, even during commercials. It draws on the vast resources of the global Bloomberg organization, including more than 1,600 reporters and editors in 94 bureaus around the world. Bloomberg Television reaches over 100 million TV-watching households through national cable distribution, the USA Network, DIRECTV, and the Bloomberg service, and it airs three half-hour television shows: Bloomberg Business News, Bloomberg Personal, and Bloomberg Small Business. Bloomberg Television offers the top 50 major news stories each half-hour, around the clock. As mentioned earlier, since 1997 Bloomberg has integrated a major news feed from AFP into its multipanel information screen. The news feed is produced in London and aired on Canal Satellite, the all-digital French direct broadcast system. CEO Bloomberg, who is also the mayor of New York City, owns 72 percent of the firm, Merrill Lynch owns 20 percent, and Bloomberg employees hold 8 percent.

Besides their media endeavors, Bloomberg is also a supporter of modern art. In 2002, the company opened Bloomberg SPACE, a public gallery located at Bloomberg's headquarters in London.

Bloomberg is a latecomer to the global wire and video service business. Yet it came into the business at a fortuitous time and has an entrepreneurial leader in Michael Bloomberg. With the expansion of cable channels, particularly all-news, and the internet, Bloomberg has found a ready market and a viable niche. The company's various services, with a clear economic focus, are available to clients who reside nearly exclusively in core and semiperipheral nations. As peripheral nations become economically viable and interact with greater frequency with core-based enterprises, subscribing to Bloomberg will make sense, particularly for government and business leaders.

Dow Jones & Company

Founded in 1882, Dow Jones & Company (DJC) has been publishing the major global newspaper of business, *The Wall Street Journal*, since 1889. In 1976 the company began the *Asian Wall Street Journal* and in 1983, *Wall Street Journal Europe*. DJC also publishes major financial magazines such as *Barron's*, since 1921, and the *Far Eastern Economic Review*, since 1946. In the 1990s, DJC started a joint venture in Russia, where it publishes *Hedomosti*. DJC also controls the Ottaway newspaper chain with 19 dailies and 15 weekly newspapers in the United States. With its financial orientation, Dow Jones competes directly with Bloomberg for the corporate and government clientele. On the electronic side, the Dow Jones news wires have over a million subscribers globally. Dow Jones also owns half of CNBC Europe and CNBC Asia. In 1999 DJC joined with Reuters to establish a new interactive electronic global service for business information to corporate and professional clients.

In late 2004, DJC won a fierce bidding war to acquire MarketWatch Inc., a highly profitable online financial news and information provider, for $519 million. MarketWatch's two sites are the popular CBS MarketWatch and BigCharts.com, and combined they attract 8 million unique visitors per month.

Finally, DJC is known for its Dow Jones Industrial Average (DJIA), which was established in 1896 and consists of a pool of 30 blue-chip US stocks. The DJIA appears globally in newspapers and magazines, and on radio and television business programs. It recently removed Chrysler Corporation from its portfolio when Chrysler merged with Daimler-Benz of Germany, because the DJIA only covers US-owned blue-chip stocks. Also in 1999, DJIA made one of the biggest changes in its 103-year history. Originally, only New York Stock Exchange stocks were included in the 30 stocks that make up the DJIA barometer. Now the Chicago-based NASDAQ stock-market has 2 in the list of 30: Microsoft and Intel. Also added were Home Depot and SBC. The four stocks dropped to make room for the newcomers were Chevron, Sears, Union Carbide, and Goodyear. All four had been in the DJIA since at least 1930. Even Woolworth Corp. was dropped in 1997 to make room for Wal-Mart Stores. In 1991, Walt Disney joined the index as US Steel was dropped. General Electric joined the index in 1928. News Corp., Viacom, Google, and Time Warner are not on the index, nor is any advertising agency.

Currently, the 2005 DJIA consists of the following major US blue-chip stocks: Alcoa, Altria, American Express, American International, Boeing, Caterpillar, Citigroup, Coca-Cola, Disney, DuPont, Exxon Mobil, General Electric (parent of NBC Universal), General Motors, Hewlett-Packard, Home Depot, Honeywell, IBM, Intel, J. P. Morgan Chase, Johnson & Johnson, McDonald's, Merck, Microsoft, Pfizer, Procter & Gamble, SBC, 3M, United Technologies, Verizon, and Wal-Mart. The DJIA reflects the evolution in the US economy from industrial society to an information, media, and high-technology orientation. Also, all 30 firms have significant global activities and all are major stakeholders in the global economy. The next round of changes will likely see additional information-based corporations added.

Xinhua

China's leading integrated news company is the Xinhua News Agency. It is striving for a global role by delivering media services to the regions of China through print and the internet, as well as online advertising and web solutions throughout Asia. Xinhua was established in 1931 and is the state news agency of the People's Republic of China. It is headquartered in Beijing and operates a large number of bureaus in China and globally. Xinhua employs more than 7,000 journalists who report on Chinese and world affairs. It publishes several periodicals, has a public-relations group, and runs a journalism school. Xinhua is tightly controlled and watched by senior Chinese government officials, particularly in the wake of the violent suppression of protesters in Tiananmen Square. Xinhua is known for its long, dull articles that avoid any criticism of Chinese government officials or actions, and "all foreign news made available to Chinese publications and broadcasters is first processed by Xinhua translators and editors."[6] In addition to its print products, Xinhua is moving into internet activities, but its content is still dull and heavily censored.

Inter Press Services

Inter Press Services (IPS) was started in 1964 by Roberto Savio in Rome. IPS has become a major news agency and has developed into an innovative system for intercultural communication. The agency operates in a manner different from other global news services by promoting a horizontal flow of news on a cooperative basis among developing countries; it also distributes information about developing-nation clients to industrialized countries. IPS is a worldwide, nonprofit association of journalists and others in the field of journalism that aims to promote a global communication strategy. That strategy is to bring together civil societies, policy-makers, and national and international media.[7]

IPS operations consist of IPS News, IPS Telecommunications, and IPS Projects. IPS News service is an independent global news wire. IPS Telecommunications offers technical expertise for the upgrading of developing nations' communication and information infrastructures. IPS Projects was established to design, manage, and report on projects in the fields of training, information and exchange, and increasing public and media awareness of the importance of global issues.

IPS also has connections with nongovernmental organizations (NGOs). For the most part, NGOs have gained widespread recognition for their work with the poor and the oppressed. NGOs have developed as important and increasingly major actors within certain societies, which are mainly in peripheral nations. IPS and NGOs have developed a strategy for cooperation in the twenty-first century. The strategy consists of five major objectives:

- To be active and useful instruments for linking NGOs from the South (mostly peripheral nations) and from the North;
- To identify suitable partners among development NGOs in the South and their counterparts in the North, which can help strengthen IPS's reporting on self-reliant, grassroots development;
- To use NGOs in the South as privileged sources of news for the media of the North, and to disseminate news of relevance to NGOs from the North to the South;
- To cooperate with NGOs of the South in offering services that can improve their presence in the North and in the media of the North;
- To offer a forum for joint discussion between NGOs and IPS management staff and journalists on innovative ways to report development action from a grassroots perspective.

A network of journalists in more than 100 countries backs IPS, with satellite communication links to 1,000 outlets. In addition, IPS has regional editorial centers that operate in Africa, Asia, the Caribbean, Europe, Latin America, and North America. More than 250 journalists provide news and information services. To date, IPS has two-thirds of its correspondents in peripheral nations who are natives of the countries in which they work. IPS focuses its news coverage on events and the global processes affecting the economic, social, and political development of peoples and nations. IPS reports more than news that is considered "emergency" or negative news; its stories concentrate on issues such as the gap between rich and poor, international trade negotiations, human rights, refugees and international migration patterns, conflict and peacekeeping, environmental protection and sustainable development, population issues, and international debt crises. The IPS World Service news report is delivered via satellite to subscribers. These services are available through online computer facilities, electronic databases, and printed bulletins. An Asian television station also uses IPS feature stories as pegs for documentaries.

IPS products include printed publications, bulletins, columns, and tele-communications. It operates five newspapers under its printed publications division. *Terra Viva Conference Daily* is an independent tabloid newspaper published during major UN conferences such as the 1996 World Food Summit in Rome Terra Viva. *Europe Daily Journal* is produced at the United Nations in New York. Contents include a daily faxed selection of highlights from the IPS wire aimed at policy-makers and decision-makers. The *G-77 Journal* is published for the 77 developing countries within the UN system. *IPS Features* is a package of 10 IPS features, special reports, and columns mailed to media clients in the Pacific Rim region. *Rural Development* is a monthly bulletin produced by IPS Africa and the weekly *Africa Bulletin*. News and information covered in the bulletins includes developments, drugs, human rights, religious affairs, environment, investment, energy, population, arts and entertainment, technology, and Latin American integration. The IPS Columnist Service provides a series of exclusive columns written by statesmen and stateswomen, officials, opposition leaders, opinion-makers, leading cultural figures, and experts offering insight on major issues. The last product offered by IPS is a telecommunications carrier service, an international information carrier for a variety of organizations.

In conclusion, IPS represents a model of development journalism. It seeks out positive development news from and among peripheral nations. IPS has found an ally in NGOs, and they work together to assist peripheral-nation causes and activities. IPS is seldom used by major core newspapers or broadcasters.

Conclusions

The major global news agencies operate in a highly competitive environment. On a daily basis, the Associated Press competes with Reuters and to a lesser extent with Bloomberg and Agence France Presse. Both AP and Reuters have added television news services as part of their product lines. Collectively, they also are active in internet services. New services with a financial focus, such as Bloomberg and Dow Jones, appear to be thriving, while historically broad service companies such as UPI appear to be in organizational and fiscal crises.

The major services are all based in industrial, core nations, with an extensive bureau network in other core nations and nearly all semiperipheral nations. The peripheral regions lack bureaus, have only stringers, or are inundated with core news crews when a major coup, earthquake, or bizarre event occurs that affects the core nations' interests or catches editors' attention.

The wire services will in all likelihood continue to thrive and even grow in influence as the cost of placing foreign correspondents abroad escalates rapidly. Many managing editors now are willing to accept wire-service copy or news footage from outside organizations such as RTV or APTN rather than have to bear the expense of placing correspondents abroad. With modern airline transportation and satellite feeds, major news outlets dispatch reporters abroad on a crisis-by-crisis basis instead of having a large number of foreign bureaus. This practice is frequently referred to as "parachute journalism." Finally, networks and others let CNN set the agenda, so when CNN covers a foreign news story, the other networks and services simply match the coverage. But if CNN does not cover a foreign event, the event most likely will go unreported by other major media outlets, such as some of the civil wars and famines in Africa.

Electronic colonialism permeates the wire services, which both directly and indirectly promote a core-based focus and emphasis in reporting values. Their journalists, editors, and management are almost all products of elite universities, have a superb command of the English language, and enjoy decent – and in some cases substantial – salaries. This group is not about to promote a revolution or seriously question the economic structure of the global economy that is providing them and their firms with a sound financial future. This in part accounts for the emphasis on financial news and information, rather than on general-interest news, detailed pieces on major social problems, or development issues. Although the wire services were major players in the early days of the NWICO debate, they now completely ignore the debate and concerns raised by either peripheral nations or academic critics from core nations. Their philosophy and outlook is straightforward: basically, they do what they do because it works and is profitable.

They are encouraging their own lifestyle and outlook in other nations, particularly in semiperipheral and peripheral regions, so that these areas become future customers for their expanding range of services, which are quickly morphing into internet e-journalism product lines.

By default they are leaving to the newly emerging blogging world on the internet many stories which the wire services now consider too controversial. More is discussed about the blogging phenomenon in chapter 12, dealing with the internet and related issues.

Notes

1 Oliver Boyd-Barnett, *The International News Agencies* (London: Constable, 1980); William Hachten, *The World News Prism* (Ames, IA: Iowa State University Press, 1999); Peter Golding and Phil Harris, eds., *Beyond Cultural Imperialism: Globalization, Communication and the New International Order* (Thousand Oaks, CA: Sage, 1997), by the same authors, "How News is Shaped," *Journalism and Mass Communication Quarterly* 77(2) (Summer 2000), pp. 223–72.

2 Donald Read, *The Power of News: The History of Reuters* (Oxford: Oxford University Press, 1992).

3 Oliver Gramling, *AP: The Story of News* (New York: Farrar and Rinehart, 1940); Peter Arnet, Vincent Alabiso, Chuck Zoeller, and Kelly Smith-Tunney, eds., *Flash! Associated Press Covers the World* (New York: Harry N. Abrams Press, 1998).

4 Jean Huteau, *AFP: une histoire de l'Agence France-Presse: 1944–1990* (Paris: R. Laffont, 1992).

5 Michael Bloomberg and Matthew Winkler, *Bloomberg by Bloomberg* (New York: John Wiley, 1998).

6 Jon Swan, "I Was a 'Polisher' in a Chinese News Factory," *Columbia Journalism Review* (March/April 1996), p. 27.

7 Much of IPS's coverage focuses on major United Nations conferences dealing with global topics. An examination of amount and kind of coverage provided by IPS, AP, and Reuters is found in C. Anthony Gifford, "The Beijing Conference on Women as Seen by Three International News Agencies," *Gazette* 61 (July 1999), pp. 327–41.

Chapter 8

Media in the Middle East and North Africa

by Ralph Berenger

Introduction

Long-time observers of the Middle East mediascape have never been more optimistic. Change, they sense, is in the wind. This is coming at a time when the region is a source of major news events on a daily basis. Iraq, Iran, Israel, Palestine, Saudi Arabia, oil, war, and tensions catch the front pages and newscasts around the globe. The regional Arab television network, Al Jazeera, is now one of the most recognized media outlets in the world.

Once dominated by protocol news, low production values, stale and sterile reporting of insignificant events, official secrecy and censorship, and tightfisted government control of news and information, Middle East media are moving slowly toward a form of journalism most Westerners would recognize, the so-called international standard of objective journalism, as practiced mostly by the United Kingdom, the United States, and other core countries.

Considerable technological advances have taken place in international broadcasting. This advent of transnational and global broadcasting has insinuated the region into the worldwide public consciousness. For the Arab world the "Al Jazeera Effect" has replaced the "CNN Effect,"[1] and the ripples of change are spreading through the region. Each year another private broadcasting facility or privately operated newspaper appears, and advertising is increasingly becoming a media staple on international satellite channels. Now most companies enter the satellite realms for prestige, national honor, or as a public-relations gesture.

Mass media is an essential component of the creation and survival of democracy in the Middle East/North Africa (MENA) region (also known as the Arab World or Islamic World after the dominant ethnic group and religion). This feature has long been a goal of successive US administrations as a way of stabilizing the volatile oil-rich region. Open news and entertainment media, free of governmental intervention or intimidation, are essential to the exchange of free ideas, transparent government, and liberal economies, which along with free elections and an independent judiciary are the key elements of democracy. Since the 2003 Iraq war, for example, between 100 and 200 newspapers, circulars, and magazines were started throughout that country, varying widely in quality, according to one press account.[2]

Nowhere has international media taken off so rapidly in recent years as in the MENA, home to 480 million Arabs, Jews, Africans, and Persians in the broadly defined 26-country region that mainly follows the Mediterranean from the Straits of Gibraltar to Turkey, and from the Red Sea to the Indian Ocean down to Comoros islands.[3] In percentage terms the region is one of the world's fastest growing places for adopting the mechanisms of international communication: satellite dishes, mobile telephony, computers, televisions, and internet service providers. But in the race for modernity, the region started well behind the pack and has considerable ground to make up. Despite the gains of recent years, MENA remains on the lower end of the knowledge-gap chart, just above Sub-Saharan Africa, its southern neighbor. (See figure 8.1.)

To close the knowledge gap, the United Nations Development Program has called for "exponential growth" in knowledge acquisition, creation, delivery and utilization systems, most notably mass-media and education institutions.[4] Given the growing popularity of American-style higher education in the region and new transnational publishing and broadcasting systems, the beginning of an exponential curve might well be underway. But seeing the task to completion will be daunting as it involves politics, religion, and altering the schema of most of the people in the region and their leaders. Yet it is only by embracing modernization, including a free press, that some in the MENA region will be able to secure core status in the foreseeable future.

The arc of instability, turmoil, conflict, crisis, and despair

Hardly a daily broadcast of international news anywhere in the world fails to mention the Middle East or North Africa region. Among the story lines are speculation about war or peace, the disparity between the rich and poor, rising or slumping oil prices, religious factionalism and fanaticism, the excesses

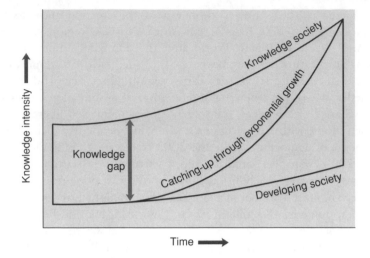

Figure 8.1 Exponential growth needed to close the knowledge gap
Source: UNDP Arab Human Development Report 2003 (New York: United Nations), p. 40. Reproduced by kind permission.

of the oil-rich elites, support or rejection of terrorism, demonstrations of anti-American, anti-Israel, anti-Western sentiment, sectarian violence, and suppression of females through culture and in practice. The United States and allies have sent more troops to the region than any other place since the 1970s as combatants in Iraq, Kuwait, and Somalia, and peacekeepers in Egypt's Sinai, Lebanon, Saudi Arabia, Bahrain, Qatar, Eritrea, Sudan, Ethiopia, Morocco, and Israel. American and British warships cruise the Persian Gulf, the Red Sea, the Mediterranean, and the Indian Ocean – available to evacuate nationals from trouble spots or provide humanitarian assistance, as has happened in Somalia, Bangladesh, and innumerable islands affected by the 2004 Christmas tsunami. The US Navy's Fifth Fleet is based in Bahrain.

MENA is the heart of what various scholars and internationalists have called the "arc of turmoil," the "arc of instability," the "arc of crisis," "the arc of conflict," or the "arc of despair." Generally, the various arcs form an s-wave swath from Western Sahara, through North Africa and the Middle East, down the Red Sea and bending northward through Arabia and into Pakistan and Bangladesh to Indonesia. Some scholars have various arcs extending from Moscow to Rwanda, but all run through the Middle East. The mediascape of MENA countries shares several common characteristics:

1. Egypt, 76.1 million	6. Algeria, 32.1 million
2. Iran, 69 million	7. Saudi Arabia, 25.8 million
3. Ethiopia, 67.9 million	8. Iraq, 25.4 million
4. Sudan, 39.1 million	9. Yemen, 20 million
5. Morocco, 32.2 million	10. Tunisia, 10 million

Figure 8.2 Most populated countries in the MENA region in 2004
Source: CIA Factbook.

- Generally low median ages and high youth unemployment often lead to civil unrest in the "Arab Street," a media construct that often substitutes for public opinion research in the Arab press;
- They have lower education levels, especially for females, than most regions of the world;
- Media markets are highly dynamic;
- Newspaper readership per thousand of population is low because of high illiteracy rates;
- Each country has suffered a "brain drain," particularly of scientists and technicians, lured to the West by quality education, higher salaries and intellectual freedom;
- Broadcast rather than printed messages have greater population penetration, but the number of radio and television receivers still lags behind the developed world. FM dominates AM and short wave as the type of radio medium most preferred;
- Islam is MENA's dominant religion, though measurable percentages of Christians and Jews can be found in most populations, sometimes as the majority;
- News reporting tends to be narrative and descriptive rather than interpretative or analytical. News is presented as a succession of isolated and unrelated events that make audience comprehension and schema-building difficult;[5]
- To varying degrees they all have militant Islamist movements, which have filled the void left by the collapse of the Soviet Union in 1991, and the political suppression of the nonsecular Arab Left;
- Through cultivation by political and social forces, there is a general distrust of the West, with some historical justification, and Western media products, which are selectively censored. News critical of the region is personalized and generally discounted as propaganda;

- They all have an inordinate desire "to correct false images" of the region in Western media; particularly movies, they feel, "tarnish the image of Arabs." Scholars have been jailed for presenting papers or addresses at academic conferences critical of regimes in their country for "tarnishing" their countries' image abroad;[6]
- Limited personal freedoms of expression are partly caused by social customs but mostly by government suppression;
- While relying on foreign-produced media products, technologies, and expertise, international influence appears to be ebbing as local technology and talent improves;
- They have low levels of formal education, averaging from less than 2 years in Somalia, Sudan, Ethiopia and Mauritania, to around 6 years for the total populations over age 25. By contrast Israel has an average of 9.23 years, and the United States has 12.25 years for the same population group;[7]
- They have mostly state-operated media, especially terrestrial broadcast systems, upon which the majority of citizens rely for news and entertainment;
- Regional channels such as Al Jazeera and Al Arabiya are regarded as "local" and thus are preferred over CNN International and BBC World Service, and even their own national channels;[8]
- Half to two-thirds of the population are under 30, and programs targeted to them by international broadcasters are popular. This has been called "The Radio Sawa Phenomenon";[9]
- Few women are in leadership or management positions, and men dominate reporting roles by wide margins in most countries;[10]
- All countries have been created, colonized, administered, influenced, or occupied within the last 150 years by Europeans, whose legacy includes the region's various forms of mass media in Arabic, Persian, Berber, and other indigenous languages, as well as in English, French, and German;
- All suffer under authoritarian regimes and leaders, many with secret police or security forces to spy on their fellow citizens, and which have weak opposition parties, if any, though the trend in some countries has been toward economic and political liberalization and transparency, if not democracy;
- Stubbornly poor economic conditions plague half the total population – over 200 million people – who earn less than US$2 a day, while some elite families are among the world's richest.

Over the last generation, MENA has spawned tyrants and terrorists that Western or core nations' governments fear since they threaten stability, if not the modern technological civilization itself.[11] All of the 9/11 hijackers came from Egypt or Saudi Arabia, as did their spiritual, financial, and strategic leader, Osama bin Laden. The plans for the March 11, 2004, Madrid train bombing were hatched by Moroccan terrorists with links to the shadowy Al Qaeda terrorist organization. The Palestinian suicide bombings in Israel, which precipitated steel-handed responses in the occupied territories of the Gaza Strip and West Bank of the Jordan River that destroyed homes and uprooted olive groves, were steered through various jihadist organizations, including Hezbollah and Hamas, which support through words and deeds continued violence in the occupied territories of Palestine and in Israel itself. Many of these factions, especially in Lebanon, have their own print and broadcast outlets. Hezbollah, for example, operates Al Manar satellite channel, which is more critical and harsher on the US and Israel than other Arab satellite channels. Al Manar has greater viewership among the dispersed Palestinian diaspora than other Arab nationalities.

Scatterings of jihadist groups bent on fulfilling Huntington's clash-of-civilization prophecy are active throughout the region.[12] Arab governments in the region had declared three wars on Israel since its founding in 1948 (1948, 1967, and 1973) before settling into a protracted guerrilla war which various Arab neighbors seem unwilling to end. Israel continues to be blamed in the conspiracy-minded Arab press for plane crashes, corruption, economic conditions, and any social disorder. A large percentage of the Arab population, for example, still believes Israel was behind the 9/11 attacks and the crash of Egyptian Air 900. The Arab media do little to dispel these public misperceptions, and often disseminate them without fact-checks.

Meanwhile brutal strongmen such as Khadafy in Libya, the al-Assad family in Syria, numerous warlords in Somalia and parts of the Sudan, and until recently Saddam Hussein in Iraq each held on to absolute power for over a generation. Most MENA countries have a mixed bag of authoritarian leadership. Most are titular republics such as Algeria, Egypt, Lebanon, Libya, Eritrea, Ethiopia, Mauritania, Sudan, Syria, Tunisia, and Yemen. Some have monarchies such as Bahrain, Jordan, Kuwait, Morocco, and Saudi Arabia, or emirs such as Qatar (home to Al Jazeera) and United Arab Republic. Others are struggling out of "failed states" like the Western Sahara and Somalia (including a breakaway, unrecognized republic, Somaliland, which has its own government and media systems). Recognizable democracies can be counted on one finger: Israel. All press systems mirror their governments in the degree of openness and transparency they will allow. What freedoms exist, with the exception of Israel and increasingly the Emirates, come from the largess of regimes in power. As we shall see, press systems generally reflect the aspirations of those regimes.

A presidential assassination – at times the succession method of choice in the region since free and fair elections are illusory – plunged Lebanon into a 17-year civil war beginning in 1975. The effects can be seen today on the streets of Beirut and the careful, politically correct discourse of the Lebanese who survived it. Saddam Hussein led his peoples into disastrous wars, which are the lengthy war (1980–8) against Iran, and Gulf Wars I (1990–1) and II (2004) against predominantly Anglo-American forces. Between the final two, Saddam turned his military and security forces lose on Shi'ah Muslims in the South, and Kurds in the North, reportedly killing thousands of his own people who tried to rebel against what they had wrongly assumed was his weakened rule.[13] In 2000, Yasser Arafat, the late president of the Palestinian Authority, urged his people to rebel against Israeli occupation of the West Bank and Gaza Strip. That Intifada has had a devastating impact on the psyche of the region, and colors almost any media discussion of regional tranquility. The Palestinian issue "has poisoned the air" in the Middle East and has become an excuse by states not to move forward with modernity, personal freedoms, free press, and democracy, which surveys have shown as top priorities of the majority of the residents in the region *after successful resolution* of the Palestine issue. While Islamists seek comfort in the seventh-century customs and clarity attributed to the Holy Koran and the traditions of the Prophet Muhammad, intellectuals and scholars pine for a return of a golden age like that in the tenth through fifteenth centuries, when the region led the world in philosophy, chemistry, political economy, literature, medicine, pharmacology, science, astronomy, and agriculture.

A legacy of knowledge acquisition and distribution

Once benefiting from its geopolitical position as the gateway to European markets for the riches of the silk- and spice-rich Orient carried in caravans and ships, the region traded equally with the Far East, Africa, Near East, and emerging cultures in central and western Europe.

The Middle East emerged as the world's center of knowledge, brimming with intellectuals, linguists, and teachers of sciences and the arts in the eleventh through fifteenth centuries, such as Nizam al-Mulk Tusi, who wrote an influential book on government and statecraft centuries before Machiavelli, and in the eleventh century started the *madrassa* education system that exists today throughout the Islamic World. Abu Hamid al-Ghazali used Aristotelian and neo-Platonic arguments to reconcile Islam, philosophy, and Sufism in the twelfth century. Ibn Khaldun, the polymathic intellectual who was equally articulate in history, political science, and sociology, espoused economic principles that presaged by nearly five centuries similar views by Adam Smith in *The Wealth of Nations.* Ibn Taghribirdi, a fifteenth-century historian and linguist, wrote definitive histories of Islamic military techniques, and is highly regarded as one of the premier historians of the early Ottoman Empire. To name a few.

Arabs gave the world the concept of zero and the base-10 mathematics system, algebra, geometry, the mariner's compass and astrolabe that contributed to the European navigational feats of the fifteenth century, and new forms of literature and storytelling that revolutionized medieval literature. Arabs perfected printing papers and maintained a near monopoly on the process, selling reams at a premium price to sixteenth-century European printers. Today's printing term for quality paper, *bagdhadi*, pays homage to the center of the paper-making art. The Middle East had universities considerably older than those in Europe, and a near-reverence for the printed word – in any language. In fact, while European Christians were burning the ancient Greek manuscripts as heretical in the Dark Ages, Arab scholars were translating into Arabic every Greek manuscript they could find.

The Caliph of Cordoba in Spain reputedly had a personal library of over 200,000 such translated volumes.[14] Much of what the world knows today about Plato, Aristotle, Herodotus, and the Greek playwrights, came from the rediscovered books safely preserved by a Muslim that were retranslated from either Greek or Arabic into Latin and the European languages during the Renaissance, and reproduced throughout Europe in the sixteenth and seventeenth centuries by replicas of Gutenberg's recently invented printing press.

By the late eighteenth and early nineteenth centuries, European growth of development of science and technology, literature, and military might eclipsed the social development in the Middle East. Eventually, the Europeans exploited the weakness of the Ottoman Empire and colonized the Middle East, bringing with them the instruments of mass communication. Napoleon, for example, introduced the first printing press and newspaper in Egypt in the early 1800s, a technology that was readily adapted by other Middle Eastern population centers.

Theories of the Arab press

With few exceptions, the MENA media follow an authoritarian model of the *Four Theories of the Press* by Siebert, Peterson, and Schramm.[15] Most media scholars in the region find simple description of media types in the Middle East too broad to be of much value.

In his functionalist analysis in *Arab Mass Media*, former US ambassador to Yemen, William A. Rugh (2004), thinks the newspapers in the region break down into four subcategories under the authoritarian model: mobilization, loyalist, transitional, and diverse. While Rugh was writing about daily newspapers, which offer considerably more diversity than state-controlled broadcast media, the ideological underpinnings could well apply cross media.

Mobilization press

Despite differences in age, size, and quality, media in this press type share certain characteristics: they may or may not be owned by political agents loyal to the government and they refuse to criticize the central government. Municipal problems can be reported on and minor national figures criticized, but scrutiny stops well below the governing regime because of censorship, rarely overtly applied. The red lines are clearly understood and respected by all. The media are nationalistic and rarely send mixed messages about the direction of national policy. Government regards them as tools to mobilize populations to behave in ways desired by government, a near-classic definition of the goals of propaganda.

Loyalist press

Media in these countries are fiercely loyal to the regime in power regardless of the type of ownership. In fact, wealthy elites or members of royal families own many publications and have a stake in successful outcomes of governmental policies. In addition to outside financial support, governments are the largest sources of advertising revenue and publishing subsidies and thus are able to reward and punish publications financially as a method of control in addition to various press laws that can restrict information and operations.

Transitional press

The status of media in countries with this media type is debatable, and careful readers can discern slight movement toward liberalization. Government might control outright all broadcast media and most of the print media, though some political parties and private individuals might also own newspapers and magazines. While the publications editorially cherish free speech as an ideal, in practice they are careful what they say about the ruling elite, who use various public laws to delimit free speech. Some private ownership is occurring, but at a slow pace. While opposition parties criticize policy, they never criticize the military, security forces, or the top ruling elites. In Egypt criticism of the minority Copts can result in newspaper closure by government, as happened in 2002 when a popular press printed dozens of pictures off a videotape of a defrocked Coptic monk *in flagrante delicto* with different women in his bedroom. Copies of *Al Nabaa*,[16] a sensational publication, were confiscated off newsstands, and the publication was fined and suspended. Governments in these countries also exercise controls by owning printing companies that can restrict newsprint consumption; licensing processes for reporters and media companies that are expensive and restrictive; space band restrictions; and even enactment of emergency laws such as the 1967 law has been renewed recently in Egypt that essentially restricts free reporting and publication.

Diverse press

Media in this category are a mixed bag of group and private ownership that has appeared late in the last century. They are diverse because they are distinctively different from one another in content, quality, political orientation, and style, according to Rugh. Though still under the authoritarian press model, media in this group demonstrate the best and worst journalism has to offer. While some countries' media have characteristics of the other media models, careful readers can detect a difference. There are some movements toward a less controlled press, as in the case of the Lebanon *Daily Star*, which prints the Middle East edition of the *International Herald Tribune* and inserts a four-page local edition of the *Star* for weekly regional distribution. As in the other models the media exercise self-censorship, though the breadth and scope of media criticism varies country to country. In all countries there are prohibitions, legally defined or understood, against criticizing the head of state or Islam, or promoting civil disorder. Some have specific domestic taboos, such as criticizing Syria for occupying parts of Lebanon and occasionally interfering in Lebanese political life.

Liberal-democratic press

If Americans could read Hebrew or any of the other dozen languages of newspapers in Israel they would be familiar with the daily and weekly print media. News organizations are tough, independent, and at times skeptical of government pronouncements. They are free from government control, they are careful about providing opposing viewpoints in their articles and finding multiple corroborating sources for controversial stories. Their professionalism protects the reader from overtly biased news coverage, and the media organizations are protected by an independent judiciary that tends to uphold the media's liberal-democratic ideals, as it did in 1988 when it supported a *Ha'aretz* reporter in a libel suit brought by soon-to-be prime minister Ariel Sharon. Arab critics note that the Israeli press has not been as rigorous as it ought to be in covering the ongoing destruction of Palestinian houses and olive groves, and the killing of bystanders in retaliation raids on the part of the Israeli Defense Force.

Rugh admits categorizing media in different countries with various social orders into four categories, namely mobilization, loyalist, transitional, and diverse, is difficult. Often the lines that distinguish one category from another can blur under different circumstances. Some Arab scholars have criticized Rugh's taxonomy as insufficiently specific or quantitative, while others have suggested the ambassador's Western orientation overlooks a more moralistic and self-responsible model. Still others say the Middle East's sociolinguistic patterns and geography should have been taken into account, since lumping Morocco (from the Maghreb), Lebanon (from the Mashreq), and Kuwait (from the Gulf) as diverse media types makes little sense because the regions are so different. Another criticism is that the Rugh taxonomy categorizes media based on one variable, their relationship to government, and not the type of news and editorial comments those media make.[17]

The Nature of Arab News

News is whatever a news organization says it is. By that definition if events go unreported in the media they cannot be news. All news stories are social constructs. A reporter's personal schema and *weltanschauung* determines what he or she will write. Their editors' similar orientation will determine what that publication or broadcast station will brand as news for its readers, viewers, and listeners. In other words, what is or is not news in the Middle East is dependent on factors other than the significance, proximity, interest, and timeliness of the event itself, which Western journalists and editors define as news.

What often puzzles Western journalists is what the state-influenced media decide is news. They are even more perplexed about what is not considered. East and West, clearly, have different journalistic traditions and different ideas of what the public ought to know.

Most Western journalists, you have already read, hold objectivity as an important newsroom value. They try to report information truthfully, fairly, with balanced points of view, and with no apparent bias. That is the international standard now being taught in journalism education programs in the West and increasingly in the Middle East as well. However, the Middle East journalist scoffs at the notion of objectivity, and in fact believes such a rarified idea exists nowhere but in Western media myth. As the Middle East journalist sees it, their job is to educate readers and listeners; to protect the established order, particularly the regime; to act as a tool of national development and unity; and to burnish the country's image.

As we have seen earlier, the media critics often regard the Middle East press as shackled by governments and elitist interests, unfree to report news, and representative of the top-down authoritarian model of the press, with elements of the developmental and communitarian press thrown in for good measure. While the overarching press type seems authoritarian, many journalism scholars in the region demur, saying the media practices social responsibility. It is the job of Arab journalists to express their opinions in news stories, even if the stories are unlabeled by editors as editorial pieces. In part this is *homage* to the storytelling skills of Arabs during their golden period. News reporting often takes on the feel of one-sided propaganda when only one point of view is presented, or on occasion when two-sided viewpoints are expressed, one is less credible than the one favored by the writer. Reporting scandals or high-level mistakes serves no real purpose, they say, if those reports undermine the personalities in power, and tarnish the country's image abroad. The 2003 UNDP's Arab Human Development Report characterized the common feature of Arab media messages as authoritarian, one-dimensional, official, and sacred.[18]

The comings, goings, and doings of the head of state are dutifully reported and usually lead the hourly news broadcast. Known as protocol news, these pro forma reports can be carried too far. For example, Tyler Brûlé of the *Financial Times* wrote about monitoring international news of the 2004 Christmas tsunami that devastated South Asia, costing 150,000 lives from his plush hotel room in Muscat, Oman, flipping through the international news channels, such as CNN International, Deutsche Welle, Sky News, and BBC World, readily available via satellite. Then he turned on the local station:

> On the day the story broke, Omani state television treated the tsunami as the third piece on its late-evening English language bulletin. It takes about five minutes on the ground to grasp that no matter what's happened in the world, Sultan Qaboos comes first.
>
> The leading story of the bulletin was a short report about the Sultan receiving a letter from Jacques Chirac, the French president. Item two was about the Sultan sending a telegram to the Indian government to express his grief over the death of former prime minister Rao.[19]

Arab journalists have long shrugged off the trappings of neutral observers and they often "critically evaluate" how their reports will affect Arab public opinion, the mythical Arab Street.[20] However, the Western journalistic ideal is not that alien to what Arabs used to believe in the golden era referenced above. Ibn Khaldun, over half a millennium ago, defined objectivity as the main prerequisite for reporting news or history, stressing the responsibility of the reporter or historian to discern truth from falsehood. Various ethical codes adopted by news organizations and syndicates (unions) in the region stress the importance objectivity and of fair and balanced news reporting.[21] To the Western mind, however, few Arab journalists and editors seem to value truth, balance, or fairness over *perceived* national interest.

Coverage of local and national controversial events are usually muted, while news reports, photographs, and cartoons are highly critical of almost everything Western. The coverage is borderline cynical of any attempts at modernity, accommodation, democratization, or cultural exchange – if the initiative is undertaken by core governments or nongovernmental organizations headquartered in the West. Motives are usually questioned and answered in news stories as the West's interest in dominating the region politically or culturally, especially its oil reserves.

In the past, Western diplomats would grin and bear it, but that was not the case in the wake of the September 11, 2001 terrorist attacks on America, and the joyous response of the Arab Street. While many newspapers in the region expressed brief, perfunctory sympathy for the people of the United States, there was hardly a respite in criticism of US culture and foreign policy. In fact *Al Ahram Weekly*, a government-controlled English-language publication in Cairo, printed several letters to the editor and columnists critical of the US and suggested it was responsible for the events of 9/11 as early as September 13. Clearly, the party line had not yet been established.[22] The next week's edition featured a story on Mohamed Atta's father saying his son was an innocent victim of an Israeli plot to tarnish Muslim images abroad. They also allowed the elder Atta to repeat the rumor that 4,000 Israeli workers at the Trade Centers heard in advance of the planned crash and did not go to work on 9/11. Several years after the tragedy, the newspaper has yet to issue a correction. The coverage of the 9/11 event and subsequent criticisms of US foreign policy in its war on terror was the tipping point for US Ambassador David Welch, who criticized the style of journalism practiced out of Cairo. In a letter in Arabic, Welch chastised current Egyptian journalistic practices and urged reporters and editors to try to do better. Predictably, Welch was vilified in the Egyptian press for "interfering in Egypt's internal affairs."[23] In the buildup to the Afghanistan and Iraq invasions, regional nerves were drawing taut. And the Arab media took an anti-American perspective.

Transnational Newspaper Publishing

While MENA since the nineteenth century had a mixture of foreign, colonial, and local newspapers, the era of transnational publication did not take hold until the 1970s, partly as a response to pressures from the United Nations to open borders to ideas from the outside with minimal governmental interference and taxation. Though expensive for the average reader, these offshore publications quickly found a market with the educated elite who could understand the European languages that made up most of the publications.

In the late 1970s a new creature made its appearance in the region, Arabic-language newspapers supported financially by wealthy Arabs, some of them related to royal families. Initially published in places like Beirut and Paris, the transnational Arabic press soon found a home in London, where they were printed and airlifted to Arab countries for distribution, often days after coming off the presses.[24]

The better-known dailies are *Al-Sharq-al-Awsat* (The Middle East) and *al-Hayat* (Life), and editors from each are regularly interviewed on BBC World and CNN International to provide expert opinions on happenings in the region. Founded in 1977, *Al-Sharq-al-Awsat* is the most widely circulated for the dailies, with 60,000 copies distributed worldwide. Owned and financially supported by a Saudi prince, *Al-Sharq-al-Awsat* was the first to employ the new satellite technology that allowed simultaneous printing in London and Riyadh. *Al-Hayat*, founded in 1988 by another Saudi prince, prints and distributes 40,000 copies using the same method. Both papers are critical of US foreign policy and especially its occupation of Iraq following the 2003 Iraq war, but so is nearly every national paper in the region. Other important offshore daily publications include *al-Quds-al-Arabi* (Arab Jerusalem), which is owned by Palestinian businessmen, prints in London, New York, and Morocco, and distributes 15,000 copies of a tabloid-style publication; and the feisty *al-Arab* (The Arab), which is owned and edited by Abdal Munim al Hawni, a former Libyan information minister, and produces 10,000 copies in Tunisia and London. That publication often runs afoul of censorship laws in some Arab countries, who refuse to distribute them.

Many influential weeklies, published in London, have also found audiences. The two largest are *al-Hawadith* (The Events), with 25,000 circulation, and *al-Majalla* (The Magazine), with 20,000. The American newsmagazine, *Newsweek*, launched an Arabic edition in 2000 that differs in style and substance from its parent.

Censorship is more an issue with offshore publications than local media, and even the large dailies have problems. For example, Saudi Arabia banned *al-Hayat* in October 2002 because it carried an open letter from 67 American intellectuals calling on Saudi Arabia to denounce "militant jihadism."[25] In Egypt, where a value-added tax is applied to nationally produced publications that generally practice self-censorship, foreign publications are known collectively as the "Cyprus Press," because of the ease of getting an offshore publication license. These publications, which make up the bulk of newsstand offerings, trade censorship for tax forgiveness on circulation and advertising sales. All foreign-published publications must undergo the censor's visor before being allowed distribution. Some offshore publications, such as *The Middle East Times*, get around the censorship issue by complying with government wishes in the print edition, while posting the redacted or banned news stories on its website under a separate heading, "Censored."[26]

Transnational Broadcasting

The modern era of transnational broadcasting in the Middle East did not begin with the launch of Arabsat, a communication satellite dedicated to serving the region in its footprint in 1985. Transnational broadcasting actually began decades earlier in the Middle East during the movement toward pan-Arabism fomented by Egypt's President Gamal Abdel Nasser. Nasser used radio speeches to crystallize then-disparate Arab nations into a union, the Arab League, and to support the idea that radio could be used for development and mobilization. In addition to reaching Arab states, which regarded the distinctive Egyptian linguistic styles as almost mythical,[27] Nasser's broadcasters expanded pan-Arabism into a broader context, the notion of nonalignment. Under his aegis Egypt retooled its radio messages in a variety of languages aimed directly at a new hotbed of independence movements in Africa in the early 1960s. Egypt was one of the numerous Soviet-sympathetic models in Africa in the early days of African independence movements. However, "The Voice of the Arabs" suffered an unrecoverable blow in credibility during the 1967 Arab–Israeli war and retreated in influence.[28] During that war, Egypt's broadcasting structure was used for propaganda and told Arabs fabricated stories of Israeli defeats and one-sided Arab victories. Only after the war was it clear of Israel's lopsided victory. Some Middle East media scholars say pan-Arab media have never fully recovered.

While Arab readers could find an increasingly wide selection of newspapers, broadcasting was an exclusive state-run monopoly.

The transnational communications revolution in the Middle East took root in 1990, five years after Arabsat's launching, and was based on several converging factors:

1 New technologies allowed satellite reception on smaller, less expensive dishes that were affordable not only by individuals but by entrepreneurs who, often against the law, distributed programming to nearby homes.
2 The increasingly apparent disintegration of the Soviet Union resulted in a need to combat the influences of "The Other" in media products entering the region, primarily newspapers, movies and television entertainment programs, and the fear that Islamic fundamentalism would fill the void left by the collapse of Soviet influence in the region.
3 Improved programming by Middle East broadcasters by technologically raising the quality of their signals as well as improving the content of programming.
4 An eagerness on the part of Arabs to be part of a greater Islamic world. In particular, the desire for pan-Arabism and the Islamic concept of *ummah*, or community, increased consumer demand.
5 The growing trend of unlicensed publications distributed in various countries but printed elsewhere or in free-trade zones within the country of distribution greatly opened media spheres in many countries, forcing government-owned publishing houses to become competitive. These "offshore publications," some written in Arabic, often outnumber domestic publications on newsstands through Arab capitals.
6 The emergence of modern journalism-teaching facilities in the Middle East.
7 The Gulf War of 1991 and around-the-clock coverage by CNN and BBC World influenced Arab entrepreneurs that 24-hour news could empower pan-Arabism and inoculate the Arab viewing public against what they saw were culturally and politically biased reporting of the Arab world.

Mired in political squabbles on the ground, Arabsat floated silently in space, little used. One of the problems was that Egypt, which had always led the region as media innovator, was boycotted from using the satellite because of its peace treaties with Israel. But that all changed December 2, 1990, when Egypt ushered in the era of transnational broadcasting when it began broadcasting its terrestrial channels to southern Europe and MENA via Arabsat.[29] A second channel soon followed in 1991, the privately owned Middle East Broadcast Centre (MBC), uplinked to the satellite from London with entertainment, news, and commentary that was truly pan-Arab in intent. The media revolution was underway.

Soon nearly every MENA country had its own satellite channel as a matter of national pride and pan-Arab solidarity, including three all-news channels by 2004: Al Jazeera from Qatar in 1996; the London-based Arab News Network (ANN), financed in part by a branch of the Syrian ruling family, in 1997, and Al Arabiya from Saudi Arabia in 2003. The channel offerings were expanded with the launch of Nilesat 101 in 1998 and Nilesat 102 in 2000, both enabled with digital technology.[30]

Today the belt around the equator at 35,000 kilometers from terra firma contains over 60,000 communication satellites and includes two from Egypt, three from Saudi Arabia and two from Israel.

Chronicling the rise of satellite-based transnational broadcasting was its own online journal, *Transnational Broadcasting Studies Journal*, published by the Adham Center at American University in Cairo. The popular and often-quoted journal gave a particular focus to the issue in the Middle East. Originally intended to cover the spectrum of transnational broadcasting issues around the world, the publication refocused itself in 2003 to concentrate on transnational broadcasting issues in MENA, the Indian subcontinent, and Indonesia. In Fall 2004 the Adham Center announced it would co-publish the journal in electronic and bound copy form with the Middle East Centre, St. Antony's College, University of Oxford.

Even the United States senses the power of Arabic transnational broadcasting. In 2003 it launched Radio Sawa (Together), which quickly became the most popular radio show in Beirut because of its modern, pop-music format that mixed Western and Arab pop music.[31] Radio Sawa has experienced phenomenal growth in the Middle East since its introduction, especially on the FM band.[32] A survey conducted in six media-savvy countries in July 2003, a few months after Radio Sawa's introduction, showed its audience share running between 30.4 and 40.8 percent among all listeners, and 40.1 to 51.6 percent among listeners under 30, its target audience.[33] A similar project started December 19, 2002, called Radio Farda (Radio Tomorrow) whose upbeat, youth-oriented programming is aimed at Farsi speakers in Iran. Radio Farda is a project of the Voice of America and Radio Free Europe and is broadcast over medium and short-wave frequencies into Iran. Little is known about the impact of this broadcasting effort since no research has been conducted within Iran.[34]

The impact of its news coverage is widely regarded as American propaganda, even though it attempts to replicate the Western model of pursuit of truth, unbiased reporting, and fair and balanced coverage even if it is unfavorable to the United States, according to its news director, Muafac Harb. On Valentines Day, 2004, the US launched a satellite television channel in Arabic, Al Hurra (The Free One).[35] Even before its launch the

Arab media predictably dismissed it as American propaganda, or an exercise in futility.[36]

> From a public communications standpoint, US international broadcasting will have a difficult time achieving its goal of reaching mass audiences in the Arab and Muslim world in order to further US public diplomacy because: (1) the research is lacking, (2) the audience is highly resistant to the messages, and (3) the strategies and messages lack cultural appropriateness.

The effects of the American experiment remain to be seen and studied.

Four of the more popular transnational broadcasting channels are profiled below.

Al Jazeera (The Island)

Arab viewers had never seen anything like it. Right there in their living room, in living color, an Arab commentator in Arabic was criticizing their Arab government and, more shockingly, their Arab leaders. Al Jazeera, the satellite news and commentary station from the tiny Persian Gulf state, Qatar, made its presence felt in 1996 by "creating ripples in a stagnant pool" that was Middle East broadcast journalism.[37] The reaction in the early years to Al Jazeera's take-no-prisoners journalism was mixed, though it reminded media historians of the rough-and-tumble newspaper period in the United States during the nation-building years in the eighteenth and nineteenth centuries. Governments from Morocco to Iraq closed down bureaus and expelled the broadcasters' reporters without much of a whimper from viewers. Initial viewership was fueled by curiosity, and soon tired of the harangues against their governments. After all, what gave Qatar the right to criticize important leaders from its "matchbox" studios in a country few around the world could pinpoint on a map?[38] But it took three invasions – first in the Palestinian Territory in 2000 by the Israeli Defense Force in the second Intifada; then in Afghanistan in 2001 to remove the Taliban; and finally in Iraq in 2003 – to build Arab credibility and become the most-watched, most-valued transnational broadcaster in the world among Arabs scattered throughout Europe, Oceania, and the Americas. It has an estimated audience of regular viewers at between 35 and 50 million worldwide.[39]

A 2002 uses and gratifications study of 5,379 Arabic speakers in 137 countries found that over 7 of 10 viewers found the channel credible, truthful, accurate, fair, trustworthy, unsensationalized, moral, and factual. Nearly 9 in 10 thought the reporters were well trained.[40] Another study found more

Arab men than women watched Al Jazeera for news in the United States, but favored watching other Arabic programming from other channels that gave them a sense of identity with their homeland and helped them cope in their adopted country.[41] In a separate study in 2003 by the Conference of International Broadcasters' Audience Research Services (CIBAR), Al Jazeera was rated highly in the Arab World as a credible (61 percent) by 57 percent of the television set owners in Egypt, Jordan, Morocco, UAE, Kuwait, and Qatar, who regarded the channel as their primary information source.[42]

Enhancing Al Jazeera's image in the Arab World was its relationship with Osama bin Laden before and after the World Trade Center and Pentagon attacks of 9/11. In fact, Al Jazeera was the only news organization to remain in Kabul after the Taliban expelled all other foreign news organizations. To Arabs this was first-rate journalism, but it made Western leaders and media nervous. Through its Kabul office – which was bombed twice during the Afghanistan invasion – Al Jazeera had access to Taliban leaders, including bin Laden. CNN and BBC scrambled to purchase tapes that had been previously broadcast to the Arab world, drawing the ire of Bush administration officials who labeled Al Jazeera as the "mouthpiece for Osama bin Laden,"[43] and American journalists who piled on the criticism. An Israeli-American columnist for a New York daily chimed in:

> Al-Jazeera is far from legitimate. It is an Arab propaganda outfit controlled by the medieval government of Qatar that masquerades as a real media company . . . Al-Jazeera is the favorite network of bin Laden. It provides him with an unedited forum for his calls to jihad. Some American news executives think it might be dangerous to rebroadcast bin Laden's screeds because they could contain encrypted messages to his followers. They can relax – bin Laden has better ways to get out his message.[44]

To journalism idealists, who believe that good reporting comes from access to good sources, Al Jazeera was doing the right thing by giving at least a muted Israeli point of view during broadcasts of the Intifada, and trying to get opposing views, though sometimes the polarity of issues resulted in something approximating "boxing rings."[45] Arab viewers were uncertain. Shia's were skeptical that Al Jazeera seemed to favor rival Sunni's. While some Saudis felt insulted by some of Al Jazeera's reporting, the rest of the Arabic-speaking world was enthralled. *This*, they reasoned, was truth, accompanied by pictures of suffering Arabs, who would not be suffering had it not been for the military invasions. Critics, of course, say Al Jazeera was silent when the Taliban allegedly slaughtered tens of thousands Afghans, nor did it show excesses in violence by al Qaeda sympathizers against Iraqis or the demonstrative support for Saddam's overthrow in some parts of Iraq.

As it did in the Israeli invasion of the Palestine territories, Al Jazeera focused on individual suffering that tugged at the collective Arab heartstrings. This was augmented with fiery talkshows that consistently criticized the West for its Middle East policies. Those pictures did not sit well with US military and diplomatic sources that pressured Qatar's ruler to rein in the channel. Emir Sheikh Hamad bin Khalifa, who created the station as part of his vision of democratic speech in the Arab world (except in Qatar itself, where published and broadcast speech is still self-censored when it comes to the ruling regime), simply reminded the West that the channel was just doing its job. Abdallah Schleifer, director of the Adham Center for Television Journalism at the American University in Cairo, thinks Al Jazeera reporters' reliance on field reporting gives them an edge on the competition. Listen to what he had to say recently:

I have the distinct feeling that Al Jazeera is more loyal to television journalism's cardinal craft of field reporting than the BBC, CNN, or the US networks, who all increasingly seem to be passing over the chance to do solid TV journalism. That means a reporter takes the time to actually check out a story, then go out into the field, shoot it, and then write up a script and voice it over for a final product that illuminates the images on screen, but that's being increasingly passed up in favor of the easier, quicker on-the-scene live appearances from the reporter, who usually can do little more than interpret an event already described by the anchor/presenter using wire copy for substance and asking his or her own reporter, by satellite, to respond with some instant and generally obvious analysis.[46]

Al Jazeera's broadcast of gory pictures, including beheaded captives, has drawn international criticism. The station dismisses such outcries as "cultural differences," and points to the hypocrisy by the US military for releasing the photos of Saddam Hussein's dead sons, which one Arab commentator called "disgusting."[47]

A major effort now seems underway at Al Jazeera to put some of its excesses behind it, and establish itself as a key international media player like BBC World and CNN International. In fact, the channel has announced plans to launch an English-language version of the channel in November 2005. To the chagrin of the US State Department, which never liked the Arab network, the new international network will have bureaus in Washington, London, Kuala Lumpur, and be based in Qatar. The network will seek out a global audience in direct competition with CNN and BBC World as it sets out an Arab perspective on world events. The channel wants to be taken seriously as a pan-Arab voice. In July 2004 it adopted a code of ethics to guide its 40–50 reporters around the world.[48]

For most non-Arabic speaking Westerners, however, Al Jazeera was defined for them by their political leaders, who were often upset with the kind of coverage given US and UK forces preparing then prosecuting war in the region. That "tarnished image" in the West was burnished in 2004 with the major theatrical release of *Control Room*, the exceptional documentary by Jehane Noujaim, which covered Al Jazeera covering the early days of the 2003 Iraq war.[49]

Al Arabiya (The Arab)

The second 24-hour news channel in the Arab world was born March 3, 2003, a few weeks before the 2003 Iraq war, in Saudi Arabia, and immediately found itself linked by the US administration with Al Jazeera as a potential propaganda arm for anti-American interests in the region. But something in the style and format of Al Arabiya set it apart: it was more interested in credibility than sensational reporting. Something else set it apart from its competitor, Al Jazeera: it was well planned and funded by a consortium of private businessmen that included interests close to Saudi royalty from the start, and it attracted considerably more advertising revenue than its competitor.

With a US$300 million initial investment and promises of advertising contracts, the tone was class not crass; Al Arabiya's reporters asked questions more diplomatically and professionally than their Doha counterparts; and its news presenters seemed less prone to offer opinions. Though it sometimes rankled heads of state – it was banned several times before and after the 2003 Iraq war from Baghdad, and suspended by the new provisional government for an interview with Saddam Hussein and for showing hooded terrorists who later beheaded their captives – it was less a "street fighter" than Al Jazeera.[50]

The distinction was not missed by the Arab viewing public, estimated at over 50 million worldwide. In a 2003 survey in selected Arab countries before the station had gained any appreciable market share, Al Arabiya ranked second behind Al Jazeera by a wide margin, 49 to 17 percent, in recognizability. In which news station people considered most credible, Al Arabiya did not even show up on the screen. Nor did it record significant results when asked about favored news sources.[51]

However, a poll by the US Department of State found that among Iraqis with satellite dishes in seven Iraqi cities in October 2004, 37 percent picked Al Arabiya as their preferred news source, followed by Al Jazeera (26 percent), with the US-run Iraqi Media Network (renamed Al Iraqiyah TV) at 12 percent.[52]

With Al Arabiya, the only Arab satellite channel granted an interview by George W. Bush in 2004, and Al Jazeera racing to establish themselves as the most credible, fair, and truthful transnational broadcast outlets, the Arab audience will indeed be seeing something different.

Arab News Network (ANN)

Arab News Network was the second 24-hour independent Arab news service. Owned by Sawmar Al Assad, a cousin to Syrian president, Bashar Al Assad, the station is based in London and licensed by the UK's Independent Television Commission (ITC), which sets standards and monitors broadcasters.

The channel was launched in May 1997 to cover international news with a focus on the Arab Gulf states, the Middle East, North Africa, and Europe. The channel broadcasts a news bulletin on the hour, and programming includes political and social features, debates, talkshows, business analysis, sports, and scientific and cultural documentaries.[53] Though connected to the ruling family, the channel was critical of Bashar Al Assad assuming the Syrian presidency on the death of President Hafiz Al Assad in 2000. Since it has no advertising, various donors, some of whom might be connected to the Saudi royal family, support the station.[54]

ANN started with 15 bureaus and 20 correspondents, but due to financial constraints it now has 9 bureaus worldwide in Palestine, Baghdad, Muscat, Tehran, Cairo, Tripoli, Morocco, Paris, and Washington. It relies on free-lance correspondents in other locations. However, the biggest cutback came in 2002 when the channel stopped its transmission via the Egyptian satellite Nilesat – reasons varied from costs to Egypt's alleged meddling with proposed news stories – while remaining on Arabsat and EutelSat.

Middle East Broadcast Centre (MBC)

Five years before Al Jazeera, MBC broke ground in the Middle East with quality broadcasting from its offices in London. Funded by two wealthy Saudi entrepreneurs, Sheiks Saleh Kamel and Walid bin Ibrahim al-Ibrahim, MBC began broadcasting news and features in Arabic in October 1991, and quickly established itself as the premier channel for Arabs living abroad or for the few hooked up to cable or satellite in the Middle East. Many of the techniques later adopted by Al Jazeera were pioneered by MBC, including the concept of political talk radio, and, more importantly, airing both sides of a story. It was the first to regularly interview Israelis as well as Hamas and Hezbollah representatives.

In 1993, Sheik Ibrahim pulled out of MBC and started Arab Radio and Television in Abu Dhabi, and MBC started to increase its entertainment offerings in addition to news. The shift in emphasis paid off as satellite dish installations boomed in the region, even though some countries, such as Saudi Arabia, Iran, and Iraq, had banned satellite television dishes.[55]

In a recent 2003 survey of the six most technologically advanced countries in the region – Egypt, United Arab Emirates, Morocco, Jordan, Qatar, and Kuwait – MBC was the most-watched satellite station in the region, outpolling Al Jazeera 30 to 17 percent overall and winning by a wide margin of 42 to 9 percent over Abu-Dhabi television as the number one source for entertainment programming.[56] Because of its high viewership by Arabic speakers in the region, MBC opened MBC2 in Dubai Media City, offering viewers cultural programming from the Middle East as well as its standard programming from US and UK entertainment producers.

To provide programming for the various satellite networks, as well as cinemas in the region, governments in Jordan, Egypt, and Dubai have invested millions in media cities with tax breaks for production of exported media material. In state-of-the-art studios that rival those in America, the United Kingdom, or India, the countries hope to fill the thousands of hours of broadcasting created by the new transnational delivery systems. Egypt was the first to recognize this potential when it constructed the Egyptian Media City in 1995 on 3.5 million square meters of land (including a Hollywood-like back lot) to produce local programming for its many Nile System channels, and to lure foreign movie-makers away from countries like Morocco and Jordan, where most of the movies featuring desert scenes are filmed, including the *Star Wars* epics, *Hidalgo*, *Alexander the Great*, *The English Patient*, the *Mummy* films, and many others. The forthcoming *Cleopatra* and *Nefertiti* will be shot in Egypt. Many of the expatriate broadcasters have also been contacted and have moved their operations, at least in part, from London and Rome. The media exporting zone idea has yet to earn sufficient revenues to cover their initial investments.[57]

While internet usage in MENA lags the rest of the world, every major city (and even some minor ones) have internet cafes and access to the Net. All the major newspapers, realizing the potential of extending their influence beyond borders, also have websites, often in English, which reach out beyond the Arab world. These websites, through discussion boards, provide opportunities for international, cross-cultural dialogue never before available. Translation programs are readily available, some on search engines such as Google or Yahoo!, that aid in understanding as well.

Educated Middle Easterners, mostly male, are making use of the technologies, and individual webpages are proliferating. So, too, are webpages for jihadist groups and those allied formally or sympathetically with groups seeking change in the region. For example, much of what Al Jazeera or Al Arabiya learned about hostage executions and some Al Qaeda operations in Iraq in 2003–4 came initially from websites, Islamist bloggers, or emails.

In addition, two of the biggest controversies or scandals of the 2003 War involved internet sites: the photographs of flag-draped coffins were posted initially by a Seattle woman on a private page; and the Abu Ghraib prison scandal was fueled, not by an article by Seymour Hersh, who broke the story, but by pictures lifted by news media off another private webpage put together by the wife of a Navy Seals.[58] Such digital images of civilian victims of war were transmitted at the speed of light around the Arab World to heighten the anti-American mood.

The region might be years away from sufficient internet penetration to be of value for widespread economic development, but the beginnings are there and most governments are allowing, if not encouraging, internet usage.[59]

Advertising and Public Relations

The dearth of privately operated print and broadcast media, depending on paid advertising for its survival, has stalled development of an advertising industry in the region. The lack of accepted circulation auditing bureaus has also contributed to the skepticism of international advertising agencies even as they rush to the region to set up shop. Frankly, circulation figures given by various media are suspect and often wildly variable depending on the source of information. Advertising agents often prefer billboards, off-shore publications, and international publications to reach audiences rather than rely on publisher statements of circulation and cost per thousands. Advertising that builds a company or product image seems the preferred product marketing strategy. Since the region has a high illiteracy rate, and commercial radio is in the neophyte stage, advertisers must rely on print media, and billboard advertisements are purposefully simple and aimed at passive audiences. Few give consumers an urgent reason to buy the product or use the service being advertised.

State-run print media often set advertising quotas for salesmen but do not often reward those salesmen who exceed the quotas. Generally speaking, newspapers in the region carry considerably less advertising per issue than do their core counterparts. Data on the amount of advertising sold in the region are difficult to find, but there are indications this may be changing rapidly as more and more advertising agencies from Europe and the

United States set up offices in Middle East capitals, and more independent radio and television stations – still few in number – gain in popularity.

Opinion-makers in the region generally do not hold the public-relations and advertising fields in high regard. One publisher recently likened PR practitioners to "pizza delivery boys."[60] The blame might rest with the PR practitioners themselves.

> The PR industry, which has mushroomed in size in the last five years . . . continues to make a rod for its own back by failing to complete the education of clients, as well as the media – seeing it as an "us versus them" scenario, rather than the "win-win-win" situation it should be in a developed and professional marketplace.[61]

A 2002 survey by one major PR company found a general skepticism among publishers, one of whom commented that no public-relations stories would be printed unless accompanied by advertising, and journalists routinely receive gifts from the companies they write stories about. Meanwhile governmental and corporate public-relations organizations remain the largest employer of female graduates with journalism and mass communication degrees.

The global PR business generated $2.5 billion in 2003, but the Middle East's contribution was a scant $25 million, about one percent of the international figure despite MENA representing 7 percent of the global population. The publisher mentioned above predicts, however, that the 2003 figure could quadruple by 2006.[62] While regional spending on public relations was miserly by global standards, advertising was another story.

While authoritative information about advertising revenues is difficult to come by in the Middle East, there are some indications that private radio and television stations might be financially beneficial. According to William Rugh, the most lucrative television advertising market is Saudi Arabia, where $270 million was spent in 1995. Of the $186 million spent on pan-Arab television ads, MBC, ART, and Egypt took 62 percent of it. As an industry, advertising in the Middle East is "woefully underdeveloped."[63]

While commercial advertising is lagging, Arab governments generally recognize its importance to favorably positioning their countries in the West, particularly to attract foreign investment and tourists. The events exacerbated the need to improve images of Arabs in the West, and many countries such as Saudi Arabia, Egypt, and Lebanon, contracted with international advertising agencies in London, Paris, and New York, to do the job of shaping perceptions of the Islamic World. In Egypt, for example, the government owns the largest advertising agency, Al Ahram, or The Pyramids Advertising.

Currently, Arab countries and businesses market their image, services, and goods primarily over the internet. Egypt, Kuwait, and the United Arab Emirates have increased their e-commerce efforts since 1990. Saudi Arabia, on the other hand, seems less inclined to develop e-commerce and concentrates its efforts in public-relations work in the United States. The same tactic was used by the Kuwaiti government, which hired Hill & Knowlton in 1990, to appeal for worldwide intervention and support after Iraq invaded and tried to re-annex the country. This led to the 1991 Iraq war.[64]

The 2000 Palestinian *intifada* (uprising), the 9/11 attack and the West's response to it, and the phenomenal growth of transnational – and global – broadcasting companies have raised the level of awareness about the power of advertising and public relations in the region among businesses and governments alike. Many of the major international advertising and public-relations agencies are opening branches in MENA, a large number of them located in Dubai Media City to serve the entire region.

However, while Western-style advertising and public-relations techniques are growing in MENA, the impact of advertising messages is still unclear. Some scholars have even predicted dismal results for American products in the Middle East based on the US government's political policies in the region, namely its support of Israel.[65] However, anecdotal evidence suggests foreign products, including those from the United States, are still popular among those Arabs who can afford them.

Conclusions

While mass-media products from around the world are available – and sometimes preferred because of their high production values and storytelling prowess – readers, listeners, viewers, and surfers have a bewildering array of locally produced television programming, internet sites, and local and foreign-produced publications in Arabic. This increased flow, while lagging other developing regions around the world and falling far short of what is available in the OECD countries, is considerably better than it was five years ago.

With the increased media come increased parental concerns in the Middle East about the effects programs have on their culture and children. Like parents everywhere, MENA mothers and fathers worry about the increasing sex and violence and culturally "inappropriate" materials entering their homes through television sets. Despite tamed-down versions of MTV, new satellite channels have started up within the region that push acceptable norms, especially displays of scantily clad females writhing to the beat of music videos, even though the beat has a definite Mediterranean sound. Academics have their work cut out for them in media-effects studies, given the generally suspicious nature of audiences and governments toward social research.

Transnational broadcasts carried over international and, increasingly, regional satellites have opened minds and markets to other points of view as never before. On individual levels, access to the internet has been accelerating in the region as well. The transition from "electronic colonialism" to "electronic self-determinism" has not gone smoothly but is noticeable. Its effect on authoritarian regimes has been palpable, as they are finding censorship an increasingly arcane practice. Some scholars have suggested that transnational media might be transforming the Middle East and pan-Arabism much like political parties have transformed the cultures in which they function.[66]

An increasing number of voices are questioning the concept of cultural imperialism in light of what is happening primarily in the Middle East.[67] While still a theory popular with development communication scholars, antiglobalism factions, and most Middle East intellectuals, recent developments of intraregional and extraregional broadcasting, telephony, and internet technologies have allowed Middle Eastern broadcasters, online newspapers, and internet bloggers to reach unparalleled numbers of Arabic-speaking people around the world. Viewers in Rabat and Asmara, Boston and Los Angeles, Madrid and Stockholm, and Bogotá and Buenos Aires can see in real time news and commentary on Al Jazeera, Al Arabiya, Iqra'a, a religious channel, or even Al Manar, or scores of satellite channels carried by Orbit or Showtime Arabia.

If the question about cultural imperialism is about *disparity*, then the OECD nations probably will always have an advantage. But there is no longer a void which broadcasters exclusively choose Western media products to fill. Exponential distribution of knowledge through media products may be unrealistic given the inequity of resources between the Middle East and core nations, but with the advent of media production centers in Egypt, Dubai, Jordan, and elsewhere, the gap is narrowing.

The biggest change caused by transnational broadcasting in MENA might be political, as authoritarian regimes sense the writing on the wall and adopt at least the façade of democracy, which would include a free press.

The current leaders of Libya, Saudi Arabia, Egypt, Mauritania, Palestine, and Israel are ironfisted septuagenarians. A new generation of mostly young leaders has taken over in Morocco, the United Arab Emirates, Syria, and Jordan. All were educated in the West and schooled in public relations rather than secretive application of power. They grew up with television and the internet and they have considerably different aspirations and visions for their countries than their forebears. Perhaps their bureaucrats and populations will hear the recent words of Crown Prince of Dubai and General Sheikh Mohammad bin Rashid Al Maktoum:[68]

> Fortunately, this period of Arab history is nearly at an end. It is no longer possible to sell illusions, to justify failure with manufactured excuses or to re-label defeats as victories. The Arab media needed to gain credibility in a period of change in which there was friction between the old and the new. Information, like anything else, must be reformed and changed. It also plays a major role in reform and change. . . . This message will not be successful without real openness about the actual situation in the Gulf with all its achievements, aspirations, problems and defects. If our media do not take the initiative and deal with local issues with courage, responsibility and reason, then foreign media will, but with their own point of view and to serve their own interests.

Or listen to his brother-in-law, King Abdullah of Jordan, who delivered a keynote address at a conference for journalists in 2004:[69]

> We are enacting laws to restructure state media organizations, and disengage the government from direct control. Laws have been drafted to liberalize the sector and to open the public airwaves to private TV and radio stations. And we abolished the Ministry of Information . . . Lasting change is deep change, and deep change does not come overnight. But Jordan has made its choice, for progressive reform, optimism, and peace. And many throughout the region agree . . . The Arab media has an important role if regional reform and peace are to succeed. Dispassionate, knowledgeable reporting; fairness; credibility – these are all essential to constructive public dialogue. Extremists don't seek dialogue; they seek platforms and exposure. Responsible journalists deny it to them, just as they deny the hatred and violence terrorists incite.

With bold, new leaders focusing on openness and a free press, optimists sense that change will be occurring sooner rather than later in the region, and that with media leading the way in knowledge distribution that the region will climb from its mired developmental stage to join the developed countries of the world. But exponential growth does have a price, such as opening up centuries-old tribal societies and adopting modernity as a social norm. Cynics say the price might be too steep.

Notes

1   The impact of CNN on the Middle East's current media atmosphere cannot be understated. ANN, Al Jazeera, MBC, and Al Arabiya adapted many of the

techniques and technologies employed by CNN. For a better understanding of the Middle East mediascape see Hussein Amin and Douglas Boyd, "The Development of Direct Broadcast Television to and Within the Middle East," *Journal of South Asian and Middle East Studies* 18(2) (Winter 1994), pp. 37–50.

2 Stephen Schwartz, "Free the Iraqi Press: The last thing they need in Baghdad is another statist medium," *The Weekly Standard*, May 17, 2004. Accessed Jan. 12, 2005, at http://www.weeklystandard.com/Content/Public/Articles/000/000/004/072kcdat.asp?pg1. Also see report on Donald Rumsfeld's view of the Iraqi press at http://www.iraqcoalition.org/pressreleases/20040423_rummy_press.html.

3 For the purposes of this chapter, the region has been expanded from traditional descriptions of the Middle East to include the new country of Eritrea and its former parent, Ethiopia, which most taxonomies place in Sub-Saharan Africa. We have also included Israel and Iran in the region as comparatives, even though their media products are distributed widely. Turkey, which is a Muslim country, and sometimes Cyprus, an island republic with a third of its land under occupation from Turkey, is included in the Middle East picture by some scholars. They are excluded here because of their development and orientation toward the Organization for Economic Cooperation and Development (OECD).

4 UNDP, *Arab Human Development Report 2003* (United Nations: New York), pp. 39–40.

5 Ibid., p. 61.

6 One of the more celebrated cases was the conviction and brief imprisonment of Saad Eddin Ibrahim in Egypt in 2001 until the high court intervened to drop all the charges against him. Dr. Ibrahim, an Arab democrat with dual Egyptian–US citizenship, is a political sociology professor at the American University in Cairo.

7 R. J. Barro and J. W. Lee, "International Data on Educational Attainment: Updates and Implications," CID Working Papers No. 42, April 2002.

8 Oliver Zollner, ed., *Beyond Borders: Research for International Broadcasting*, 2003 (Bonn, Germany: Conference of International Broadcasters' Audience Research Services, 2004), pp. 78–9.

9 Ibid., p. 79.

10 For a varied discussion of women in Middle East media, see Naomi Sakr's *Women and Media in the Middle East: Power Through Self Expression* (London: I. B. Tauris, 2004).

11 See Benjamin R. Barber, *Jihad vs. McWorld: How Globalism and Tribalism are Reshaping the World* (New York: Ballantine, 1995).

12 See Samuel P. Huntington, *Clash of Civilization and the Remaking of World Order* (New York: Simon & Schuster, 1996).

13 Gassing of Kurds in Halabja by Saddam Hussein is disputed. While it is generally accepted as fact, Stephen C. Pelletiere, Douglas V. Johnson II, and Leif R. Rosenberger, of the Strategic Studies Institute of the US War College at Carlisle, Pennsylvania, issued a report in 1990, prior to the 1991 Gulf War, questioning the assumption that Hussein had gassed his own people in 1988,

saying the Kurds in Halabja were caught in a cross-exchange of chemical agents during the Iraq–Iran war and corpses actually showed signs of chemical agents used by Iran. Al Jazeera reported these claims as fact. However, still other scholars point to 39 other incidents where Saddam Hussein's regime gassed Iraqi Kurdish civilians.

14 See H. G. Wells, *The Outline of History*, vols. 1 & 2, 3rd rpr. (St. Clair Shores, MI: Scholarly Press, 1974 (1920)), for an account of early Muslim contributions to the European Enlightenment.

15 Fred S. Siebert, T. Peterson, and W. Schramm, *Four Theories of the Press* (Urbana: University of Illinois Press, 1963).

16 According to the Berenger–Hulsman taxonomy of Egyptian newspapers (government owned or oriented; political party opposition; independent and "popular press"; and foreign published but distributed in Egypt), *Al Nabaa* was in the independent and popular press category. The "yellow newspaper" was cited for 1,211 violations of Egyptian public morality and public decency laws in the first half of 2002.

17 See Noha Mellor, *The Making of Arab News* (London: Rowman & Littlefield, 2005), pp. 49–59.

18 UNDP, *Arab Human Development Report 2003* (New York: United Nations), pp. 61–2, quoting Ali Al-Qarni, *Arab Media Discourse*, 1997.

19 Tyler Brûlé, "Bridging the Gulf," *The Financial Times*, Jan. 8, 2005.

20 Abdel Nabi (1989), quoted in Noha Mellor, *The Making of Arab News* (London: Routledge, 2005), p. 87.

21 Ibid., pp. 88–9.

22 A criticism of Arab governments' use of state-run media is they allow negative framing of Western democracy, lifestyles, race relations, human rights, and popular culture. This anti-Western cultivation seems ingrained in the Arab press, and anti-American sentiment hit a high point during the 2003 Iraq war. So it seemed out of character on 9/11 not to continue criticism. The historically anti-American press was fostered after colonialism and a series of Western and American military interventions in the region. The result was a series of articles and books on the anti-Americanism phenomenon. For example, see Melvin and Margaret DeFleur's, *Learning to Hate Americans* (Spokane: Marquette Books, 2003); R. Lambert's "Misunderstanding Each Other," in *Foreign Affairs*, March/April 2003, pp. 62–74; J.-F. Revel, *Without Marx or Jesus* (New York: Dell, 1972); James J. Napoli, "Hating America: The Press in Egypt and France," pp. 3–13 in R. D. Berenger, ed., *Global Media Go to War: The Role of Entertainment and News Media in the 2003 Iraq War* (Spokane: Marquette Books, 2004).

23 For an English version of the article published in *Al Ahram* that criticized the Egyptian media, go to http://www.usembassy.egnet.net/ambassador/sp092002.htm. For translated reaction to Welch's speech, see the Middle East Research Institute's website, accessed January 3, 2005: http://www.memri.de/ uebersetzungen_ analysen/themen/usa_und_der_nahe_osten/us_egypt_ambassador_05_11_03.html

24 Information for this section from William A. Rugh's *Arab Mass Media: Newspapers, Radio and Television in Arab Politics* (Westport, CT: Praeger, 2004), pp. 167–80; and R. D. Berenger, "Tax Economics and Censorship of Foreign-licensed Publications Distributed in Egypt: The Case of the 'Cyprus Press'," *International Journal of Commerce and Management* (forthcoming 2005).

25 Alan Cooperman, "Saudis Ban U.S. Letter," *International Herald Tribune*, Oct. 25, 2002, p. 4.

26 To read the stories and the rationale for their censorship see http://www.metimes.com/censored/index.php.

27 R. D. Berenger and Kamel Labidi, "Egypt," p. 83, in A. Cooper-Chen, ed., *Global Entertainment Media: Content, Audience and Issues* (Mahwah, NJ: Lawrence Erlbaum Associates, 2005).

28 Orayb Aref Najjar, "The Middle East and North Africa," p. 285 in A. DeBeer and J. C. Merrill, eds., *Global Journalism: Tropical Issues and Media Systems*, 4th ed. (Boston: Allyn & Bacon, 2004).

29 Naomi Sakr, *Satellite Realms: Transnational Television, Globalization and the Middle East* (New York: I. B. Tauris, 2001), p. 11.

30 For the definitive history of the growth of Arab broadcasting, see Naomi Sakr's *Satellite Realms*.

31 While carried on the FM band in Beirut, Radio Sawa is less successful in Egypt, where it debuted in 2004 and is carried on the less popular AM band. However, a private radio station started up in Cairo and secured a coveted FM band spot, quickly becoming the most listened-to radio station for young, hip Cairenes. The radio station is Egypt's first commercial radio venture.

32 Radio Sawa is carried on the less popular AM/digital satellite dial in Egypt, which slightly skewed the overall impact of Radio Sawa in the study. Only 10.9% listen to the channel overall, while 20.5% of its listeners are aged 15–30.

33 Zollner, *Beyond Borders*, pp. 84–5.

34 Hansjoerg Biener, "The Arrival of Radio Farda: International Broadcasting to Iran at the Crossroads," *Middle East Review of International Affairs* 7(1) (March 2003), pp. 13–22.

35 Muafac Harb, "A New Look to Arab News," *TBS Journal* 12 (Spring/Summer 2004). Accessed January 4, 2005, at http://www.tbsjournal.com/Archives/Spring04/harb.htm.

36 Wendy Feliz Sefsaf, "US International Broadcasting Strategies in the Arab World: An Analysis of the Broadcasting Board of Governors' Strategy from a Public Communication Standpoint," *TBS Journal* 13 (Fall/Winter 2004). Accessed January 5, 2005, at http://www.tbsjournal.com/felizsefsaf.html.

37 Jihad Ali Ballout, quoted in Stephen Quinn and Tim Walters, "Al Jazeera: A Broadcaster Creating Ripples in a Stagnant Pool," p. 57, in Berenger, ed., *Global Media Go to War*.

38 Egyptian president Hosni Mubarak visited Al Jazeera in 2000 and reportedly exclaimed, "This matchbox? All this noise is coming from this matchbox?" Quoted by Thomas Friedman, "Glostnost in the Gulf," *New York Times*, Feb. 27, 2001.

39 Asserted by Hugh Miles in *Al Jazeera: How Arab TV News Challenged the World* (London: Abacus, 2005). Pre-Iraq war estimates ranged from 30 to 35 million.

40 Khalid Al-Jaber, *The Credibility of Arab Broadcasting: The Case of Al Jazeera* (Doha, Qatar: National Council for Culture, Arts and Heritage, 2004), pp. 69, 83.

41 Abeer Etefa, "Transnational Television and the Arab Diaspora in the United States," *TBS Journal* (Spring/Summer 2004). Accessed December 21, 2004, at http://www.tbsjournal.com/Archives/Spring04/etefa.htm.

42 Zollner, *Beyond Borders*, pp. 80–3.

43 Multiple sources cite Defense Secretary Donald Rumsfeld with the remark. For the relationship between Al Jazeera and US administration see http://www.cpj.org/Briefings/2001/aljazeera_oct01/aljazeera_oct01.html.

44 Ze'er Chafets, "Al Jazeera Unmasked: An Arab Propaganda Machine in the Guise of Real Journalism," *New York Daily News*, Oct. 14, 2001, p. 37.

45 Mohammed El Nawawy and Adel Iskander, *Al-Jazeera: The Story of the Network That is Rattling Governments and Defining Modern Journalism* (Boulder, CO: Westview Press, 2003). In a chapter titled "Boxing Rings: Al Jazeera's Talk Shows" the authors say the channel was among the pioneers of political talk television in the Middle East, although programs nearly always end in yelling matches and insults.

46 S. Abdallah Schleifer, "Al Jazeera Update: More Datelines from Doha and a Code of Ethics," *TBS Journal* 13 (Fall/Winter 2004). Accessed December 28, 2005, at http://www.tbsjournal.com/aljazeera_schleifer.html.

47 Elie Harb, assistant editor in chief of the Lebanese Broadcasting Company (LBC), quoted in Paul Cochrane's "To Show or Not to Show? Graphic Images in TV Media," *TBS Journal* 13 (Fall/Winter 2004). Accessed January 3, 2005 at http://www.tbsjournal.com/Archives/Spring04/harb.htm.

48 Schleifer, "Al Jazeera Update."

49 For stories and reviews of Control Room, see http://www.tbsjournal.com/Archives/Spring04/schechter.htm.

50 Samantha M. Shapiro, "The War Inside the Arab Newsroom," *New York Times Magazine*, Jan. 2, 2005. Accessed 6 January 2005 at http://www.nytimes.com/2005/01/02/magazine/02ARAB.html?ex=1105741266&ei=1&en=1d7cc4adbe081cc1

51 Zollner, *Beyond Borders*, pp. 80–3.

52 Peter Feuilherade, "Profile: Al-Arabiya TV," BBC.co.uk. Accessed January 20, 2005, at http://news.bbc.co.uk/1/hi/world/middle_east/3236654.stm

53 Noha El Hennawy, "ANN: Satellite on a Shoe String," *TBS Journal* 9 (Fall/Winter 2002). Accessed 27 December 2004 at http://www.tbsjournal.com/Archives/Fall02/ANN.html.

54 Rugh, *Arab Mass Media*, p. 239.

55 The satellite-dish ban in Saudi Arabia was largely ignored; but in Iraq it was enforced everywhere but in the Kurdish area, which began smuggling the dishes into the Kurd-controlled north from Turkey and elsewhere. The Kurds have had the most experience of all Iraqis with international television, and its

own television stations reflect it. (Personal interview with Maggy Zanger, Cairo, May 2003.) Since the fall of the Ba'athist regime in Baghdad, international communications has boomed with mobile telephony, internet, and satellite dishes being widely adopted. Iran's ban was also short-lived when government moderates, who took control briefly, lifted the ban.

56 Zollner, *Beyond Borders*, pp. 80–1.
57 See Rugh, *Arab Mass Media*, pp. 222–4; Sakr, *Satellite Realms*, pp. 109–11; and Stephen Quinn, Tim Walters, and John Whiteoak, "A Tale of Three (Media) Cities," *Global Media Journal* 2(4) (Fall 2004), accessed January 15, 2005, at http://lass.calumet.purdue.edu/cca/gmj/SubmittedDocuments/Fall2004/pdf_files/Quinn-Refereed-GMJ-F04.pdf
58 Davenport, Christian. "New Prison Photos Emerge," *Washington Post*, May 4, 2004, p. A-1. Accessed January 16, 2005, at http://www.washingtonpost.com/ac2/wp-dyn?pagename=article&contentId=A5623-2004May5&notFound=true.
59 The best practices in the region are Dubai Media City, which is completely interactive; and a new development of a similar digital city in Egypt, which provides free internet services as part of its national telecommunications policy.
60 Unnamed source quoted in editor Ben Smalley's *Middle East Media Guide 2004* (Dubai, UAE: Sandstone FZ-LLC), p. 164. http://www.tbsjournal.com/Archives/Fall02/ANN.html
61 Ibid., pp. 164–6.
62 Ibid., p. 164.
63 Rugh, *Arab Mass Media*, p. 219.
64 See Fraser P. Seitel's *The Practice of Public Relations* (New York: Prentice Hall, 2001). In an article in *O'Dwyer's PR Daily*, January 31, 2002, Seitel reported the Saudi government had paid $100,000 to Patton Boggs, an affiliate of Qorvis Communications, to lobby on its behalf in the US Congress. One also recalls the efforts of Prince Alwaleed bin Talal bin Abdelaziz bin Alsaud, the sixth richest person on earth, to gift $10,000 to the city of New York to help in reconstruction work at Ground Zero. His check was returned after a public outcry. Prince Alweed continues to be a major player in global media, however, as a major stockholder in AOL and EuroDisney, among other entertainment, hotel, real estate developments, Arab Radio and Television (ART) network, and media-related holdings.
65 Jihad Fakhreddine, "Trojan Horse? On the Arab Media as a Portal for Western Goods and Values," *TBS Journal* 12 (Spring/Summer 2004). Accessed January 4, 2005, at http://www.tbsjournal.com/Archives/ Spring04/fakhreddine.htm.
66 For a discussion on the need for a theory regarding Arab satellite broadcasting and political participation, see Kai Hafez, "Arab Satellite Broadcasting: An Alternative to Political Parties?" *TBS Journal* 13 (Fall 2004). Accessed January 15, 2005, http://www.tbsjournal.com/camphafez.htm.
67 See Michael G. Elasmar, ed., *The Impact of International Television: A Paradigm Shift* (Mahwah, NJ: Lawrence Erlbaum Associates, 2003), for questions about cultural imperialism theory in the present era, and how that paradigm might no longer be valid, if it ever was.

68 Comments made at opening of the annual conference of the Emirates Centre for Strategic Studies and Research in Abu Dhabi, January 9, 2005. Reported in the Gulf News, January 10, 2005, "Be Bold in Tackling Issues, Mohammad Tells Media," accessed January 15, 2005, at http://www.uaeinteract.com/news/default.asp?ID=42.

69 Keynote Address by His Majesty King Abdullah at News Xchange 2004, Algarve, Jordan, November 18, 2004. *TBS Journal* 13 (Fall/Winter 2004). Accessed January 15, 2005, at http://www.tbsjournal. com/kingabdallahkeynote.html.

Chapter 9

The Role of Global Advertising

Introduction

Commercial advertising thrives in a free-enterprise environment. Market-driven economies require advertising in order to succeed in merchandising goods and services both domestically and globally. Today, cultural industries, like others, seek marketing and advertising campaigns in order to create consumer awareness and increase sales. They do this nationally and increasingly internationally. As major multimedia corporations became ever more global, so their need for global advertising increases. And as the global economy expands, so does the need for global products, global brands, and global services such as advertising. Marketing and advertising globally has cost and brand image advantages. British Airways, Coca-Cola, Ford, GM, BP, GE, Microsoft, Disney, McDonald's, and Procter & Gamble have created persuasive global strategies involving a global corporate vision with a single voice or theme. For example, in 1994, "IBM announced the appointment of one advertising agency with the prime responsibility for executing IBM's strategic voice singularly around the world."[1] Now many multinational corporations seek out a single ad agency with global reach to provide a broad range of advertising-related services. The biggest unresolved issue in global advertising is still focused around a historical debate concerning standardization of all advertising versus adaptation of copy as well as strategies to local markets and tastes.[2] In the future the scales will likely tilt toward the standardization approach as multinational firms seek greater economies of scale, and with the huge advertising budgets, company headquarters will demand a greater role in the decision-making process.

The expansion of major multinational advertising agencies has become a key component in international communication for three major reasons:

1 Corporations themselves are going increasingly global and taking their advertising agencies with them. This includes communication corporations as well as other sectors such as transportation, food and beverages, natural resources, credit cards, etc.

2 As multimedia outlets – from privatized radio and television networks in Europe to new media and print outlets in Latin America – expand, they require successful advertising campaigns in order to generate the revenues and attract new customers necessary to succeed as viable commercial enterprises.

3 The growth of satellite-delivered broadcasting channels, along with a rapid expansion of cable systems and networks, have in turn generated demand for increased use of advertising agencies in order to develop a sufficient customer base for either the new services themselves, or the products they advertise.

The following sections highlight the major global advertising agencies that now themselves rank among the biggest firms in the world. They are not the advertising agencies of an earlier era that offered a limited menu of services to a few corporations within a single nation. Today, these advertising agencies are truly global in scope. Many are working with global products and offering a vast array of services far beyond print,[3] graphics, and placement advice, services that include everything from accounting practices, to training, to total quality management (TQM) practices, to data collection and analysis, all to assist with the development of corporate strategy plans and to web-based activities.[4] The modern advertising agency is a major partner with its clients in order that both become successful commercial undertakings. It is difficult to conceive of international communication in the current and future global environment without global advertising agencies as a key component.

The top 10 advertisers in the world contain only four US-based multinationals, namely Procter & Gamble, General Motors, Ford, and Time Warner. Of the top 10, two are communication corporations: Time Warner and Sony (see figure 9.1). Collectively they spend over $11 billion annually on competitive advertising globally. This is the basic reason why every major global ad agency has to have a significant corporate presence in the United States. Also, every one of the 10 largest advertisers has major global markets outside the United States, and therefore their ad agencies have to go global in order to keep and properly service these lucrative and prestigious accounts.

1. Procter & Gamble	6. Time Warner
2. Unilever	7. Daimler Chrysler
3. General Motors	8. L'Oreal
4. Toyota	9. Nestlé
5. Ford Motor Company	10. Sony

Figure 9.1   Top 10 advertisers in 2004
Source: Datamonitor.com.

These major advertising agencies are based in core nations and carry with them into all semiperipheral nations and some peripheral nations values, attitudes, and business practices. For example, these agencies employ the latest in research[5] including surveys, focus groups, knowledge management,[6] and demographic analysis, so that foreign customers look to these agencies rather than to local, frequently small firms, which do not have the arsenal of services, staff resources, or highly educated professionals with MBA or Ph.D. credentials they would need in order to compete effectively. Finally, the issue of advertising is not restricted to narrow concerns such as the availability of services from major multinational advertising agencies; rather, there is a larger, more conceptual concern of market economies functioning in a free-enterprise and democratic environment. Advertising does not fare well or serve any substantial purpose, for example, in totalitarian countries. In such countries, there are frequently only a few products of substantial value to purchase, or when such products are available, few except the ruling elite have the funds to purchase them. Advertising is a necessary ingredient, however, in the expanding market-based global economy, in which nation-states, whether in the periphery or semiperiphery regions, not only have to contend with foreign media, but they also have to contend with foreign advertising agencies. With deregulation, privatization, and expanding economies, the strategic goal of more and more nations has to take into account as a high priority the consequences of advertising on consumers as well as on their cultures as a whole. Thus, the impact of global advertising has become an important ingredient in an examination of international communication. A good example of the growing role of advertising is the deregulation sweeping western Europe that is resulting in a substantial increase in the number of radio, television, and cable services. This broadly based philosophic and economic movement has consequences for other nations as well, particularly those in eastern Europe:

The different East European regimes were confronted not only with the dangers inherent in the importation of programs. They also had to face the more serious dangers inherent in the importation of a mode of organization of the audiovisual sphere inspired by the logic of private enterprise, and of a matrix governed by values in total contradiction with those which they continued to defend.[7]

Today, few defend or call for a return to government-owned and -controlled media, a media with no advertising. More media, more choice, along with plenty of advertising, is the accepted environment being promoted by multinational conglomerates, clients, and ad agencies alike.

The following global agencies, all with multiple subsidiaries, services, and clients, are discussed in this chapter.

1) Omnicom Group Inc. (United States)
2) WPP Group (United Kingdom)
3) The Interpublic Group of Companies Inc. (United States)
4) Dentsu Inc. (Japan)
5) Publicis (France)
6) Havas Advertising (France).

The hallmark of global advertising is the trend embracing mergers and acquisitions. For many years the British firm WPP Group held the number one spot. But in 2001, the number three global giant, Interpublic Group, announced the purchase of the fifth-largest firm, True North Communications, for $2.1 billion. As a result, Interpublic became the largest advertising firm in the world. Not to be outdone and knocked to second place, WPP in 2004 purchased Grey Global Group of New York for nearly $1.5 billion. But during this time Omnicom Group emerged as number one with other acquisitions and expansion.

The important question is why are there so many mergers in this industry? The answer is fourfold. First, they hope some type of positive synergy will come about as a result of the expansion. Second, in some cases, the firms want to acquire creative talent not available in-house. Third, others seek to acquire a strategic niche to complement current strengths. And fourth, some firms realize they have to be aggressive and expand before a competitor attempts a takeover of either them or a rival they are looking at. Havas of France may be in this position since it failed to win the bidding war with WPP for Grey Global. It is very difficult for mid-sized advertising firms like Havas to survive in the highly competitive global arena.

Finally, all ad agencies have creative talent, but the ability to have one's commercial stand out among the rest is a daunting task. Since there are thousands of commercials seeking our attention, it takes imagination and creativity to get one's message to stand out. Frequently this means being on the cutting edge or pushing the ad or marketing envelope. If an ad goes too far, controversy often results. Two companies known globally for pushing the envelope are Benetton and Nike. For example, Nike ran racy ads during the 2000 Olympics and some media pulled the ads. Also in 2004 Nike had a large media campaign in China featuring Le Bron James of basketball fame. In the commercial he slays a dragon, a symbol of Chinese culture and historic pride. Nike finally pulled that ad. On the other hand, Benetton uses provocative ads to promote social issues. One of their global ads had an oil-drenched duck in a pool of oil. That was it; no clothes or other products in the picture.

Omnicom Group Inc.

Omnicom Group is the world's largest advertising organization and is headquartered in the United States. It was formed in 1986 and is a strategic holding company. Its 2003 sales exceeded US$8 billion. They like other global advertising firms have been experiencing slower growth since 9/11, but appears to be moving forward with many of the top industry talent. Omnicom employs 59,000 people and has grown recently with the addition of new affiliates. High-profile clients include PepsiCo, Anheuser-Busch, McDonald's, GE, Air France, and Daimler Chrysler. Omnicom provides marketing and consulting services through its Diversified Agency Services unit, which includes Communications Consulting Worldwide, the world's largest public-relations firm.

The Omnicom Group operates three global agency networks (BBDO Worldwide, DDB Worldwide, and TBWA Worldwide), plus a range of independent agencies including Cline, Davis & Mann (CDM), InterOne Marketing Group, Goodby, and GSD&M Advertising. The three global agency networks all rank in the top 10 global advertising agencies.

BBDO Worldwide, headquartered in New York City, operates nearly 300 agencies in 76 countries. From 1994 through 1998, BBDO received 200 broadcast advertising awards in the 5 major global competitions, substantially more than any other agency. In 2001 it was chosen as the leading global agency of the year by several trade publications. Major global business is from Dell Computer, Frito-Lay, and Duracell. DDB Worldwide, headquartered in New York City, operates over 206 offices in 96 countries. At the 45th International Advertising Festival in Cannes, DDB agencies won a total of 34 Lions (Oscars of the advertising world), more than any other advertising agency network, for the third year in a row. Major global accounts are the Sheraton Hotels and FTD.

TBWA Worldwide is the last of the three networks of Omnicom and it is also headquartered in New York City. TBWA Worldwide operates 237 offices in 75 countries. In the United States, for the second year in a row, Creativity Magazine named TBWA Worldwide Creative Agency of the Year. Major companies with TBWA Worldwide global accounts are Master Foods, Nextel, NatWest Bank, Société BIC, and Levi's.

TBWA/Hunt Lascaris Holdings, South Africa's second largest ad firm, was mandated in 1999 by Omnicom to sell a portion of its equity to black investors. The move came amid growing pressure on local agencies to attract minority investors. Those unable to do so could fall out of contention for government ad accounts. Omnicom Group's agency brands are consistently recognized as among the world's creative best. The company is at the top of the international market and provides advertising, media planning, marketing research, and broad array of consulting services to an expanding customer base in over 100 countries.

Ketchum PR Agency: ethics issue

Omnicom Group owns public-relations firm Ketchum. (It also owns another major public-relations firm, Fleishman-Hillard, which also got into billing troubles in California.) In 2005 Ketchum received much unwanted media attention for laundering a large Federal government contract with the Department of Education. It turns out that Ketchum hired a prominent conservative commentator, Armstrong Williams, to covertly hype an Education program without disclosing that he was on the payroll of Ketchum. Nor did he or Ketchum say openly which federal Department was paying for Omnicom's PR agency. Another of the commentator's clients for his newspaper columns was the Tribune Company, which immediately fired him for his ethical lapse. It turns out that Williams did a number of shows on radio and television, as well as print pieces, without divulging that he was being well paid for propaganda pieces for the Federal Government. The PR professional association, Public Relations Society of America, and many others deplored this ethical mess which Ketchum created. After weeks of negative media attention, Ketchum finally admitted its ethical lapse. It will be interesting to see, if over time, other clients, such as Cingular, Home Depot, Kodak, or Pepsi decide to leave this ethically challenged agency – or what the parent conglomerate, Omnicom Group, does about the image nightmare Ketchum has created for it.

WPP Group

WPP Group is the second-largest advertising and communication services group in the world. It consists of over 75 companies with 1,700 global offices operating in 104 nations. WPP employs more than 69,000 people. The company is largely the creation of English businessman Martin Sorrell, who made his name as financial director of advertising at Saatchi & Saatchi, joining that firm in 1977 and playing a key role in its growth through acquisitions.[8] However, in 1986 Sorrell set out to create his own advertising firm, the WPP Group. In the first half of 1987, WPP turned its attention to the United States market and acquired several US companies. It is the world's second largest communication group, providing services to local, multi-national, and global clients, including more than 300 of Fortune's Global 500. WPP is engaged in advertising, media planning and buying, market research, consulting, public relations, and specialist communications. More than 50 percent of WPP's sales come from advertising, and it derives more than 80 percent of its sales from outside the United Kingdom. This full-service agency specializes in the planning, production, and placing of advertising for clients in all categories, from radio commercials, to posters and print, to interactive television commercials, to internet and business. Although advertising makes up half its sales, WPP also offers clients media planning and buying, market research and consulting, public relations, and specialty communications. Some of WPP's global clients are IBM, American Express, Kimberly Clark, Merrill Lynch, Nestlé, and Unilever. WPP's most important single territory is the United States, which accounts for almost half of its income. The United Kingdom accounts for about 16 percent. The 2003 revenues were close to $4 billion. This is a significant increase from the early 1990s, when WPP was forced to suspend all dividend payments and refinance its considerable debt.

Some of WPP Group's major subsidiaries are Young & Rubicam, J. Walter Thompson Group, Ogilvy & Mather, Scali, McCabe, Hill & Knowlton, Kantar Group, and Research International Ltd. Through WPP's subsidiaries, the Group is moving into new areas such as the internet, data mining, behavior modeling, and customer retention work. In 2000, WPP purchased Young & Rubicam in a $4.7 billion acquisition to form the world's largest advertising and services group. In 1999, Young & Rubicam (Y&R) was the third largest US ad agency, with 12,000 employees in nearly 350 offices in over 70 countries. Y&R offers a broad range of ad, media, and communication services as well as the controlled public-relations giant Burson-Marsteller. Y&R was an employee-owned private company until 1998 when it went public to raise funds for further global expansion. Y&R utilized a number of globally based videoconferencing sites for both management and clients.

Through these sites, Y&R attempts to focus its creative resources, regardless of location, to meet clients' needs. It has a major new global marketing subsidiary called Winderman Cato Johnson (WCJ), which takes a technology focus in order to assist clients with e-commerce and internet-based marketing needs and solutions. WCJ has over 3,000 employees working in close to 50 nations. Some of its major global clients are Ford, AT&T, Xerox, and Sony. Ford alone accounts for 10 percent of Y&R billings. In 2003 WPP acquired Cordiant and a 25 percent equity position in ZenithOptimedia. Both these US-based firms increased WPP's presence in the strategic North American market. In 2004 WPP took over Grey Global Group and added major clients, such as 3M, Oracle, Sprint, and Proctor & Gamble. WPP also recently bought a Washington PR firm, a Japanese agency, and part of Mediapro Group. With their new subsidiaries, WPP's global revenue stream will increase considerably. WPP offers major clients world-class advertising, public relations, and marketing research to help them expand globally.

Interpublic Group of Companies Inc.

The world's number three advertising group, The Interpublic Group of Companies (IPC), is headquartered in New York and employs over 43,000 people. It serves a total of more than 4,000 multinational, regional, and local clients. The company roots trace back to 1930 when two firms merged to create McCann-Erickson. Now IPC has five global operating divisions: Constituency Management Group, FCB Group, Independent Agencies, McCann-Erickson Worldwide, and The Partnership. The various divisions serve the advertising, marketing, and other strategic needs of clients including global companies such as Coca-Cola, Unilever, and General Motors. IPC's net income in 2003 was nearly $6 billion. In 2000, however, it lost the Burger King account. In 2005 it picked up Intel. Over the last 20 years, IPC's revenue has increased by more than 1,100 percent and net income has risen 1,800 percent.

IPC has offices in more than 120 countries. Its international public-relations unit is one of the largest PR firms in the world. Interpublic is the parent organization of a growing number of leading advertising agencies and marketing communications companies. As the holding company, IPC creates ads through its four global networks: McCann-Erickson World Group, Ammirati Puris Lintas, the Lowe Group, and DraftDirect. The McCann-Erickson World Group was formed in 1997 and employs 12,000 people. As a new worldwide communications firm, it is dedicated to providing a full spectrum of high-quality marketing, research, and communication services.

It is one of the most powerful networks of ad agencies in the world and has a rapidly expanding portfolio of marketing communications companies that operate parallel with the ad agencies. IPC has over 50 subsidiaries, which cover all aspects of advertising and marketing. They serve clients on every continent.

Interpublic as part of the ad industry's consolidation trend purchased True North Communications. It is based in Chicago and has over 200 offices in close to 100 countries. It has three major brands: in advertising, FCB Worldwide; in public relations, BSMG Worldwide; and in marketing, Marketing Drive Worldwide. True North is particularly strong in North America and South America. Major clients include Coors, Compaq, Amazon.com, Jell-O, and Major League Baseball. In 2000 True North lost the Chrysler Group account worth about $140 million, or about 10 percent of its revenue.

True North owns about 50 percent of the internet firm Modern Media, and also is a part owner of Springer & Jacoby, a progressive German agency. A key company goal is to expand the number of clients with global brands who are seeking full-service agencies.

Dentsu Inc.

Dentsu is the fourth-largest global ad agency and number one in Japan. The roots of Dentsu date back to 1901 when Hoshiri Mitsunaga founded Japan Advertising and Telegraphic Service Company. By 1946, Dentsu had become a commercial broadcasting, public relations, and advertising entity that modernized its efforts through extensive reliance on market research. In 1951, Dentsu incorporated its radio and television divisions and produced Japan's first television broadcast. By 1959, Dentsu had expanded to the United States by opening an office in New York. Two years later, in 1961, Dentsu joined with Young & Rubicam, the US-based agency, to become a joint venture firm for several major accounts. Dentsu agency continued to expand globally with offices in Chicago, Los Angeles, Honolulu, Paris, Melbourne, and Taiwan. By the mid-1970s, Dentsu was ranked the number one global advertising agency. By the 1980s, it was broadening its efforts with its Total Communication Service and the opening of additional offices across Europe and the Middle East. The company has over 14,000 employees and is headquartered in Tokyo, Japan. It maintains and operates 32 offices in Japan and has subsidiaries and affiliates in 27 countries around the globe. Dentsu is particularly strong in the United States, Asia, and the Middle East. Dentsu dominates by collecting half of Japan's primetime billings. Dentsu has over 6,000 clients and some of the major global clients are Canon, Sony, Hitachi, Bell Atlantic, and Toyota. It also has a division that specializes in sports marketing.

Dentsu corporate philosophy was restructured in 1986. Originally developed to define Dentsu's role as a full-service communications company, the corporate philosophy is now composed of corporate objectives, employee qualifications, 10 work guidelines, and the slogan that reflects the company's commitment: "Communications Excellence."

The managers of Dentsu Inc. offer a Total Communication Service that includes account services, market research and strategic planning, creative development, media services, sales promotion, corporate communications, sports marketing, event promotion, new media and digital advertising, and advertising support systems. Dentsu is committed to making sure each client's message reaches its designated target through its Total Communication Service.

Dentsu has a strategic partnership with Young & Rubicam (acquired by WPP in 2000) as well as a 15 percent stake in the major French advertising conglomerate Publicis.

Publicis Group

Publicis is the largest agency in Europe and was founded in 1926. It has over 20,000 employees in 80 nations. It has 150 subsidiaries offering a broad range of communication services worldwide. Since 1998 one of its main subsidiaries is San Francisco-based Publicis & Hal Riney. This provided Publicis with a strategic foothold in the lucrative North American market. Major clients are Sprint and Hewlett-Packard, but in 2002 they lost the $300 million Saturn account.

In 2000 Publicis Group purchased Saatchi & Saatchi for $1.9 billion as part of its global expansion. In 1999 Publicis bought 49 percent of Chicago-based Burrell Communications. Burrell is a large ad agency specializing in African American markets. It has several major clients including Coca-Cola, McDonald's, Procter & Gamble, and Sears. In 1997 Publicis purchased 51 percent of Israel's leading agency, Ariely Advertising.

Through a series of major strategic acquisitions, including buying out major rival Saatchi & Saatchi in 2000, Publicis is seeking to become a European and global agency offering a broad range of services. It is trying to move into emerging multinational markets by responding to industry pressure to add foreign subsidiaries. Brothers co-founded Saatchi & Saatchi in 1970. The company used to be part of the advertising giant Cordiant, which in 1997 split into two firms, Cordiant Communications and Saatchi

& Saatchi. Since the split of the giant company, business has been good for both parties. Both have a large European focus.

The international holding company Saatchi & Saatchi currently has operations in advertising, marketing, and communications. In 2005 the company employed 7,000 workers. Its namesake advertising agency, which generates more than 80 percent of the company's sales, has about 150 offices in more than 90 countries and serves global clients such as Procter & Gamble, Toyota, DuPont, and General Mills. The company provides worldwide marketing communications services and media services through Rowland Communications Worldwide, has a 70 percent interest in the Facilities Group, and now owns Zenith Media Worldwide.

The Saatchi brothers made some individuals wealthy when they overpaid for venerable agencies in their misguided strategy to buy their way to the number one spot. For example, when Charles and Maurice Saatchi purchased Bates, then the third largest US ad agency, for $400 million down in 1986 and another $50 million in 1998, it was the highest price paid for an advertising agency. The brothers also paid a premium for two other US agencies that year, Dancer-Fitzgerald-Sample and Backer & Spielvogel. One year later, the brothers attempted to buy J. Walter Thompson, the United States' oldest advertising agency. The ongoing global acquisition frenzy in the ad industry can be traced back to the Saatchi brothers.

In 1994 Maurice Saatchi was dismissed as chairman of the holding company; Charles Saatchi left a short time later. The company continued without them and managed to acquire major accounts such as Toyota and Procter & Gamble. More than half of its worldwide billings come from North America. Saatchi & Saatchi is key in assisting Publicis in becoming a more dominant global agency.

In 2002 Publicis purchased US-based Bcom3 for $3 billion. Bcom3 was the result of a merger in 2000 among BDM, The Leo Group, and The MacManus Group. Bcom3 was 20 percent owned by Dentsu. The merged firms provides a broad range of communication services such as advertising, public relations, marketing, research, and media buying and planning. One of the partners, Leo Group, has a proud history. Leo Burnett, the founder, has been responsible for creating some of the most successful marketing icons in the United States, including such campaigns as Tony the Tiger, the Marlboro Man, the Pillsbury Doughboy, and the Jolly Green Giant. Founded in 1935, the company provides a full range of advertising, marketing, and communication services to clients such as Coca-Cola, Nintendo, Walt Disney, General Motors, Kellogg's, and Procter & Gamble. The former employee-owned company employs 9,000 in its 80 offices worldwide. Burnett has a 49 percent stake in UK-based Bartle Bogle Hegarty. Burnett's international billings alone were close to $7 billion, and several of its blue-chip clients have been with the firm for decades. Over $4 billion in billings come from non-US-based offices, reflecting Burnett's effective global strategy. Yet the merged firm was still only mid-sized in a land of ad giants, and thus to survive it was sold to Publicis. In turn Publicis, which has acquired several key firms, now provides its international clients with seamless and multi-faceted ad and marketing advice.

Havas Advertising

Havas Advertising is a leading pan-European agency. With over 300 subsidiaries, it operates in over 88 countries in addition to Europe, employs over 16,000 people worldwide, and had billings of close to $2 billion in 2003. Europe represents 60 percent of its revenue, with France the major player. The United States provides over 30 percent of Havas Advertising's revenue. Since 75 percent of all global advertising is by US firms, global advertising agencies that are not US-based require an effective network of subsidiaries in the United States to succeed as global firms. In Latin America, Havas Advertising operates in Mexico, Brazil, and Argentina. It also has a major sports planning and marketing subsidiary. Major clients include Kraft, Microsoft, Volvo, and Airbus.

Havas had been aiming to become one of the top five global advertising agencies in the next decade, but recently missed the buy of US-based Grey Global to the British ad conglomerate WPP. As an international agency, Havas needs to add to its international activities through a global strategy of meeting the needs of clients and their products through a larger network of global brand managers. Havas's global ad agency is known as Euro RSCG Worldwide.

Conclusions

The premier global advertising and communication service agencies are in a highly competitive market for creative talent as well as additional customers. The global agencies, all based in core nations, are primarily located in North America and Europe. The European and Japanese agencies need to have a major presence in North American markets because that is where the bulk of the corporations that engage in substantial international advertising are located. All major advertising firms have an extensive network of subsidiaries and offices in core, semiperipheral, and a few peripheral nations. Many of the offices are located in former colonies, particularly those of Britain and France. During the past decades, a substantial amount of consolidation has taken place in the industry. The large firms are becoming larger in order to offer a broader range of services to current and prospective clients. Given the continuing global privatization of media outlets as well as the increase in channel capacity due to technological innovations such as digital systems, in the future there will be a growing demand in industrialized and emerging nations for commercially effective media advertising. The merger mania is also likely to continue.

Finally, critics of cultural imperialism blame US ad agencies for their global reach on behalf of multinational clients. Yet the actual picture is quite different. The second-largest ad agency in the world – WPP Group – is British. In fact, nearly half of the top global ad agencies are non-US-owned or -controlled. In addition to WPP, the number four agency is Dentsu (Japan), number six is Publicis (France), number seven is Havas (France). In reality, a set of core nations – the United States, France, Britain, and Japan – collectively are spreading the advertising mantra around the globe for an increasing number of multinational firms. These giant ad firms and their clients have a strong vested corporate interest in the global economy.

The role and impact of global advertising is a key component which helps define and substantiate both world-system and electronic colonialism theories. The following list outlines the key links between global advertising agencies and world-system and electronic colonialism theories:

- The major global ad agencies are all based in core nations. They act as savvy electronic imperialists on behalf of their global clients.
- All major agencies have to be based in or have major subsidiaries in the United States. US multinational firms purchase the bulk of global ads.
- All major agencies have offices in major cities of other core nations.
- All major agencies have offices in semiperipheral nations.
- Due to the saturation and maturity of core markets, ad agency expansion is available primarily through two routes: (1) through corporate expansion to additional major cities in the semiperipheral zones, particularly in Latin America or Asia, and (2) through acquisition of medium- and small-size ad agencies, or related businesses in core nations. The big will get bigger in this industry.[9] Interpublic's bid to take over True North, WPP buying Grey Group, and Publicis's purchase of Bcom3 are excellent examples of this trend.
- Mid-sized ad firms, such as Havas, are poorly positioned or equipped to succeed in an industry of global giants.
- Major ad agencies employ extremely creative personnel plus cutting-edge research techniques to produce effective marketing and media

commercials for their clients. As a result, they are major players in the electronic colonialism of the global marketplace.

- There are no major agencies headquartered in peripheral nations. Nations in this least affluent zone consider themselves fortunate to host a branch office of some core-based major agency. The major agencies offer such a plethora of sophisticated services that indigenous ad firms in other zones find it virtually impossible to compete effectively for large international accounts.

Finally, the major agencies have branched out to offer full-service, seamless packages ranging from accounting, to management training, to assessment, to strategic planning, so that clients in the lesser two zones become ensnared in electronic colonialism practices without fully contemplating the long-run behavior, impact, and attitude shifts required.

In the lesser two zones, those countries with market-driven economies and expanding media outlets will experience more competition from core-based agencies seeking new accounts, including the strong possibility that core-based agencies will invest in local ad agencies as fully or partially owned or controlled subsidiaries. From the perspective of electronic colonialism, advertising has a greater role and impact on foreigners' minds, lives, values, and ultimately purchasing behaviors than the audio or video programming or print copy these ads accompany or surround. The goal of ad agencies is to influence others attitudes, behaviors, and ultimately lifestyles. Their goal is to replace traditional buying habits with new behaviors leading to the consumption of core nations' goods and services. To some extent, global ad agencies are the foot soldiers of electronic colonialism theory. They are promoting core nations' values and products to an ever-increasing number of individuals and nations across the globe on a daily basis.

In the future, with the expansion of the global economy and markets, along with more media technologies, new commercial opportunities will appear for aggressive global ad agencies. This will clearly extend beyond cable, wireless, and satellite channels to include the internet. Major agencies are experiencing industry pressure to achieve broader scale and scope by expanding their services and acquiring subsidiaries as they themselves confront global competition. For all major agencies, more than half of gross revenue now comes from global billing. Domestic billing, even in the United States, is no longer sufficient to sustain a major player among the global agencies. All stakeholders need a plethora of clients in an expanding range of foreign countries Advertising is an industry in which the chief stakeholders need to continue to grow and acquire other firms or they may find themselves being acquired by some other aggressive firm based in Europe, Japan, or the United States.

Notes

1 Wayne McCullough, "Global Advertising Which Acts Locally: The IBM Subtitles Campaign," *Journal of Advertising Research* 36 (May–June 1996), p. 12.

2 M. Agrawal, "Review of a 40-year Debate in International Advertising Practitioner and Academician Perspectives to the Standardization/Adaptation Issue," *International Marketing Review* 12 (March 1995), pp. 26–48.

3 Industry Overview: "Press: Still the Largest Medium," *International Journal of Advertising* 18 (Aug. 1999), pp. 405–11.

4 Wossen Kassaye, "Global Advertising and the World Wide Web," *Business Horizons* 40 (May–June 1997); and Kuen-Hee Ju-Pak, "Content Dimensions of Web Advertising: A Cross-National Comparison," *International Journal of Advertising* 18 (May 1999), pp. 207–32.

5 Demetrios Vakratsas and Tim Ambler, "How Advertising Works: What Do We Really Know?" *Journal of Marketing* 63 (Jan. 1999), pp. 26–43; and Marieke de Mooij, *Global Marketing and Advertising* (Thousand Oaks, CA: Sage, 1997).

6 Michael Ewing and Doug West, "Advertising Knowledge Management: Strategies and Implications," *International Journal of Advertising* 19 (May 2000), pp. 225–44.

7 Tristan Mattelart, "Transboundary Flows of Western Entertainment Cross the Iron Curtain," *Journal of International Communication* 6(2) (Dec. 1999), p. 118.

8 WPP is a publicly traded stock on the London and New York exchanges. WPP was incorporated in 1871 in the United Kingdom as Wire and Plastic Products Limited; the WPP of today is far removed from its original focus.

9 Andreas Grein and Robert Ducoffe, "Strategic Responses to Market Globalization among Advertising Agencies," *International Journal of Advertising* 17 (Aug. 1998), pp. 301–20.

Chapter 10

The Message: The Role of International Organizations

Introduction

Historically, the United Nations Educational, Scientific, and Cultural Organization (UNESCO) has tried to avoid controversy. Yet its role, profile, and focus in the international information and communication debate are unmistakable. UNESCO, a specialized agency of the United Nations, sponsored crucial international conferences that focused on the communication debate and also directed its research program toward promoting new initiatives such as the New World Information and Communication Order (NWICO). Initially UNESCO invested much, backstage as well as publicly, in NWICO. This eventually led to major problems for the agency, the greatest of which were the withdrawals during the 1980s of the United States and the United Kingdom from UNESCO membership. When they left, they also took their crucial financial support, which had been about one-third of UNESCO's total budget. UNESCO put its efforts and credibility into supporting a call for NWICO, but with the demise of the Cold War, UNESCO was found wanting. It had made a strategic mistake in relying extensively on Soviet support for NWICO.

Before describing the critical historical meetings and stakeholders in the NWICO debate, it is important to note that the global media have two rather distinct origins. In the United States, their origins are strongly rooted in commercial media systems in which advertising and market forces play crucial roles. Initially with radio and now with television and telecommunications, the US model is one of corporate influence with private ownership and control. The US model treats media and culture as economic commodities. By contrast, in Europe and in most countries of the world, the historical model is one of government ownership or government control of the mass media. The BBC is a good example of a noncommercial radio and television network subsidized by both the government and listeners or viewers, who pay annual licensing fees. In most of the world, radio evolved as a government medium without commercials or the influence of marketplace competition. The role of electronic media was to inform, educate, and entertain; not to make money from advertisers. Broadcasting monopolies were the early pervasive global model. When television technology emerged, these same government agencies took responsibility for television broadcasting. For several decades they limited the number of national television networks to only one or two, much as they did with radio. They viewed the media as cultural partners that were necessary to promote a nation's history, culture, and the arts. When commercial television emerged, a mixed model was accepted in Europe and in many other countries. The commercial model of the United States was frowned upon until vast audiences began viewing the shows presented by new alternative commercial television stations. With deregulation and the advancement of cable and satellite technologies, several competing commercial broadcasting systems were born. These systems or networks frequently are giants and reach larger audiences than the original government-controlled and -administered networks.

It is important to keep this duality of approach in mind when considering the following debates. The debates themselves tended to move along two different tracks, the one track being more commercial, market driven, and free enterprise in orientation, the other being noncommercial, publicly funded, and government controlled and regulated in the public interest in orientation. The following sections review the history of the international communication debates, illustrating the global and fundamental differences in the origins, philosophies, roles, and environments in which global communication stakeholders have operated and, in some monopolistic, government-regulated environments, continue to operate. More than half of the nations in the world – those in the peripheral regions – still place some type of restriction on journalists or media outlets. Even though the commercial, advertiser-supported networks have attracted by far the largest audiences internationally, there is still a dedicated and loyal niche audience supporting public broadcasting, led by outlets such as the BBC. Many non-Americans view the international communication debate from a much different perspective. "Decolonization in itself has not made the world more just and peaceful. The evidence shows more news and images come from the Western world and the access to non-Western culture in terms of information, knowledge, entertainment and images becomes more scarce."[1]

UNESCO: Backdrop for the NWICO Debates

Acknowledging in its constitution that "since wars begin in the minds of men, it is in the minds of men that the defenses of peace must be constructed," UNESCO originated in Great Britain in 1945. Based on this lofty ideal, UNESCO has transformed itself from a passive force into an active force in international affairs. It views its mission as that of a catalyst for and supporter of development:

> Both on the theoretical and the practical level, UNESCO has a vital role to play. . . . The current economic relations between industrialized and developing countries must, certainly, be transformed, but they cannot on their own change the political and socio-cultural factors, which shape integrated developments. Thus UNESCO has the task of helping: to enlarge the scientific and technological bases which permit each country to use its natural resources better; . . . to increase and improve communications and information systems; . . . to promote the progress of social sciences so that each society can undertake its own studies and utilize the instruments of change without losing its own identity.[2]

Formally established as a specialized agency of the United Nations in 1946, UNESCO entered the international arena with 20 member states, the vast majority being core nations. Its budget is drawn from a levy imposed on each member state. Its General Assembly, comprised of all member states, meets every two years to determine the agency's programs and budget. A 45-member Executive Board supervises the implementation of the programs, and the day-to-day operations of the agency are carried out by the Secretariat. Although based in Paris, the Secretariat draws its personnel from all member states.[3] In the early years, all members were core or semiperipheral nations. Peripheral nations began joining UNESCO after the Second World War. Many were former colonies of European core nations – this created a tense working environment. Today, delegates from several peripheral nations hold senior positions in UNESCO. To a large extent most peripheral nations view UNESCO as the one specialized agency of the UN which promotes their needs and agenda with its focus on a broad range of development initiatives.

UNESCO's mandate is broad, covering educational, scientific, cultural, and communication programs and research projects around the globe. The convening and sponsoring of international ministerial and research conferences to discuss various aspects of this broad mandate is one of UNESCO's most important and time-consuming tasks. In fact, it is through this role that UNESCO became a major player in the international communication debates leading to NWICO.

Originally, the Western nations, particularly Britain, France, and the United States, dominated UNESCO. However, beginning in the 1950s and continuing today, power and influence shifted as a result of the continual addition of newly emerging nations, primarily from Asia, Africa, and other peripheral areas. Today, the Director-General is from Asia. The one-country-one-vote procedures that govern the agency have provided the peripheral nations with a voice. During the 1960s, the shared ideological and economic conditions of several of these peripheral nations led to the development of a power bloc or lobby known as the Group of 77. Although this bloc has grown to include well over 100 nations, its role and that of these newly emerged nations within UNESCO is fraught with contradictions. As Richard Hoggart explains, "The new nations, who were, in general, creations of the early sixties, tend to take the UN seriously though ambiguously. Since the UN was set up by the victorious allied powers, it has the stamp of Western ways of thinking. On the other hand, its record in anti-colonialism is good and it has made a considerable contribution to the emergence of some new states. Their relationship to the UN is therefore rich in ambiguities."[4]

This ambiguity is no better illustrated than in their attitudes toward global communication. On the one hand, many of these nations want, some desperately, to become modern industrialized countries with color digital television, personal computers, cellular phones, and all the media trappings that money and technology permit. Yet, as noted earlier, most lack even the basic telecommunication infrastructures for telephone, let alone sophisticated ground terminals for satellite television transmission, or fiberoptic cable for internet access. At the same time, many of these nations reject Western culture – Hollywood films, Madison Avenue commercials, and core-nation or foreign-produced television programming. For many in the peripheral zone, only pure, indigenous domestic media products are acceptable. The dilemma, of course, is that core-nation technology and shows are easily accessible and cheaper than the production or creation of indigenous systems or software.

Throughout its existence, UNESCO has had its critics. Part of that criticism is a result of the periodic negative assessment of its parent, the United Nations. Another flash point, during the mid-1970s, was a decision that excluded Israel from the European regional grouping, creating a barrage of criticism from the Western press, and leading the United States to temporarily withhold its contribution to UNESCO, an amount equal to about 25 percent of the agency's total budget.

Paradoxically, another cause for criticism was the consistent demand of peripheral countries for better development initiatives. UNESCO's initial response to critics was to focus on education, which culminated in the publication of the 1972 Faure Commission report, *Learning to Be*.[5] But with the completion of that effort, a substantive policy vacuum developed that permitted the introduction of a series of resolutions by republics of the Soviet Union concerning the development of national media and communication policies. UNESCO, core governments, and multinational media corporations largely ignored the issues and questions being raised because they underestimated the strength, determination, and depth of animosity felt by peripheral nations. These peripheral nations had a long list of grievances about international media flows. The lack of substantive policy permitted the Soviets and several peripheral nations to hijack UNESCO's planning agenda in the late 1970s. The result was the eruption of the NWICO debates, which dominated the activities of UNESCO for more than two decades. This chapter highlights the major forums in which the media and communication debates crystallized. Even today, many nations around the world are critical and concerned about the impact of foreign software on their domestic values, attitudes, and beliefs.

Identifying the Issues and Taking Sides

The debate officially began in 1970[6] when UNESCO's General Assembly outlined the need to articulate national communication policies and a series of publications dealing with this issue began to emerge. This examination, by the peripheral nations in particular, led to increased documentation and greater awareness of the one-way flow of media messages from core to peripheral nations. It also became apparent that national communication development policies for semiperipheral and peripheral nations could not be produced when so much of their media were produced or controlled by foreign firms based in London, Paris, New York, or Los Angeles.

Subsequently, three significant resolutions were introduced that increased the visibility and divisiveness of the global media issue. The first related to the rapid development of direct broadcast satellite (DBS) technology. DBS allowed media outlets to transmit their messages directly to receiving sets throughout the world. Whereas traditional ground-station broadcasting signals could be controlled or blocked to prevent the widespread transmission of alien messages, DBS signals could easily circumvent these restrictions and procedures. In response, UNESCO passed a resolution – by a vote of 100 to 1, with the United States as the only dissenter – to require satellite broadcasters to obtain the prior consent of national governments before transmitting messages to a foreign territory. Even though there was no technical way to enforce the resolution, its passage represented a bold-faced rejection of US "free press" and "free flow" rhetoric, practice, and ideals.

The second resolution called for regional meetings of experts to discuss national communication policies. This resolution received the unanimous support of the General Assembly, but dissension arose when it was decided to hold these meetings in peripheral regions and not in the core industrialized nations, as had been UNESCO's tradition. A few of the early meetings were held in Latin America.

The third contentious resolution, which was introduced by the USSR, sought to acknowledge both the right and the responsibility of national governments to control the media messages' availability to their citizenry. Although the resolution failed to pass, it was attractive to many peripheral nations, which were heartened to have the support of at least one of the superpowers. Although peripheral nations had achieved a significant presence in UNESCO, this Soviet "sharing of the minds" with respect to communication policy lent strength to their votes, opinions, and influence. For their part, the Soviets had no journalistic qualms or ethical dilemmas about extending international government control of media; clearly, their major objective was to aggravate the United States and other core nations.

The Nonaligned Movement

As the process of decolonization continued to release newly emerging nations from the foreign-policy mandates of their former colonizers, many began to fear becoming satellites or pawns of one of the two superpowers, the United States or the Soviet Union. Consequently, a new pressure group emerged. In 1973 a summit meeting of foreign ministers of nonaligned countries met in Algiers. During this meeting, participating nations acknowledged their desire to develop a unique foreign-policy stance independent of both the United States and the USSR. They wanted to create a "third option" to reflect their independence. Many of the policy positions postulated sought to overcome the consequences of past colonization. Among these was a demand for the decolonization of information.

A series of nonaligned conferences followed in Peru, Tunisia, Mexico, India, and Sri Lanka. At each successive meeting, the rhetoric and action progressed from attacking transnational communication corporations to developing an action plan for the establishment of a wire service, Inter Press Services, which would begin as a pool of contributing government information services.

Additional issues included debate about the New International Economic Order (NIEO) and awareness of the growing power of a nucleus of oil-rich, nonaligned countries in the Middle East, known as the Organization of Petroleum Exporting Countries (OPEC).

In addition to the nonaligned summit meetings, a crucial seminar was held at the University of Tampere in Finland. Finland's President Urho Kekkonen, in addressing the issue of cultural imperialism, asserted that the theory of the "free" flow of information was really a rationale for a "one-way" flow. Not coincidentally, a major research study also was presented at the conference that documented the pervasive influence of US and British television program sales internationally.[7] As research increasingly revealed evidence of the one-way flow of media products, particularly wire services, anti-Western rhetoric escalated.

Latin America Meetings

While the nonaligned countries proceeded to articulate their complaints and develop communication strategies, several UNESCO-sponsored meetings were convened to investigate the disparities in international information flows and participation in national communication policy development. The major issues quickly became the relationship between communication policies and economic, social, and cultural development, and the role of governments in promoting the latter by controlling the former. A major conference to examine these questions was set for July 1976 in San Jose, Costa Rica, but two background meetings were held in Bogota, Colombia, July 4–13, 1974, and Quito, Ecuador, June 24–30, 1975. These meetings provided significant impetus and research for critics of Western media. Background papers, data, and research documents were presented outlining several grievances about a broad range of international communication issues. Foreign wire services, particularly those headquartered in New York, London, and Paris, came in for considerable criticism about their coverage of Latin America.

It should be emphasized that all parties to the debate understood that these regional conferences were creating momentum for a major international conference focusing on media and information-flow issues. Global information flows and media policies dominated the debate at UNESCO just as education had in the 1960s. However, while there had been a general consensus about the positive role and impact of education, a strong and highly divisive polarity of opinion (free press versus government control) was developing concerning global information policies.

The 19th UNESCO General Assembly, Nairobi, 1976

The vital role of information and the debate about how to promote development through information policies were the focus of the 19th UNESCO General Assembly. By this time, most peripheral countries had abandoned the desire for and rhetoric about a free press in favor of a development press, one that would assist in the positive development of their nation-states. They wanted a cultural stamp of their own making and not one imported from core nations or "Made in the USA." The Director-General of UNESCO, Amadou-Mahtar M'Bow from Senegal, Africa, could not have agreed more.

The major document before delegates at the Nairobi conference was a resolution similar to the one that had been introduced by the Soviet Union in 1971 entitled "Draft Declaration of Fundamental Principles Governing the Use of the Mass Media in Strengthening Peace and International Understanding and in Combating War, Propaganda, Racialism and Apartheid." This declaration, specifically Article 12, requiring that national governments take responsibility for all media systems, guaranteed extensive attention from the Western press. Once again, most of the Western media coverage was negative. The negative focus affected Director-General M'Bow as well as the media debate.

Before outlining the major events in Nairobi, it is necessary to remind readers of a situation during the early 1970s that again cemented Western, particularly US, faith in the value of a free press. Without dwelling on the details, two junior reporters for the *Washington Post*, Carl Bernstein and Bob Woodward, pursued a lead that ultimately resulted in the resignation of Richard Nixon as president of the United States. Like nothing else might have, the Watergate scandal reinvigorated a latent distrust of government regulations and demonstrated to the people of the United States and other core nations the need for a press free from government control. Even the mere suggestion of increased government control of the media was anathema to the US public and Western journalists. In a similar fashion, British control of the national press during the Falkland Islands invasion in 1982 irritated many British reporters and publishers as well as the British public. Consequently, the Western model of the press as the "fourth estate" had been strongly reinforced in advance of the Nairobi conference.

After years of preliminary discussions concerning the role of the media, the Nairobi debate boiled down to a signal draft declaration consisting of 12 articles. Given the heightened profile of the issue within UNESCO and on the news agenda of the global wire services, a means to avoid a direct confrontation between East and West was sought. Leaving aside other issues, it was Article 12, calling for state responsibility for media activities, that dominated the conference. In the "spirit of Nairobi," a compromise was reached, mainly backstage, to shelve the draft declaration and to reduce pressure among the peripheral nations and nonaligned militants by forming a new group to study the issue further. UNESCO created the International Commission for the Study of Communication Problems, headed by Senator Sean MacBride of Ireland.

Having accurately analyzed the strong Western objection to development journalism and government oversight or control of press activities, Director-General M'Bow wanted to avoid an outright showdown, as well as save his career. Although he was able to delay the debate and vote until the next General Assembly, to be held in Paris in 1978, he also exacerbated the problem by linking the debate over a new international information order to the proposed new international economic order.

The New International Economic Order (NIEO) ———

In order to provide a complete picture of the rise of the nonaligned movement, it is necessary to describe the development of the New International Economic Order (NIEO). During the early 1970s, the United Nations and its member agencies became major vehicles for change, offering hope to emerging peripheral nations. Many observers were surprised by the extent to which the resolve and the magnitude of change adopted by the United Nations was misanalyzed not only in terms of NWICO, but also with respect to the underlying NIEO. It took Western economists several years to come to grips with NIEO, and only a few understood its link to international communication and NWICO. This point is highlighted in a report published by UNESCO, which also addressed the changing balance of power within the international agency.

> Just what was the NIEO that the United Nations, and therefore UNESCO, were supporting? In effect, it represents a major change for the West, which traditionally controlled the United States and its organizations. This is clearly not the case any longer. When 146 nations met in Paris for 5 weeks of UNESCO meetings in the fall of 1978, the largest group, 106 Member States, represented Third World, or so-called nonaligned, nations. They were originally labeled the "Group of 77," and this label is still used despite continually increasing size and influence.[8]

Given the shift, it should not be surprising that the pressure for changes to enhance the development opportunities of peripheral nations became a pressing issue on the agendas of the United Nations and its specialized agencies. In response, on May 1, 1974, the United Nations General Assembly passed a resolution to adopt a major program of action establishing a New International Economic Order. The declaration encouraged member states to:

> work urgently for the establishment of a New International Economic Order based on "equity, sovereign equality, interdependence, common interest and cooperation among all states," irrespective of their economic and social systems which shall correct inequalities and redress existing injustices, make it possible to eliminate the widening gap between the developed and the developing countries and ensure steadily accelerating economic and social development and peace and justice for future generations.[9]

The result was a flurry of research and conferences conducted to clarify the issues and develop strategies for achieving the goal.[10] Despite all the activity, enhanced economic development for peripheral nations failed to occur. However, the peripheral nations found an unexpected opportunity for change when the Organization of Petroleum Exporting Countries (OPEC), originally founded in Baghdad in 1960, was able to force a substantial increase in the price of oil, a basic commodity throughout the world.[11] During the 1970s, OPEC quickly became a model for peripheral nations to emulate in hopes of obtaining the economic concessions and achieving the financial growth that had escaped them.

The changes in economic orientation and philosophy brought about by NIEO influenced all aspects of UNESCO's activities. Everything from the influence of transnational corporations to the role of the major wire services and the impact of popular culture was examined in light of either NIEO or NWICO. The anticolonial rhetoric of the new order was harsh. Colonial domination, neocolonialism, racial discrimination, apartheid, media images, cultural imperialism, and violations of human rights were all subject to severe criticism. Although the goals of the new order were lofty, its real objective was to shift international power from Western, core nations to a loose coalition of peripheral regions, Arab OPEC regions, nonaligned nations, and socialist (namely, the USSR) countries. The next goal was to effect a change in sociocultural priorities under the protection or guidance of NWICO.

The Debate Begins in Earnest

As UNESCO prepared for the next general meeting, the future of Director-General M'Bow rested on how he handled the contentious draft declaration on the mass media. He realized that the "spirit of Nairobi" was a false one built on acrimony and distrust. The agreement to establish the MacBride International Commission as a means of buying time and reducing the building pressure had been worked out backstage at the last moment to avoid a walkout by Western delegations. That compromise was no longer sufficient to withstand the mounting strain.

M'Bow also had to do something to polish UNESCO's image, which had become severely tarnished. UNESCO's Secretariat perceived the problem as one created by the Western press, which had emphasized negative aspects of UNESCO's leadership, initiatives, and programs. In reality, however, UNESCO's public image was more negatively affected by its shift from a passive, pro-Western agency to an activist, pro-development, peripheral-oriented agency. Its ideological commitment to fundamental change, through NIEO for example, was little understood and was perceived as a threat to the free markets and economic security that core nations had taken for granted since UNESCO's inception in the 1940s. But new peripheral nations looked to this specialized agency of the United Nations to take care of their international grievances.

As for the plight of peripheral nations, "it was as though they had moved from military colonialism to technological neocolonialism without a thought beyond the purely practical and profitable."[12] Many peripheral nations had rushed to accept Western technology and software designed for other cultures and other needs, and now conceded that Western-controlled aid was not the answer to their problems. They had seen aspects of electronic colonialism and they did not like what they were seeing. As a result, peripheral nations approached the media and culture debate with a call for greater distributive justice bolstered by their five-year discussions of the need for a NIEO. They had flexed their muscles, voted, and received attention; now they were prepared to go after the Western mass media.

In his opening address to the 1978 General Assembly, Director-General M'Bow set the framework for UNESCO's future agenda. Noting that "the establishment of a new international economic order constitutes . . . one of the major contexts, and no doubt the largest, within which the activities of the Organization will take place," M'Bow continued by asserting that the imbalances between the West and the peripheral nations were not limited to "solely the production and exchange of information and knowledge."[13] In this way, M'Bow ensured that NWICO would become further intertwined with the NIEO. After reviewing several other UNESCO activities including human rights, education, disarmament, and science and technology, M'Bow turned to communication. He acknowledged "the task awaiting the international community in this field over the next few years represents a real challenge, since it is a task which is at one and the same time immense, complex, essential and urgent."[14] Then M'Bow proceeded to review the

MacBride Commission and highlighted specific areas that required further research and clarification, including disparities in global communication.

In closing, M'Bow criticized his opponents and urged them to adopt NWICO:

> I believe very sincerely that the draft now before you could meet with a large measure of agreement, provided that it is read objectively and dispassionately, and that form of words are patiently sought which dispel the ambiguities of hidden motives that some people still read into it. In this way, the large measure of agreement that the General Conference considers necessary could be achieved.[15]

M'Bow lost ground quickly as Western nations, in response to his address, spoke against the submitted draft declaration. Activities in plenary sessions, in corridors, and in media briefings cumulatively portrayed UNESCO as divided along East–West lines, with the East (socialist) receiving support from many peripheral and OPEC nations. It was clear that the controversial draft declaration on the role of the mass media would have significant implications. It represented a distinct change from the free flow of information policy established by the United Nations and supported by the United States in the 1940s.

Moreover, peripheral nations clung to their objections to the Western media. Their criticisms reflected three primary issues. The first argument was a straightforward anticapitalist approach that criticized the commercial orientation of the press, radio, television, and film industries. The second line of attack focused on the one-way flow of information from the United States, through wire services, television programming, and Hollywood productions, to other nations, with little if any reciprocal trade. Some peripheral nations, particularly those in Africa, that were former colonies of European powers, also attacked the BBC, Reuters, and Spanish and French broadcasting interests, although less vociferously. Fear of electronic colonialism motivated the third argument, which featured a dislike of the history, norms, morals, language, lifestyles, and cultural aspects conveyed through the content of core nations' press, radio, television, advertising, and film productions.

For many Western delegates, the issue boiled down to one of state control over the mass media. Secretary of State for Canada John Roberts, MP, delivered one of the strongest speeches during the entire assembly. In explaining Canada's reservations about the Declaration, Roberts stated:

> I am making no secret of my disquiet, and that of the Government of which I am a member, concerning the Draft Declaration on the Mass Media . . . On

every continent there are some people who think that governments should regulate journalists, should tell them, in the public interest, what to write, or should pass judgment on their accuracy. Canadians do not believe that either politicians or public servants should have anything to say in the management, direction or correction of the media. Quite the contrary. In their view, only a free press can guarantee that the decisions of the state power are in harmony with the wishes of the people. Governments have no means of knowing what the needs of society are for its own well-being, unless they are told by an informed public.[16]

Roberts went on to list reasons for a postponement of the adoption of the contentious text. The address was well received, and because Canada has stature in UNESCO, the Western wire services gave coverage to Roberts' remarks. In response, Dr. Phillip Muscat from Malta summed up the major peripheral nations' grievances:

The service that emanates from the big international press and news agencies sometimes tends to be slanted against the developing countries of the Third World and their leaders. Great prominence is given to certain news items of minor importance, while national achievements in vital sectors are barely mentioned or wrongly reported. Moreover, in certain instances the international press is used as a destabilizing factor against the governments whose only crime is generally that of standing up for their rights, their sovereignty and independence.[17]

Following the plenary session, M'Bow began, as he always did, by criticizing Western press coverage of the issue. He then called for the development of a universal journalistic code of ethics to govern the actions of media and journalists. Many feared that such a code would lead to some type of system that ultimately could be used to restrict journalists' freedom. The Soviets and authoritarian nations thought they had an ally in M'Bow, and an issue, NWICO, with which to restrict the Western media.

Ultimately, UNESCO's 20th General Assembly approved a compromise draft declaration on the mass media that endorsed freedom of the press. This represented a significant diplomatic reversal in favor of the West and moderate developing nations and a temporary reprieve for Director-General M'Bow. Although it was M'Bow who initially presented, endorsed, and pushed the first controversial draft declaration, the Western press uniformly and correctly blamed the Soviet bloc for the attack on their free-press philosophy. One suspects that M'Bow, finding his back against the wall and his career on the line, abandoned what he had cherished in October to pacify the Western nations and thereby retain their substantial funding. Of course, it is likely that M'Bow also recognized that the forthcoming final

MacBride International Commission Report and the next UNESCO General Assembly provided opportunities for him to regroup and present his NWICO tenets once again.

UNESCO in the 1980s

As described in the previous section, it took a reluctantly accepted eleventh-hour compromise to pull the 20th General Assembly's session on mass communication out of the fire in 1978. Yet the delegates to UNESCO general assemblies continued to put at least the face of consensus and unanimity on the international communication discussions that invariably tottered on the brink of open warfare and collapse. Once again, this time in Belgrade in 1980, the General Assembly adopted a mass-media resolution by consensus when nobody called for a vote on it. As unbelievable as it may seem, that resolution actually won approval because it simultaneously advocated proposals based on the principles of both sides of the debate. The result was an uneven and inconsistent declaration.

Despite its equivocal language, reciprocal concessions, and unanimous approval, the resolution was "one of the most bitterly fought over in UNESCO's history."[18] It revealed the extent to which the Western and developing world positions on NWICO were irreconcilable. Even though concessions were made by both sides, the peripheral nations, acting with the support of the Soviet bloc, seemed to get the better of the West. According to several observers, their advantage appeared to turn on the inclusion of some principles that could be interpreted as anti-free-press.

The launching at the 21st General Assembly of the International Programme for the Development of Communication (IPDC) also created a great deal of controversy and suspicion. A 39-member intergovernmental council was established to administer the program and set out its priorities and policies. IPDC continues today with the goal of aiding communication projects in peripheral nations. Because council members were to be elected on a rotating basis to ensure regional representation, peripheral nations would have considerable leverage within IPDC. Another controversial issue concerned the funding for IPDC. Many peripheral nations wanted an international fund to be established within the UNESCO framework. The United States refused to pledge to such a fund and suggested that the money needed to initiate the program should be diverted from UNESCO's regular mass communication budget.

In retrospect, the 21st General Assembly was remarkable for the decisions made. It not only approved a version of the NWICO, but it also accepted the MacBride Commission report, which clearly endorsed activities that would promote development journalism and communication, and it created the IPDC to implement some of those policies. What was unclear at the time was the degree to which the hostility brewing against Director-General M'Bow would, by mid-decade, reach sufficient intensity to justify the withdrawal of both the United Kingdom and the United States from UNESCO.

The 22nd General Assembly of UNESCO convened in Paris on October 25, 1983. One hundred sixty-one countries participated in the five-week conference, which turned out to be one of the most critical in the history of UNESCO. Just a few weeks after the meetings were adjourned, US State Department dissatisfaction with a number of UNESCO issues led to the announcement of their intention to withdraw from UNESCO at the end of 1984 unless its demands for substantial change were met. The United States not only withdrew, but remained a nonmember for a number of years.

The meetings began with the presentation of "The Draft Programme and Budget for 1984–1985," which was prepared by the UNESCO Secretariat on the basis of the consensus reached by the delegates. Of most relevance to this discussion is "Major Programme III, Communication in the Service of Man," outlined below:

PROGRAMME 111.1: STUDIES ON COMMUNICATION

a) to stimulate the development of research, especially concerning the socio-cultural impact of new communication technologies, the democratization of communication and the future of books and reading;
b) to further elaborate the concepts of "the right to communicate" and access to and participation in communication, and to continue to study the idea of the responsibility of communicators;
c) to continue the study of methods for planning, programming and financing of communication, with special reference to the communication industries.[19]

The program continued by encouraging the reduction of current international communication imbalances through the development of a plurality of information sources and through cooperation and collaboration. It acknowledged that the activities listed in the program would "facilitate a detailed examination of a new information and communication order, with a view to promoting its establishment."[20] The proposed budget for the three major programs listed in Programme III was almost $30 million, an increase of more than 33 percent over the previous budget. So much for the cost containment sought by the United States and the United Kingdom.

It had been hoped that the freedom of the press issue and NWICO, which had divided UNESCO for over a decade, might be only a minor topic at this meeting. On the first day of debate, however, two serious and contentious issues arose. The first was the substantial increase in the budget for communications. The second was a Soviet Union proposal calling for curbs on press freedom as part of NWICO.

The Soviet delegation realized that the First Amendment was sacred in the eyes of the US press, and its intention was to aggravate the US and other Western delegations. The Soviet draft urged UNESCO to draw up a list of "mass-media organs" whose reporting had violated the guidelines that the organization had enunciated earlier. These were the same guidelines that most Western governments had criticized as hostile to the freedom of the press. The Soviets were forced to withdraw their contentious resolution, but its introduction had heightened distrust of NWICO by providing a concrete illustration of its threats to press freedom.

Although the media debate was a key issue, the size of the budget increase created another serious problem for the United States. The United States was the only one of the 161 nations to vote against the $374.4 million budget. At the final vote, 10 other countries abstained after asking for a budgetary freeze. The final budget adopted was about $12 million less than that first proposed, but the cuts did not go deep enough for the United States, which had been seeking "zero growth" in all UN agencies.

Although the United States failed to achieve as much as it had hoped, it certainly was more successful than it had been in the past decade. It had curbed the development of NWICO, and there was an emerging shift toward the Western perspective on press matters. Although the final budget did not represent zero growth, it was only 2.5 percent higher than the previous one. What, therefore, prompted the US decision to pull out of UNESCO less than one month later?

Shortly after the close of the 22nd General Assembly, stories began appearing in the US press about the possible withdrawal of the United States from UNESCO. According to a *New York Times* report, the proposal was being considered in the State Department and a decision was expected soon.[21] Gregory J. Newell, Assistant Secretary of State for International Organization Affairs, said that his office had conducted a study of the performance of some 19 organizations and noted that in addition to mismanagement and lack of budgetary restraint, there were problems of politicization within many UN agencies. He asserted that internal studies had shown what the Reagan administration viewed as improvement in many UN multilateral agencies, but that UNESCO had responded inadequately. Newell then ordered a complete review of UNESCO that would later justify US withdrawal.

Opponents of the withdrawal pointed to the improvements made at the 22nd General Assembly. They feared that withdrawal would leave the organization vulnerable to those who opposed US interests. Moreover, the United States Commission for UNESCO, although acknowledging problems, voted by an overwhelming majority to continue membership and fight for change from within. But Newell recognized the vulnerability of UNESCO and used it to condemn and threaten the entire UN system.

Following the reviews, the US State Department recommended, on December 21, 1983, that the United States file notice of its intention to withdraw from UNESCO on January 1, 1985. The decision had to be made by December 31, but the US would have one year in which to reassess the situation. President Ronald Reagan sent a formal letter of withdrawal to Director-General M'Bow on December 29, making it clear that the departure was temporary and that the United States retained the right to rejoin. According to a State Department spokesperson, the decision was taken because "UNESCO has extraneously politicized virtually every subject it deals with, has exhibited hostility toward the basic institutions of a free society, especially a free market and a free press, and has demonstrated unrestrained budgetary expansion."[22]

Officially, the State Department recommendation to withdraw from UNESCO was based on what it identified as three major behavioral problems: (1) the politicization of issues; (2) the promulgation of statist concepts; and (3) mismanagement and fiscal irresponsibility. The United States officially withdrew from UNESCO in January 1985. (It has returned under President Bush and now has an ambassador in Paris and a National Commission in Washington.)

UNESCO Without the United States

By the time the 23rd session of the UNESCO General Assembly was convened in Bulgaria on October 8, 1985, not only had the United States withdrawn from the organization, but the United Kingdom also was reconsidering its membership. Given this Western power void, the socialist bloc was anxious to put its own stamp on the meetings.

In fact, the selection of Sofia, Bulgaria, as the site for meeting was part of a Soviet strategy to enhance its own power and position within UNESCO. Given the budgetary limitations facing the agency, it made fiscal sense to hold the conference at UNESCO headquarters in Paris where it would not be necessary to house and feed 1,000 UNESCO employees for the six-week assembly. But it was precisely that expenditure, in addition to the revenues generated by the presence of 3,000 additional delegates to the conference, that caused the Soviet Union to lobby strongly on behalf of the Sofia site. Moreover, by convening in Bulgaria without an official US delegation, many socialist countries saw this as an opportunity to strengthen their role within UNESCO and use it as a vehicle to promote anti-West projects and administrators.

Once again, the most sensitive issue to emerge during the General Assembly was the discussion of NWICO. NWICO emphasized the disparities among nations and suggested means, sometimes contradictory and contentious, for reaching a new order and balance in international information, media, and communication flows. Although NWICO was still a relatively modest concept, the major problem was the fact that it was systematically perceived as being structurally different by the two major groups of nation-states. Western, core nations viewed NWICO as troublesome, vague, and potentially harmful. On the other hand, the socialist bloc, peripheral nations, and nonaligned nations contended that NWICO was both a practical program and a theoretical concept to encourage and legitimize a more activist indigenous production capacity. It was considered to be a paradigm from which to facilitate infrastructure developments along pro-peripheral-nation lines. This cleavage was reinforced by the US withdrawal from UNESCO.

The United Kingdom played an interesting role at the 23rd General Assembly. Basically, the UK's position was a difficult one because it had given notice in December 1984 that it intended to withdraw from UNESCO at the end of 1985. As a result, the British were almost as powerless within UNESCO as the United States. As diplomatic eunuchs, their efforts to exert influence became somewhat melodramatic. Most of the peripheral nations saw no reason to consider the UK's views, complaints, or objectives, and even its Western allies and Commonwealth partners realized that its actions were intended to legitimize its decision to withdraw as of January 1986.

New Era, Leaders, and Strategy

M'Bow left the director-general position at UNESCO in 1986. He also left a weakened UN agency to his successor. Federico Mayor, from Barcelona, Spain, was elected as the new director-general of UNESCO in 1987 and held the office until 1999. From 1978 to 1981, Mayor had served as deputy director-general of UNESCO. When he left that post, he was elected to the Spanish Parliament and served as minister of education. During his tenure, he altered UNESCO's role and did not support NWICO.

Mayor assumed the leadership of UNESCO at arguably the lowest point in the agency's history. Its budget had been slashed as a result of the withdrawal of the United States and the United Kingdom; and particularly negative Western newspapers, magazines, and other media coverage had tarnished its reputation. Director-General Mayor's immediate goal was to establish a climate of trust in the hope that the United States and the United Kingdom would return to full membership. He also sought to decrease the size of the bureaucracy and improve administrative management. By the late 1990s, Mayor convinced Great Britain to return, but had little else to show for his efforts at significant reform.

At the 25th UNESCO General Assembly in 1989, Director-General Mayor issued a new communication strategy. This new approach stressed the Western principles of freedom of press, freedom of expression, and the development of an independent and pluralistic media. This philosophical and ideological shift was not only more attractive to the West, but it also coincided with the fall of the Berlin Wall in November 1989, which had raised expectations for an independent press throughout central and eastern Europe.

In order to implement the new communication proposals, Mayor announced that a series of UNESCO meetings would be convened in Namibia, Kazakhstan, Chile, and Yemen. At each of these regional meetings, UNESCO's free-press communication proposal was to be enunciated, and ideas to promote press freedom and media pluralism in the regions would be explored. For example, the Windhoek Resolution, emerging from the 1991 Namibia conference to promote a pluralistic and free African press, declared that:

1   Consistent with article 19 of the Universal Declaration of Human Rights, the establishment, maintenance and fostering of an independent, pluralistic and free press is essential to the development and maintenance of democracy in a nation, and for economic development.
2   By an independent press, we mean a press independent from governmental, political or economic control or from control of materials and infrastructure essential for the production and dissemination of newspapers, magazines and periodicals.
3   By a pluralistic press, we mean the end of monopolies of any kind and the existence of the greatest possible number of newspapers, magazines and periodicals reflecting the widest possible range of opinion within the community.
4   The welcome changes that an increasing number of African States are now undergoing towards multi-party democracies provide the climate in which an independent pluralistic press can emerge.

5   The worldwide trend towards democracy and freedom of information and expression is a fundamental contribution to the fulfillment of human aspirations.[23]

Wherever Director-General Mayor went during the 1990s, he promoted the new UNESCO communication strategy. His activities and comments were directed toward persuading two audiences: the current UNESCO membership and the United States. Not only did he advocate resolutions supporting new free and pluralistic press initiatives throughout the regions of the world, but he also sought to convince the United States that UNESCO's communication policy was very much in line with the US free-press traditions.

For example, in his opening address to the conference in Bulgaria in September 1997, Mayor asserted:

> The indisputable success of that Round Table certainly gave new impetus to UNESCO's work for the development of independent and pluralistic media in both the public and private sector and encouraged us to continue along the same lines in other parts of the world – firstly in Africa (Windhoek, Namibia, May 1991), then in Asia (Almaty, Kazakhstan, October 1993), in Latin America and the Caribbean (Santiago de Chile, May 1994), and in the Arab region (Sana'a, Yemen, January 1996). The four Declarations and the corresponding plans of action adopted at those meetings have become real milestones in UNESCO's struggle for freedom of expression and of the press.[24]

He proceeded to emphasize this point and went on to stipulate the steps that must be taken to achieve the goal:

> The most crucial requirements today include:
>
> Building up pluralistic and independent media – public and private alike – to replace the former monopolistic state-controlled news agencies, newspapers, and radio and television networks;
> Transforming media legislation unsuited to democratic requirements;
> Providing the skills and know-how to meet the challenges of a democratic and competitive society including new areas of specialization such as marketing, advertising, media management and public relations.[25]

This revised communication policy at UNESCO paved the way for the return of the United Kingdom, but it did not persuade the United States. In fact, UNESCO's critics in Congress, the State Department, and outside of government remained adamant that the United States stay out of

UNESCO. For example, in 1995, despite the positive changes undertaken by Mayor and the return of the United Kingdom, the Heritage Foundation argued, "Rejoining UNESCO . . . would be a serious mistake."[26] Its rationales were delineated in "Executive Memorandum no. 403." They were:

1 UNESCO has serious management shortcomings.
2 Rejoining UNESCO would send the wrong signal about UN management reform.
3 UNESCO's mission lacks focus.
4 UNESCO activities are redundant.
5 The United States already benefits from the best of UNESCO.[27]

The memorandum concludes with a plea to the US government to spend elsewhere the $65 million annual dues due UNESCO. President Clinton stated in 1995, "I assure you that US membership in UNESCO remains on my list of priorities for the future."[28] Also on his list for the 1990s was paying back the $1.6 billion in dues owed to the United Nations that Congress had refused for years to approve but finally relented to do in 1999.

UNESCO in the 1990s

In the early 1990s, as a result of dramatic but peaceful political revolutions, the former Soviet Union and its client states rapidly abandoned totalitarian structures, including their press systems. Consequently, many journalists and editors from newly independent states of eastern and central Europe began to participate in the new communication strategy debate within UNESCO. The general conferences, which continued to be held every two years, produced several resolutions supporting the goals of the new strategy. In particular, there was considerable support for independent and free media along the lines of the Western model. In addition, the International Programme for the Development of Communication (IPDC) encouraged proposals that facilitated the founding of free and open press activities in peripheral nations. Director-General Mayor also created a new unit within UNESCO entitled "Freedom of Expression and Democracy." Its goal was just that – to promote freedom of expression and other democratic ideas, including a free and pluralistic press. Moreover, under Mayor's leadership, UNESCO began to work against the imprisonment and expulsion of journalists around the world. In response to these policy changes, the United Kingdom rejoined UNESCO in 1997.

The United States' Reaction

Director-General Mayor's efforts and the revised international communication policy did not go unnoticed in the United States. When the US
National Security Council established an interagency working group in 1993
to examine UNESCO, all relevant activities ranging from the administration
of the agency to its media-related strategies underwent thorough scrutiny.
The working group's findings were positive, and it recommended that the
United States rejoin UNESCO by mid-decade. Simultaneously, a small group
in the US House of Representatives initiated favorable discussions concerning UNESCO and suggested that it was time for the United States to
return. Educators also began to lobby informally for US reentry. Mayor also
traveled extensively in the United States to promote good relations between
UNESCO and the US. Despite the goodwill created by Mayor, his successor, and UNESCO's free-press initiatives, it was not until 2001, under
President Bush, that the US rejoined UNESCO.

A New Focus

In the late 1990s, UNESCO produced a major document titled "World
Information Report" that began to chronicle information resources in
almost 200 countries around the globe. Its publication marked a change in
emphasis within UNESCO to the examination of the global information
highway, including the internet. The "World Information Report" provided
extensive documentation of computer-based information processing, including
the shift toward multimedia, telecommunications, and electronic databases.
   The report is divided into three parts. The first section describes the
information services in individual countries or regions. The second section
details the infrastructures for information industries and focuses on technical
issues including multimedia and telecommunications. The final section dis-
cusses issues and trends such as the emergence of the information society,
information highways, economic implications, copyright matters, and other
social or legal questions. The report concludes with a chapter outlining the
necessity for international cooperation in order to ensure access for all through
the interconnection of global information technologies. Mayor emphasized
the importance of these issues and UNESCO's new direction in 1998:

> We need to make a new start, founded on the principles and values enshrined
> in UNESCO's Constitution, which stipulates that, for a just and lasting peace,

"intellectual and moral solidarity" is a necessary condition. Here, the new communication technologies and especially the development of the information highways have the potential to give concrete form to global solidarity by including the excluded, because the networks they form can reach all human beings, wherever they live.[29]

Part of the new focus is to promote practical and concrete programs that can help peripheral regions. For example, now in UNESCO documents the push concerning communication is to provide "equal access to information and communication technologies."[30] UNESCO is also sponsoring regional conferences focusing on a free and pluralistic press.

Mayor's Successor: An Asian Leader

In October 1999, two important events occurred in UNESCO. First, a new director-general was elected after major candidates had emerged from Australia, Saudi Arabia, Egypt, and Japan. Ultimately, the Japanese ambassador to France, Koichiro Matsuura, was elected director-general. He began his six-year term immediately and presides over the annual budget of $300 million; this budget is now closer to $400 million since the United States rejoined. The DG's current term ends in 2005. Since the last two DGs are from core nations, Spain and Japan, it is likely that a new DG would be from a peripheral nation.

The second event concerned allegations of cronyism and mismanagement, specifically that the French government had used the Paris-based UNESCO to place former government aides on UNESCO's payroll throughout the 1990s. The UK paper *The Guardian* ran extensive stories documenting the administrative problems, going so far as to report that almost half of UNESCO's appointments in the 1990s failed to meet the administrative criteria for credentials and for fair and open competition for senior appointments.[31]

In 2004 DG Matsuura organized a meeting to draft a global convention on the protection of cultural diversity and artistic expression. This followed an earlier 2004 meeting with over 600 delegates from 132 UNESCO member states, plus numerous NGOs, that discussed the protection of cultural goods and services. This includes the mass media for many of the participating nations. Such a convention, if ratified, would put UNESCO on a likely collision course with the WTO. The WTO is seeking to expand its mandate by including cultural industries in such a way as to reduce all protectionist measures – such as quotas, grants, subsidies, license fees, and a host of other protectionist tariffs. This entire matter has the potential to become a major global public-policy issue.

Finally, UNESCO is also heavily involved in the World Summit on the Information Society (more is discussed about the WSIS in the following chapter). UNESCO is providing assistance for many of the WSIS action-plan areas under the umbrella of UNESCO's major initiative labeled "Knowledge Societies." Some critics of the WSIS claim that it seeks to promote governments having a role in media oversight, and to them it sounds like a phase or stage two of the discredited NWICO. Given that the second meeting of WSIS is in anti-free-press and authoritarian Tunisia, the outlook is dim for all agencies, including UNESCO, which sponsor WSIS and support the bizarre selection of the location of Tunisia for a major international conference.

Conclusions

Although the UNESCO General Assembly has always addressed 13 major programs, beginning with the 1976 meeting in Nairobi its conferences have been dominated by the single communication program, NWICO, and its fallout. Like a lightning rod, NWICO attracted all the media attention. Not only was it an issue of distinct interest to the media, but it also polarized the delegates to the point that the United States and the United Kingdom withdrew. It also created significant public image problems for the agency and threatened its internal operations and financial stability. Today, UNESCO still has major fiscal and image problems. Historically, the debate was about aspects of electronic colonialism that the core nations did not want to hear about, deal with, or come to terms with. Peripheral nations were concerned that their cultures, values, and influence were being displaced by slick, heavily advertised sounds and images from a few core nations.

Although there is little doubt among those familiar with UNESCO that the organization does sound work in several areas ranging from literacy and environmental concerns to scientific and educational topics, these efforts receive scant attention at the general assemblies and in global media coverage. This imbalance is clear when one realizes that UNESCO's communication sector receives less than 10 percent of the agency's budget, but clearly receives well over 90 percent of its media coverage. The problem is complicated further because that coverage, particularly in Western nations, is overwhelmingly negative. It is difficult, therefore, for concerned individuals and governments to be supportive of UNESCO when the public at large is not favorably impressed, and when the uninitiated believe that all UNESCO does is debate communication and promote anti-free-press policies.

The historical role of the Soviet Union is also clear. It was obvious to many that the Soviet Union was promoting an anti-free-press agenda and that it had considerable rein within the halls of UNESCO. To a large extent, without the United Kingdom or the United States at the negotiating table, UNESCO became a captive of the socialist nations that offered token support to peripheral nations. A second challenge related to internal leadership. After 11 years as director-general, M'Bow had failed to respond to the growing negative perception of UNESCO, even within the UN system. His term came to an abrupt end in 1987. Finally, and perhaps most surprising, was the implosion of the Soviet Union, which spelled the end of its role as the great benefactor, champion, and savior of UNESCO and NWICO. When the USSR exited from the world stage, so too did the influence and funds it lent to UNESCO.

Despite the problems NWICO created, the overall debate in UNESCO has been informative. It not only forced a reanalysis and reaffirmation of values, but it also accentuated the need for hard data and planning practical strategies in order to enhance communication development throughout the world. NWICO continues to evolve in its search for practical and applied measures aimed at redressing media imbalances and promoting greater concern for cultural sensitivity and indigenous software. The peripheral nations still cling to NWICO in the face of greater core-nation media pressure to adopt Western philosophies, products, and practices. Director-General Matsuura wants none of the divisive rhetoric and is promoting a media-friendly UNESCO. Finally, a small group of academics and journalists from around the globe continue to promote the aims of NWICO. Under the banner of the MacBride Round Table, they meet every two years to examine the state of affairs in peripheral nations.[32] They are an advocacy group created in 1989 to examine the global communication imbalances identified in the 1980 MacBride Report, titled *Many Voices, One World*,[33] commissioned by UNESCO. They are expanding the research agenda to include internet issues as part of the NWICO legacy.

Finally, UNESCO is moving into two areas loaded with contention. They are a global convention on cultural diversity and strong affiliation with the WSIS. Either of these hot-button issues could once again see major donor nations reexamine their commitment to UNESCO and its programs.[34]

Notes

1   Ali Mohammadi, *International Communication and Globalization* (London: Sage, 1997), p. 2.
2   UNESCO, "What Is UNESCO" (Paris: UNESCO, 1977).

3 For an excellent look at the internal workings and problems of UNESCO's Secretariat, see former Assistant Director-General Richard Hoggart's *An Idea and Its Servants: UNESCO from Within* (London: Chatto and Windus, 1978).

4 Hoggart, *An Idea and Its Servants*, p. 64.

5 Faure Commission report, *Learning to Be* (Paris: UNESCO, 1972).

6 Some analysts date the beginning of the NWICO debate to 1968, when the Declaration on Human Rights was amended to include the notion of a balanced and free flow of information. Given the subsequent differences in interpretation, policy decisions, and political maneuvering related to this phrase, it is interesting to note that it was the United States that first introduced the amendment.

7 Kaarle Nordenstreng and Tapio Varis, "Television Traffic – A One Way Street? A Survey and Analysis of the International Flow of Television" (Paris: UNESCO, 1974).

8 Brenda Pavlic and Cees Hamelink, *The New International Economic Order: Links between Economies and Communications, Reports and Papers on Mass Communication 98* (Paris: UNESCO, 1985).

9 United Nations, Declaration on the Establishment of a New International Economic Order, G.A. Res. 3201, Sixth Special Session, UN Supp. (No. 1), UN Doc A/9559.

10 See, for example, UNESCO, *Moving towards Change: Some Thoughts on the New International Economic Order* (Paris: UNESCO, 1976).

11 The history of OPEC is also viewed by communication scholars as a classic case study of initial Western media inattention, and then biased reporting, once OPEC was able to establish itself as a major instrument of political and commercial power – extending to the gas pump.

12 Hoggart, *An Idea and Its Servants*, p. 193.

13 UNESCO 20C/Inf. 9. 28 October (Paris: Author, 1978), p. 4. Reprinted by permission of UNESCO.

14 Ibid., p. 14.

15 Ibid., p. 15.

16 John Roberts, UNESCO document 20C/vr (prov), 6 November 1978 (Press Release, n.p.). Reprinted by permission of UNESCO.

17 Phillip Muscat, UNESCO document 20C/vr (prov), 4 November 1978 (Press Release, n.p.). Reprinted by permission of UNESCO.

18 *New York Times*, Oct. 25, 1980, p. 14.

19 UNESCO, Draft Programme and Budget for 1984–1985, III, Communication in the Service of Man, 22C/5 (Paris: Author, 1983), p. 2.

20 Ibid., p. 3.

21 *New York Times*, Dec. 15, 1983, p. D1.

22 *New York Times*, Dec. 30, 1983, p. D4.

23 UNESCO, "Declarations on Promoting Independent and Pluralist Media: Declaration of Windhoek" (Paris: UNESCO, May 3, 1991, mimeographed), p. 4.

24 Federico Mayor, "Address at the Opening of the European Seminar to Promote Pluralistic and Independent Media" (Paris: UNESCO, Sept. 10, 1997, mimeographed), p. 1.

25 Mayor, "Address," p. 2.

26 Thomas P. Sheehy, "Executive Memorandum no. 403: Stay Out of UNESCO" (Washington, DC: Heritage Foundation, Jan. 1, 1995, mimeographed), p. 1.

27 Ibid.

28 www.Reuters.com, Information Service, Nov. 15, 1995.

29 Federico Mayor, "Opening Address: Human Rights on the Eve of the 21st Century" (Paris: UNESCO, Dec. 17, 1998, mimeographed), p. 2.

30 UNESCO 160 EX/48. Final Report of the Task Force on UNESCO in the Twenty-First Century. Oct. 11 (Paris: UNESCO, 2000), p. 6.

31 Jon Henley, *The Guardian*, Oct. 18, 19, 21, 1999.

32 This group seeks to examine issues of access, ownership, equality, and trends in global communication in the tradition of the MacBride Report. See, for example, Richard Vincent, Kaarle Nordenstreng, and Michael Traber, eds., *Towards Equity in Global Communication* (Crosskill, NJ: Hampton Press, 1999).

33 Sean MacBride, *Many Voices, One World* (New York: Unipub, 1980).

34 Events at UNESCO are a lot like history on the run. To keep up with matters discussed in this chapter, including if a new DG has been selected for the 2006–12 term, see www.unesco.org.

Chapter 11

The Medium: Global Technologies and Organizations

Introduction

Although most of the concern about global broadcasting focuses on ownership, content, impact, or cultural issues, the global telecommunications infrastructure, or the medium by which content is transmitted, is now emerging as a significant topic as well. Global information superhighways are not without their socioeconomic consequences. The penetration of satellite dishes, the laying of fiberoptic cables, the internet, and the deployment of cellular telephones are all part of Marshall McLuhan's "global village." This chapter seeks to detail the major stakeholders in the evolution of telecommunication systems around the globe. As core nations continue to move into the Information Revolution, their telecommunication systems are central to their success. The global telecommunication system is the central nervous system of the global economy. Global broadcasting could not exist without an internationally functioning technical transmission system or infrastructure.

The primary global telecommunication agency is the International Telecommunication Union (ITU), a specialized United Nations agency. However, there are other major players, such as Intelsat, that bring to the telecommunications table a mix of philosophical, ownership, technical, and public-policy perspectives. Core nations have long dominated ITU, but now semiperipheral and peripheral nations are calling for major structural changes to reflect their needs and concerns.

International Telecommunication Union (ITU)

Today the struggle between core and peripheral nations over the question of NWICO is at an uneasy compromise. The sense of victory felt by core nations over minimizing major tenets of NWICO has been short-lived. Observers note that another arena, the International Telecommunication Union (ITU), based in Switzerland, has become a battlefield between core and peripheral nations. The ITU sponsors major global conferences that look at global technical standards and other issues affecting global telecommunications. At these meetings, participants confer to assign worldwide frequencies from the usable electromagnetic spectrum available for broadcasting and a wide variety of communication services.[1] Historically, these meetings attracted little attention as technicians and engineers from various nations around the world divided the spectrum with great concern for technical matters. Issues such as microwave interference among neighboring nations, standards, or equipment interconnection protocols dominated the meetings. When nations sent delegates to ITU meetings, industrial nations assumed that a highly technical and engineering delegation would suffice. Little attention was paid to social, cultural, or economic concerns. But times have changed. Peripheral nations now want a major voice at ITU.

Global conferences are convened and organized by ITU, which is charged with coordinating the international use of telecommunication systems worldwide. The nations represented at these global conferences are members of ITU. These conferences review and amend existing ITU international radio regulations. For instance, conference participants are empowered to amend regulatory procedures for settling differences between nations and for notifying, coordinating, and registering radio frequency assignments. They also are authorized to set new rules concerning technical and performance standards of telecommunication systems, including satellite issues. Probably the most significant set of regulations the general conferences review is the international Table of Frequency Allocation.

By virtue of the range of their global authority, all ITU conferences are profoundly significant events. During the years between ITU conferences, technological innovations such as satellite communications or cellular phones, and methods for using more and more of the high ranges of the spectrum, particularly microwave frequencies, have revolutionized telecommunications. Major ITU conferences have been held twice in North America: in 1949 in Atlantic City, New Jersey, and in 1998 in Minneapolis, Minnesota. The 1998 conference lasted four weeks and set the ITU's general policies, adopted strategic and financial plans, and elected members of the ITU council.

New developments in communication exercise a profound influence on social, cultural, economic, and political organizations and have so radically transformed the way most people live and interact with each other and their environment that the present era has come to be known as the "information age." All core nations have the latest in communication technologies, whereas the peripheral nations have few computers, cellular phones, or digital services.[2]

History and structure of the ITU

In 1865 the International Telegraph Union, the ITU's forerunner, was formed under the International Telegraph Convention signed by 20 European nations in Paris. This makes the ITU the oldest international organization surviving today. At that time, the organization dealt exclusively with technical problems. The establishment of international standards for the Morse code was among its first endeavors.

The invention and implementation of wireless systems such as radio and cross-border telephoning complicated the process of setting international regulations. In 1885 the Union established the first international rules governing telephony. At the 1906 Berlin conference, the first international conference to deal with radio and to set standards for equipment and technical uniformity, certain sections of the radio frequency spectrum were allocated to specific radio services, most notably the wireless frequencies used by ships at sea. The 1927 International Radio Telegraph Conference decided the next major advance in radio spectrum management. At this conference, a Table of Frequency Allocations was created.

John Howkins points out the rather simple procedures involved in early ITU activities:

> Users notified the union about the frequencies, which they were already using or wished to use, and the union registered these in its master list. Neither the union nor the user owned the frequency. What happened was that, through the union's processes of registration, the user had a squatter's right to a specific frequency. Furthermore, the union's recognition of a particular usage gave the user some protection in international law.[3]

This simple squatter's right on a first-come, first-served basis did not, however, take into account the limited nature of the resource. Also, the first comers were mainly from North America and Europe, core nations. This procedure has been largely responsible for the congestion in some popular frequency bands, a problem that today makes efficient allocation a difficult proposition requiring regional meetings to sort out conflicting claims.

Initially, spectrum usage was confined to maritime activities such as radio navigation and ship-to-shore communication. During the 1920s, due to technological advances that provided new means of utilizing higher frequencies, the types of services that the radio spectrum enjoyed multiplied rapidly. As new radio services began to compete for spectrum space, fears grew that unless each new type of service was given a separate and distinct band within the spectrum, overcrowding and interference among the services would occur.

The ITU responded to this concern at the 1929 World Administrative Radio Council (WARC), resolving that the various uses of the spectrum be coordinated by allocating a certain stretch or band of frequencies to each particular service. By the 1947 Atlantic City conference, further advances in telecommunications capacity necessitated revision of procedures for registering and securing recognition of spectrum uses. More detailed plans for services were adopted for each of the three newly created regions: Region 1 for Europe and Africa, Region 2 for the Americas, and Region 3 for Asia and the South Pacific.

As early as 1959, the ITU's approach to telecommunications management came under criticism. Critics noted that huge areas of the spectrum, such as the high-frequency bands, were unplanned, and they pointed out that the ITU stepped in to coordinate national assignments of frequencies only after congestion and conflicting uses had occurred. Generally, the ITU gave priority to those nations that had the economic and technological sophistication to occupy a frequency first. These were not necessarily the nations that needed the frequency the most. The fortunate nations were primarily core nations that relied on the squatter's-rights tradition to claim prime spectrum positions.

Misgivings about the basic machinery of the ITU escalated in the 1980s and 1990s. The regulations the ITU had originally adopted to make international telecommunications manageable were becoming either overextended or obsolete with the rapid introduction of new demands such as frequency space for cellular telephones.

To restate the original point, the history of the ITU has been punctuated by problems and doubts about the efficiency of its structural framework. The problems and doubts turn on questions that are essentially of a technical or administrative nature. One prime reason for this technical orientation was articulated in the *Economist*, which noted, "the ITU is full of engineers terrified of controversy and terrified of the press."[4] This fundamental fact is part of the ITU's culture today.

In recent years, critics of ITU have cautioned that although this narrow technical focus may have been tolerable when decisions about telecommunications were of concern only to a limited circle of specialists within the industry, it is no longer adequate. In an age in which telecommunications have become highly politicized because of their profound effects on the complexion of national and international roles, many nations are not only concerned about which medium or frequency they are carried on, but they are also concerned about many nontechnical matters. Semiperipheral and peripheral nations are aware of the pivotal role telecommunications play in the global economy. They also are demanding prime spectrum allocations well in advance of their actual use.

ITU has received prompting from many quarters to implement structural and administrative reforms designed to furnish mechanisms for recognizing and absorbing political and socioeconomic input. Currently, ITU has developed neither the ability to deal with political or ideological concerns nor the necessary administrative structure through which such conflicts could be channeled without crippling itself.

When peripheral nations threaten to turn ITU conferences into ideological and rhetorical contests, they trigger much apprehension. With no experience in dealing with such developments, ITU talks could collapse before technical issues could be resolved. This would jeopardize global spectrum management decisions and leave matters in an uncomfortable state of suspension. Of course, this is the last thing core nations want, with billions invested in global telecommunications systems. These systems represent the central nervous system of the global economy. Therefore, core nations have a keen interest in maintaining a manageable and predictable telecommunications environment through ITU.

Current concerns

Two chief reasons that the international community devoted more attention and preparation to recent ITU conferences were the increase in the number of countries represented and the fact that peripheral nations, which accounted for almost all the increase, now constitute a majority in the ITU. In the 1950s, fewer than 100 nations were members of ITU. But by 2005, there were 189 nations in the ITU family. The level of preparation and negotiating skill required to manage a meeting of over 2,000 delegates from over 150 countries and some 50 NGOs dealing with issues of unusual technical and social complexity was unprecedented in ITU's 130-year history. They are also being confronted with the rapid pace of innovation in the telecom and information technologies sectors.

The new majority status of the peripheral nations contributes to the high profile of these conferences, and these nations have been the source of a feature previously unheard of at ITU meetings – namely, the use of political and ideological criteria in arriving at decisions concerning the Digital Divide, spectrum management and allocations, as well as other issues which impact peripheral regions. Decisions at ITU are made on an one-nation, one-vote basis. Core nations worry that if peripheral nations act in unison they will be

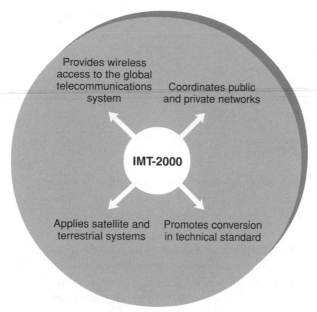

Provides wireless access to the global telecommunications system

Coordinates public and private networks

IMT-2000

Applies satellite and terrestrial systems

Promotes conversion in technical standard

Figure 11.1 Facets of the IMT-2000 Initiative

able, by virtue of the majority they command, to push through measures relating to NWICO and thereby guarantee access for the developing world to highly desired spectrum space and geostationary orbits for satellites, as well as committing funds to reduce the Digital Divide. Many of the proposals concern the core nations, particularly the US, which will have a great deal to lose or which will have to bear the brunt of new expenditures.

Because the more prominent issues associated with NWICO concern cultural imperialism, such as concentration of ownership, growing private control of media, and imbalances in news flow, peripheral nations are quick to point out imbalances in spectrum allocations.

Currently, a major initiative at ITU is promoting a global international mobile system called IMT-2000. This initiative will provide wireless access to the global telecommunication system through application of both satellite and terrestrial systems. It will provide guidance for coordinating related technological developments in order to promote conversion in technical standard for wireless access technologies. This initiative also seeks to coordinate both public and private networks, which are emerging at various rates in different regions of the world (see figure 11.1).

The role of the ITU has expanded enormously due to technological innovation and the multiplicity of new stakeholders ranging from governments, to broadcasters, to manufacturers, so that it has become the major global organization dealing with the substantial telecommunications sector. Currently, ITU consists of 189 member states along with 727 corporations and organizations, which represent both public and private interests. Many of the member states and related organizations now expect the ITU to take into account the cultural, social, and non-economic dimensions of the world in making allocations and other major decisions.

Geostationary orbits

Technically, the most effective positioning of a communication satellite is 22,300 miles above the equator in a geostationary or geosynchronous orbit (see figure 11.2). At such an altitude, a satellite completes one orbit of the earth in the same time it takes the earth to revolve once around its axis, that is, once every 24 hours. Because the satellite is traveling at the identical speed as the earth, it is always hovering over the same area and thus can provide continuous communication service to the same region. Satellites placed at lower or higher altitudes such as 15,000 or 30,000 miles above the earth do not travel at the same speed as the earth and thus over time disappear over the horizon. To provide continuous communication with such satellites, as one satellite disappears over the horizon, another satellite must simultaneously

Figure 11.2 A satellite orbiting the Earth

appear to replace it. This requires expensive and elaborate antennae or receivers that can track this new satellite as it enters into view. Because synchronous satellites are always over the same spot on earth, simple receivers or ground stations are able to pick up their signals. Moreover, because of the altitude of synchronous satellites, their beams cover much greater amounts of territory, called a footprint, than lower-altitude counterparts.

Unfortunately, there is limited space for satellites in the thin slice 22,300 miles above the equator in which such satellites can operate or park for their lifetime. This is why the question of allotting orbital slots in advance, on a country-by-country basis, has become a pressing issue for peripheral nations, which trail far behind in satellite technology. If and when they catch up, there will not be sufficient usable prime parking spots remaining for their additional geostationary satellites.

The issue of geostationary parking spots took on additional symbolic meaning in the 1980s. Because the only position for these satellites was above the equator, and because the equator covers parts of peripheral regions in Latin America and Africa, some delegates from these regions seized on this important point. They began to express the idea at ITU meetings that the outer space above these nations should be reserved for them so that they would have appropriate parking spots for future satellite deployment. As already mentioned, these allocations historically have been awarded on a first-come, first-served basis, which meant that core nations and the former Soviet Union came first to the table to make specific requests for operational satellite parking spots. By the time peripheral nations, even those at the equator, are ready to operate satellites at some future point, there will be no prime parking spots available, only suboptimal spots. And these suboptimal spots will be over some other nation, not the prime spots above their own nation-states. Naturally, the traditional operating mode of first-come, first-served displeased peripheral delegates not only about satellite orbital spaces, but also about spectrum allocation and management. The peripheral regions wanted to replace the first-come, first-served process of ITU's spectrum management with a new system whereby they could reserve frequencies of all types for their own future use. They argued that this strategy would promote fair and equitable access to the international radio spectrum. Because older industrialized nations entered the field of radio telecommunications at a much earlier date than many newly emerging peripheral nations, core nations by default obtained the rights to all prime frequencies. Just as naturally, industrialized nations, led by the US, objected to any shift in criteria for allocation issues coming before ITU conferences. Core nations claimed that the new policy would leave many allotted frequencies and orbital slots empty, awaiting some future point in time when the peripheral nations would be able to afford new technology.

The outcome of the push by peripheral nations for greater consideration in the allocation of the international communication spectrum, including orbital parking spots, eventually saw substantial compromise. Even the US agreed to allow Intelsat (discussed later in this chapter) to promote the deployment of satellite communications in an equitable fashion across the world. This meant that peripheral nations would have appropriate ground stations for both uplinking and downlinking signals from the vast number of Intelsat satellites deployed around the world.

The Maitland Commission

A number of factors discouraged peripheral nations from pushing NWICO at the ITU. First, they realized there would be other global meetings sponsored by the ITU at which they could state their case and make gains in their movement toward a fairer share of the radio spectrum and orbital parking spaces. Second, many nations, particularly the US, applied pressure and collected on debts to ensure that an orderly spectrum remained intact, particularly for satellites. Third, almost all nations have some type of domestic system, regardless of how rudimentary, and want to see it continue operating without major adjustments. Fourth, divergent and often conflicting national interests among peripheral nations prevented the formation of a powerful, united, and well-orchestrated voting bloc that could have presented resolutions and amendments demanding radical changes in ITU policies and procedures.

Although industrialized nations sought to avoid the coming controversy over the crucial role that telecommunications play in economic, cultural, and social developments, peripheral nations persisted in their criticism of the ITU. In response, during the 1980s the ITU established the Maitland Commission, chaired by Sir Donald Maitland of the United Kingdom. The formal title of the study group was the Independent Commission for Worldwide Telecommunications Development.[5] The two-year study submitted its report to the ITU in January 1985. The report addressed the inequities in the distribution of telecommunications systems and services between core and other nations. It looked, for example, at telephone penetration levels and made some startling comparisons. Three-quarters of the world's population lives in countries with fewer than 10 telephones per 100 people, and more than half of the globe has access to less than one telephone per 100 people. In the Western core industrialized world, however, individuals enjoy the use of more than one telephone per two people. The commission concluded that this imbalance could no longer be tolerated: "It cannot be right that in the latter part of the twentieth century a minority of the human race should enjoy the benefits of the new technology while a majority live in comparative isolation."[6] Moreover, the commission highlighted the benefits to the entire world if the disparities were removed:

> Given the vital role telecommunications play not only in such obvious fields as emergency, health, and other social services, administration, and commerce, but also in stimulating economic growth and enhancing the quality of life, creating effective networks world wide will bring immense benefits. An increase in international traffic will generate funds, which could be devoted to the further improvement and development of telecommunications services. The increased flow of trade and information will contribute to better international relationships. The process of creating effective networks worldwide will provide new markets for the high technology and other industries, some of which are already suffering the effects of surplus productive capacity. The interest industrialized and developing countries share in the world-wide development of telecommunications is as great as in the exploitation of new sources of energy. And yet it is far less appreciated.[7]

The Maitland Commission argued that although telecommunications systems were once considered a luxury, they are now viewed as essential components of development. Indeed, one may argue that a telecommunications infrastructure is a prerequisite for any type of social or economic development in peripheral nations. For example, the benefits of telecommunications include increased economic, commercial, and administrative efficiency; improved social and emergency services; and more equitable distribution of the social, cultural, and economic benefits of development. In addition, "The absence of a system which enables timely information to be sent and received engenders a sense of isolation and frustration, and so raises a barrier between different sections of the population. This cannot but undermine the process of development."[8] The Maitland Commission concluded that the best way to redress the imbalance and enhance the telecommunications ability of the developing world was through the expansion of telecommunications networks.

A final set of recommendations involved the role of the ITU and how it might be strengthened. The commission reasserted that telecommunications development should be given a higher priority. It charged the secretary-general of the ITU with monitoring the implementation of the recommendations offered in the report, reporting on the progress made, and stimulating further progress where necessary. The report concluded:

> There is no single remedy. A range of actions over a wide front and at different levels is required. Progress will be made only in stages. But, if the effort is sustained, the situation worldwide could be transformed in twenty years. All mankind could be brought within easy reach of a telephone by the early part of next century and our objective achieved.[9]

Maitland follow-up

The Maitland Commission forever altered the traditional role of ITU. No longer was ITU a simple technical and engineering meeting. In the future, it would have to take into account the peripheral nations' concerns about issues such as access to and equitable distribution of the radio spectrum. The Maitland Report focused on the inequities among nations, particularly the fact that core nations control telecommunications research, manufacturing, and fiscal resources. Although everyone knew that a telecommunications infrastructure was necessary for the promotion of telemedicine, education, banking, tourism, and eventually access to the internet, peripheral nations realized they were not going to become part of the electronic global village if they did not receive support from ITU. Therefore, peripheral nations did not want to tear down the ITU, but rather reform it from within. Many of these reforms and genuine concerns become prevalent at ITU in the 1990s and up to the present. But new major issues emerged involving the role of the private telecommunications sector within ITU's decision-making apparatus, along with discussions about the privatization of major stakeholders such as Comsat and Intelsat. These crucial matters are dealt with in the following sections.

International Telecommunications Satellite Organization (Intelsat)

Intelsat was formed in 1965 to provide international satellite communication services. From the beginning, the United States was the major participant in Intelsat and the leading core nation in the ITU. Intelsat was controlled and owned by 144 member nations. It provided the satellite technology necessary to complete the global communication systems that were in place by 1969. Intelsat global satellite systems bring video, audio, voice, data, and internet services to users in more than 200 nations around the globe. Basically, Intelsat operates as a wholesaler providing satellite services to users through Intelsat members in each country. The US member was Comsat Corporation. Intelsat achieves this by operating a system of high-powered spacecraft in orbit as well as thousands of earth stations around the world. Intelsat customers are primarily major telecommunications operators in each nation throughout the world. In addition, Intelsat provides satellite communication services to major broadcasters, airlines, banks, multinational corporations, and international newspaper distributors, as well as disaster relief, healthcare, and telemedicine organizations around the globe.

In the mid-1960s, Intelsat launched the world's first communication satellite, and by 1969 it provided global television coverage of the moon landing to an audience estimated to exceed 500 million people. In 1978, Intelsat linked the World Cup football matches to over 1 billion TV viewers in 42 countries. By 1997, Intelsat had established three regional support centers to increase market awareness and develop further telecommunications business. These offices are in the Pacific Rim, Southeast Asia, and Europe. In 2000, Intelsat made possible the broadcast of the Sydney Olympic Games to a record 4 billion people around the world, using 10 of its satellites.

In July 2001 Intelsat became a private company incorporated in Bermuda. Before it could issue shares to the public it was acquired by a group of private investors in 2004. This new consortium plans to expand the fixed satellite services beyond the current 200 nations and territories. The investors view Intelsat as the "gold standard" in the fixed satellite services sector.

In a major move under new ownership in late 2004 Intelsat acquired the major US-based Comsat General Corporation. This purchase brought not only private business but also governments which with greater frequency rely on satellites to communicate with their embassies around the world.

Separately in 2001 ViaSat acquired Comsat Laboratories, Comsat's thinktank and technical laboratories. This new division of ViaSat provides a broad range of engineering and technical advice for both wireless and satellite clients.

Intelsat competition

Part of the global telecommunications environment Intelsat faces is the reality of two new strong competing forces. First, there are a series of other satellite providers now operating in direct competition with Intelsat. For example, several companies now provide satellite-centric telecommunications services to a range of clients and compete directly with Intelsat for high-volume users and transoceanic telecommunications business. The second major competitor is transoceanic fiberoptic cable systems. These cables have exceptional broadband width, reliability, and speed, and the systems now account for substantial amounts of telecommunications traffic over high-volume routes. These two competing groups service those routes that provide considerable profitability. They do not serve peripheral nations, less populated areas, or low-profit routes where there is little demand for high-capacity, high-speed digital communications. Intelsat is the lifeline provider for universal access to satellite service, thanks to its historic ownership and participatory structure. Clearly, however, this field of telecommunications could radically change with privatization.

After 30 years, Intelsat is confronting a new reality. The competitive and regulatory international environment for satellites is substantially different from the environment of a global central monopoly that was present when Intelsat was first formed in the 1960s. Now the environment is rife with deregulation, competition, liberalization, and privatization. The original 144 partners in Intelsat find themselves with increasingly different goals, owners, and domestic policies. Many of the national partners have or will be privatized. This is happening at a time when the other global partners are vigorously advocating their own, different business goals and policies. One aspect of particular policy concern is the total privatization of Intelsat, which occurred in 2001. Intelsat functioned as an intergovernmental operating organization based on a consensus that followed a series of negotiated global agreements. Because there is no global regulator of international telecommunications services or prices, Intelsat tended to promote agreements that would protect all members – core, semiperipheral, and peripheral alike. But now the peripheral group is fearful that its interests would be totally neglected in a privatized environment in which the sheer weight of economics and profitability will dominate future decision-making. Some peripheral nations could even lose their lifeline access to Intelsat's satellites. Without access to Intelsat's infrastructures, they could lose connection to the outside world. In times of national disasters, such as the Asian tsunami, such lack of connectivity to the outside world could make a crisis even greater.

ITU's Changing Role and Expectations

When ITU was founded in 1865, it was established to coordinate agreements between 20 nations concerning interconnecting telegraph networks for international telegraph traffic. Over time other nations joined, and equipment manufacturers and telecommunication carriers from both the public and private sectors participated in working groups to assist ITU in establishing appropriate technical standards. The private-sector firms never had any voting authority but provided needed technical studies so that ITU could develop appropriate international agreements to permit the orderly deployment of telecommunications technologies.

During the first decades of ITU's existence, most telecommunication carriers were monopoly providers already owned by governments of various nations. For example, the government of France owned the Office of the Post Telegraph and Telecommunication, known as PTT. But with the rapid expansion of the global economy, along with rapid innovations in the tele-communications sector, a new environment confronts ITU. The demands of the information society and global economy find telecommunications systems and services being privatized in an era of deregulation. Liberalization, along with new stakeholders who have little or no connection to their own governments through ownership, oversight, or control, are now part of the telecommunications landscape. Thus, the balance of power has shifted with the liberalization of the telecommunications environment to the private sector. This movement is further complicated by the conversion of tradi-tionally distinct analog technologies to digital communications. Tele-communications firms and broadcasting and computer corporations work with essentially the same basic digital technologies. Now Hewlett-Packard, Microsoft, Intel, IBM, and others are some of ITU's private-sector members. They are providing the much-needed technical expertise as both wireless telecommunications and satellite technologies continue to evolve. The current situation in the ITU is becoming awkward, with the private-sector members estimated to provide over 90 percent of the intellectual and technical con-tribution that underpins ITU's recommendations and technical standards. This new reality needs to be dealt with in order for ITU to retain its global technical decision-making role. Speed and broad participation is not a hall-mark of ITU's style of bureaucratic management, yet the private sector wants greater influence at future conferences, and these firms want a say in ITU's future directions. Faced with this growing private-sector call for shared power arrangements, ITU has been slow to respond even though liberalization and privatization have been part of the global information economy for over a decade. In 1998, at ITU's Minneapolis conference, the new environment confronting ITU was discussed in conference materials. Documents supplied to delegates stated:

> With an increasing number of new fora created by the market itself, many users and experts now question the relevance of a slow-moving body such as the ITU, where all power is vested in government representatives rather than in those organizations who are investing in and developing new technologies.
>
> However, before writing off the ITU one should bear in mind that it is the only truly global impartial organization whose membership spans all aspects of the industry, from PTOs to manufacturers to satellite system operators to service providers and even user groups. Even in its current form ITU can largely take single-handed credit for the successful development of the world's current telecommunications networks over the last 100 years.[10]

ITU's slow and cumbersome procedures could cause regional groups to take over its technical standards-setting role. The same document goes on to state:

Most ITU Members – State and private sector – at least agree that a declining role for the ITU is not desirable. Despite the burgeoning growth of industry- and technology-specific forums and lobby groups, the ITU still represents the only truly global, impartial telecommunications organization. It has no vested interests, represents the needs of the poor as well as the rich countries, and has succeeded where all other industry groups have failed – that is, in pulling together competing organizations and governments in a spirit of cooperation. And, in the ITU's case, this cooperative effort is much more than mere words; it has led to almost faultless interconnection of the global telecommunications network and a shared approach to radio frequency spectrum use for radio communications.[11]

Finally, peripheral nations enjoy their voting status at ITU and do not want to see it diluted by adding private-sector voting rights. They are also concerned that private-sector voting rights will go to multinational corporations based in core regions such as the United States, Europe, or Japan. Over time the marginal voices of the peripheral nations could become even weaker if ITU takes heed of the private sector's discontent with its current status. Yet ITU realizes that if it fails to respond, many major telecommunications players could shift their interests, role, and advice to other regional groups – to the ultimate detriment of ITU in the twenty-first century.

ITU has not been blind to the calls for reform. In developing a strategic plan for 1999–2003, ITU's major planning document recognized the crucial role that international telecommunications play within the broader context of the global economy. The strategic planning document notes, for example, the following trends within the telecommunications sector:

- rapid technological developments which improve the efficiency of existing products, systems, and services and permit innovation in all these areas;
- sharply declining costs for information processing and transmission capacity, accompanied by sharply rising costs for software, marketing, and customer service;
- the privatization of government telecommunication operators (between 1984 and 1996, some 44 PTOs were privatized);
- the establishment of independent regulatory bodies; the liberalization of domestic and international markets for telecommunication products and services under sector-specific policies and regulations;
- the emergence of "global" telecommunication operators capable of providing end-to-end services across national borders either by establishing a commercial presence through subsidiaries, acquisitions, partnerships and strategic alliances, or by supplying services across borders;
- the increasingly important role being played in the telecommunication sector by general competition, trade, and commercial policies and

regulations, most notably through the work of the World Trade Organization Group on Basic Telecommunications (WTO/GBT), which recently reached agreement on a set of fundamental principles that will serve as the basis for a global telecommunication regulatory framework;

■ the convergence of telecommunication, computer, broadcasting, and information technology, which is leading to competition between these previously distinct industry sectors, and raising questions about how to reconcile the different policy and regulatory frameworks which have governed these sectors in the past.[12]

The document does show concern for the increasing gap between "the information rich" and "the information poor," or the Digital Divide as the literature now refers to it. Yet at the same time, as ITU is attempting to reposition itself in the international telecommunications debate, it appears to be a potential big loser as large organizations such as Comsat and Intelsat are privatized. If this occurs, these organizations will have to answer directly to their shareholders rather than seek solutions that take into account the needs of other nations.

The World Summit on the Information Society (WSIS)

The United Nations (UN) endorsed the WSIS in 2001. The Summit is to be held in two phases: the first phase was held in Geneva, Switzerland, in 2003 and the second phase is to be held in Tunis, Tunisia in late 2005.[13] Both phases are being coordinated by the ITU.

In general, the Summit is taking a global approach to the impact of the Information Society (IS). It is seeking ways to make the IS equitable and inclusive by discussing issues such as access, capacity, and connectivity. Particular attention is being paid to e-learning/education, e-governance, e-media, and c-trade. A final plan of action aimed at reducing the digital divide will likely emerge from the second phase, but there are already three areas of contention.

The first is the selection of Tunisia itself as the site for the second phase. It is a country with a poor track record concerning a free press, plus now it is jailing cyber dissidents. To hold such a major Summit calling for good intentions, political will, and openness in an authoritarian nation known for hostility to the international press and which opposes the free flow of information, particularly on the internet, makes little sense.

The second issue deals with NWICO. As discussed in earlier chapters, UNESCO, the ITU, and the UN all played some part in the contentious debate about NWICO. Yet, even in the tamer confines of the first phase in Geneva, issues such as reducing imbalances in IT systems and calls for greater diversity of media ownership appeared in the declaration of principles. These reflect aspects of the earlier NWICO feud.

The third and perhaps most explosive issue deals with the governance of the internet. As detailed in chapter 12, the current assignment of internet names is being performed by the Internet Corporation for Assigning Names and Numbers (ICANN). But the second phase is going to take up the issue of changing this so that peripheral regions have some influence in future decisions.

World Trade Organization (WTO)

In 1947 most of the industrialized nations established the General Agreement on Tariffs and Trade (GATT), the basic aim of which was to establish international rules for promoting freer trade by reducing tariffs, government grants, or subsidies. The agreements were multilateral in focus, meaning that several nations agreed to a certain timetable to mutually reduce tariffs in order to facilitate growth in trade and the global economy. On January 1, 1995, the World Trade Organization (WTO) succeeded GATT. Currently, the WTO has 148 member nations and is headquartered in Geneva, Switzerland. The entry of China represents a significant market for all core nations.

As global trade increases, including a substantial number of mergers and acquisitions internationally in the communications sector, the roles and influence of WTO have taken on additional importance. Yet the roles played by WTO are not without controversy or consequence. The 1999 meeting in Seattle, Washington, saw substantial protest from environmental activists, labor groups, and anarchists. Although the protest focused on environmental and labor issues, several of the peripheral nations' delegates complained that the imposition of US environmental regulations or salary and working conditions mandated by US labor unions was merely another form of imperialism, which the peripheral nations rejected. Peripheral nations, as well as some core and semiperipheral nations, were also concerned about the impact and relevance of the US labor practices on their cultural industries. An important point of contention is that the United States views media properties such as film, books, and magazines as economic entities, whereas many other nations view these products as central to their history, national identity, and culture. As a result, several parties outside the US vigorously defend their right to exclude cultural industries and products from WTO negotiations. The major NGO contesting WTO's attempts to include audiovisual or cultural industries is the International Network for Cultural Diversity (INCD).[14] The 8-year-old INCD seeks to counter the homogenizing effects of the globalization and commercialization of culture. They seek to preserve diversity and promote choice in the cultural market-place. This includes the production and distribution of indigenous goods.[15] The INCD is a citizen's movement with over 500 members from 70 nations. It is a prime mover in terms of supporting UNESCO's draft Convention on the protection of the promotion of cultural diversity. This Convention legitimates government's subsidies, grants, etc. to their cultural industries and opposes the WTO's commercialization of this sector.

A related controversial issue facing the WTO is intellectual property rights. Intellectual property refers to artistic and literary creations, most of which are protected by copyright. With the expansion of global communication corporations, the ability to reward and determine ownership of creative works is becoming more problematic. And with the expansion of international commerce, the WTO's role in establishing ground rules for all trade is receiving much greater attention.

Currently the WTO appears stuck on the Doha Round, which focuses on agriculture because core nations will not drop tariffs and thus permit access to peripheral nations. Disputes between nations may be resolved through a complicated dispute settlement process. Such a process is preferable to that of earlier times when colonial disputes about trade frequently led to skirmishes, some escalating into open warfare.

Organization for Economic Cooperation and Development (OECD)

The OECD was established immediately following the Second World War. Canadian and US foreign aid under the Marshall Plan was initially adminis-tered by the Organization for European Economic Cooperation (OEEC). The goal of this organization was to rebuild Europe, which had been dev-astated by the war. Much of the motivation for funding what was a success-ful program was the effort to stop communism from spreading across Europe, which had been devastated by the war. In 1961 the Organization for Eco-nomic Cooperation and Development was formed by 20 nations in Europe and North America. Since then, 10 additional nations have entered, most recently the Slovak Republic in 2000. The OECD also has relations with 70 other nations and several NGOs. Under the leadership of Secretary General Donald Johnson, a Canadian, the OECD has been attempting to add more development activities to its research agenda. The member nations and the date of entry in OECD are as follows:

Australia 1971	Hungary 1996	Norway 1961
Austria 1961	Iceland 1961	Poland 1996
Belgium 1961	Ireland 1961	Portugal 1961
Canada 1961	Italy 1961	Slovak Republic 2000
Czech Republic 1995	Japan 1964	Spain 1961
Denmark 1961	Korea 1996	Sweden 1961
Finland 1969	Luxembourg 1961	Switzerland 1961
France 1961	Mexico 1994	Turkey 1961
Germany 1961	The Netherlands 1961	United Kingdom 1961
Greece 1961	New Zealand 1973	United States 1961

OECD members support research to develop international economic and social policy research. They investigate a broad spectrum of public-policy issues that seek to identify the impact of national policies on the international economy. Currently, much of their work focuses on the impact of global trade, including everything from video to the internet. For example, the OECD provides member nations with cutting-edge research on a variety of topics relating to the mass media. The following are examples from the over 50 reports produced by the OECD which seek to assist member nations in planning for various aspects of media policy and emerging trends (figure 11.3).

Two other sectors within their research divisions that impact global communication, are, first, Information and Communication Technologies, and second, Digital Economy and the Information Society.

1. Media Mergers

2. New Social and Economic Approaches to a Multimedia World

3. The Implications of Convergence

4. Global Information Infrastructure

5. Competition and Regulation in Broadcasting

6. Competition Law and Policy

7. Telecommunications Regulations: Institutional Structures and Responsibilities

Figure 11.3 Examples of OECD's mass media research reports

OECD attempts to forecast macroeconomic developments on behalf of the 30 member countries, which produce two-thirds of the world's goods and services. In a way, OECD is a thinktank for core and some semiperipheral nations. It provides them with expert advice on how to further frame and expand international trade rules so that the cooperation among member nations as well as others increases and creates a stable and expanding global economy. Most of their work is from an economic perspective. New members are admitted to OECD, which tends to be an exclusive club, as long as they have a commitment to a democratic system of national government and function with a market economy.

Conclusions

The US withdrawal from UNESCO was not an isolated event; in fact, it reflected the widespread and somewhat negative view of all UN multilateral agencies in which the United States should play a vital role. In addition to problems with UNESCO, which hosted anti-Western projects, particularly with reference to NWICO, the United States has expressed similar concerns about ITU.

US withdrawal from ITU would be a disaster for the long-term development of national and international communication. The fact that an individual can place a call between almost any pair of telephones in the world is no small feat of international coordination, both technical and political: it represents one of the unambiguously constructive achievements of any UN agency. The importance of international coordination is demonstrated by the fact that in the one area where coordination has failed – namely, high-frequency broadcasting – chaotic interference has ensued. If the United States were to leave ITU, it has been suggested that the US could continue to collaborate with the technical committees on standards and on spectrum competition. This ignores the politically charged nature of all intergovernmental agencies; ITU is no exception. With only 4 percent of the world's population, the United States is the largest user of global telecommunications systems and services, made possible, in large part, by the ITU.

ITU is no longer the most private domain of technicians and engineers dealing with communication technology from a purely technical point of view. It is part of the international concern that sees economic, social, cultural, development, and political aspects as part of the global decision-making process. ITU's character shift has, of course, drawn sharp criticism from those who either used to benefit from or control the "clubby" technical atmosphere that core nations fostered. Some critics downplay the role of

ITU as well as its current changes, but a proper analysis indicates that ITU is not only central to the future of international telecommunications, but also central to the global economy. On any scale, the United States is the major net beneficiary of the global economy. Telecommunications is the central nervous system of the global economy, and the United States would be the biggest loser should ITU fail in its various roles. Yet several peripheral nations within ITU push a parochial agenda that continues to frustrate core nations.

A global village with a fractured ITU, or an Intelsat weakened because of privatization, would set the scene for potential chaotic, conflicting, and competing assignments of the international frequencies related to the electromagnetic spectrum. Even though such a situation would adversely affect other nations, this would pale in comparison to the turmoil and commercial losses that core governments would suffer, as well as their vast private sector, which relies on instantaneous telecommunications every second of every hour without end. More attention to ITU issues by core nations will be required because the consequences of neglect could cripple the global economy.

Basically the ITU is seeking to retain global leadership as the preeminent intergovernmental organization where public (government) and private businesses work to develop global telecommunications and information services networks in an orderly and fair manner. This is no small challenge.

Finally, the outcome of the WSIS is still to be written. Some critics are claiming that it will be a back-door attempt to resurrect aspects of the NWICO saga. If this happens then the ITU, its major patron, will be blindsided and this could hasten its demise. The other area of possible contention is the idea of UNESCO promoting an international convention on cultural diversity at the same time the WTO is looking at cultural industries as a new frontier for its trade rules. These rules make subsidies; grants; radio, television, and film content regulations; and quotas illegal. This has the potential to even ensnare the publicly funded BBC.

Notes

1   It is appropriate here to introduce the concept of digital communication. Digital communication represents the emerging technological standard for the transmission of voice, video, audio, graphics, and data. As a technology, it decodes incoming messages into electronic bytes that are then transmitted via a telecommunication medium, whether a wired system, such as fiberoptics, or a wireless technology, such as satellite or cellular. The receiving technology reconstructs the digital information into the appropriate original format, such as a color telecast of an international media event such as the Olympics, or data being transferred from one multinational corporation to its various subsidiaries around

the globe. Over time all current analog-based technologies will migrate to a digital format. This digitalization of telecommunications will eventually mean that traditional telephone companies will be able to broadcast television services or carry the internet, and vice versa. This is a large part of the engine of change that is propelling so many mergers across broadcasting and telecommunication entities that historically were separate. The convergence phenomenon began to overtake many regulatory bodies and their rule making in the 1990s. In the twenty-first century, both national and international regulatory agencies will be found wanting as digital technologies and other technical innovations simply outpace the ability of regulators to devise appropriate guidelines to provide appropriate oversight or structure to a plethora of competing global digital services.

2　Documentation of the interconnection of global communication networks, trade, and services is contained in George Barnett et al., "Globalization and International Communication: An Examination of Monetary, Telecommunications and Trade Networks," *Journal of International Communication* 6(2) (Dec. 1999), pp. 7–19.

3　John Howkins, "How the ITU Works," *Inter Media* 7(5) (1979), pp. 22–3.

4　"Will You Keep My Space?" *The Economist*, Sept. 1978, p. 18.

5　Independent Commission for World-Wide Telecommunications Development Report: *The Missing Link* (Geneva: ITU, 1985).

6　Ibid., p. 31.

7　Ibid., p. 65.

8　Ibid., pp. 7–8

9　Ibid., p. 69.

10　www.itu.int, "Opening Documents, ITC Press and Public Information Service, October 12, 1998," p. 6.

11　Ibid., p. 6.

12　ITU Document, "Towards a Draft Strategic Plan for the Union 1999–2003," pp. 5–11.

13　For more up-to-date information on the Summit see www.itu.int/wsis.

14　For additional information on the INCD see www.incd.net.

15　For a comprehensive discussion of the impact of globalization on popular culture see Peter Grant and Chris Wood, *Blockbusters and Trade Wars* (Vancouver: Douglas & McIntyre, 2004).

Chapter 12

The Internet: The New Frontier

Introduction

The internet is to the information age what the automobile was to the industrial age. The internet is now a mass medium that has created a new dimension for global communication. It had its origins in the 1950s as a response to a crucial military question: namely, how could the United States send strategic information across long distances electronically with a maximum guarantee of accuracy and the likelihood of reaching its ultimate destination? A team of leading scientists was assembled from leading universities across America. They set in motion research that established the foundations for the electronic transfer of information over vast distances. It was to become a marriage of computer technology and the internet.

Before describing in detail the series of activities and decisions that collectively formed the foundation for the modern-day internet, one needs to note that only a few major innovations have affected international communications. The inventions started slowly: the printing press, the telegraph, and telephone in the nineteenth century, but following the Second World War the infrastructure of global communications finally had been put in place.

In the nineteenth century there were newspapers, which traveled by rail or private mail, and writing, which traveled as letters via the international postal services. Electronic message systems primarily consisted of the telegraph, which tended to expand in tandem with railway systems. Following the telegraph came the telephone, which saw a rapid expansion along with a telecommunications infrastructure during the twentieth century. Wireless signals started as ship-to-shore devices and morphed into radio. Radio broadcasting and the creation of networks emerged in the early part of the last century. At the same time, the movie industry was taking shape in both Europe and the United States. The laying of submarine telephone cable under the Atlantic and then the Pacific Oceans further expanded international communications capacity. Shortly thereafter, satellite and cable broadcasting were introduced to further expand the telephone, radio, television, data, and other forms of telephony. Now, the introduction of digital technologies, bringing convergence, and the internet represent the next new wave of global mass communication. The internet relies extensively on the interconnection of widely dispersed, global, and interconnected personal computer systems.[1]

Background

The internet system began in the Cold War era of the 1950s. With a high level of anxiety over issues such as national security, the spread of communism, the Russians' successful launch on October 4, 1957, of Sputnik,[2] and the potential for nuclear destruction created the public will to undertake research on a massive scale. When one combines these fears with the military background of President Eisenhower, in retrospect it is easy to understand how funding and the intellectual critical mass needed for the creation of a system that would eventually become the internet were established during the 1950s. For example, during this era it was widely discussed that the United States was vulnerable to a potential nuclear attack and that such an attack could disrupt nationwide communication systems. Both commercial and military systems were vulnerable. The other concern was the high cost of computing, along with the physical size and awkwardness of mainframe systems, which used punch cards and bulky tapes. As a result, in 1958 the US government established the Advanced Research Projects Agency (ARPA) to promote advanced research in computing and investigate related telecommunication matters. ARPA had the task of determining how computer technology could be successfully applied to military activities. About the same time, the Rand Corporation produced a national security report that documented the extreme vulnerability of the US national communication infrastructure in the event of a catastrophic event. Basically, Rand proved that national communication systems between the East Coast and the West Coast could be interrupted or severed by a nuclear attack. This, of course, had tremendous ramifications for a coordinated military and civilian response. The collective outcome of these concerns was to build what is described as a distributed network, internet's precursor, called ARPANET.

ARPANET was constructed in 1969 as a national network basically consisting of a number of stand-alone, remote systems. Each system controlled all necessary data, like a number of backup systems. These systems collectively moved data from one system to another. This distributive network allowed for different possible routes, so if one system was down, the message or data would be relayed through an alternative telecommunication route that was part of ARPANET. For example, if the network in Chicago was down, the system would reroute the data through St. Louis or Houston until it reached its final destination, say Los Angeles. Eventually the entire message would be reconstructed as the data communication, arriving via several different networks, reached its final destination. The military thinking was that given a catastrophic nuclear attack in one part of the country, there would be enough ARPANET systems to bypass affected regions so that the Pentagon could communicate with military bases located strategically in the Midwest or on the West Coast, for example. Today the ARPANET system might appear archaic, but it did generate a large number of high-end host computers that had clear commercial applications for the technology and software being developed and supported by extensive federal research funds available through military and national security initiatives.

A second major outcome of the early computer activities that eventually led to the internet was the extensive utilization of university talent. ARPANET was a project to interconnect the technical workings of four academic research groups based at the University of California Los Angeles, the University of California Santa Barbara, the University of Utah, and Stanford University. These groups were selected because they were working on technical design issues and signal protocols for computers in different locations in an effort to communicate with each other and share resources. These academics were the first generation of computer scientists. At the same time, the US Department of Defense was supporting networking and engineering projects at Harvard University and the Massachusetts Institute of Technology that would serve as the nucleus for East Coast high-technology research initiatives. Similarly, ARPANET provided the intellectual critical mass on the West Coast that was necessary for the application of communication technologies to various military initiatives. Over time, universities and technical thinktanks such as the Rand Corporation began to promote other nondefense uses of the networks. In the early days, newsgroups expanded based on academic disciplines. For example, physicists began to communicate with other physicists electronically, mathematicians with other mathematicians, economists with other economists, and so on. This produced an expanding universe of electronic mail users who were using personal computers or laboratory computers to communicate across a publicly switched network, which initially was under the control of the Department of Defense. ARPANET had become a packet (data) switching network that allowed researchers, via different computers in different regions, to communicate using computer machines. By 1972 the initial 4 sites had grown to 23, all networked together and pushing the frontiers of new hardware and software design. By 1987 the Department of Defense had transferred responsibility to the National Science Foundation (NSF), in part recognizing the substantial expansion of the internet system that had replaced ARPANET by this time. The NSF was a logical choice because a large number of nonmilitary applications and protocols were being pursued, and NSF wanted to create a university-based network for a wide variety of academics. Also, a number of commercial computer manufacturers were supporting research to create compatibility and open architectural features to assist an expanding market.

By 1990 the internet was seeing substantial use by people who had significant computer programming experience. It was completely text based, and people had to learn computer operating systems in order to send or receive email or participate in discussion groups. During the 1990s, the creation of the World Wide Web, the mouse, icons, browsers, and search engines that were user-friendly enabled the internet to expand globally and rapidly. During the same period, the rapid decline in the cost of personal computers also enabled widespread applications in homes, schools, and businesses, which had not been foreseen by the developers of the ARPANET system. In order to encourage the widest possible use of the internet, in 1995 the NSF turned over control of the internet to a number of commercial organizations and networks. Thus, today no one organization, government, or corporation owns the internet. Rather, it is a global interconnection of telecommunications systems controlled by protocols and rule-making on a voluntary basis.

Although the internet system was initially a technical medium for scientists and engineers, it has evolved into a mass medium. It has now become a network of networks. The internet consists of four major elements or electronic services: email, FTP (File Transfer Protocol), newsgroups, and two chat areas – IRC (internet relay chat) and collaboration. Each of these elements has international communication potential.

The US Department of Defense provided the initial funding, but since that time the internet has become a global network with major commercial applications. The internet economy now is growing faster than other sectors of the economy. For example, according to a 2000 University of Texas study, e-commerce now employs more workers than insurance, public utilities, or the airlines. The same study forecasts an additional 62 percent annual growth rate for e-commerce companies.[3] The internet did not become a global network overnight, but certain events have focused its ability to bring together millions of geographically separated individuals. For example, when Princess Diana died, cyberspace became a popular meeting place for mourners. Other examples include the publication of NASA's Path Finder pictures from Mars, or the popularity of stock-market information. On certain days, thousands of investors switch to internet financial webpages provided by internet sites, broadcasting networks, cable systems, or investment houses.

Initially, the Web was viewed as an alternative news source, but now it is a mainstream news source. The Web is a mixture of special-interest information providers, ranging from governments, to commercial systems, to global broadcasters such as CNN, the BBC, or Time Warner.

The World Wide Web

The World Wide Web (WWW) is an internet-based process that came about through the convergence of advancing technologies and increased sophistication in programming languages. The rapid development of the Web is a result of distributed processing, which includes storing, displaying, searching, and formatting computer-based information; the global interconnection of PCs; the development of hypertext and a coding standard, HTML; and browsers. Browsers are a key component and basically represent client application software that knows how to communicate through the internet and capture appropriate documents. Browsers also include built-in tools for searches, email, organizing information, and so on.

During the 1990s, there were two major browsers in competition with each other: Netscape Navigator, which was acquired by AOL, and Microsoft's Internet Explorer. Netscape dominated the browser market during the early years, but Microsoft overtook the browser market in the late 1990s. This domination of the browser market came to the attention of the US Department of Justice. In 1999 the Department of Justice found that Microsoft engaged in monopolistic tactics through its marketing and by embedding its browser within Microsoft's operating systems, Windows, to the detriment of competition. Microsoft appealed the decision in the US successfully, but the EU continues to seek some remedies from the firm.

History of the WWW

As a physicist at CERN Laboratories in Geneva, Switzerland, Tim Berners-Lee wrote a seminal paper in 1980 entitled "Enquire-Within-Upon-

Everything." It contained a program that linked arbitrary computers but had the additional capacity to sort information by certain categories. The computers could be located anywhere and search for select information, perhaps on particle physics. By 1990 Berners-Lee and others had progressed to the stage of writing papers and software using hypertext for the purpose of allowing European physicists to communicate with each other by computer. Berners-Lee proposed using a single simple interface to search various information sites spread about the internet system without regard to location. He captured the concept of using Hypertext Markup Language (HTML) to select certain words and then search a vast range of documents to discover similar words, listing them as a result of a computer search. The list also contained the remote computer's address (a URL) to obtain the referenced document. This became the basis of the modern World Wide Web. Initially the Web was limited to professional and academic organization users, but in 1993 the National Center for Supercomputing Applications (NCSA) at the University of Illinois developed user-friendly client browsers they called Mosaic. Prior to this development there were about 50 web servers worldwide. By 1994, with the introduction of Mosaic, there were over 1,500. By 1995 the Web became the dominant mode for accessing information from remote personal computers over the internet.

In 1994 Mosaic guru Marc Andreessen left NCSA to form the Mosaic Communication Corporation which in turn changed its name to Netscape Communications Corporation. Netscape produced the first version of Netscape Navigator, the early dominant browser for web users. In 1996 Microsoft released the Internet Explorer 3.0 version, which was to provide overwhelming browser competition for Netscape. The Microsoft browser was able to retrieve remote documents and provide greater speed and display capacity than its competitors. Each generation of browsers added several unique features, which further expanded the utilization of the Web for home, business, school, and a plethora of other users.

With the advent of the fifth generation of browsers, the differences between Microsoft and Netscape are now so pronounced that each system interfaces with external pages that are dependent on the programming language of a specific browser. Thus, users who want the complete universe of pages or sites for any particular subject area have to load both browser programs in order to retrieve webpages that are systematically linked with one or the other of the browser architectural protocols. In part, it was this phenomenon that attracted the Department of Justice's attention, because the dominance of Microsoft's Explorer browser was inclining new website developers to develop software that could interface with Microsoft's Windows but not necessarily with the Netscape browser, or others. Because Microsoft has popular Windows products preloaded on almost every new

PC, this permits Internet Explorer to be embedded within Microsoft's product lines. PCs arrive with preinstalled Explorer browsers for users who then either have little need or the sophistication to seek out the competing Netscape browser. Microsoft's browser, claiming to be faster, smaller, and offering more features, has thus become the gateway to the Web almost to the exclusion of other competing browsers.

Video games

Any history of the internet would not be complete without acknowledging the role of video games. Whether Atari, Nintendo, Sega, or PlayStation, these video games have created a generation of computer users who appreciated high speed, enhanced graphics, and interactivity. Successful video games have served as a backdrop against which computer manufacturers must judge each new generation of PC. As a result, video games continue to set new and higher standards for graphics, speed, and sophistication that each generation of PC has to at least match, if not exceed. The other related phenomenon is that video games are a global enthusiasm. Early on, much of the software originated from Japan, but North American, European, and other affluent cultures quickly became willing markets for and manufacturers of these increasingly complex games. Games became common property of teenagers in core nations.

Currently, video games are either preprogrammed within a cafeteria of software that is preloaded on PCs, or else they are available externally through the internet to be downloaded for personal use. A major point is that video games, although a separate technology using either a modem and a standard TV monitor or a hand-held device, had an impact not only on the technology of the internet, but also on software development, particularly graphics capabilities. Games set the visual benchmark for PC graphics. It turns out that moving from a controller to a mouse is a small step for game users.

Internet Timeline ───────────────────────────

The following timeline represents the major historical events that cumulatively aided the global system called the internet.

1955   US President Eisenhower approves funding for US satellite development.

1957   USSR launches first satellite program, Sputnik, which consists of four satellites.

1958   US Department of Defense establishes the Advanced Research Projects Agency (ARPA).

1960s   A series of isolated academic papers in Europe and North America appear detailing packet switching, batch processing, spooling systems, time sharing computers, and network alternatives.

1961   April: Soviets put first man in space.
        May: United States puts man in space.
        President Kennedy calls for massive funding for research and space exploration.

1965   Ted Nelson describes hypertext, a concept using word association to find similar words electronically.

1969   ARPANET created with four university host sites.
        CompuServe established for home and business customers.
        United States succeeds with moon landing and walk on lunar surface.

1970s   Several new ARPANET host sites established, including European sites.

1971   USSR establishes first orbital space station.

1972   First email program written.

1973   United States establishes first US space station, Skylab.

1975   Microcomputers introduced.
        Paul Allen and Bill Gates found Microsoft to develop programming languages.

1976   Apple Computers reach market.

1977   Owners of Apple, Radio Shack, Atari, Commodore 64, Texas Instruments, and others begin marketing personal computers designed for schools and home.
        University of Wisconsin supports research to interconnect over 100 computer scientists via email.

1980   Apple issues public stock to raise capital for extensive research and development infrastructure. Leads to 1984 introduction of Apple Macintosh desktop computers.
        Physicist Tim Berners-Lee of CERN Laboratories (Switzerland) writes program to link colleagues' PCs.

1981   IBM enters personal computer market with two key partners, Intel and Microsoft. Because of size and market penetration, IBM sets new PC architect standards. Smaller, lighter, and cheaper clones begin to appear as well, using Intel and Microsoft products and protocols.
        Bitnet for email and file transfers established between Yale and City University of New York; IBM adopts Bitnet protocol to link IBM university computers.

Several Big 10 universities begin to establish protocols for networking services, email, and list server activities among campuses.

1983   Desktop workstations established by scientists through grants from NSF.

1984   Newsgroups are organized by researchers at universities, research institutes, and computer manufacturers.

1985   America Online (AOL) founded.

1986   Microsoft issues public stock and introduces Windows. Screen icons become the industry model.

1989   Steve Jobs creates new computer company, NeXT. This system introduces many innovations for desktop systems. Berners-Lee and others create web browser for NeXT workstations.
Commercial email offered in limited markets by MCI and CompuServe.
Berners-Lee writes a paper detailing a system using hypertext (HTML) that would become the programming basis for the www.

1990   ARPANET is disbanded.
McGill University (Montreal) supports Archie, a primitive search protocol.

1991   University of Minnesota supports Gopher, an early search engine.

1992   University of Nevada supports Veronica, a somewhat advanced search engine.

1994   Netscape developed as internet browser and establishes early lead.
Amazon.com launched.

1995   Real Audio is developed for PCs audio use.
Netscape issues shares as public company.
Microsoft introduces browser, Internet Explorer 4.0, to challenge Netscape.
Yahoo! and eBay founded. Beginning of online auctions.

1998   More PCs sold than televisions.
CompuServe and Netscape acquired by AOL.
Hacker creates viruses infecting internet programs.
Google search engine launched.

1999   Microsoft is charged by US Department of Justice with engaging in antitrust activities.
AOL customer base exceeds 20 million.
Melissa virus swamps email systems.

2000   AOL and Time Warner announce merger to create the largest global communications conglomerate.
Love Letter virus originating in Philippines attaches to email addresses and infects hard drives around the globe.

Globally, old media companies begin to look for potential new media (internet) companies for mergers, acquisitions, or partnership.

2001   Microsoft enters the video game market with Xbox.

White House website infected with virus.

2002   Verizon introduces high-speed 3G cell networks.

2003   Digital cameras outsell film units.

Blaster worm spread worldwide.

Lawyers for recording artists and studios go after file sharing and music downloading.

2004   Google goes public with share offering.

Sasser worm and MyDoom virus create internet difficulties.

800 million internet users worldwide.

Online advertising exceeds $10 billion; most coming from newspaper advertising.

2005   Spyware and adware are growing problems, as is junk email.

France announces plan to counter Google's library digitalization project.

MPAA lawyers sue movie downloaders.

Apple's iPod sales set record.

Impact of the Internet

The internet has had a major impact on many areas of life, from e-commerce to distance education. The following paragraphs highlight a single narrow yet important area: government reports. This example illustrates some of the many unexpected influences of the internet.

The availability of government documents on the internet has changed not only the access issue, but also the way information is now provided in an unfiltered fashion. Political pundits no longer have free rein to put their own personal spin, whether of the Left or the Right, on issues in order to direct viewers, listeners, or readers to an "appropriate" point of view. Because of the internet, individuals can apply their own thoughts, ideas, and background to the interpretation of new information.

The internet phenomenon began to expand rapidly in the 1990s. The system has grown enormously, much of the fuel for growth generated by the creation of widely advertised commercial services. The original internet system was designed as a narrow-casting system in which selected users would access select and unique data, or share specialized information. Now it has become a 24-hour system, a mass medium in effect, ranging from

1. Google

2. Yahoo!

3. MSN

4. AOL

5. Ask Jeeves

Figure 12.1   Top 5 search engines in the US

full-service web information, to portals,[4] to news websites such as MSNBC or CNN, in addition to services aimed at the more limited high-tech users. Many utilize the internet's search engine feature. (See figure 12.1.)

One of the internet's largest usage periods was Friday, September 11, 1998, when the Starr Report was released. Another was 9/11, the World Trade Center attack in 2001. In 1998 millions around the globe flocked to the internet when independent counsel Kenneth Starr released his report about President Clinton. It contained graphic details about the president's relationship with intern Monica Lewinsky. Many websites, in fact, crashed or were delayed because of the record volume of web traffic: internet tracking groups collectively reported that about 6 million Americans read the text of the report over a three-day period. In addition, about 10 times more people downloaded the 445-page Starr Report than the White House's 73-page response. The Starr report also increased the number of viewers of cable and network news on Friday, the day of the report's release. CNN reported its viewership average in excess of one million households, which is three times its daily norm. MSNBC averaged about double its normal audience, and FOX News Channel also reported double the number of households for an average day. The Starr report made communication history, not just in the United States but around the world. Globally, over 20 million people accessed the report within 48 hours of its electronic release. Not only was the volume record-setting, but also the availability to the average citizen was also astonishing. Average people around the world were reading the report at the same time as Congress, White House staff, news media executives, and reporters. For example, America Online, the world's largest web-based provider, recorded in excess of 10 million hours online on the day the report was released. Other online web ramps also reported either a staggering volume or technical slowdowns due to unprecedented traffic that day. A similar phenomenon occurred with the 9/11 Commission in 2004. Televised hearings, numerous press appearances and finally a bestselling government report all watched by internet users led to significant pressure on the US Federal Government to act. Demand for copies of *The 9/11 Commission Report: Final Report of the National Commission on Terrorist Attacks Upon the United States* swamped Amazon.com and other sales sites.

The important communication point to be made in all of this is that no longer were news editors, pundits, politicians, the US president, or others able to act as gatekeepers to restrict, alter, spin, or limit the information in the report. Rather, millions of average people around the world now have access to the full, unedited government reports at the same time they are presented to the national legislatures.

The Starr Report and summaries of the 9/11 Report on the internet changed in a fundamental way the potential for mass dissemination of information to a global audience. The reports represented unprecedented and unique examples of the pervasiveness of the internet as a mass communication system. It represented the democratization of the mass media in that politicians or media elites were no longer able to control, filter, or interject their editorial viewpoints about a significant government document.[5] Average individuals in the United States and elsewhere with access to the internet were able to download the entire report, consume it themselves, and draw their own conclusions. They did not have to rely on the door-to-door newspaper the next day, or condensed soundbites on national newscasts to inform them about a major government document. Even the President of the United States, along with his substantial staff of spin doctors and press spokespersons, were left to consume these and other reports from their computers at the same time that millions of people around the globe were doing exactly the same thing.

As a result of the internet, the global public is better informed. They can act as a more informed public jury concerning major political events, such as the invasion of Iraq. But the changes are not by any means limited to politics. The internet is changing the nature and perception of the human environment. Users are creating a third culture, such as that Featherstone referred to in an earlier work on the origins and growth of a global culture.[6] There is a difference between users and nonusers of the internet. And this phenomenon is more pronounced among heavy users. To some extent Marshall McLuhan foresaw this as early as the 1960s when he was theorizing about the mass media being so pervasive as to totally consume all aspects of a person's being – and leaving no aspect of one's being untouched.[7] Finally, along similar lines, electronic colonialism is about the mind being shaped more and more by external media, of which the internet is simply the latest player. The internet does alter, affect, and influence people in psychological ways yet to be foretold or completely understood.

As such, the internet is a major player in the evolving "Empire of the Mind" phenomena. The internet is also primarily in English and has a US-centric bias. These two realities have clear cultural consequences for internet users around the globe. From rural villages in India with computer access to Starbucks internet cafes in almost ever major capital of the world, electronic colonialism is on a steady march 24/7.

The internet has an obvious downside. It is capable of relaying, internationally, sordid details about what historically tended to be personal matters. It also can spark erroneous claims that could end a politician's or CEO's career. When an internet site runs a story, the story goes global. It is not restricted to a city, state, or even nation. Rather, it becomes instantaneously available worldwide.

A final note is that the internet's global and instantaneous communication ability, for good or ill, changed public life forever. In the age of the internet there is no privacy. (Just ask the bloggers. They are covered in more detail later in this chapter.) The release of government reports have made internet history, but they also opened the door for a two-way information superhighway. Various constituents in record numbers emailed their elected representatives with their thoughts and ideas about how to vote. Rather than sending a letter by mail, they now quickly – and for free – mail a message to even obscure members of local and national governments. Many representatives are reporting that they have to reassign staff to deal with the flood of email as the public uses the same computers to reply to the contents of government reports as to influence the position of their elected representatives. The messages tend to be short and full of typos, but in the final analysis, the sheer volume of email likely has a collective impact. Politicians, or government agencies such as the US FCC or the UK Ofcom, do not have to wait for weeks for the regular mail to arrive to determine where their constituents stand on vital issues.

The Internet and Global Television Issues

The story of video on the internet has yet to be written. The video materials available, whether they are television programming or feature movies, have tremendous implications for current producers. With the ability of the internet to broadcast video live, along with worldwide dissemination, current copyright holders could potentially see their materials appear anywhere in the world without their authorization or compensation. The following two examples illustrate the potential problems.

In June 2000 in California, a group of movie studios filed a suit in Los Angeles to close down a website that was allowing viewers to record television shows online. The site was attracting a large number of users and therefore caught the attention of television executives. Applying traditional copyright laws, the movie studios' legal team sought to close down the site immediately for unauthorized taping and redistribution of the video content, which originated from a series of entertainment companies and was available via cable in the Los Angles area for a cable subscription fee.[8]

A second situation reflecting the convergence of television and the internet is represented by a company based in Toronto, Canada: iCraveTV. Beginning in December 1999, with nearly one million customers during its first month of operation, iCraveTV offered 17 online television stations. It provided free internet access for its advertising-supported rebroadcast of Canadian and US television channels.[9] The 24-hour, live streaming service included NBC, CBS, ABC, FOX, and PBS. Within Canada, internet broadcasting services are not regulated under the Canadian Broadcasting Act. What iCraveTV had done was to create 10 Canadian internet superstations for a potential global audience. Providing the integration of television with the internet has not been without its critics. Some claim that the internet site violated copyright laws and constituted trademark infringement. For example, the US-based National Football League was part of a group that took legal action because US internet users are able to access NFL games through stations rebroadcast live on the iCraveTV internet site. Other plaintiffs in the suit were ABC, CBS, FOX, Disney, and Time Warner. Using internet video streaming or other internet services could place firms in legal difficulties if prosecuted under US law. US law is aimed at protecting the copyright provisions of not only the major broadcasting networks but also major sporting events, which are contracted on an exclusive basis with US-based networks. The internet's role was clearly not anticipated even a few years ago in terms of providing a competing global alternative for the rights holders.

These examples will likely be replicated when some entrepreneurial web provider makes European soccer globally available on the internet. Also, American baseball, which has a substantial following in Japan and elsewhere, may see its signals being broadcast on the internet. The National Hockey League, which has a large following in Europe and other nations, is also likely to see its product on some internet portal in countries where it has never been broadcast before. The International Olympic Committee is also a group that aggressively protects its trademarked products and symbols. To some, this is innovative and a new application for the internet; for others, these users are mere content pirates and rights thieves.

The Internet and Hollywood Films

Industries that have been surprisingly slow to change, such as Hollywood and the feature film studios, have been forced to reexamine their global distribution policies because of the internet. Traditionally, Hollywood's major studios would release their films within North America first, and then later, sometimes many months later, would distribute them around the world, primarily to other core nations and then semiperipheral nations. In a few instances, it could take a year for a major feature film to open in theaters in smaller nations or eastern Europe. Now Hollywood is confronting the emergence of the global entertainment market. This market is increasingly sophisticated, with potential moviegoers using websites to obtain information about newly released Hollywood films; others are purchasing films through e-commerce businesses that specialize in film distribution, primarily DVD disk technology. A new Hollywood policy of rolling out global distribution of major movies within weeks is a direct response to the changing environment created by the internet. All the major studios are reexamining their global marketing of new films, and the major reason is that Hollywood's hype machine has finally met a force it cannot control – the internet.

Gone are the days when Hollywood could sell its movies in domestic isolation, with little fear that the US marketing message would spread quickly to countries where the films wouldn't be seen for months.[10] An example of this phenomenon was the co-production of Columbia and Universal Pictures, which arranged a global release for Julia Roberts' feature film *Erin Brockovich*. During the opening week, the film became the number one attraction in seven major markets, including the United States, Canada, and five European nations. The global market for films is being approached more as a single market than as a series of isolated markets. Sony is also marketing new releases on an international rather than a national basis.

There are three other interesting facets of this new policy shift, which recognizes the globalization of the Hollywood feature film industry. The first is that the new releases come out only in English; dubbed or translated versions are not available on the initial release date. The second byproduct of the change is that the marketing strategy and advertising copy, including photos, for these releases are now all standardized. Identical promotional materials are used across the globe in other core nations. The promos seen in the United States for Hollywood's latest blockbuster are now the same promos being seen in Europe and other nations. Hollywood's approach to the global market had to change or face a growth in the pirating of films or alternative purchasing, which would have adversely affected the profitability of the studios' investments in what are in most cases pricey feature films. This is what has led to the third policy shift. In 2005, following the lead of the music industry, which was going after illegal online file sharing through the courts, the Motion Picture Association of America (MPAA) began a series of lawsuits to stop illegal online copying of movies. MPAA is seeking to reduce file swapping or peer to peer (p2p) activities involving Hollywood productions. Although the copyright violation and movie sharing is only about 2 percent of online illegal activity (music represents more than 60 percent) the movie industry is really worried about the future. Today the enormous size of digital movie files makes downloading a long process, plus it occupies a great deal of disc space. But with each new generation of computers both speed and space will be less of a problem or deterrent. Complicating matters for MPAA is that each new version of file-sharing software is becoming more user friendly and more difficult to track. Facing these technical realities Hollywood studios are seeking to make some online pirates pay and use these cases to stop others. Even if successful in US courts, the studios still have little hope of legal standing for the enormous threat to their property rights outside the US.

Internet Users

Yet another example of how the internet has caused a reexamination of traditional ways of doing business concerns internet users. According to Computer Industry Almanac Inc.'s *Internet Industry Almanac*, the top 10 countries with the highest internet usage in 2004 were:

1 United States 202.5 million users
2 China 87.0 million users
3 Japan 66.5 million users
4 Germany 47.2 million users
5 United Kingdom 34.9 million users
6 South Korea 30.7 million users
7 Italy 28.6 million users
8 France 23.2 million users
9 Canada 20.5 million users
10 Brazil 19.3 million users

The United States alone accounts for over 50 percent of the global internet usage.[11] Europe accounts for 25 percent of global usage. It is obvious that core nations were the early inventors and adopters of the internet and now continue to expand and dominate global usage. The core nations have all three requirements for internet access: technical expertise, the financial resources to buy the required computers and hookups, and communication infrastructures to deliver interactive internet services. In many cases, peripheral nations lack at least one of these requirements, and in some cases they lack all three.

Not surprisingly, the US is the internet superpower. According to SUNY-Buffalo communication professor George Barnett, "the United States is . . . the nucleus of internet traffic," and it is the most central nation on the international networks of both hyperlinks (bandwidth) and infrastructure. In cyberspace, peripheral and semiperipheral nations rarely communicate directly; almost all internet traffic flows through the US. The nature of the internet today can be partially explained using world-system theory, with language, technological, and cultural advantages that help the US remain the most powerful and influential nation. According to Barnett, the US "has the structural capacity to act as an information broker or gatekeeper for the international internet."[12]

Another factor that seems to encourage greater internet use is geography. Six nations have geographically isolated populations yet have substantial per capita users. These are the Scandinavian countries of Finland, Sweden, and Norway, as well as Australia, Canada, and New Zealand.

It is projected that by 2010 over a billion people worldwide will have access to the internet from their work and homes. This will allow core-based broadcasters and advertisers, particularly those with a global brand or strategic plan, to market their services via the internet on an unprecedented scale. Semiperipheral nations in central and eastern Europe will likely see the largest per capita gains in new internet users. E-commerce on the internet is now generating significant revenue in all core nations. This will fuel additional demand for internet access as well as growing commercial competition as the market share for electronic purchases of goods and services around the globe expands at a rapid pace.

Finally AOL represents an interesting application of both electronic colonialism and world-system theories. Currently, AOL has about 30 million subscribers around the world. It is by far the number one provider in the United States. Internationally, primarily through a series of joint ventures, AOL is attempting to strategically focus future growth in international markets. It is the number two internet provider in Germany, France, and Canada; in Brazil it is fourth, and in Japan it is tenth. Globally AOL and its subsidiary, CompuServe are available in 16 countries. Offshore, however, AOL frequently does not use the name America Online for fear of anti-US reaction among the computer literate, but simply goes by AOL. The expansion of AOL is targeted in the short run to semiperipheral nations, and it is anticipated that by the year 2010, a majority of AOL subscribers globally will be from outside the United States.

Computer Viruses

With the advent of the internet came the birth of computer viruses. Some are merely nuisances, while others, such as the Melissa, Love Letter, Trojan horse, Mydoom, and Resume viruses, have affected electronic mail and other files with extremely damaging results. Major corporations have had to shut down their systems due to some of the more pernicious viruses. These have the potential to erase data, release secure data, change data, or totally freeze or take over computer systems. It is estimated that there are now over 100 new viruses per week. With e-commerce expanding on a daily basis, the impact of viruses can be catastrophic and within a matter of minutes run into the millions of dollars in lost time and business. Although computer viruses first appeared in the early 1980s, macroviruses that spread worldwide with the extensive use of the internet system are a more recent phenomenon. There are also many reports of hoaxes, which are more than major annoyances. Given the recent impact of viruses that embedded themselves in complex and massive ways, even hoaxes have to be taken seriously.

Cyber crime is another new byproduct, as well as a legal challenge, of the internet. For example, the I Love You worm code that originated in the Philippines in May 2000 moved via email across Asia to Europe and from there to North and South America. Thousands of individual users were infected, as well as major organizations such as the British House of Commons, Yahoo!, the US Central Intelligence Agency, CNN, and the Ford Motor Company. Although the overall cost of damage from this email worm is difficult to assess, it was well into the millions of dollars.

Basically, computer viruses are uninvited guests that run on your PC. They can attach themselves to other files – mainly email addresses. As computer-programming languages become user-friendlier, and because they are transferable, virus programmers have realized that viruses can now switch from one platform to another without any difficulty. The virus problem is huge because viruses can be initiated by novice programmers, but the consequences can be truly catastrophic as the viruses worm their way globally and in seconds from system to system. Malicious hackers or simply nerdy computer groupies can unleash viruses at any time. Today there is anti-virus software that has helped to reduce the problem. Yet new categories like adware, pop-ups, spyware, and malware continue to infect computers. Removal software is available from several vendors.

Finally, in 2004 in the first felony prosecution of spammers in the US, a jury convicted two spammers of sending vast bulk email messages. They face up to 10 years in prison. Antispam laws with tougher sanctions are being enacted in several jurisdictions.

Blogging

A new internet-driven phenomenon called web logs or web diaries, and popularly called blogging, arrived in the mainstream media by 2004. Historically, some early bloggers, such as engineers or technicians, were adding personal or political comments to their discussion websites as early as the mid-1990s, but a few seminal events occurred in the early 2000s, which moved blogging to a new level.

The first substantial blogger-driven event was a rather focused internet attack in 2002 on the then powerful Republican Senator, Trent Lott. Lott had made some inappropriate and racist comments at a party and the mainstream media as usual covered the matter, but only for a few days. But some tenacious bloggers kept the heat on Lott for weeks and called for his resignation as senate leader. This web-based chorus forced the national media to take another look at the entire episode. Lott did resign. He did so because bloggers were able to build pressure via the internet that put Lott back on the evening newscasts and talkshows in a negative light. A decade earlier he would have avoided such scrutiny and shame.

In 2003 other creative blog users were able to mount a substantial fundraising drive via the internet for Howard Dean, a candidate for the Democratic presidential nomination. His star rose rapidly as the internet favorite, but he and the others lost out to Senator John Kerry. Dean also set the "gold standard" of fund raising by using the internet in creative ways. Then in 2004 bloggers became mini-celebrities by being accredited as media representatives at both the Democratic and Republican national conventions.[13] Blogging became a household word, much as Google did, in record time. Finally, in late 2004 Dan Rather and CBS carried a piece on documents alleging that President Bush was not as solid a National Guard soldier as the latter had claimed. The documents turned out to be false. Again it was the bloggers who kept the profile and bias of the CBS network alive and forced the mainstream media to again pursue the entire issue. Eventually both Rather and CBS issued apologies for their major ethical lapse. CBS was forced to set up an investigation, and as a result other senior CBS personnel were fired. In addition, some websites were calling for Rather to be fired as well. Rather announced his retirement and he left in 2005. Eason Jordon of CNN fame was also roadkill for some vengeful bloggers that same year.

A related newer stage of this phenomenon is video blogging. This combines the text-based blog with some appropriate video. The Asian tsunami and amateur video enthusiasts on vacation in the region provided a windfall for v-bloggers on several continents in 2005. There are no protocols, permissions obtained, or copyright concerns by the v-bloggers. Future dramatic footage, be it a televised confrontation or a natural disaster, will find its way around the world thanks to the growing cadre of vbloggers.

So the debate about the role and eventual fate of bloggers is still to be written. Some claim that they are pretend journalists in t-shirts with a laptop, while others see the new phenomenon being the next significant trend in journalism. Bloggers can be rude, crass, and seem to spend a great deal of their time discussing sex, yet they have made the political process more open and clearly have a voice and opinion on high-profile issues, whether people or political parties like it or not.

ICANN

The Internet Corporation for Assigned Names and Numbers (ICANN) has become both powerful and controversial. It is the outcome of years of recognizing the significance of the internet for the global economy. Domain names and various internet protocols, which carry a unique numerical address, are at the center of the internet's orderly expansion. All computers need an address in order to participate in the internet's growing role in all aspects of modern life. The global internet community "created a need for a new kind of social contract."[14] Milton Mueller refers to the various functions that ultimately provide for unique internet names and addresses as "the root."[15] It is clear that ICANN has become powerful because it controls the rights to top-level domain names, such as .com, .edu, .net, or .org. ICANN is a private company which controls the technical standards of cyberspace. To some extent it controls global information-sharing in the online environment. It raises the bar on the construct of power.

Internet names and related protocols emerged out of and along with the growth of the American Research Projects Agency (ARPANET). Since the funding for ARPANET came from the US military at this early stage, some controversy over who was getting the preferred names was bound to emerge. ARPANET was disbanded in 1990. The US-funded National Science Foundation took over part of the naming function for a period, and then in 1993 the US Federal government gave governance control to Network Solutions Inc. A rash of "cyber squatting" took place where people would register domain names with the hope of selling them later.[16] By 1998 this and other problems led the US Department of Commerce to create a private entity, ICANN, based in California. ICANN was given substantial gatekeeper control over new access to the internet's registries. Challenges to what appeared as a powerful monopoly role emerged.[17] In the US much of the challenge to the functioning ICANN came under the umbrella of antitrust laws, specifically the tough Sherman Antitrust Act.[18] Even though ICANN is governed by an international Board of Directors, who attempt to ensure that technical elements of the internet's infrastructure serve global needs, this oversight has not kept the global community of users included or content. Currently there are calls for a shift from the US-centric coordinating role of ICANN to a multilateral organization and environment.[19] This controversial matter has unexpectedly been taken up with zeal by some peripheral nations within the World Summit of the Information Society (WSIS). It will see a politicized tone for what ICANN and others see as technical rule-making in nature.[20] It also means that the future of internet governance may benefit the ITU or the OECD – as possible new ICANN oversight and structures – or the WSIS could end in turmoil – since Tunisia, the host country for the second phase of WSIS, has a fondness for arresting internet users as well as free-press advocates.

In closing, the above is not a trivial matter. The future of the internet and how and who governs it internationally is central to the emerging electronic information environment. If fair and equitable access is not spelled out, then it is the peripheral regions that will fall further behind in the digital divide chasm. The core nations to date have controlled the "global village" with its internet connectivity through ICANN and its predecessors. Some opening up of rule-making and greater access is now being challenged in several fora.

Conclusions

Any description of the internet, as well as projecting the future of global communications, deals with history on the run. Given the major technological and software advances being promoted by major corporations and research institutions, there are going to be several additional generations of internet hardware and software. Likewise, the merger phenomenon of old media stakeholders and new internet players, such as Time Warner, is in its infancy. In the future, there are likely to be more mergers of transnational corporations, whether they are based in Europe, North America, or Japan. The internet personifies a dynamic, rather than static, state of affairs. The internet economy is growing at a "much faster pace than the Industrial Revolution that began in the 18th century. Perhaps more importantly, the potential scope, size and overall economic impact of this economic system is much larger than what we can comprehend today. The key characteristics that distinguish the new economy are information, knowledge, and speed."[21]

Before drawing some general conclusions, a significant point relates to indigenous internet sites. It is true that various linguistic or ethnic groups have created sites that focus on and promote smaller cultural sectors. Many of these are aimed at keeping expatriates informed or aiding children with their ancestral roots. Yet for every page on the internet which is non-English, there are at least 100 pages of English text. The internet is both US-centric and English dominated. That is a major reason why the internet is a leading purveyor of electronic colonialism around the globe.

An excellent example of the internet as an English purveyor is the US-based search engine Google's initiative to digitalize knowledge from five of the world's greatest English-language libraries. The libraries are Harvard, Stanford, Michigan, Oxford, and the enormous New York Public Library. This project will ultimately provide a global and Anglo-Saxon electronic universal library. Realizing that this represents yet another marginalization of the French language as well as its literature, culture, and history, the president of France and the French National Library announced an effort to digitalize that library's vast holdings to ward off American cultural hegemony. But with Google's multimillion-dollar project and expectation of making 4.5 billion pages of English text available around the world, France's and every other non-English library may be rendered quaint local storage houses for historical artifacts. Defining the future of knowledge in the electronic digital environment through this Google project will have profound implications for what is considered information. If it is not in the database is it less worthy, and will it even survive? This has the French and many other authorities, correctly, concerned.

Even so, we can draw four general conclusions. First, although the origins of the internet may be traced back to the 1950s with the strong leadership of the US Defense Department, it is still safe to say that the origin, description, and role of the internet as it has evolved to date occurred within core nations. Innovations and expertise in North America, Europe, and to some extent Japan permitted the development and rise of the hardware technology and software necessary to establish a global internet system. Semiperipheral nations played only a catch-up role as they attempted to mimic innovations first established and demonstrated within core-nation markets. Semiperipheral nations also tend to face the dual problem of the lack of investment capital to underwrite new internet ventures, and a lack of the high-tech entrepreneurs needed to develop and promote more indigenous internet sites and services. For peripheral regions, the situation is exacerbated.

The internet revolution is in progress. Some nations with progressive public policies that encourage foreign capital and reward entrepreneurs will benefit, but other nations may stall or regress over time to weakened global economic and social positions. Semiperipheral and peripheral nations are distant users of the internet. In those regimes where the internet exists, it is available only to elites, whether they are government officials, academics, business leaders, or religious and tribal leaders. In far too many cases, the average person in peripheral regions is waiting for a first telephone, not preoccupied with browser technologies, e-commerce, iPods, or MP3 files.

Second, the internet represents change. Its impact among information gatherers and providers, whether they are in the media, business, or universities, has been profound. The situation will continue to escalate as e-commerce activities begin to displace traditional mechanisms and modes within the marketplace. Just as Amazon.com revolutionized the bookselling industry, so virtually every industry will experience similar internet intrusiveness and some global opportunities in the near future.

Third, e-commerce and e-multimedia will take on greater global trappings. The ability to advertise and market on the internet is a global electronic phenomenon. It has transformed commerce beyond the traditional bounds of the nation-state. The BBC, MTV, CNN, and other media enterprises have long recognized this, but particularly with the merger of AOL and Time Warner, there is a clear demarcation between the old media firms and the new. A firm without an internet presence is destined to a strategic reality of declining market share and influence. The internet represents the globalization of the marketplace in a fashion unprecedented in human history. It brings with it values and economic rituals such as credit cards and advertising that reflect the electronic colonizing of both the mind and the marketplace. Internet global advertising exceeds $10 billion and increases annually. Much of the online ad revenues appear to be coming primarily from newspapers and to a lesser extent from network television. Strategically, over time, since the amount of online advertising is going to increase, some newspapers will likely close.

Fourth, capturing consumer behavior and consumer purchasing power for products and services offered over the internet will become a greater economic force and reality over time. The global success of the Big Four, which are Amazon.com, eBay, Google, and Yahoo!, as both viable commercial and electronic leaders bodes well for not only them but many others as well.

It is not so much an issue of cultural imperialism, as some critics have maintained, as the economic common sense of following the success of various individuals, corporations, and systems that have migrated successfully and quickly to the world of the internet. This phenomenon might more reasonably be called electronic imperialism. The internet is to our future what automobiles and transportation were to our past. Now we are looking at digital nations, virtual spaces, e-commerce, and global systems that link individuals and the internet without regard for time or space. Whereas time and space were the defining characteristics of the industrial era, so now the internet, where time and space no longer pertain, is the defining medium of the information age.

Finally, internet technologies are not neutral. They impact a broad range of behaviors from information-processing, to research strategies, to e-commerce, and e-living. Just as the invention of the printing press had widespread consequences for the Industrial Revolution over the course of the last two centuries, so too the internet will impact this and future centuries in profound ways. Marshall McLuhan (1911–80) detailed the printing press's impact on society and individuals in his seminal work, *The Gutenberg Galaxy* (1962). A similar classic has yet to be written about the impact of the internet, but there are early indications that this impact will be substantial. For example, with reference to the internet and information technologies, Alan Hedley states, "what is at stake are the very thought processes of those dominated. Only powerful nations currently have the ability to choose the type of information society most compatible with their cultural institutions."[22] This viewpoint is fully consistent with the theory of electronic colonialism. Basically, the internet, whether it is in China, the United States, or some remote part of India, will have parallel consequences for social systems (e.g., education, commerce, and discussion groups) and the mindsets of individual users. Internet users, regardless of time or space, will mentally converge over time with other widely dispersed users. They will come to have more in common with individuals scattered around the planet than with nonusers in their neighborhoods, schools, or work.

Notes

1   This chapter seeks to highlight salient aspects of the history and current role of the internet. There is a vast literature on the subject; a few sample pieces include: J. Levine, C. Baroni, and M. Young, *The Internet for Dummies* (Foster City, CA: IDG Books Worldwide, 1999); K. Hafner and M. Lyon, *Where Wizards Stay Up Late: The Origins of the Internet* (New York: Touchstone Books, 1998); and Paul Ceruzzi, *A History of Modern Computing* (Boston: MIT Press, 1998).

2   The symbolic role of the Russian series of four Sputnik satellites cannot be underestimated. These relatively unsophisticated satellites successfully launched by the Soviet Union demonstrated to US military, political, and industrial leaders that Soviet technology was more advanced than many had believed. The same rocketry that could fire a satellite into orbit could also be easily modified to launch a nuclear payload aimed at North America. In response, in 1961 US President John F. Kennedy committed the nation to putting a man on the

moon by the end of the decade. Thus began the space race, along with the necessary rocketry to propel not only satellites into space but also manned orbital missions. In July 1969, the Apollo 11 module landed on the moon with Neil Armstrong and Buzz Aldrin.

Although Sputnik's signal lasted only 18 days, it was sufficient to galvanize the United States to engage in a space race with the Soviet Union. The space race would provide substantial funding for the development of satellites for broadcasting as well as military uses, and the development of manned space vehicles led to the miniaturization and increased sophistication of computer systems. Although it is highly possible that US academics and scientists would have eventually developed much of the communication technology of today even without Sputnik, Sputnik provided the impetus, focus, and substantial federal funding required to propel the US into the global leadership role it currently holds in computers, satellites, and telecommunications.

3   *USA Today*, June 6, 2000, p. lA.

4   Portals are essential navigating tools for searching the internet. They fall into two categories. The first type of portal, available through AOL, Yahoo, MSN Worldwide, Excite, Lycos, and others, helps users search for general-interest and broad categories of content. The audience for these major portals has given rise to a second category called niche portals, which specialize in more narrow areas and condensed searches. Good examples are portal sites for graphic artists, gardening, golf, sports, gambling, or health, or sites in Spanish such as quepasa.com for the global Latino market. These specialty portals have unique features that appeal to specific segments or niches of the broader internet audience. Over time, as new niche segments are identified, these types of portals will expand significantly and ultimately draw users from the general portal sites.

5   The internet has changed the nature and role of the mass media. Just how much is a story yet to be told. At this point, some may argue, with good reason, that the traditional media still set the agenda of public discourse and that the internet traffic is a function of the old media, which still retain elite power. But we are rapidly reaching the point in core nations where the internet will set the agenda and traditional media will be forced to follow.

6   Michael Featherstone, ed., *Global Culture: Nationalism, Globalization and Modernity* (London: Sage, 1990).

7   Marshall McLuhan and Quentin Fiore, *The Medium is the Message* (New York: Bantam Books, 1967).

8   *Wall Street Journal*, June 16, 2000, p. B8.

9   In the early 1990s, Mark Cuban, now a Yahoo! Inc. executive, married a PC with a high-speed telephone line to get a distant college basketball game. He subsequently created an internet site using similar connections for distant events that became so popular that he sold it to Yahoo! in 1999. Yahoo! now offers its users close to 500 radio stations and nearly 70 television stations and cable networks. Yahoo! pays all necessary fees up front for audio and video programming that appears on the internet by way of Yahoo!'s portal.

10 *Wall Street Journal*, June 12, 2000, p. Al.

11 Ken Cukier of *Communications Week International* (France), in a 1999 paper titled "Bandwidth Colonialism? The Implications of the Internet on International E-Commerce," makes the case that the internet is US-centric. The global topology of the internet is US dominated because bandwidth, cost, and technology favor the United States. Cukier cites as an example the fact that Paris-based FranceNet's most powerful server was located in California.

12 George A. Barnett, "The Role of the internet in Cultural Identity," University of Buffalo (SUNY) Department of Communication, August 2004. George A. Barnett, "The Structure of International Internet Hyperlinks and Bilateral Bandwidth," University of Buffalo (SUNY) Department of Communication, June 2004.

13 Matthew Klam, "Fear and Laptops on the Campaign Trail," *The New York Times Magazine*, Sept, 26, 2004.

14 Milton Mueller, *Ruling the Root: Internet Governance and the Taming of Cyberspace* (Cambridge, MA: MIT Press, 2002).

15 Ibid., p. 6.

16 Lily Blue, "Internet and Domain Name Governance: Antitrust Litigation and ICANN," *Berkeley Technology Law Journal* 19 (2004), pp. 387–403.

17 Susan Schiavetta and Konstantinos Komaitis, "ICANN's Role in Controlling Information on the Internet," *International Review of Law, Computers and Technology*, 17(3), pp. 267–84.

18 Blue, "Internet and Domain Name Governance," p. 393.

19 Wolfgang Kleinwachter, "Beyond ICANN VS ITU?" *Gazette* 66 (2004), pp. 233–51.

20 Milton Mueller and Lee McKnight, "The Post-.com Internet: Toward Regular and Objective Procedures for Internet Governance," *Telecommunications Policy* 28 (2004), pp. 487–502.

21 Anitesh Barua and Andrew Whinston, *The Internet Economy Indicators* (Austin: University of Texas, 2000), June 8, p. 2.

22 Alan Hedley "Technological Diffusion or Cultural Imperialism? Measuring the Information Revolution," *International Journal of Comparative Sociology* 39(2) (June 1998), p. 210.

Chapter 13

Summary and Conclusions

Introduction

This chapter reviews major aspects of the theories and landscape of global communication. Although currently there is relatively little concern about NWICO and the role of specialized UN agencies such as UNESCO, there is still concern about the cultural, social, and economic impact of global communication trends. Unexpected exceptions are the ITU's role with the yet to be finalized World Summit on the Information Society (WSIS); and UNESCO's support for a legally binding global convention or law supporting cultural and linguistic diversity. With widespread utilization of the internet, transnational corporate acquisitions and mergers among media, telecommunications, and advertising corporations, and the expanding economic role of cultural industries, the issue of global communication has moved to a new and larger stage.

The issue and impact of communications corporations is no longer a trivial or marginal matter for policy-makers, researchers, or investors. All core nations rely for their economic health and viability on the success in foreign countries of their communications corporations. In previous decades, other leading corporations, such as those in the agriculture, automotive, or aerospace industries, made major contributions to the creation of new jobs and new wealth, but that is no longer the case. Particularly with the end of the Cold War, the aerospace industry, which includes military aircraft, has seen a substantial reduction in employment, impact, and influence. As a result, the success of cultural industries, domestically and in foreign markets, has become a vital component of successful international

trade. Those nations that enjoy successful global communication corporations such as Disney, Time Warner, Viacom, Sony, News Corporation,
Bertelsmann, and NBC Universal clearly count on these firms having continued success in order to keep domestic employment high, as well as keep
their balance-of-trade ledgers "balanced" in a favorable direction.

Cultural industries are a concern of national and international policy-
makers as well as major corporations in North America, Europe, and Asia.
With the drive to increase market share, coupled with more sophisticated
technology and advertising, many new markets are being inundated with
media fare created and owned by large foreign stakeholders. Now even
more and larger foreign communication stakeholders are competing aggressively with each other in nations and markets on other continents – frequently several time zones and cultures away. This is particularly true
in semiperipheral nations, which are the next frontier for multinational
communication corporations. Core-based firms are aggressively developing and promoting new media opportunities in semiperipheral nations in
order to increase market share. Whether these firms are building new
multiplex movie theaters or expanding access to the internet, the semiperipheral nations have become the commercial battlefield for core communication stakeholders. Also, sponsored media seminars and workshops
dealing with the values and practices of Western free-press traditions are
increasingly offered in semiperipheral nations. UNESCO now sponsors many
of these seminars. In this collective process indigenous cultures are at significant risk.

Finally, the proliferation of global music, movies, tapes, advertising, and
websites for preteens and teenagers has led to a new generation and culture
gap. These groups now experience in common audio and visual materials,
activities, language, topics, and in many cases clothing and values that cut
across this key demographic segment in North America, Asia, and Europe.
These audio and video materials give them similar expressions and worldviews
that are increasingly remote or different from those of their parents or even
their older siblings. For the adolescents (who are particularly heavy media
consumers) in this growing global segment, including MTV groupies, Britney
Spears look-alikes, and Bart Simpson wannabes, their attitudes, dress, language,
and behavior are increasingly at odds with their parents' or their teachers'
generation. Between these kids and their grandparents, particularly those
who emigrated from another nation and speak a non-English language, this
phenomenon has created an even greater cultural and behavioral divide.

In sum, because of the impact of global communication, many teenagers
around the globe have more in common with each other than they do
with any other normative group with which they interact, including
parents, relatives, and teachers. The long-run implications of this relatively

recent global media phenomenon have yet to be determined, researched, or fully understood.

Summary

As outlined in the beginning chapters, international communication theory is going through a transformation. Earlier attempts at theorizing have failed to develop models or research agendas that match the reality of the contemporary role of global communication. Theories of modernization, dependency, and cultural imperialism have failed to satisfactorily explain global communication. The old theories only explain part of the global picture.

The theoretical failings are partly a function of three related events. The first is the end of the Cold War era and the parallel decline in influence of socialist media critics, whose ideas and rhetoric became stale. The second event comprises numerous technical advances such as the creation of a new major global communication phenomenon, convergence, digital environments, the internet, or the reach of the latest satellites. The third event is the emergence of several major global communications stakeholders, many of which are non-US owned and controlled. Europe, Japan, Canada, Mexico, and others have major stakeholders in this important and expanding sector. Collectively, these events have led to the need to reanalyze and reformulate the theoretical underpinnings of the discipline of international communication. That is what this book is all about. It proposes a new theoretical perspective that unites world-system theory (WST) with electronic colonialism theory (ECT): "Empire of the Mind." This combination places the discipline on a contemporary theoretical foundation for the purpose of explaining the global communication landscape. Various activities continue to increase the need for understanding the many components that collectively influence international communication. The preceding chapters cover the salient features as well as the expanding globalization of the corporate giants in this field. Even though some of the stakeholders shift, through mergers etc., the underlying core analysis – WST and ECT – as laid out in this book remains viable and credible.

Before reviewing these components, remember that the impact on international communication at the end of the Cold War should not be underestimated. First, much of the research undertaken in the 1970s and 1980s focused on issues or media content that had a distinct ideological focus and slant that emphasized a dichotomy between capitalist and socialist worldviews. This outmoded dichotomy renders many of the studies and their conclusions marginal or suspect in the new post-Cold War environment.

Second, the volume of international news was higher during the Cold War because many publishers, editors, and journalists set their priorities according to the Cold War dichotomy and resulting international tensions. It was a great deal simpler for editors when the thrust of US foreign policy could be summed up in two words: stop communism. With that old dichotomy almost invisible, the interest and attention paid to international news has shifted because of terrorism and 9/11. Third, after 9/11, international news came back on the media's radar in a big way. The global war on terrorism, the Afghanistan war, and the Iraq war – the trifecta of international agenda-setting – reclaimed the front pages and face-time of television news around the globe. Fourth, as the global economy continues to expand through a series of mergers and acquisitions in the communications and other sectors, we would expect global business news coverage to increase in order to monitor the expanding global economy. Finally, the United States is looking for a new role within UNESCO, and for a number of years it has also played precarious roles within the United Nations, including withholding its substantial financial dues for a considerable period in the 1990s.

Rather than promoting global organizations and encouraging greater multilateral cooperation through the UN and specialized UN agencies and organizations, the United States has never appeared as either a team player or a major leader in multilateral organizations. This US attitude is anomalous considering that the vast majority of global corporations are headquartered in the United States. The US corporations have the greatest vested interest in global peace and stability as well as in economic and monetary systems that are functional and stable. Yet with the end of the ideological confrontation of the Cold War era, the US government seeks only peripheral roles, if any, in almost all global agencies that influence, examine, monitor, or set rules affecting international communication. In some cases, isolationists in Washington adopt a fortress mentality, or support only global communication policies that clearly benefit the United States, frequently at the expense of other nations. More is discussed concerning this aspect under "McPhail's Paradox," below.

NWICO

The New World Information and Communications Order (NWICO) dominated international communication debates for several decades. A combination of newly independent nations, many of which were former colonies of core nations, plus the ideological interests of communist republics, propelled the issue of news flow and the role of the mass media into a contentious position. Industrialized core countries view the press as independent and nongovernmental – that is, as public shareholder-owned broadcasting and communication corporations as well as delivery systems. Although the shrill ideological rhetoric of the supporters of NWICO has faded, when one examines more closely the underlying issue of what determines international news flow, it is clearly not a balanced process. Some of these matters are now playing a role at the WSIS and NWICO, which is on life support, may get an unexpected boost as an outcome of deliberations at the WSIS.

Global mass media do not work in a vacuum; they work in an environment in which certain factors dominate the decision-making process, which virtually guarantees that certain news will be covered extensively whereas other news will be almost ignored. For example, two broad roles have emerged from global media studies that account for a great deal of what does or does not get covered: gatekeeper roles and logistical roles.[1] Examples of gatekeeper roles include wire service decision-making, negative news such as the Asian tsunami, or the coups-and-earthquakes syndrome. The logistical roles include economic interconnectedness, cultural affinity, such as being a former colony, speaking the English language, or regionalism. From a straight economic perspective, much of what happens in peripheral nations is of little monetary consequence to core nations. The major exceptions are significant deviances from the norm, such as when there are major earthquakes, coups, tidal waves, or civil war, particularly if the event is covered by CNN. Peripheral, developing-nation news reaches the front pages or television sets in major industrialized core nations when it is bad news. Otherwise, the vast number of nations in the periphery zone receives no media attention at all year after year.

Aspects of NWICO position are supported by empirical research produced in North America and Europe. NWICO proponents calling for solutions involving some type of government control clearly fall on deaf ears in boardrooms and newsrooms in industrialized core nations. Many of the issues raised by NWICO are placed in a better and more meaningful perspective when viewed through the dual theoretical prisms of electronic colonialism and world-system theories or perspectives as outlined in previous chapters. A brief synopsis follows.

Electronic Colonialism Theory

Electronic colonialism theory[2] (ECT) posits that foreign produced, created, or manufactured cultural products have the ability to influence, or possibly displace, indigenous cultural productions, artifacts, and media to the detriment of receiving nations. On one level, ECT examines economic transactions through which a number of large multinational communication corporations engage in the selling of culturally imbedded goods and services abroad. These corporations view the transactions as revenue-producing activities that increase market share and maximize profits for themselves and their shareholders. All of this is accomplished in unison with other firms, particularly advertisers, and multilateral agencies such as the WTO, ITU, or the OECD. Yet ECT also looks at the social and cultural impact of these same economic activities. Effects include attitude formation, particularly among young consumers who seek out foreign cultural products, ranging from comic books, to music, to videos, which represent distant cultures and dreams – products that are produced and manufactured primarily in a totally different environment, culture, and often in a different language.

ECT provides the theoretical backdrop for examining the long-run global consequences of core nations' multimedia offerings in semiperipheral and peripheral nations. It provides a means for examining and understanding some of the broader issues, particularly in regard to semiperipheral and peripheral nations, concerning the plethora of cultural products, messages, and industries from a global perspective. Over time these images and sounds will lead to the creation of a new type of global empire. It will be an "Empire of the Mind."

The major communication industries tend to be located in a few wealthy core nations, whereas their customers are dispersed around the globe and come from different linguistic, social, economic, religious, and political environments. Yet over time ECT speculates that these differences will shrink in favor of the producing nations, which frequently work in English. This movement toward English as the language of the "global village" even applies to the EU. The EU consists of 25 nations with 20 different languages. The only language that most Europeans speak, other than their native tongue, is English.

Three important factor factors are evident in figure 13.1. First all these companies are located in a single zone – the core region. Not a one is even

1. Time Warner	6. News Corporation
2. Viacom	7. Bertelsmann
3. Disney	8. Associated Press / Reuters (tie)
4. British Broadcasting Corporation	9. GE's NBC Universal
5. Sony	10. Omnicom / WPP (tie)

Figure 13.1 The 12 most important communication companies in the world

from the semiperipheral zone. Second, the language of the global media is English and over time will continue to even be more so. Third, except for the BBC, all have and need to have a strong presence in the crucial US market.

Over time, most of the corporations described in the preceding chapters will have more customers and make more revenue outside their head offices' nations. They are truly global and not national entities.

Let us look at two examples to illustrate this point. First, in their advertising, more corporations are moving toward a single, global strategy. Firms such as the Ford Motor Company are seeking to consolidate their advertising and marketing expenditures within a single advertising agency that has a global reach and workforce. The Ford advertising budget is over a billion dollars a year. This requires a vast number of employees from Ford's advertising agency – the WPP Group of the United Kingdom[3] – to carry out an effective global marketing and advertising campaign. Only a few years ago, large corporations such as Ford would have utilized perhaps half a dozen agencies in various parts of the world to carry out their corporate advertising. Now they view this fragmentation as both too expensive and counterproductive.

The second example is Coca-Cola.[4] This is a $2 billion account for Interpublic Group of New York. Coca-Cola's offshore sales exceed domestic distribution of its global brand. Previously, Coca-Cola had over 30 advertising agencies handling its products around the world. Now it is attempting to focus on a global strategy and a global message in order to increase foreign sales substantially.

The purpose of providing these two examples is to make the point that global activities on behalf of major corporations take place in order to maximize sales and thus profits in more and more foreign nations. These nations and customers are concentrated in other core as well as semiperipheral regions.

World-System Theory

World-system theory[5] (WST) is a means of organizing from a theoretical perspective global activities in the international communications field. WST basically divides the world into three major sectors: core, semiperipheral, and peripheral. Core nations, relatively few in number, exercise vast economic influence and dominate relationships and transactions with the other two zones. The United States, the European Union, and Japan are some of the dominant stakeholders in the core group. This group has the power to define the rules, timing, and content of transactions with nations or regions in the other two zones. Some current core nations, such as Australia, Norway, Canada, and New Zealand, are becoming increasingly concerned that they may slip into the semiperipheral zone if they are not able to attract, finance, and keep information industries, entrepreneurs, and educated workers. The loss and impact of News Corp. shifting from Australia to the US is an example of how important the leading core nation, the US, is in terms of centrality to the global economy. Barnett and Salisbury examined WST with reference to communication/information. Looking at data from the international telecommunications network, they conclude "The results indicate that the network is composed of a single group with the United States and the other Western economic powers at the center and the lesser developed countries at the periphery. A nation's centrality in the network is significantly correlated with its GDP per capita."[6]

Semiperipheral nations are substantial in number and are those nations that interact with core nations but currently lack the power and economic institutions to join the elite core group. China, Mexico, Brazil, India, and some of the Middle East nations, which were discussed in chapter 8, are trying to reposition themselves as core nations. Some others are attempting to fast-track their entry into the core region by requesting membership in the European Union. That is why the current 25-nation EU community will likely grow to 30 or so over time.

Finally, the peripheral zone is made up of developing nations. These nations and regions have relatively little if any power, and their economic dealings with the semiperipheral and core nations benefit these two last zones. Many African, Latin American, and most Asian nations belong to the periphery. They are basically exploited by the other zones and have few media exports, little education, little technology, poor health, and much poverty.

World-system theory's characterization of global nations does provide a theoretical framework for addressing the question of why communication industries located in core nations have the market and economic advantage in dealing with the other two zones. To some extent, WST is an extension of the one-way flow argument developed decades ago, but when we look at the traffic patterns, whether in music, movies, the internet, or any other cultural product, clearly the core zone dominates, the semiperipheral is next, and the peripheral is at the bottom of the hierarchy. All major communication corporations, whether advertising, print, wire service, movies, electronics, video, or internet, have their world headquarters in core nations, have extensive dealings with semiperipheral nations, including purchasing subsidiaries to ensure market penetration, and have relatively little corporate presence in the periphery.

The theories of electronic colonialism and world system form a continuum that, together, describe and explain the underlying essential elements in international communication. ECT focuses primarily on the impact or attitudes of individuals and groups. It deals with what happens to individuals when they are repeatedly exposed to foreign-produced communications with a cultural cache. These messages convey foreign personalities, foreign dress, foreign history, foreign norms, foreign values, and foreign tastes. Frequently these values are at variance with indigenous cultures and lifestyles, particularly in peripheral nations. Individuals and groups are viewed as customers, and when combined or aggregated, they are equated with market share. To a large and expanding extent, the goal of global communication corporations is to make electronic colonies of large segments of the population around the globe in order to increase market share and maximize profits. ECT explains events through a cultural lens or perspective.

WST moves the analysis into the economic territory that underpins the global trading system within which communication industries operate. WST focuses on the substantial activities and power within communication industries located in core nations, and how they utilize their economic power for systematic advantage in their relationships with semiperipheral nations and peripheral nations. WST focuses more on the macroeconomic and policy dimensions of the corporate decision-making process, whereas ECT focuses more on the impact of foreign products, ideologies, and software on individuals, or their minds.

ECT Plus WST

Combining the two theories provides the most powerful explanation of the contemporary phenomenon of global communication that is available to students, policy analysts, corporate planners, and researchers alike. The failures of modernization, development, and cultural imperialism theories, as well as other scattered attempts to explain certain narrow microsegments of the international communication field, have not moved the discipline much beyond either anecdotal impressions or ideologically laced charges. These charges and lack of data to support them are particularly transparent and obvious in NWICO activities. As the role of international communication continues to expand, these two combined theories represent an opportunity for greater insight and understanding of this most significant global phenomenon.

McPhail's Paradox: The US, modernity, and future actions

There is no doubt that the US has the greatest vested interest in the global economy. As a nation-state it has the largest number of multinational companies, many in the communication sector, which depend on global commerce and transactions as a major source of jobs and income. The US needs global order and rules to keep its industries functioning and growing. They are the prime beneficiaries of global rules. They need the UN and its specialized agencies, like the WTO and ITU, to function effectively. But there is within the US a clear cultural chasm or disconnect between the progressives, concerned, educated, and those threatened by change, immigrants, international agencies, and new ideas. But the US needs the global economy and the global economy needs the US.

Yet the US population in general and the Federal government specifically are among the harshest critics of international agencies. They stand against modernity. They are threatened by transnational agreements and frequently are in violation of them. The US openly bashes the UN system. The loss of faith in the UN is a byproduct of the US continuously circumventing it or appointing people to it that dislike it. They were out of UNESCO for years and withheld funds to the UN for years thanks to Senator Jesse Helms. The US is one of the most frequent violators of WTO's rules promoting free trade. The recent imposition of steel tariffs by the US is a case in point. In other sectors the US simply refuses to participate, ratify, sign, or support global measures even though it is a major stakeholder.[7] The Kyoto environmental Protocol, the Law of the Sea, the Landmines agreement, the global Convention on the Rights of the Child, the Convention on Elimination of Discrimination against Women, the International Criminal Court, and other international initiatives designed to produce an orderly, safer, and better world are lacking a US signature.

Or take the case of the Geneva Convention that supports humanitarian actions in times of war. The US signed this one. Yet recently it has come to light that they have done everything to avoid complying with the Geneva provisions at their several military prisons around the world. The startling contortions and twisted logic that the US Department of Defense and the Pentagon went through to justify avoiding or simply ignoring the Geneva Convention would make the Cirque du Soleil envious.

Rather than promoting international tolerance, cooperation, and furthering global social justice, they promote a parochial "America First" mantra. The US casts an image of not wanting to be a global team player. They do not get the larger picture. Although the most powerful nation on earth, they avoid global leadership roles in the UN system and multilateral organization elsewhere. It is as if they fear the consequences, or they desire to shun modernity. Yet they should be leading and supporting all global rules, laws, practices, and organizations. Clearly the US-based multinational communication conglomerates need all of the preceding global rules and standards. In contrast, the EU, Australia, Canada, the Nordic nations, and many others promote social justice through multilateral organizations. Not the US.

Canada, the US's largest trading partner, is a symbolic "case study" of American ethnocentrism. Canada is in endless trade fights with the US. The US is quick to initiate bilateral trade fights across a number of sectors: fish, lumber, steel, beef, and cultural industries. The smaller nation of Canada does not look for magnanimous consideration from the US. Even compromise is outside the rhetoric of the US State Department for its largest trading partner – Canada. They seek to crush their Canadian trading partner, and play hardball at every turn. Even though Canada on the world stage is a relatively minor actor in the global economy, the US, as a policy strategy, treats them as an enemy. Never mind that Canada allowed hundreds of US commercial airlines to land in Canada after 9/11. Or that Canadian hydroelectric companies routinely assist US states hit by natural catastrophes. The US foreign policy is to protect and maximize American interests. No compromise, no concessions. In the new, post-Cold War era, the US business empire rules. It is no longer the British Empire which rules the waves, but the US empire which rules the global airwaves and most of the international media.

An example of the above is the US's complaint to the WTO against Canada. The issue is mainstream culture. Canada, where 80 percent of magazine sales are US magazines, had sought a modest relief position – not to be, since the US considers any attempt to protect an indigenous cultural industry as unacceptable. The issue was a "split-run" of US imported magazines where token Canadian advertising and content were required by Canadian regulations but were strongly protested against by US publishers. When is 80 percent of a foreign market not enough? When it is an American media conglomerate in cooperation with the US federal government. The US won the WTO complaint and now enjoys more than 85 percent of Canadian domestic magazine sales.

The global economy is the life-blood of a vast number of American multinational firms; just consider a few such as General Electric, IBM, Microsoft, Time Warner, Disney, News Corp., or Viacom. Yet who is the first to criticize the UN, or UNESCO, or other international agencies and agreements? The US. And several of the US media, such as the *Wall Street Journal*, Fox network, Sinclair Broadcasting, the *National Review*, and the *New York Post* champion this paradoxical stand. It is not as if they are discussing small nations such as Iceland, Greenland, or New Zealand. They would be relatively unscathed if the global trading system collapsed. The US would be devastated. But they and many in the media, like Rush Limbaugh, Brit Hume, and Bill O'Reilly, are the biggest complainers across a broad range of issues when it comes to the UN, social programs, bilingualism, outsourcing, immigration, global trade, or international bargaining and agreements. It is clearly a paradox seemingly better understood by foreigners than Americans themselves at all levels of work, government, and the media.

As many core nations move beyond modernity to postmodernity, the position of the US on the world stage stands in stark contrast in terms of their overall response to the possibilities of being a global communication leader.[8] They are more likely to be perceived globally as a rather narrow minded, somewhat vindictive, disliked nation in international fora. In the future, how the US handles the delicate issues of culture, media, and diversity, and participates in multilateral agencies and fora will likely determine the outcome of this paradox. US history and recent nominees to UN posts do not provide encouraging signs.

Conclusions

It is difficult to formulate conclusions when dealing with international communication. The field is in a state of flux, and global changes affect it on a daily basis. The three major engines driving the change are innovations in communication technologies, the global war on terrorism, and the global economy. The world is a different yet better place because of international communication. Many citizens are better informed and major corporations are able to experience success, including expanding employment opportunities, because of the possibilities and potential provided by innovations in international communication. But beyond broad generalizations, there are still a few more specific conclusions that can be drawn from an understanding of the various stakeholders, nations, as well as global communication corporations. The following four conclusions focus on media expansion, sovereignty, continued globalization, and the internet. Clearly, other conclusions may be drawn, but given the rapid pace of change in this sector, the following are the most likely predictions.

First, the audio and video history of international communication has been dominated and will continue to be by US music, television, feature films, and internet portals. Starting with the likes of Disney cartoons and animation movies, *I Love Lucy*, *Melrose Place*, *Dynasty*, *Dallas*, *Baywatch*, *Cheers*, *Star Trek*, *The Simpsons*, to *Friends*, *The Sopranos*, and *Sex and the City*, American television shows have dominated television sets around the world. The same is true for CDs, DVDs, and movie screens as well. In fact DVD sales now represent a major tertiary (following the primary screening on television or in theaters, then syndication rights) source of windfall profits for rights holders. Some of the leading DVD sales that are once again contributing to the financial health of the studios are *Lord of the Rings, Shrek, Star Wars, Harry Potter, Spider-Man, Seinfeld*, and *The Simpsons*. Networks and studios are scrambling to put out additional releases of old stock at a rapid rate as most US and other core-nation homes acquire DVD players.

The important fact about all this is that no one is forced to watch these shows or listen to the music. There is no gun to anyone's head to watch US television or movie productions. They do it because the scripts, production values and sets, acting or singing talent, and budgets create world-class materials. Also, foreign buyers from commercial and noncommercial television networks from around the world flock to New York, Hollywood, and Las Vegas trade shows to bid for the syndication rights to US television network or cable shows and series.

This demand by offshore buyers has been increased by the proliferation of new television stations and movie multiplexes, cable systems, satellite channels, and DVD or iPod players. The increase in leisure time, the fact that more individuals in more core and semiperipheral countries have disposable income, and are increasingly able to understand English, particularly teenagers, all these factors contribute to the escalating global demand. When you add the fact that the internet is American-centric, mainly in English, and carries more and more audiovisual content, this tends to assure the continuing influence of American multimedia conglomerates. The influence is also cultural in nature. Since core nations are highly competitive and exhibit mature markets at home, the greatest impact of these latter phenomena is likely to be most prevalent in semiperipheral nations. Finally, the marketing and advertising budgets of the global media conglomerates are huge. Their sophisticated approach to their customers around the world leaves little to chance.

As a collective result of the above, the electronic colonization of vast numbers of people not only continues but, just as the British ruled the globe by controlling the seas, so now also the US and a few others rule the airwaves, television and movies screens, and the emerging digital universe. The minds of the many, without regard to time or space, are clearly influenced by the flow and content of a vast range of core-nation media products and options. Google's ability to act as a global editor with it digitization of mostly Anglo-Saxon knowledge is a clear and potent example of this trend. As a result, ECT is becoming more powerful as a theory for understanding and organizing the impact of global communication on cultures over time.

Second, the plethora of transborder activities among major media, advertising, telecommunications, and internet firms is rendering historical national boundaries, and in some cases policies, obsolete. The ability of US communication firms to transmit information or products globally, as well as for foreign firms to sell their cultural products in the lucrative US market, is making national communication policies and political boundaries an issue of the past rather than the future. For example, CNN, FOX News, MSNBC, the BBC, AP, Reuters, Euronews, and others go wherever there is news. Time Warner, Disney, Sony, Bertelsmann, Viacom, NBC Universal, and even the BBC seek foreign markets or audiences where there is a viable consumer base and a potential for profitability. The internet goes wherever there is a modem, a computer, and some type of internet access, which may be hardwired or wireless. Thus, as global communication companies, along with their advertising agencies, expand markets and merge with more and more foreign firms, the concept of a single head office of a single nation controlling, taxing, or regulating global communication firms is becoming increasingly problematic. This alteration of sovereignty received an unexpected boost with the collapse of the Berlin Wall and the eventual lessening of international tension that was prevalent during the Cold War. There were no longer two dominant superpowers, each with enormous arsenals of propaganda and weapons to protect their nation-states. During the 1990s a vacuum emerged, as only a single global power remained – the United States. Into this vacuum moved the major stakeholders in the global economy. Multinational corporations simply usurped economic power and some political power in order to promote their interests across national boundaries.[9] For example, today several multinational corporations are more powerful and have greater reach and greater influence than any nation in the periphery. We now live in a world where a single individual, Bill Gates of Microsoft, is wealthier than the entire group of nation-states in the periphery. It appears that although the concept of the nation-state has lasted about 600 years, policy-makers and corporations alike are now questioning it. This phenomenon will push multinational organizations and transnational regional agreements into increasingly important roles, because domestic, national control is now clearly a pre-internet phenomenon. Institutions such as the UN, UNESCO, ITU, WTO, and OECD, and the European Union are willingly adopting entirely new regulations, currency, and ways of doing things in the postsovereignty era. This is the postsovereignty reality. Yet at the same time, many of these same firms and phenomena, such as the internet, are fueling a resurgence of nationalism and localism, and some hope that they are a means of protecting and reinforcing indigenous cultures, groups, and languages.

Third, a fundamental aspect of the global economy will dominate the current and future global landscape of international communication. Specifically, the economies of scale are driving substantial corporate mergers and acquisitions.[10] This is true in every aspect of the cultural-industries phenomenon, starting with advertising agencies and moving on to global media, wire services, and internet corporations. Old media in particular, for which print products are the predominant revenue generator, will have to either acquire new media themselves or be bought out by some aggressive new media entrepreneur. There will be no standstill in the global communications sector. Stakeholders will either move aggressively to expand market share through innovation, mergers, and acquisitions, or they themselves will become targets for either friendly or hostile takeovers. The global economy is not user-friendly or cost effective to small players in the communications sector.

The transfer of concepts, philosophies, and practices of liberalization, deregulation, and privatization across all core and semiperipheral nations has meant that the communications sector, which tended to be focused mainly within nation-states, has now taken on truly global dimensions. This is true across all elements of the industry – advertising, media, audio and video, as well as in technology, particularly the internet. The leading globalizing nation is the United States, but the European Union has also been extremely active in the globalization process. This is particularly true in two ways: (1) the activities and strategic plans of Japan's Sony, Germany's Bertelsmann, France's Publicis advertising, and the UK's Reuters and WPP are informing and influencing others about how to compete in the global economy; (2) all major European communication firms recognize that they must have some type of presence in the United States in order to be an effective global stakeholder. All major communication industries, regardless of national origin, have identified the North American market as essential for major stakeholder status in the globalization process. Finally, another aspect of globalization is the combination of old media and new media. The merger of AOL and Time Warner, despite their missteps, defines the phenomenon, but it also reinforces and expands the globalized role that all communication industries need to identify, deal with, and ultimately take on.

The globalization of the communications industry has several consequences. First, the original thrust of cultural imperialism was to loudly criticize the Hollywood feature-film industry. This is now an uninformed perspective, because Hollywood is no longer totally owned by US interests. Instead, foreign communication conglomerates such as Sony of Japan and Bertelsmann of Germany have substantial global media holdings. The global communication industry is not a monolithic empire, but rather a phenomenon that is now widely dispersed among core nations, with a few semiperipheral nations desperately trying to obtain core-like status through their own expansion via select mergers and acquisitions, particularly in the film industry. Within the communications sector, strategic planning is about global planning, not domestic or national planning.

Fourth, the role of the internet is still evolving. Just a decade ago the internet was a relatively isolated technical phenomenon for which scientists and other experts were still developing key components and applications for scientific or primarily industrial applications. A mere 10 years later, the internet has become a major phenomenon affecting global communication and commerce in unheard-of ways. The volume of usage, the depth and breadth of users worldwide, and the dramatic impact on e-commerce, e-learning, and e-public policy are astonishing. Yet, in spite of its significant role across core nations in particular, the internet is still in its infancy. The internet of today is analogous to the invention of the printing press, the early days of the assembly line, or the early applications of the computer chip. We are in the early phase of what will become a mature industry, which will likely be replaced eventually by some other technological invention, or by a mix of technologies and other factors.

One other significant aspect of the internet is that it has empowered the individual to make different choices in different ways. Individuals may obtain news directly from the internet without the filtering of publishers, editors, or journalists. Or they can create their own blogs or v-blogs and seek an audience for their musings. Blogging has taken on a life of its own and will continue to grow in prevalence and impact. As the wire services and many news outlets become more conservative in stance, this news vacuum will now be filled by anxious bloggers on the lookout for anything from tiny errors to major scandals. Individuals anywhere on the planet may also purchase cultural products or view them through their terminals without leaving their home, school, or place of business. This phenomenon is not just available to individuals in a single or a few nation-states; it is a globally dispersed phenomenon in which geography becomes irrelevant, particularly as wireless internet connections pop up around the globe. The prevalence of the internet is related to the sovereignty issue because the information on the internet is as portable as the technology itself. Industrial-era concepts such as space, location, control, bricks and mortar, and monopoly are marginalized in the age of the internet.

Finally, as evidenced by the mergers of AOL and Time Warner as well as others, the communications industry recognizes that multinational conglomerates will become the model and new benchmark for global communication stakeholders. This will involve a blurring of traditional boundaries of all communications sectors, as the global economy forces the application of the internet into every segment of the international communications market. The digital world of core nations will speed the internet into homes and villages around the globe in record time. Over time, more semiperipheral nations will mature into core nations, and then the issue will become how and which peripheral nations will evolve into the semiperipheral zone. The cutting edge of innovations influencing the internet, however, will continue to appear first and quickest across core nations.

Notes

1 Denis Wu Haoming, "Investigating the Determinance of International News Flow A Meta Analysis," *Gazette* 60 (Dec. 1998), pp. 493–512.

2 Thomas L. McPhail, *Electronic Colonialism* (Newbury, CA: Sage, 1986).

3 "WPP Leads Way in Global Ties to Clients," *Wall Street Journal*, Dec. 1, 2000, p. B6.

4 "Coke Gives Nod to Interpublic for Ad Contract," *Wall Street Journal*, Dec. 4, 2000, p. B12.

5 Thomas R. Shannon, *An Introduction to the World System Perspective* (Boulder, CO: Westview Press, 1996). A look at the variables underlying globalization may be found in James Mittelman, *The Globalization Syndrome: Transformation and Resistance* (Princeton, NJ: Princeton University Press, 2000). It is informative concerning the resistance to cultural hegemony.

6 George Barnett and Joseph Salisbury, "Communication and Globalization: A Longitudinal Analysis of the International Telecommunication Network," *Journal of World Systems Research* 2(16) (1996), p. 20.

7 The issue of US isolationism is not new. For example, the US has never ratified the 1919 Treaty of Versailles, which formally ended the First World War. The Treaty included a League of Nations, which was heavily promoted by US President Woodrow Wilson. Despite extensive efforts by Wilson, including a cross-country speaking tour to get support from radio, magazines, and newspapers, the ethnocentric isolationists in Washington prevailed. Other nations that signed the Treaty were France, Germany, England, Italy, and Japan. Also the noted US aviation hero Charles Lindbergh and other fascists, campaigned aggressively against the US entry into the Second World War, which commenced in 1938. They were prevailing and supporting Hitler until the bombing of Pearl Harbor in December 1941, what one might regard as an earlier version of 9/11.

8 Noted media scholar William Hachten has a similar take on the situation. He states, "the fact remains that international society is marked by the absence of collective procedures, by competition rather than cooperation, and by the lack of a commitment to a common goal – in other words, a situation that approaches anarchy." *The World News Prism* (Ames: Iowa State University Press, 1999), p. 12.

9 For a discussion of the failure of the US to do the empire walk well, see Deepak Lal, "An Imperial Denial," *Yale Global Online*, Jan. 6, 2005. It may be found at http://yaleglobal.yale.edu.

10 "Cross-Border Mergers Soared Last Year," *Wall Street Journal*, July 19, 2000, p. A18. This article traces merger activities, and it notes a 50 percent increase over the 1998 rate. This rate continues today following a lull after 9/11. The United States, United Kingdom, Sweden, Germany, France, and Canada dominate the global buying. One sector, advertising, is particularly active.

Select Bibliography

The 9/11 Commission Report: *Final Report of the National Commission on Terrorist Attacks upon the United States.* Washington: Replica Books, 2004.

Albarran, Alan B. and Chan-Olmsted, Sylvia M. *Global Media Economics: Commercialization, Concentration and Integration of World Media Markets.* Ames: Iowa State University Press, 1998.

Alexander, Alison, Owers, James, and Carveth, Rod, eds. *Media Economics: Theory and Practice.* Mahwah, NJ: Lawrence Erlbaum, 1998.

Ansu-Kyeremeh, Kwasi. "Indigenous Communication in Africa: A Conceptual Framework." In Kwasi Amsu-Kyeremeh, ed., *Perspective on Indigenous Communication in Africa.* Legon, Ghana: School of Communication Studies Printing Press, 1998.

Artz, B. and Kamalipour, Y., eds. *The Globalization of Corporate Media Hegemony.* Albany: State University of New York Press, 2003.

Bagdikian, Ben. *The Media Monopoly.* Boston: Beacon Press, 2000.

Banks, Jack. "MTV and the Globalization of Popular Culture." *Gazette* 59(1) (1997): 43–60.

Barber, Benjamin R. "Democracy at Risk: American Culture in a Global Culture." *World Policy Journal* 15(2) (1998): 29–42.

Barnett, G. A. and Salisbury, J. G. T. "Communication and Globalization: A Longitudinal Analysis of the International Telecommunication Network." *Journal of World Systems Research* 16(2) (1996): 1–17.

Barnett, George A., Salisbury, Joseph G. T., Kim, Chul Woo, and Langhorne, Anna. "Globalisation and International Communication: An Examination of Monetary, Telecommunications and Trade Networks." *Journal of International Communication* 6(2) (1999): 7–49.

Barua, Anitesh and Whinston, Andrew. *The Internet Economy Indicators.* Austin: University of Texas, 2000.

Beltran, Luis. "Alien Premises, Objects and Methods in Latin American Communication Research." *Communication Research* 3 (1976): 107–34.

Berenger, Ralph. *Global Media Go to War: Role of News and Entertainment Media During the 2003 Iraq War*. Spokane, WA: Marquette Books, 2004.

Bloomberg, Michael and Winkler, Matthew. *Bloomberg by Bloomberg*. New York: John Wiley & Sons, 1998.

Boyd-Barrett, Oliver. "National and International News Agencies." *Gazette* 62(1) (2000): 5–18.

Barnett, Robert. *The Global Jukebox: The International Music Industry*. New York: Routledge, 1996.

Campbell, Robert. *The Golden Years of Broadcasting: A Celebration of the First Fifty Years of Radio and TV on NBC*. New York: Scribner, 1976.

Carveth, Rod. "The Reconstruction of the Global Media Marketplace." *Communication Research* 19(6) (1992): 705–24.

Cave, Martin and Collins, Richard. "Regulating the BBC." *Telecommunications Policy* 28(3/4) (2004): 249–72.

Chang, T. K. and Lee, J. W. "Factors Affecting Gatekeepers' Selection of Foreign News: A National Survey of Newspaper Editors." *Journalism Quarterly* 69 (1992): 559–61.

Chase-Dunn, C. *Global Formation: Structures of the World-Economy*. London: Blackwell, 1989.

Chin, Tony. *CBS: The First 50 Years*. New York: General Publishing, 1999.

Coase, R. H. *British Broadcasting*. London: University of London Press, 1950.

Cohen, Y. "Foreign Press Corps as an Indicator of International News Interest." *Gazette* 56 (1995): 89–100.

Coombs, Tim. "The Internet as Potential Equalizer." *Public Relations Review* 24 (1998): 289–303.

Corner, John, Schlesinger, Philip, and Silverstone, Roger. *International Media Research: A Critical Survey*. London: Routledge, 1997.

Cowen, Tyler. "French Kiss-off: How Protectionism Has Hurt French Films." *Reason* 30(3) (1998): 40–8.

Crystal, David. *English as a Global Language*. Cambridge: Cambridge University Press, 1997.

Cullity, Jocelyn. "The Global Destiny: Cultural Nationalism on MTV India." *Journal of Communication Inquiry* 26(4) (2002): 408–25.

De Beer, Arnold and Merrill, John. *Global Journalism*. Boston: Allyn & Bacon, 2004.

Defleur, Melvin and Ball-Rokeach, Sandra. *Theories of Mass Communication*. New York: Longman, 1975.

Dieckmann, O. "Cultural Determinants of Economic Growth: Theory and Evidence." *Journal of Cultural Economics* 20(4) (1996): 297–320.

Elasmar, Michael G. "Opportunities and Challenges of Using Meta-Analysis in the Field of International Communication." *Critical Studies in Mass Communication* 16(3) (1999): 379–89.

El-Nawawy, Mohammed and Iskandar, Adel. *Al-Jazeera*. Boulder, CO: Westview Press, 2002.

Featherstone, Michael, ed. *Global Culture: Nationalism, Globalization and Modernity*. London: Sage, 1990.

Flournoy, Don M. and Stewart, Robert K. *CNN: Making News in the Global Market.* Luton, UK: John Libbey Media, 1977.

Fox, Elizabeth. *Latin American Broadcasting.* Luton: University of Luton Press, 1997.

Gershon, Richard A. *The Transnational Media Corporation: Global Messages and Free Market Competition.* Mahwah, NJ: Lawrence Erlbaum, 1997.

Giddens, Anthony. *Modernity and Self-Identity.* Stanford, CA: Stanford University Press, 1991.

Giffard, C. Anthony and Rivenburgh, Nancy K. "News Agencies, National Images, and Global Media Events." *Journalism and Mass Communication Quarterly* 77(1) (2000): 8–21.

Golding, Peter and Harris, Phil, eds. *Beyond Cultural Imperialism: Globalization, Communication, and the New International Order.* London: Sage Publications, 1997.

Grant, Peter and Wood, Chris. *Blockbusters and Trade Wars.* Toronto: Douglas and McInytre, 2004.

Grein, Adreas and Ducoffe, Robert. "Strategic Responses to Market Globalization among Advertising Agencies." *International Journal of Advertising* 17(3) (1998): 301–19.

Hachten, William and Scotton, James. *The World News Prism: Global Media in an Era of Terrorism.* Ames: Iowa State University Press, 2002.

Hall, Thomas D. "The World-System Perspective: A Small Sample from a Large Universe." *Sociological Inquiry* 66(4) (1996): 440–54.

Hanink, D. M. *The International Economy: A Geographic Perspective.* New York: John Wiley, 1994.

Hedley, Alan. "Technological Diffusion or Cultural Imperialism? Measuring the Information Revolution." *International Journal of Comparative Sociology* 39(2) (1998): 198–223.

Hersh, Seymour. *Chain of Command: The Road from 9/11 to Abu Ghraib.* New York: HarperCollins, 2004.

Hills, Jill. *The Struggle for Control of Global Communication.* Urbana: University of Illinois Press, 2002.

Hoggart, Richard. *An Idea and Its Servants: UNESCO from Within.* London: Chatto and Windus, 1978.

Hojman, David. "Economic Policy and Latin American Culture: Is a Virtuous Circle Possible?" *Journal of Latin American Studies* 31 (Feb. 1999): 167–90.

Hopkins, Mark. "A Babel of Broadcasts." *Columbia Journalism Review* 38(2) (1999): 447.

Hoskins, Colin, McFadyen, Stuart, and Finn, Adam. *Global Television and Film: An Introduction to the Economics of the Business.* New York: Clarendon, 1997.

Hudson, Heather. *Global Connections: International Telecommunications Infrastructure and Policy.* New York: Van Nostrand Reinhold, 1997.

Huteau, Jean. *AFP: Une histoire de l'Agence France-Presse: 1944–1990.* Paris: R. Laffont, 1992.

Janus, N. "Transnational Advertising: Some Considerations of the Impact on Peripheral Societies." In R. Atwood and E. McAnany, eds., *Communication and Latin*

American Society: Trends in Critical Research, 1960–1985. Madison, WI: University of Wisconsin Press, 1986.

Joshi, Lalit and Malcolm, Derek, eds. *Bollywood: Popular Indian Cinema*. London: Dakini Books, 2002.

Keeyton, Jeffery. *Not Teflon: MTV Design*. New York: Universal Publishing, 2004.

Kennedy, Paul. *The Rise and Fall of the Great Powers*. New York: Vintage Books, 1989.

Kim, Kyungmo and Barnett, George. "The Determinants of International News Flow: A Network Analysis." *Communication Research* 23(3) (June 1996): 323–52.

Knightley, Phillip. *The First Casualty*. New York: Harcourt, Brace and Jovanovich, 1975.

Kraidy, Marwan. "The Global, the Local, and the Hybrid: A Native Ethnography of Globalization." *Critical Studies in Mass Communication* 16 (1999): 456–76.

Lee, Raymond. "Globalization and Mass Society Theory." *International Review of Sociology* 12(1) (2002): 45–60.

Linden, Ank. "Overt Intentions and Covert Agendas." *Gazette* 61(2) (1999): 153–75.

MacBride, Sean. *Many Voices, One World*. New York: Unipub, 1980.

Madden, Normandy. "Cable, Satellite Media Lure Influential Viewers." *Advertising Age International* (Oct. 1999): 36.

Malek, Abbas. "Introduction: News Media and Foreign Policy: A Field Ripe for Research." *Journal of International Communication* 4(1) (1997): 1–10.

Martinez, Arnando. "The New World Order and What We Make of It." *World Policy Journal* 16(3) (1999): 692.

Mattelart, Tristan. "Transboundary Flows of Western Entertainment Across the Iron Curtain." *Journal of International Communication* 6(2) (1999): 106–21.

McChesney, Robert W. "The Internet and US Communication Policy-making in Historical and Critical Perspective." *Journal of Communication* 46(1) (1996): 98–124.

McCullough, Wayne. "Global Advertising Which Acts Locally: The IBM Subtitles Campaign." *Journal of Advertising Research* 36 (May–June 1996): 11–15.

McDonald, Ian R. and Lawrence, Regina G. "Filling the 24 × 7 News Hole: Television News Coverage Following September 11." *American Behavioral Scientist* 48(3) (2004): 327–40.

Mckee, Kathy Brittain. "Why I [Still] Want My MTV: Music Video and Aesthetic Communication (Book Review)." *Journalism & Mass Communication Quarterly* 81(3) (2004): 718–20.

McLuhan, Marshall. *The Gutenberg Galaxy*. Toronto, Canada: University of Toronto Press, 1962.

——. *Understanding Media: The Extension of Man*. New York: McGraw-Hill, 1964.

—— and Fiore, Quentin. *The Medium is the Message*. New York: Bantam Books, 1967.

McPhail, Thomas. "Direct Broadcast Satellites: The Demise of Public and Commercial Policy Objectives" (with S. Judge). In Indu Singh, ed., *Telecommunications in the Year 2000: National and International Perspectives*, pp. 72–9. Norwood, NJ: Ablex, 1983.

——. "The Communication Economy Sweepstakes: Few Winners, Many Losers – A Canadian Case Study." *Informatologia Yugoslavia* 17(1–2) (1985): 97–105.

——. *Electronic Colonialism.* Newbury, CA: Sage Publications, 1986.

——. "The International Politics of Telecommunications: Resolving the North–South Dilemma" (with Brenda McPhail). *International Journal* 42 (1987): 289–319.

——. "Canadianization of European Broadcasting: Is an Electronic Berlin Wall the Answer?" In *Broadcasting and Research: Experiences and Strategies*, pp. 15–30. Amsterdam: ESOMAR, 1988.

——. "Inquiry in International Communication." In M. Asante and B. Gudykunst, eds., *Handbook of International and Intercultural Communication*, pp. 47–66. Newbury, CA: Sage Publications, 1989.

——. "Television and Development Communication: A Canadian Case Study." In Andrew Moemeka, ed. *Communicating for Development: A Pan-Disciplinary Perspective*, pp. 191–218. Albany: State University of New York Press, 1994.

——. *Global Communication: Theories, Stakeholders, and Trends.* Boston: Allyn & Bacon, 2002.

—— and Barnett, George. "An Examination of the Relationship of United States Television and Canadian Identity." *International Journal of Intercultural Relations* 4 (1980): 219–32.

—— and McPhail, Brenda. *Communication: The Canadian Experience.* Toronto: Copp Clark Pitman, 1990.

Melkote, Srinivas, Shields, Peter, and Agrawel, Binod, eds. *International Satellite Broadcasting in South Asia.* Lanham, MD: University Press of America, 1998.

Merrill, John, Berenger, Ralph, and Merrill, Charles. *Media Musings: Interviews With Great Thinkers.* Spokane, WA: Marquette Books, 2004.

Mishra, Vijay. *Bollywood Cinema.* New York: Routledge, 2001.

Mitchell, Tony. "Treaty Now! Indigenous Music and Music Television in Australia." *Media, Culture, and Society* 15(2) (1993): 299–308.

Mittelman, James H. *The Globalization Syndrome: Transformation and Resistance.* Princeton: Princeton University Press, 2000.

Moemeka, Andrew. "Development Communication: A Historical and Conceptual Overview." In Moemeka, ed., *Communication for Development: A Pan-Disciplinary Perspective.* Albany: State University of New York Press, 1994.

Mohammadi, Ali, ed. *International Communication and Globalization.* London: Sage Publications, 1997.

Menge, Peter. "1998 ICA Presidential Address: Communication Structures and Processes in Globalization." *Journal of Communication* 48(44) (1999): 142–53.

Morris, Merrill and Ogan, Christine. "The Internet as Mass Medium." *Journal of Communication* 46(1) (1996): 39–50.

Mueller, Milton. *Ruling the Root: Internet Governance and the Taming of Cyberspace.* Cambridge, MA: MIT Press, 2002.

Nostbakken, David and Morrow, Charles, eds. *Cultural Expression in the Global Village.* Ottawa, Canada: Southbound, 1993.

Paek, Hye-Jin and Pan, Zhongdang. "Spreading Global Consumerism: Effects of Mass Media and Advertising on Consumerist Values in China." *Mass Communication & Society* 7(4) (2004): 491–515.

Park, Hong-Wan. "A Gramscian Approach to Interpreting International Communication." *Journal of Communication* 48(4) (1998): 79–99.

Paterson, Chris A. "International Television News Agency Coverage of Conflict." *Journal of International Communication* 4(1) (1997) 50–66.

Ramaprasad, J. "Content, Geography Concentration and Consonance in Foreign News Coverage of ABC, NBC, and CBS." *International Communication Bulletin* 28 (1993): 10–14.

Read, Donald. *The Power of News: The History of Reuters.* Oxford: Oxford University Press, 1992.

Ries, Al and Trout, Jack. *Positioning: The Battle for your Mind.* New York: McGraw Hill, 2001.

Riffe, D. "Linking International News to US Interest: A Content Analysis." *International Communication Bulletin* 31 (1996): 14–18.

Riley, Patricia and Menge, Peter. "Introduction." *Communication Research* 25(4) (1998): 355–8.

Rogers, Everett. *Modernization among Peasants: The Impact of Communication.* New York: Holt, Rinehart, and Winston, 1969.

——. "Communication and Development: The Passing of the Dominant Paradigm." *Communication Research* 3(2) (1976): 213–40.

Rosenblum, Morton. *Coups and Earthquakes.* New York: Harper & Row, 1979.

Rostow, Walter. *The Stages of Economic Growth.* New York: Cambridge University Press, 1960.

Rothkopf, David. "In Praise of Cultural Imperialism." *Foreign Policy* 107 (1997): 38–53.

Sambrook, Richard. "The Poliak Lecture: Holding on to Objectivity." Speech given at Columbia University, Oct. 27, 2004.

Schafer, D. Paul. "The Millennium Challenge: Making the Transition from an Economic Age to a 'Cultural Age'." *World Futures* 51 (1998): 287–320.

Schiller, Herbert. *Communication and Cultural Domination.* White Plains, NY: M. E. Sharpe Inc., 1976.

Schlesinger, P. "Wishful Thinking: Cultural Politics, Media, and Collective Identities in Europe." *Journal of Communication* 43(2) (1993): 6–17.

Seaver, Brenda. "The Public Dimension of Foreign Policy." *Harvard International Journal of Press/Politics* 3(1) (1998): 65–91.

Sengupta, Subir. "Analysis of Television Commercials from India and the United States." *Gazette* 57 (1996): 1–16.

Shah, Hermant. "Modernization, Marginalization, and Emancipation: Toward a Normative Model of Journalism and National Development." *Communication Theory* 6(2) (1998): 143–67.

Shannon, Thomas R. *An Introduction to the World System Perspective.* Boulder, CO: Westview Press, 1996.

Shoemaker, P. and Reese, S. *Mediating the Message: Theories of Influence on Mass Media Content.* New York: Longman, 1991.

Slater, Robert. *The New GE: How Jack Welch Revived an American Institution.* Highstown, NJ: Irwin, 1992.

Spark, Alasdair. "Wrestling with America: Media, National Images, and the Global Village." *Journal of Popular Culture* 29 (1996): 83–97.

Stevenson, Robert. *Global Communication to the Twenty-first Century.* New York: Longman, 1994.

Swan, Jon. "I Was a 'Polisher' in a Chinese News Factory." *Columbia Journalism Review* 27 (March/April 1996): 33–6.

Taylor, Philip. *War and the Media.* Manchester, UK: Manchester University Press, 1988.

——. *Global Communications, International Affairs and the Media Since 1945.* London: Routledge, 1997.

Tehranian, Majid. "Foreword." In Y. Kamalipour, ed., *Images of the US Around the World: A Multicultural Perspective.* Albany: State University of New York Press, 1999.

Thomas, Bob. *Building a Company: Roy O. Disney and the Creation of an Entertainment Empire.* Boston: Hyperion, 1999.

Thompson, J. B. *The Media and Modernity: A Social Theory of the Media.* Stanford, CA: Stanford University Press, 1995.

Thussa, D. *International Communication: Continuity and Change.* London: Arnold Press, 2000.

Tunstall, J. *The Media Are American.* New York: Columbia University Press, 1977.

Van Rossem, R. "The World System Paradigm as General Theory of Development: A Cross-National Test." *American Sociological Review* 61 (1996): 508–27.

Volkmer, Ingrid. *News in the Global Sphere: A Study of CNN and its Impact on Global Communication.* Luton: University of Luton Press, 1999.

Wagnleitner, Reinhold. "The Empire of the Fun, or Talkin' Soviet Union Blues: The Sound of Freedom and US Cultural Hegemony in Europe." *Diplomatic History* 23(3) (1999): 499–524.

Wallerstein, I. *The Modern World System.* New York: Academic Press, 1976.

Wanta, Wayne, Golan, Guy, and Lee, Cheolhan. "Agenda Setting and International News: Media Influence on Public Perceptions of Foreign Nations." *Journalism & Mass Communication Quarterly* 81(2) (2004): 364–77.

Ware, William and Dupagne, Michel. "Effects of US Television Programs on Foreign Audiences: A Meta-Analysis." *Journalism Quarterly* 71(4) (1994): 947–59.

Watts, Steven. *The Magic Kingdom: Walt Disney and the American Way of Life.* Boston: Houghton Mifflin, 1998.

Westerstahl, J. and Johansson, F. "Foreign News: News Values and Ideologies." *European Journal of Communication* 9 (1994): 71–89.

Wheeler, Mark. "Supranational Regulation: Television and the European Union." *European Journal of Communication* 19(3) (2004): 349–69.

Whittemore, Hank. *CNN: The Inside Story.* Toronto: Little, Brown, 1990.

"World Advertising Expenditure." *International Journal of Advertising* 19(1) (2000): 139–44.

Wu, Haoming Denis. "Investigating the Determinants of International News Flow: A Meta-Analysis." *Gazette* 60(6) (1998): 493–512.

Index

Note: page numbers followed by *n* refer to information in an endnote. The Arabic article al- is ignored in the filing sequence; search by using the initial letter of the word following al-.

Ansu-Kyeremeh, Kwasi, 42
anti-Americanism: in Arab media, 204, 221*n*; in Latin America, 7–8
antitrust regulation: AOL/Time Warner merger, 61–3, 132; ICANN, 309–10; Microsoft IE browser, 294, 295–6, 298
anti-Westernism in UNESCO, 250
AOL (America Online), 298, 300, 306; Time Warner merger, 61–3, 66–8, 103, 132
AP *see* Associated Press
AP-DJ, 180
AP Radio, 181
Apple Computers, 297, 299
APTN, 181
Arab League, 206
Arab News Network (ANN), 208, 213, 219–20*n*
al-Arab (newspaper), 205
Arab Radio and Television, 214
Arab–Israeli conflicts, 4, 197, 198, 206, 209
Arabic media *see* Middle East/North Africa
Al Arabiya channel, 196, 208, 212–13, 215, 219–20*n*
Arabsat, 206, 207–8
Arafat, Yasser, 198
"arc of turmoil/instability/conflict," 194
Archie (search protocol), 298
Arnett, Peter, 148, 149–50, 154
ARPANET, 291–3, 297, 298, 309
Ashcroft, Attorney General, 5
Asia: Channel News Asia, 166; Western programming, 10, 82–4, 91, 135–6; *see also* China; India; Middle East/North Africa
Assad, Bashar Al, 213
al-Assad family, 197, 213
Associated Press (AP), 41, 170–1, 175, 179–83, 190
Associated Press Television News (APTN), 177

Atta, Mohamed and father, 204
audience research, 48; Arabic broadcasting, 209–10, 212, 214; audience fragmentation, 123–4, 138; ratings companies, 106–7
audiovisual products, 92*n*, 98
Australia, 91, 97, 125–6, 323
authoritarian regimes: Arab press types, 199–201, 202, 203; in MENA region, 196, 197, 218; and NWICO debate, 253
Axel Springer, 100, 102, 107–8
Azcarraga Jean, Emilio, 112
Azcarraga Milmo, Emilio, 111–12
Azcarraga family, 111–12

Bagdikian, Ben, 16
Ball-Rokeach, Sandra, 48
Banks, Jack, 137
Barnett, George, 16, 25, 30, 306, 323
BBC, 95, 142, 159–64; as CNN competitor, 144, 162, 165, 171; as core nation broadcaster, 41; and electronic colonialism, 20, 21; funding issues, 160, 162, 163, 164, 288; Hutton Report, 4–5, 163–4; as model for public broadcasting, 20, 125, 159, 160, 242; Royal Charter, 163–4; Voice of America comparison, 168
BBC News 24, 144, 162
BBC Prime, 162
BBC World Service (Radio), 144, 162, 172
BBC World Service Television, 5, 149, 157, 162, 165
BBDO Worldwide, 230
Bcom3, 236
Beltran, Luis, 52
Benetton adverts, 230
Berlusconi, Silvio, 79, 107
Berners-Lee, Tim, 294–5, 297, 298
Bernstein, Carl, 248
Bertelsmann, 59, 95, 100–3, 118, 128, 330

Bertelsmann Music Group (BMG), 101, 129, 131, 133
bias in media: UK, 12; US, 5–6, 88–9
Bible and introduction of printing, 17–18
Big Four networks: audience fragmentation, 123–4, 138
Billboard, 129
Bitnet protocol, 297
Blair, Tony, 140n, 155
Blockbuster, 24, 50, 76, 77, 121
blogging, 5, 159, 191, 308–9, 331
Bloomberg, Michael, 185, 186
Bloomberg, 184, 185–6, 190
Bloomberg Television, 185
BMG Music Entertainment, 101, 129, 131, 133
Bollywood, 115–16
Bravo network, 86–7
Brazil, 112–13
Britain *see* United Kingdom
British Broadcasting Corporation *see* BBC
British Empire, 17, 20
British Sky Broadcasting Group *see* BSkyB
broadcasting *see* public broadcasting; radio; television
Broadcasting Board of Governors (BBG), 167
Bronfman, Edgar, Jr., 132
browsers (internet), 294, 295–6, 298
Brûlé, Tyler, 203
BSkyB network, 79, 81–2, 144
Buena Vista International, 68, 71–2
Burnett, Leo, 236–7
Bush, George W., Jr., 4, 213, 262, 308
Bush, Jeb, 157
business: news coverage, 319; *see also* multimedia conglomerates

Cable News Network *see* CNN
cable and satellite broadcasting systems: advertising needs, 227; AOL/Time Warner merger, 61–3, 66–8; and audience fragmentation, 123–4, 138; Canal Plus, 104–5; in China, 10, 11; development of CNN, 150–2; Disney channels, 71, 72; News Corporation, 79, 81–4; sports broadcasting, 79; spread to peripheral nations, 32, 39; transoceanic fiberoptic cable systems, 279; US cultural domination, 61; Viacom interests, 76, 77; *see also* MTV; satellite technology
Can West Global Communications Corp., 109–10
Canada: multimedia conglomerates, 97, 109–11; and NWICO draft, 252–3; radio cuts, 172; restrictions on US imports, 127–8, 139n, 326; US cultural influence in, 29–30, 38n
Canal de Noticias NBC, 85–6
Canal Plus, 79, 104–5, 128
Canal Satellite, 184, 185
Capital Cities/ABC, 68, 70–1
capitalist ideology: and world-system theory, 28
Carveth, Rod, 127, 128
Case, Steve, 62
Catholic Church: and Crusades, 17; and printing press, 18
CBS: blogging campaign, 308; staff reductions, 124, 140n; Viacom merger, 75
censorship: in China, 11, 93n, 187; of foreign news, 15; gatekeeping in Western media, 14, 301; internet access, 11, 13–14; in Liberia, 13–14; in MENA region, 200–1, 205–6, 214, 218; Tunisia, 283, 310
Central Intelligence Agency (CIA), 2, 9–10
CERN Laboratories, 294–5, 297
Channel News Asia (CNA), 166
Chiapas, Mexico, 7
Chile: US media intervention, 8–10
China: Hong Kong Disneyland, 11, 73, 74, 91; media growth in, 10–11,

82, 83–4, 91; Tiananmen Square coverage, 146–8; WTO entry, 93*n*; Xinhua News Agency, 187

China International TV Corp, 11

"Choose or Lose" (MTV program), 136

Christian colonialism, 17

CIA, 2, 9–10

CII (International Information Channel), 144, 172

Cinecanal, 77

cineplexes, 126–7

Circuit 7760, 181

Cisneros Group, 113

Citizen Exchange Program (CEP), 167

Clarke, Richard, 4

Clayton, Thomas, 25

Clear Channel Communications, 129

Clinton, Bill: Starr Report, 300; UNESCO membership, 261

CNA (Channel News Asia), 166

CNBC, 84, 85, 86, 87, 89, 124

CNN (Cable News Network), 22, 41, 66, 124, 142–74; CNN effect: on other media, 190, 219–20*n*; CNN effect: on politics, 156–7; competitors, 144–5, 156, 159–68, 171–2, 211; corporate background, 145–6, 156; development history, 150–2; downsizing, 156; identity crisis, 157–8; and internet, 146, 300; Spanish-language broadcasting, 146, 151; and War on Terror, 4, 5; *World Report* program, 152–4

CNN Radio, 146

Coca-Cola advertising, 322

Cohen, William, 154

Cold War: effect of end of, 1, 3, 15, 318–19, 329; space race, 297, 313–14*n*; US and Chile, 8–10; US role in international communication, 2–3

collaboration (internet), 293

College and University Affiliations Program (CUAP), 166–7

Collins, Jim, 28

colonialism: and communication patterns, 13; decolonization and UNESCO, 246–7; historical epochs, 16–20; in MENA region, 196; *see also* electronic colonialism theory

color television, 40, 161

Columbia Pictures, 96–7, 128

commercial media systems: and public broadcasting, 159, 160; US global model, 241–2; and world-system theory, 28–9, 32; *see also* advertising; cable and satellite broadcasting

Common Market, 98

communication dependency and news flows, 30

communication forces, 31–4

communication research *see* mass communication research traditions

communism *see* China; Cold War; Soviet Union

computer games, 296, 299

computer technology: origins of internet, 291–2; *see also* digital technology; internet

computer viruses, 298, 299, 307

Comsat Corporation, 278, 279

Conference of International Broadcasters' Audience Service, 210

Consumer News and Business Channel *see* CNBC

consumerism: and internet, 312; teenage global market, 317–18; and world-system theory, 28–9; *see also* advertising

Control Room (documentary), 212

Cook, John, 156

copyright issues, 131–2, 138, 285; and internet, 299, 303, 304–5

Cordoba, Caliph of, 199

core nations, 25, 26, 322; importance of telecommunications, 288; and international communication flows, 31–4; and internet usage, 305–6, 331; news agencies in, 41, 175, 190; structuralist approach to research,

International Network for Cultural
Diversity (INCD), 22, 38*n*, 285,
288
international news: CNN profile,
142–74; news flows and world-
system theory, 30; *see also* foreign
news
International Olympic Committee
(IOC), 116–17
international organizations:
communications technology,
268–89; in post-sovereignty era,
329; UNESCO, 241–67; and US,
319, 324–7
International Program for the
Development of Communication
(IPDC), 254, 255, 261
International Telecommunication
Union (ITU), 268, 269–84;
frequency allocation, 269, 270–2,
273, 275; historical context, 270–2;
and NWICO agenda, 272–3, 276,
283–4, 288; private-sector members,
281–2; and US, 287–8; and World
Summit on the Information Society,
283–4, 316
International Telecommunications
Satellite Organization (Intelsat), 268,
276, 278–80
internet, 290–315, 330–1; access
limitations, 11, 13–14; background
and origins, 290–9; blogging, 5,
159, 191, 308–9, 331; CNN
Interactive, 146; copyright issues,
299, 303, 304–5; domain name
allocation, 284, 309–10; government
documents on, 299–302; and Iraq
War, 5; in MENA region, 214–15,
217, 218; MTV interests, 134–5,
137; and multimedia conglomerates,
61–3, 66–8, 75, 87, 102–3, 110;
and music industry, 130, 131, 133,
134–5, 137, 138, 299; and news
agencies, 181–2, 192; UNESCO
World Information Report, 262–3;

as vital market share, 312, 330; and
World Summit on the Information
Society, 283, 284; *see also* digital
technology
Internet Broadcasting Systems (IBS),
110
Internet Corporation for Assigned
Names and Numbers (ICANN),
284, 309–10
Internet Explorer (IE), 294, 295–6,
298
internet relay chat (IRC), 293
Interpublic Group of Companies Inc.
(IPC), 229, 233–4, 322
IPC *see* Interpublic Group of
Companies Inc.
IPDC, 254, 255, 261
iPod, 299
IPS (Inter Press Services), 188–9
Iran: resistance to US products, 139*n*
Iraq *see* Iraq War; Persian Gulf War I
Iraq War: and MENA media, 198,
209, 210–11, 212, 215; and
Western media, 4–6, 12, 158–9,
163–4
IRC (internet relay chat), 293
Islam, 195; *see also* Middle East/North
Africa
Israel, 197, 201–2; *see also* Arab-Israeli
conflicts
Italy, 107
ITN (Independent Television News),
179
ITU *see* International
Telecommunication Union
ITV, 161
Iwerks, Ubbe, 70

Japan *see* Dentsu; Sony
Al Jazeera, 4, 196, 208, 209–12, 215,
219–20*n*; "Al Jazeera" effect, 192;
Wall Street Journal editorial, 88
Jihad, 197, 214–15
Jobs, Steve, 298
John Paul II, Pope, 17

public relations, 216–17, 231
Publicis Group, 229, 235–7, 238, 330
publishing, 76–7, 102, 104, 106

Al Qaeda, 4, 197
Qatar, 209, 211
al-Quds-al-Arabi (newspaper), 205
quotas on US imports, 61, 127–8, 139n

radio: and AP news agency, 180–1, 182; BBC, 160; CNN Radio, 146; Deutsche Welle, 164; IBB, 167–8; international news, 144, 172; ITU regulation, 269, 270–1, 275; in MENA region, 208; US multimedia conglomerates, 78
Radio Canada International (RCI), 21, 172
Radio Farda, 208
Radio Free Europe: in Middle East, 208
Radio Marti, 167, 168–71
Radio Sawa, 208; "Radio Sawa Phenomenon," 196
Rand Corporation, 291
Rather, Dan, 5, 308
ratings companies, 106–7; *see also* audience research
Reagan, Ronald, 3, 22, 56, 256, 257
Real Audio, 298
reality television, 122, 123, 125–6
recording contracts, 133
regulation: changing situation, 124–5; and internet, 293, 310; telecommunications technology, 268–89; *see also* antitrust regulation; New World Information and Communication Order
Reith, Lord John, 160
research *see* development theories; mass communication research traditions
retired military analysts, 155, 173n
Reuters, 41, 175, 176–9, 190, 330
Reuters Television (RTV), 177, 179

Rice, Condoleezza, 4
Roberts, John, 252–3
Robertson, George, 155
Rogers, Everett, 45, 54
Roman Empire, 16
Rosenblum, Mort, 14, 15–16
Rostow, Walter, 44–5
Rothkopf, David, 121
RTL Group, 102
RTV (Reuters Television), 177, 179
Rugh, William A., 199–200, 201, 202, 216
Russell, William Harold, 12

Saatchi & Saatchi, 235–6
Salisbury, Joseph, 323
Sambrook, Richard, 5
satellite technology: Arabic transnational broadcasting, 206–15, 218; direct broadcast satellite, 245–6; and international news, 147, 152, 162; regulation, 269, 274–6; *see also* cable and satellite broadcasting systems
Saudi Arabia, 14, 205–6, 212–13, 216
Savio, Roberto, 188
Schiller, Dan, 22, 48–9
Schiller, Herbert, 22, 48–9, 54, 96
Schleifer, Abdallah, 211
Schroeder, Gerhard, 140n
Scripps, E. W., 183
Seagram Company, 103, 130, 132
search engines, 298
Second World War, 160, 161, 332n
semiperipheral nations, 25, 26–7, 322–3; and internet, 311–12, 331; multimedia conglomerates in, 317; as receiving markets, 31–2; *see also* electronic colonialism theory; world-system theory
September 11 *see* 9/11 terrorist attacks
service economy, 18
Shannon, Thomas, 25–6
Al-Sharq-al-Awsat (newspaper), 205
Shaw, Bernard, 147, 148

United Nations: Universal Declaration of Human Rights, 21, 266n; and US, 325, 326–7; see also ITU
United Nations Development Program (UNDP), 193, 203
United Nations Educational, Scientific, and Cultural Organization see UNESCO
United Press International (UPI), 182, 183–4, 190
United States: and cultural imperialism, 60–1, 95–7, 120–1, 135–6, 138–9, 284, 330; domination of media, 59, 61, 122–9, 327–8; election coverage, 158; export of cultural products, 3, 120–39, 327–8; foreign news situation, 14–16; global media model, 241–2; international joint ventures, 128–9; internet domination, 305–6, 311, 328; isolationism, 15–16, 324–7; and ITU, 287–8; Middle East activity, 194; multimedia conglomerates, 59–94, 96–7; propaganda, 9–10, 167, 168–71, 208–9; space race, 297, 313–14n; superpower role, 1; and UNESCO, 3, 241, 244, 245–6, 252, 254, 255, 256–7, 260–1, 262, 319; and world-system theory, 323; see also 9/11 attacks; Cold War; US . . . ; War on Terrorism
United States of Europe (USE), 97–109, 119
United States Information Agency (USIA), 166
Universal, 86, 91, 103; see also Vivendi
Universal Declaration of Human Rights, 21, 266n
Universal Music Group (UMG), 103, 129, 130, 133
universities and internet, 292, 295, 297–8
Univision, 112, 113, 114–15
UPI see United Press International

US Civil War, 12
US Department of Defense, 2, 5, 154, 155; internet origins, 292–3, 297; retired military analysts, 155, 173n
US State Department, 2, 9–10; and CNN, 154, 155, 156–7; and IBB, 166–71; and UNESCO withdrawal, 256–7
USA Today, 89
USE (United States of Europe), 97–109, 119
USSR see Soviet Union

Varis, Tapio, 22
Venevison, 113
Venezuela, 113
Verizon, 299
Veronica (search engine), 298
Viacom, 59, 60, 75–8, 89, 124, 139; MTV, 120, 133–9
Viacom Entertainment Group, 77
Viasat, 279
video: blogging, 308–9; games, 296, 299; and internet, 302–3; rentals, 50; video albums, 130; see also MTV; television
Vietnam war: CNN's erroneous report, 154
viruses (computers), 298, 299, 307
Vivendi, 60, 84–5, 88, 91, 103, 105
Vivendi Universal Music Group, 103, 129, 130
VNU, 60, 95, 106–7, 128
Voice of America (VOA), 21, 41, 167–8, 172; Radio Farda, 208; Radio Marti, 168–71

Wall Street Journal, 88–9
Wallerstein, Immanuel, 25
Wal-Mart, 90
Walt Disney company see Disney corporation
Walt Disney Internet Group, 69
Walt Disney Television International (WDTV-I), 69

war correspondents: CNN reporters, 148, 149–50; embedded journalism in Iraq War, 158–9; history of, 11–12

War on Terrorism, 1–2; Arab media coverage, 209, 210–11, 212, 215; internet documentation, 300–1; media coverage and impact, 3–6, 157, 158–9, 319

Warner Communications, 65, 67–8

Warner Music Group, 129, 132

Washington Post, The, 15, 248

Watergate, 248

WAZ, 103

Welch, David, 204

WETV, 110–11

Wheatstone, Charles, 12

Williams, Armstrong, 171, 231

Wilson, Woodrow, 332*n*

Winderman Cato Johnson (WCJ), 233

Windows, 298

wireless technology: AOL, 66–7; international telecommunications organizations, 268–89; *see also* digital technology; radio; satellite technology

wire-service news agencies, 41, 175–91

Woodward, Bob, 248

World Administrative Radio Council (1929), 271

World Bank: *World Development Report*, 46, 54–5

World Information Report (UNESCO), 262–3

World Report (CNN program), 152–4

World Service *see* BBC World Service

World Summit on the Information Society (WSIS): and ICANN, 310; and ITU, 283–4, 316; and UNESCO, 264, 265, 283–4

World Trade Organization (WTO), 34, 93*n*, 284–5; and cultural industries, 38*n*, 109, 119, 164, 263–4, 284–5, 288; and US, 325, 326

World Wide Web (WWW), 293, 294–6

Worldnet Television and Film Service, 167, 168

world-system theory (WST), 24–31, 56, 322–4; and advertising, 237–9; and electronic colonialism theory, 30–1, 324–7; and "Empire of the Mind," 318; European multimedia companies, 99; global communication forces, 31–4; and international news services, 172; and internet usage, 306; and US multimedia conglomerates, 60, 96–7

Worldwide Television News (WTN), 179

worms (computer viruses), 299, 307

WPP Group, 22, 229, 232–3, 238, 322, 330

WTO *see* World Trade Organization

Xinhua News Agency, 187

Yahoo!, 298, 312, 314*n*

Young & Rubicam (Y&R), 232–3